DEAD STRAIGHT GUIDE TO

THE SMITHS

MICK O' SHEA

This edition published November 2019

Email: info@redplanetzone.com

Printed in the UK by TJI

Publisher: Mark Neeter

A catalogue record for this book is available from the British Library

ISBN: 978 1 9127 3333 0

REDPLANETMUSICBOOKS.COM

CONTENTS

FOREWORD

Manchester has spawned a wide and varied roster of bands and solo artists over the years: Davy Jones (of The Monkees), Mick Hucknall, 10CC, The Bee Gees, The Hollies, Buzzcocks, Joy Division/New Order, Magazine, M People, Stone Roses, James, Oasis, and The 1975 to name but a few. The band that has come to epitomise Manchester's musical heritage quite like no other, however, is undoubtedly The Smiths. Indeed, Morrissey, Marr and Co. are now lauded as being the definitive British indie rock band of the Eighties. And it could be argued Marr's innovative, jangly guitar style – his Rickenbacker 330 tuned up a full step to F# to accommodate Morrissey's keening, self-absorbed crooning – served as the blueprint for what became known as Britpop.

My own introduction to The Smiths came with catching the promo video to 'This Charming Man' on *The Tube* one Friday evening towards the end of 1983. The rest of the band's disaffected-art-student-look was par for the post-punk course, but I knew instantly that their gladioli-wielding frontman was a pop star in the making. The song's subject matter went entirely over my head as my 21-year-old self would have struggled to spell homoeroticism, let alone recognise its subtle nuances at play.

Much of Manchester's musical lineage can be traced back to the Sex Pistols' now-legendary twin outings at Manchester's Lesser Free Trade Hall during the summer of 1976. I'd no idea at the time, of course, but Morrissey is one of the fabled few that can swear to being there at both shows. His being aware of the Pistols stemmed from a fascination with the New York Dolls. This fascination prompted him to respond to one of the 'Frontman Wanted' ads future Clash guitarist Mick Jones placed in the *Melody Maker* classifieds during the spring of 1975 while trying to get the fabled London SS out of a Praed Street basement and onto a stage. Though it's pure conjecture on my part, had Morrissey been a couple of years older and lived within commuting distance of the capital, then the British mid-Seventies music scene may just have taken a left oblique.

Information wasn't as readily to hand as it is today, of course, which meant the only viable means of finding out whether The Smiths were currently on tour came via the *NME* or one of the other leading music weeklies. As luck would have it, Morrissey and Co. were indeed out on the road at the time and were set to play The Haçienda on November 24. The band's eponymously-titled debut album was still some three months from release, but with 'This Charming Man'

being two-and-three-quarter minutes of pure pop perfection it stood to reason their set would be peppered with other such gems. And so it would prove, for I came away at the end of the night with snatches of 'Pretty Girls Make Graves', 'You've Got Everything Now', 'What Difference Does It Make?' and my all-time Smiths fave, 'Reel Around the Fountain' rattling around inside my head.

I still rate that night at The Haçienda as being one of my all-time Top Five gigs, and yet I get far more mileage out of mentioning how I was in the crowd at Preston's Guild Hall in November 1986. This, of course, was the night Morrissey got pinged on the head by a coin or some other projectile launched from the audience during the opening number 'The Queen Is Dead'. At the time I remember being royally fucked off, but in hindsight, I can see why the drama that comes with an aborted show would trump an uninterrupted set. I fully expected the Guild Hall show to be rescheduled at a later date, but, alas, that wasn't to be.

As with the other titles in the series this book is exactly what it says on the front cover – a 'Dead Straight Guide'. So although the text delves into the band's private lives on occasion, it's predominantly about the music that captured the imagination of a generation.

Mick O'Shea
Still Living the Dream
February 2020

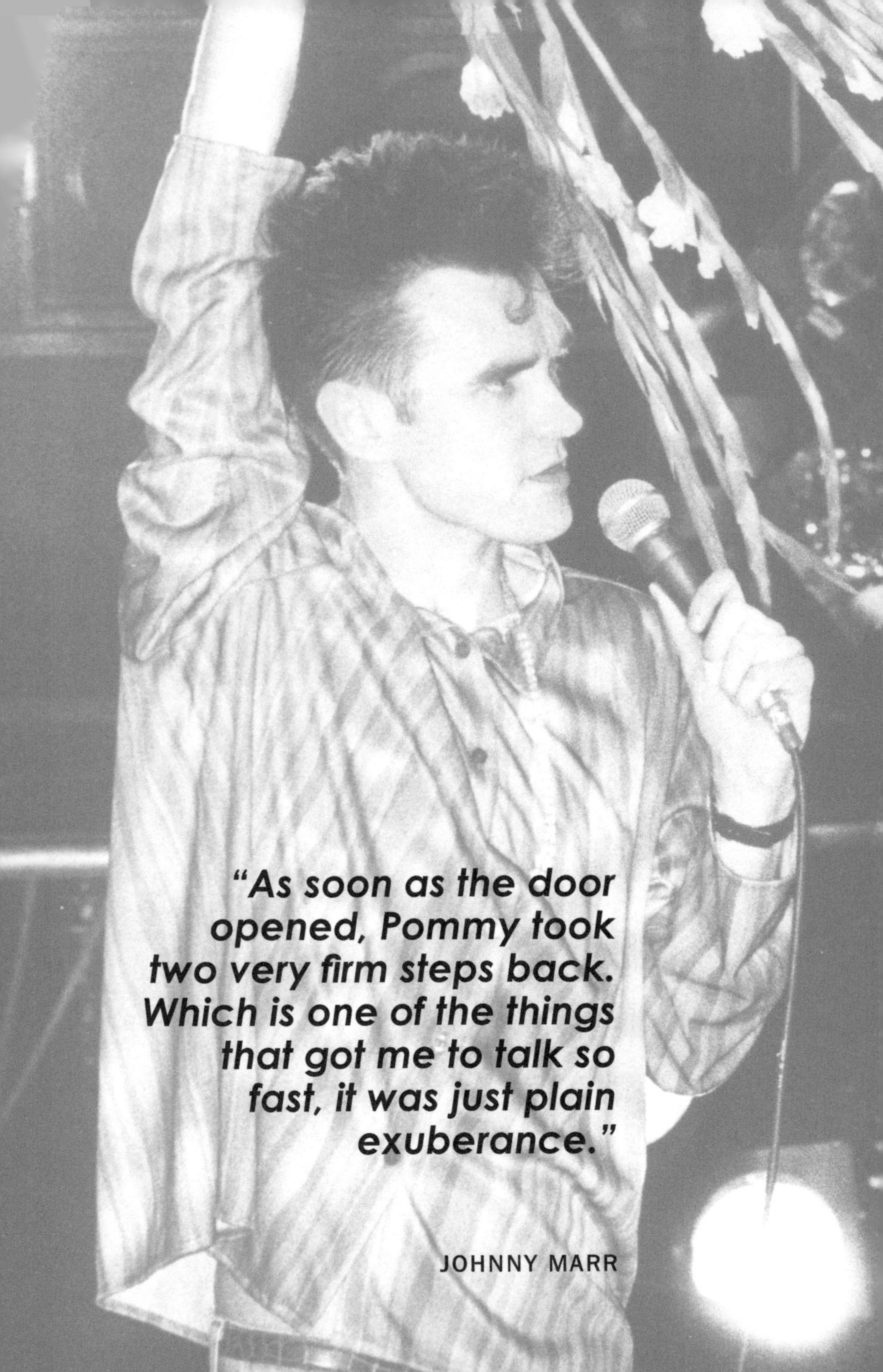

"As soon as the door opened, Pommy took two very firm steps back. Which is one of the things that got me to talk so fast, it was just plain exuberance."

JOHNNY MARR

INTRODUCTION

Johnny Marr's arriving at 384 Kings Road in May 1982 has gone down in Smiths folklore as being akin to John Lennon's encountering Paul McCartney at the St. Peter's Church garden fête. While recounting that late-May afternoon in Set the Boy Free, Marr says his impromptu decision to trawl through the streets of Stretford in search of 384 Kings Road was down to his catching the story of famous songwriting duo Leiber and Stoller on *The South Bank Show* that a mate had recorded on his newly-purchased VHS videocassette recorder. Marr was looking to speak to a guy some four years older than himself that he'd met briefly at a Patti Smith concert at the Manchester Apollo towards the end of August 1978. "On the screen, Jerry Leiber told the story of how he met Mike Stoller, and how he didn't actually know his future partner but had heard that he was someone who wrote songs," Marr would recount. "He found out where [Stoller] lived, went to his house and knocked on the door. Right then, I had a eureka moment."

Marr's electing to track down Morrissey – eureka moment or no – was one hell of a long shot as he'd neither seen nor heard anything about the latter for several years. Indeed, all he knew about the seemingly reclusive Morrissey – aside from his having briefly fronted a short-lived Manchester punk act, The Nosebleeds – was that he resided somewhere in Stretford and had written stuff in the *NME* about the New York Dolls.

It was the Dolls that had provided Morrissey with his own eureka moment after his catching the brash New York outfit's now-legendary British TV debut on *The Old Grey Whistle Test* in November 1972. The show's somewhat staid presenter, 'Whispering' Bob Harris, had churlishly dismissed the Dolls as "mock rock", but for Morrissey their trashy don't-give-a-fuck stance represented the future of rock 'n' roll – or at least the future of rock 'n' roll as he would like it to be. "The New York Dolls were just the antidote to everything," he later recounted. "I just thought they were wonderful . . . I still have vague fond memories . . . I think they were the single most important group to me as an adolescent." The Dolls featured so large in his adolescence that upon discovering that *Granada Reports*' quirky presenter Tony Wilson was lined up to host a new music show called So It Goes that was set to be broadcast in the Manchester region, he sent Wilson a dog-eared sleeve of the Dolls' eponymous debut album. Attached was a note which read: "Dear Mr Wilson, I've heard about your show. Its [sic] wonderful news. Please, could we have some music like this."

Morrissey's having penned a book on the New York Dolls gave him a certain local celebrity status while having his letters printed up in the music papers on a near-

New York Dolls.

weekly basis further enhanced his reputation as a writer. His fascination for the Dolls, and in turn the New York punk scene the dragged-up quintet had undoubtedly helped inspire, meant he soon became attuned to what was happening at the seedier end of London's King's Road during the summer of 1976. Yet while he was one of the select few that could indeed swear they were there when the Sex Pistols played the first of the aforementioned Manchester's Lesser Free Trade Hall shows on Friday, June 4, 1976 (or 1076 as the tickets advertised owing to a typo), he came away again somewhat sceptical of the Pistols' own onstage bedlam. His intrigue, however, was sufficiently piqued to pen missives to both the *NME* and *Melody Maker* – the latter ending with a caveat about how the Pistols' "audacious lyrics and discordant music won't hold their heads above water when their followers tire of torn jumpers and safety-pins."

As the world now knows, the Pistols' Lesser Free Trade Hall debut is hailed as being the catalyst that transformed Manchester's

music scene – if only owing to the likes of Bernard Sumner and Peter Hook (Warsaw/Joy Division), Mark E. Smith (The Fall), Howard Devoto, Pete Shelley, and Steve Diggle (Buzzcocks) all being in attendance that balmy summer's evening.

The Pistols returned to the Lesser Free Trade Hall some six weeks later on Tuesday, July 20. Aside from the Buzzcocks (who were making their full debut), the support bill that night included Wythenshawe-based punksters, Slaughter & The Dogs – the first band Marr ever saw live. Though clearly underage, he was allowed entry as his brother was friends with someone in Wild Ram, the support band on the night. Wild Ram would subsequently undergo a name-change to Ed Banger and the Nosebleeds (soon to be truncated to The Nosebleeds).

According to Stephen 'Pommy' Pomfret's recollections from the Pistols' second Lesser Free Trade Hall outing, Morrissey sauntered into the hall sporting a homemade New York Dolls T-shirt, with a copy of either the Dolls' eponymous debut album or the follow-up,

> *"The New York Dolls were just the antidote to everything, they were the single most important group to me as an adolescent."*

Too Much Too Soon, clutched under his arm. Pomfret would subsequently play a small, yet not insignificant role in The Smiths' story as it was he who would bring Marr and Morrissey together.

By the spring of 1982 Marr was working at the recently-opened X Clothes on Chapel Walks (an independent alternative fashion chain with shops in Sheffield, Leeds, as well as the one in Manchester). Heeding the adage that you never get a second chance to make a favourable first impression, Marr arrived at Morrissey's door decked out in style. He was

wearing biker boots, faded baggy 'Fifties Levi jeans (rolled up to the right height to show of the buckles of his boots), a Johnson's jacket and sleeveless shirt and an authentic US flying cap – as worn by Marlon Brando's character Johnny Strabler from the 1953 film The Wild One – rounding off his look. If this wasn't eye-opening enough on a sedate Sunday afternoon, his bequiffed hair was dyed varying shades of red.

Aside from allowing Marr first dibs on the latest fashions, working at X Clothes brought him into contact with the movers and shakers on Manchester's music scene as well as

"Morrissey didn't say much and just let me tell him what I wanted to do."

helping him get his own name out there. Tony Wilson would swing by to inquire if Marr was interested in joining Section 25, a Blackpool-based trio that was signed to Factory Records and about to embark on a US tour with Factory labelmates New Order. Though impressed by the songs on the tape Wilson had given him, Marr was only interested in putting his own band together. On another occasion, Factory's in-house art director, Peter Saville, came through the door with aspiring DJ and future M Person Mike Pickering, another of Wilson's faithful. The duo had apparently just attended a meeting about a new nightclub Wilson was in the process of setting up at the Palace Theatre end of Whitworth Street. They were thinking of calling the club The Haçienda. They went so far as to lay out the blueprints for the club on the desk for Marr to cast his eye over.

Situated next door to X Clothes was another fashion emporium called Crazy Face, which specialised in retro, American-influenced clothing. Crazy face's owner, Joe Moss, a 40-year-old Stockport-born entrepreneur with a dual interest in music and clothes. Back in the Sixties, he'd been a regular face at the Twisted Wheel on Whitworth Street, one of the first clubs in Manchester to

play Northern Soul. The Twisted Wheel also played host to the first-ever gig by Cream. Having built up a thriving wholesale jeans business, Moss expanded into the boutique world opening Crazy Face and another shop called Tupelo Honey on Portland Street (both names being the titles of Van Morrison songs). He also opened a shop in his native Stockport. He kept a guitar in the back room at Chapel Walks and could occasionally be found noodling away to his heart's content during his lunch hour. During his lunch break Marr would nip next door to chat with the girls that worked there; the obscure R&B, soul and rock 'n' roll blaring out of the speakers proving an equal distraction. One occasion Marr came through the Crazy Face door he espied a guy standing by the counter sporting a battered original flying jacket and a pair of American railroad baggy work pants – and bearing more than a passable resemblance to Jack Nicholson's character, Randle P. McMurphy, from One Flew Over the Cuckoo's Nest. This was Moss. Introductions were made. Given

their shared passion for the guitar, the two quickly struck up a conversation. When Moss admitted to his ongoing struggle to master the intro to The Temptations' 'My Girl', Marr offered to show him how it was done, and a friendship was born. Indeed, it was on Moss's video recorder that he watched the Southbank Show about Leiber and Stoller.

When Marr rocked up to Pomfret's that fateful Sunday announcing he was Stretford-bound with no idea as to how to locate Kings Road, the latter agreed to tag along for the hell of it – if only to witness Morrissey's expression on seeing the wannabe Black Rebel biker boy standing in his midst. Upon their arrival at the nondescript, yet pleasant-looking semi-detached red-brick house, it was Pommy, rather than Marr, that knocked on the door. Morrissey's sister Jackie answered and went back inside to summon her sibling. It was also Pommy that made the introductions. "I'd like you to meet a friend of mine," he told Morrissey. Once they were inside, Pomfret proceeded to explain how Marr was a guitarist looking to put a band together and would he be interested? "I expected him to say he wasn't interested at all," Pomfret revealed. "But he said, 'Oh yes, yes!' He was as excited as Morrissey can get. So I put him onto Johnny and they started to talk."

Marr remembers being struck by Morrissey's totally non-rock 'n' roll attire – suit trousers, buttoned-up shirt (with a T-shirt underneath) and baggy cardigan; his short, Fifties-like hairstyle exuding a bookish intellect. He admits to pondering what their host might think of his somewhat outré ensemble as they headed up to Morrissey's bedroom. However, seeing the life-size cardboard cut-out of James Dean from the doomed actor's final film Giant at the top of the stairs set his mind at ease. On entering the bedroom, his eyes fell on the typewriter nestled on the dresser. In his mind's eye he pictured Morrissey composing one the many missives he'd fired off to the *NME* and the other leading music papers.

While the visit had come out of the blue, Morrissey was at least already familiar with the name 'Johnny Marr' owing to one-time Nosebleeds' guitarist Billy Duffy having tipped him the wink about his guest's prowess on the guitar. Having narrowly lost out to Midge Ure for Glen Matlock's Rich Kids, Duffy was now playing with Theatre of Hate, whose debut album, Westworld – which had been produced by The Clash's Mick Jones – had cracked the Top 20. The album's lead single, 'Do You Believe in the West World', would reach the Top 40, resulting in an appearance on *Top of the Pops*.

"It was Pommy rather than Marr that knocked on the door and it was also Pommy that introduced him to Morrissey once they were inside"

Morrissey also remembered their brief encounter at the Patti Smith show at the Manchester Apollo. He's been loitering in the foyer with Duffy and Slaughter & The Dogs' bassist, Howard 'Zip' Bates, when Marr had stopped to say hello before sauntering through into the hall.

Once the interlopers made themselves

comfortable Morrissey went and stood by the record player. After some preamble, Marr launched into his spiel about the band he was looking to put together; talking ten-to-the-dozen for fear of Morrissey losing interest. "He (Morrissey) didn't say much and just let me tell him what I wanted to do," he later recounted.

Morrissey, of course, wasn't obliged to say anything at all as he hadn't solicited the visit. He was harbouring ambitions of becoming a music writer, and every journo of note knows the advantage of remaining silent in the hope of keeping the other party talking. The one question Morrissey did ask of the garrulous guitarist was what music he liked. Upon hearing Marr reel off The Shangri-Las, Ronettes, Crystals, and several all-girl groups, Morrissey casually nodded over to a box of 7-inch singles further along from the typewriter and asked if Marr would like to choose a record to put on. Marr hadn't needed asking twice and scrambled off the bed to peruse the collection; his already favourable impression of Morrissey intensifying as he leafed through one rare Tamla single after another. He finally settled on "Paper Boy" by The Marvelettes, the all-girl group that had scored Tamla Motown's debut US #1 with 'Please, Mr Postman' in 1961. Morrissey thought it a "good choice", but Marr instead opted for the flip side 'You're the One'.

In turn, Morrissey put on The Toys' 'A Lover's Concerto' followed by Sandi Shaw's 1965 Top 10 hit 'Message Understood', which Marr admits to having never heard before.

When the song finished, there was more small-talk about mutual friends and the current Manchester music scene before Marr set about explaining that while he didn't have anyone else lined up for his, as yet, illusory band, he did have a couple of people in mind. Morrissey then handed his prospective songwriting partner some examples of his lyrics. When the time came to take their leave, Marr suggested that they speak on the phone the following day. "We said goodbye, and as I went out of the gate and into the sun, I thought to myself: 'If he calls tomorrow this band is on.'"

Morrissey did make the call and the band was indeed on . . .

Marr would subsequently reflect on the immediacy of his bonding with Morrissey – a bonding brought about by a shared knowledge of early-Sixties pop ephemera. He would also admit that had Morrissey rejected his overtures he would never have made so bold a move again.

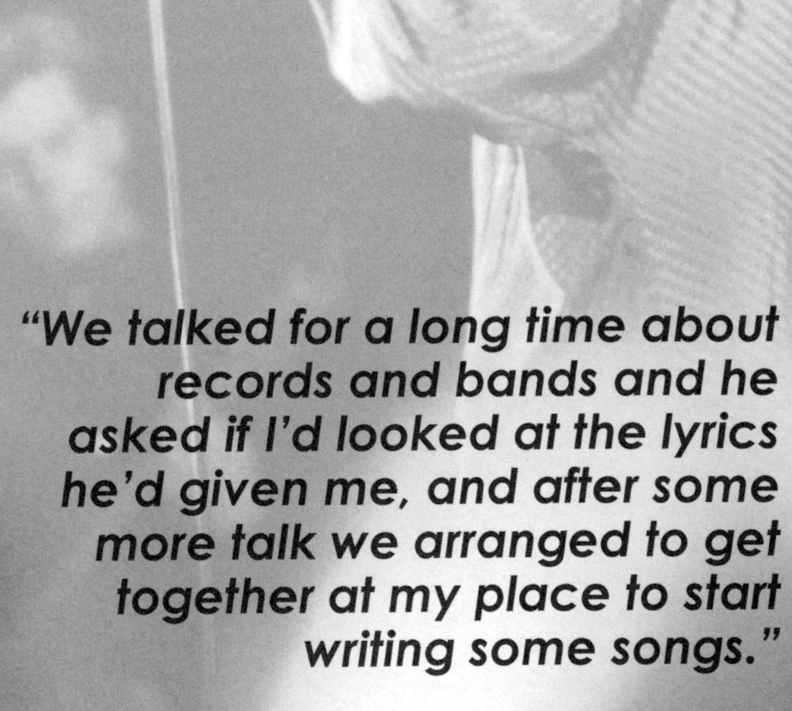

"We talked for a long time about records and bands and he asked if I'd looked at the lyrics he'd given me, and after some more talk we arranged to get together at my place to start writing some songs."

JOHNNY MARR

CHAPTER ONE

WHY PAMPER LIFE'S COMPLEXITY

While Smiths fans the world over undoubtedly view Marr and Morrissey's coming together as being a stars-aligning-in-the-firmament moment, they, in turn, have also allowed themselves to get carried away while recounting that auspicious spring afternoon of May 1982 in various interviews through the years. Indeed, in his autobiography, Morrissey waxes lyrical about how the "immaculately bequiffed" Marr reminded him of a young Tom Bell from the 1961 film *Payroll*, and of his arriving at Kings Road "almost carried away by his own zest to make meaningful music." Speaking elsewhere, their encounter takes on near-mythical proportions, with Morrissey citing it as "an event I'd always been looking forward to and unconsciously been waiting for since my childhood."

For all his bluster about unconsciously sensing his destiny, there was obviously something indefinable at play at the time of Marr's Stretford odyssey as Morrissey could have been on one of his occasional forays to London. Alternatively, he could have simply told Jackie to say he wasn't at home while maintaining a furtive watch through the upstairs front window until the interlopers had gone on their merry way. He obviously wasn't frequenting X Clothes or else Marr wouldn't have needed to mention their brief encounter at the Manchester Apollo as a way of breaking the ice. It's also worth remembering that Ian McColloch was at the top of Marr's wish-list at the time. Had the information he'd been given about Echo & The Bunnymen's impending split not turned out to be spurious, Marr would have instead beaten a path to McCulloch's door, and The Smiths might never have existed outside of Morrissey's bedroom daydreams.

Within days of Marr and Pomfret's visit, Morrissey returned the favour by boarding a train to Altrincham where he was picked up by Marr's girlfriend, Angie, and delivered to the home of Shelley Rohde, where the guitarist was renting the attic room. Rohde had started out as a journalist and was currently working alongside Tony Wilson on *Granada Reports*. She was also regarded as an expert on L. S. Lowry, and one of the first things Morrissey would have seen upon entering the house was a framed poster of the front cover to her biography on the celebrated Stretford-born artist, *A Private View of L. S. Lowry*, on the wall at the foot of the stairs. A couple of days before this second meeting, Morrissey had posted Marr a Manilla envelope containing a cassette tape and a photocopied photo of James Dean. The tape was a compilation of songs by all-girl groups the Shangri-Las, The Crystals, and The Shirelles, Marianne Faithful, and Sandi Shaw.

Morrissey had brought some more of his lyrics for them to work on. The first out of the bag was called 'The Hand That Rocks the Cradle', which would, of course, feature on The Smiths' eponymous debut album. Without thinking about it Marr started playing a E /F# /Bm /F#m /B /A# /Dm /Am /G /D /C#m /A chord sequence similar to that of 'Kimberly', the opening track on side two of Patti Smith's seminal debut album, Horses. "It seemed to scan right with the words and suggested a bass line, which I played at the same time," he explained. "I continued to play, and then Morrissey started singing the words, and within a few words the tune was born." After running through the song a couple of times, Marr recorded their efforts onto his tape machine he then overdubbed a ringing guitar line on top. "It felt like an important moment," the guitarist continued. "I was thinking about the words and how the style was almost vaudevillian, although I hadn't analysed what it was all about."

Morrissey certainly had no qualms with Marr's borrowing from Lenny Kaye as he'd waxed lyrical about *Horses* being "the most exciting rock album of the year and shows more potential than just about any other release in recent memory" in a letter that appeared in the September 25, 1976 issue of *Sounds*.

The second set of lyrics they worked on, 'Suffer Little Children' (which would also feature on The Smiths), held particular resonance for the both of them with their both being Manchester born and bred. The words relate to the harrowing Moors Murders – going so far as to reference the then three known victims (John Kilbride, Lesley Ann Downey, and Edward Evans) as well as Myra Hindley by name. In Set the Boy Free, Marr talks of photos of Hindley and Ian Brady being "an ongoing fixture in the newspapers and on the television," and of his "pick[ing] up half-heard details from the adults' conversations about tortured children and tape recordings." But this seems unlikely given that he was three weeks shy of his second birthday at the time of Brady and Hindley's arrests. Of course, with Morrissey being four years older than Marr, he would at least have had an understanding of the misery that "grip[ped] mid-Sixties Manchester as Hindley and Brady raise their faces to the camera and become known to us all."

When reflecting on that pivotal afternoon holed up in Shelley Rohde's loft, Marr says the tune to 'Over the Moors' (set to be retitled 'Suffer Little Children') practically wrote itself – as though ethereal forces were guiding his fingers up and down the fretboard. By the time the song was finished, he didn't know what to make of it other than it defined an aspect of his and Morrissey's creativity. "It said to me, 'We do things differently.'"

It's highly likely that during these initial get-togethers, Marr and Morrissey took the time getting to know something of one another's

upbringing. Marr's actual surname is Maher, but he'd since shortened it to the snappier-sounding "Marr" in homage of Marc Bolan. Another reason, of course, was to avoid any future confusion over he and Buzzcocks' drummer having the exact same name. His Irish émigré parents, John and Frances, were living in Longsight at the time Marr came into the world on October 31, 1963, but relocated to neighbouring Ancoats while he was still a babe in arms. He was five-years-old when he got hold of his first guitar – a cheap and cheerful wooden acoustic that had captivated his attention since first seeing it in the window of the local corner shop. Marr would cherish that guitar and carry it around with him wherever he went. "I don't know why I had to have it, but I was besotted with it," he reflected. The yearning most likely came from an uncle accompanying himself on the guitar while belting out traditional Irish ballads and the latest pop hits during summer holidays with his extended family in his parents' native County Kildare. Marr's father was also very musical, and aside from possessing a more-than-passable singing voice, he could also play the accordion and harmonica; the latter of which he taught his eldest son.

Morrissey's parents, Peter and Elizabeth (or Betty as she was known), were also Irish emigres, having arrived in Manchester from their native Dublin with baby daughter Jacqueline in tow a year or so before he was born in May 1959. The Morrisseys had settled in Hulme, and as Betty approached full term, it was agreed that should the new arrival be a boy they would name him either after her father, Patrick Stephen, which also happened to be the names of Peter's deceased infant brothers. In later years during the height of fame, Morrissey would claim he was named after Steve Cochran, an American stage and film actor who enjoyed a steady, if unspectacular Hollywood career until his death at the age of 48. Cochran's most memorable film role was playing opposite James Cagney in *White Heat*.

During the summer of 1965, Peter and Betty put down a deposit on a terraced house in Queen's Square, which was situated at the eastern end of Stretford and within the shadow of Loreto College; a school of local renown that was founded in 1851 by nuns from the Blessed Institute of the Virgin Mary. They would remain in Queen's Square for the next five years before relocating to King's Road. Morrissey has fond memories from his time at Queen's Square as his grandparents lived next door while an auntie also lived close-by. For a time, they were joined by Betty's younger sister, Mary, a beehive-haired Dusty Springfield look-a-like to whom Morrissey became very attached. (Mary would subsequently move to New Jersey where Morrissey visited her in 1975).

Unlike Marr, Morrissey failed his 11-plus. His time at St. Mary's Secondary Modern was to prove a far from happy one. "I had no idea that life could get any worse, or that schoolteachers could be more contemptuous than those of wilting St. Wilfred's," he reflected in his eponymously-titled 2011 autobiography. "But the snarling stupidity at St. Mary's is deathless, and its wearisome echo of negativity exhausts me to a permanent state of circumstantial sadness." Morrissey's scathing criticism of Britain's

educational system is well known, of course. "The education I received was so basically evil and brutal," he seethed. "All I learnt was to have no self-esteem and to feel ashamed without knowing why."

Despite his loathing for formal education, Morrissey continued onto Stretford Technical College where he attained three O-levels, one of which, unsurprisingly, given his passion for reading, was English Literature.

Marr had been eight when he and his family moved to Wythenshawe as part of Manchester's inner-city clearance scheme. Though only eight miles away, it seemed to his mind as though they were emigrating to another continent. Wythenshawe was out in the southern suburbs, situated close to Manchester Airport. It was, and still is, a predominantly working-class area. Originally intended as a garden city, Wythenshawe could once boast being the largest council housing estate in Europe. The Mahers' new three-bedroom home not only had gardens front and back, but all the latest mod cons including central heating and a proper bathroom.

Though yet to hit his teens, music and fashion were already featuring large in young Johnny's life. Glam rock was all the rage by this time, and the trashy guitars, stomping tribal beats played by ever-more-garishly-dressed bands such as Roxy Music, Sweet, Mud, Slade, Mott the Hoople, and T Rex captured his fevered imagination. The first record he bought was T. Rex's 'Jeepster', the song's catchy A7 riffed intro coupled with a mid-song moody chord change initiating a life-long passion for Marc Bolan. Coincidentally, Morrissey's first-ever concert was seeing T. Rex play Belle View's Kings Hall in July 1972.

Having saved up his paper round money to purchase his first electric guitar – a red Vox Ace costing the princely sum of £32 – Marr began practising in earnest. He was also picking up tips from the guitarists in a band called Four Way Street, one of whom was Billy Duffy. It was Duffy that first turned his attention to the Sex Pistols after catching the second of their Lesser Free Trade Hall shows in July 1976. More importantly, as far as the impressionable Marr was concerned, however, was that Slaughter & The Dogs and the Buzzcocks – both local acts – had supported the Pistols on the night. The Buzzcocks' self-produced EP, *Spiral Scratch*, was to have a sizeable impact on Marr's life in more ways than one. For it was while inspecting the EP's cheap Xeroxed cover that he discovered Buzzcocks' drummer was called John Maher. He'd already been toying with changing his name, but this made it something of a prerequisite.

It was Duffy who also pointed out to Marr how his rapidly-developing guitar style was highly reminiscent to that of Stooges' guitarist James Williamson. Marr had never heard of The Stooges, but a visit to Virgin Records had soon put this right. As soon as he slipped *Raw Power* onto the turntable and heard 'Search and Destroy' for the first time, he knew he was on the right path. "Everything I already felt was real," he enthused. "Iggy and the Stooges were going to a place I really wanted to be; *Raw Power* shone a light."

Morrissey, meantime, was still extolling the virtues of the New York Dolls – even

going so far as to fire off a scathing missive to Sounds' John Ingham after the latter had dared to criticise his heroes. Given his yearning to forge a career in music journalism, verbally assaulting one of the leading music weeklies' resident scribes was hardly conducive to achieving his goals. But at the end of the day, he simply couldn't allow Ingham's dissing of the Dolls to go unchecked.

The New York Dolls had self-imploded in a Florida trailer park during the spring of 1975 while under the tentative stewardship of Malcolm McLaren who would, of course, go on to mismanage the Sex Pistols. It's doubtful Morrissey would have been aware of McLaren's forlorn attempts to rejuvenate the Dolls' ailing career as the UK music papers would have seen little need to waste any column inches on his stateside venture. Mercury Records had dropped the Dolls soon after the release of the aptly-titled *Too Much Too Soon*, yet while the band's prodigious booze and drug intake was to prove a significant factor in their denouement, McLaren's having them perform in front of a hammer and sickle backdrop had served as a coup dis-grace.

McLaren had never really shown much interest in managing the Pistols, other than using the band as clotheshorses to promote the clothes he and Vivienne Westwood were selling out of their shop – SEX. However, having secured the group a recording contract with EMI, he'd thrown his energies into setting up a nationwide tour to promote their debut single 'Anarchy in the UK'. Ever the huckster, McLaren had invited Johnny Thunders and Jerry Nolan's new outfit, The Heartbreakers, onto the bill to give the tour a little Lower East Side allure. His hard work would, of course, be laid to waste in the wake of the Pistols' now-legendary appearance on *Today*, on December 1, 1976, but the Electric Circus show was one of the three original 19 tour dates that went ahead as scheduled.

Morrissey's opinion as to the Pistols' merits had wavered somewhat by the time the Anarchy Tour stumbled into Manchester. Venturing into Collyhurst after dark certainly wasn't without its risks either, and yet the chance to get up close and personal with Thunders and Nolan was simply too good an opportunity to pass up. The encounter didn't go as he might have hoped: "I approach them knowing that my heart might at the very least stop. They allow me to take photographs, but their unsmiling shrugs render conversation unwelcome. The outer reality shakes the inner life awake. Johnny and Jerry mean nothing after all."

The question still remains as to whether The Heartbreakers were responsible for introducing heroin to the UK punk scene. But with their put-upon manager, Lee Black Childers, having taken it upon himself to tighten his grip on his charges' dwindling methadone supply, Thunders and Nolan's indifference towards Morrissey could have been merely owing to their being in urgent need of their daily fix.

The Pistols' teatime tête-à-tête with *Today's* curmudgeonly host, Bill Grundy, is now seen as being punk's 'watershed moment'. While a plethora of punk bands would seemingly spring up overnight, Manchester could already boast a thriving

Photo by Kevin Cummins.

punk scene. Two days on from the Electric Circus show, an ad seeking "Dolls/Patti fans for Manchester-based punk band" appeared within *Sounds*' classifieds.

One can't help but wonder why Morrissey didn't wait till after the Electric Circus show before placing the ad as there was every chance he might find the like-minded souls he was seeking amongst the audience. His search for fellow Dolls/Patti aficionados would ultimately come to nought, however, and he would subsequently cite the night of the Anarchy Tour show as being "the start of a drawn-out process of easing myself away."

A "drawn-out process" that was to be exacerbated by his father announcing he was leaving the marital home in the run-up to Christmas.

Whereas Morrissey was slowly easing himself into self-imposed hibernation, his future songwriting collaborator was intent on grabbing a slice of the limelight with his new band – the voguish-sounding Paris Valentinos. (They had initially settled on calling themselves Paris, but were forced into adding the exotic expansion upon discovering there was a band of that name already in existence). Aside from Marr, the Valentinos' line-up was to boast another star in the making. Bassist Kevin Williams was an aspiring actor, who, after undergoing a name change to the snappier-sounding Kevin Kennedy, was to find fame as Curly Watts in *Coronation Street*.

Thanks to their drummer, Bobby Durkin, Paris Valentinos were allowed to rehearse once a week in a local school hall in return for their providing musical accompaniment at

Sunday evening services in the neighbouring church

With The Stooges having served as the first stepping stone on Marr's musical education, it was perhaps inevitable that he would gravitate towards the New York Dolls. Indeed, it was his infatuation with Johnny Thunders that led to his taking a pair of scissors to his hair and wearing eye-liner. Although only a month into his teens when the Pistols were turning the Thames TV airwaves blue, he readily embraced punk by dying his hair and having his sister Claire pierce his ear with a sewing needle. His change in appearance brought disapproving raised eyebrows at St. Augustine's – as did his refusal to answer to Maher during registration – but Marr had found his path and wasn't for turning.

Though happy to adopt a punk look, Marr had no interest in mimicking The Clash or The Damned in playing Ramones-esque three-chord thrash. Instead, he turned his pierced ear to pop's rich pageantry – particularly the Motown melodies of Holland/Dozier/Holland. Having worked up an eclectic set of covers including the Stones' 'Jumpin' Jack Flash', Tom Petty and the Heartbreakers' 'American Girl', Thin Lizzy's 'The Boys Are Back in Town' and 'Don't Believe a Word', and Rod Stewart's 'Maggie May'. The Paris Valentinos would make their live debut at a Jubilee Day street party on the Wythenshawe estate in early June 1977. The performance was marred (no pun intended) somewhat by an afternoon of frivolous underage drinking. Yet the quartet nonetheless came away feeling exalted. "I knew we were scrappy, and I felt like a kid," Marr reflected, "but at least I was a kid in a band."

Unbeknown to Marr, his future Smiths confederate Andy Rourke also happened to be enrolled at St. Augustine's. Marr was aware of who Rourke was, of course, if only because of a shared disregard of the school's regimen. As such, there was the usual rivalry – who could grow their hair the longest or look the more dishevelled before a summons to the form master. When reflecting on their time at St. Augustine's, Marr says that Rourke was sociable to a point yet seemed to lack self-esteem or confidence. This was due in part to his mother relocating to Spain following his parents' separation. In turn, Rourke remembers Marr strutting about as though he was the cock of the walk. "He wasn't particularly hard, but thought he was, and used to act it."

Rourke was the third eldest of four brothers. With their father (Michael) having to work away from home three or four nights a week, his sons had the run of the house to do pretty much as they pleased. More often than not, Rourke would skip school in favour of hanging out with the kids from the local council estates. He started experimenting in soft drugs and when he did deign to put in an appearance at St. Augustine's he often fell asleep at his desk. It was, of course, only a matter of time before Rourke's recklessness caught up with him. He was caught in possession of certain drugs while on a school trip to the continent and duly placed under the supervisory care of a social worker upon his return to Manchester.

Marr says he'd been kicking his heels during one of the school's breaktimes when

Rourke had ambled over and – indicating to the Neil Young badge Marr was sporting – sparked a conversation by singing 'Tonight's the Night' (the opening track of Young's 1975 album of the same name). On discovering Rourke was teaching himself guitar, Marr agreed to their getting together up for a jam at Rourke's house in Ashton-on-Mersey the following day.

Borrowing an acoustic that belonged to one of Rourke's brothers, Marr ran through 'Ballrooms of Mars' from T. Rex's *Slider* as well as a couple of his own riffs. In turn, Rourke played Neil Young's 'The Needle and the Damage Done' from the Canadian rocker's *Harvest* album. Marr came away suitably impressed. "His playing was assured and accomplished, and it was obvious that he was a natural musician. We passed the guitar backwards and forwards and, in those moments, Andy and I made a connection that would take us through times and places we couldn't even imagine."

Marr's prowess on the guitar wasn't his only talent as he was also showing great promise on the football pitch. He was already playing for the Manchester Boys team when the call came for a try-out with his beloved Manchester City. During a fantastical three-year-period from 1968 (the same year their devilish rivals in red had lifted the European Cup) through to 1970, City won the First Division title, the FA Cup, League Cup, and European Cup Winners' Cup. The club's fortunes had dipped somewhat in recent years but a cheeky Dennis Tueart overhead had delivered the League Cup again during the 1975-76 season. However, seeing the determination and dedication the other boys were putting into their game made Marr realise his heart was set on making music – that, and his being the only one on the pitch wearing eye-liner.

The Paris Valentinos were forced into a temporary hiatus when Marr accepted an invitation to join a Velvet Underground-inspired outfit operating out of Manchester's red-light district in Whalley Range called Sister Ray. The offer came via Kev Williams, whom someone within Sister Ray's set-up had tracked down to make their approach. Despite Kennedy's warning about Sister Ray's frontman, Clive Robertson, being something

I was okay with being the leader and I liked the sound of the band around me"

of a loose cannon Marr was sufficiently intrigued to attend a rehearsal. "They were a group of vagrant biker nasties," he later recounted. "[They were] a lot older than me and had a few gigs that got them a bit of notoriety because the singer was crazy."

Just as in Collyhurst, Whalley Range was another of Manchester no-go areas after dark – especially for a 15-year-old kid clutching a guitar. Marr, at least, was savvy to the situation and took to timing his runs to and from the bus stop so that he wouldn't be on the street a heartbeat longer than necessary. His one and only live outing with Sister Ray came with their opening for The

Freshies at the Wythenshawe Forum. The Freshies were fronted by Chris Sievey who would find subsequent fame with his alter-ego Frank Sidebottom. "It was a fierce set and a baptism of fire," says Marr. "The singer went mental and got into an altercation with one of the other bands after we played."

Andy Rourke, Kevin Williams, and the other Valentinos came along to offer support, but Marr had already made up his mind that his time with Sister Ray was at an end.

Marr would find himself taking on vocal duties with the Paris Valentinos following singer Chris Milne's departure. Andy Rourke was brought in on rhythm guitar, and his and Marr's twin-guitar attack led to the band taking a power-pop direction covering songs such as Eddie and the Hot Rods' 'Do Anything You Wanna Do', and 'Another Girl, Another Planet' by the latter guitarist's current favourite band, The Only Ones. "I was okay with being the leader and I liked the sound of the band around me," Marr continued. "Vocally I was going for something between Johnny Thunders and Patti Smith, and the next step was to turn the riffs I had into songs of our own.

'It was around this same time that Marr first encountered the girl of his dreams – and future wife – Angie Brown. A friend was throwing a party while her parents were away, and Marr was sitting with Durkin musing over the merits of Blondie's Parallel Lines when he espied a lovely elfin Siouxsie Sioux look-a-like standing on the other side of the room. It was one of those 'kismet' moments where the world stops turning on its axis. Marr was utterly transfixed. His senses were swimming. So much so, that he blithely informed Durkin "I'm going to marry that girl." Already fuelled on Dutch courage, he idled across and tentatively struck up a conversation. He can no longer remember his opening patter, only that at some point he asked Angie when her birthday was; discovering they were both Halloween babies only intensifying his moon-eyed emotions. It later transpired he needn't have fretted as Angie knew exactly who he was and was just as smitten. She just had a better poker face.

Marr set about turning his new ideas into songs but playing them to half-hearted youth club crowds wasn't what he'd had in mind when forming Paris Valentinos. If the band was going to get anywhere, they needed to seriously up their game. Realising Williams' heart was no longer in what they were doing, Marr co-opted Rourke into switching to bass, and they continued as a three-piece. They were rehearsing one evening when Rob Allman – who'd been the driving force behind Four Way Street – swung by to check them out. He was impressed by what he heard – so much so, that he proposed their starting a new group. Marr held Allman's talents in high regard and hadn't needed asking twice.

Calling themselves White Dice, the quartet started rehearsing regularly. With Allman's friend and musical collaborator, Paul Whittall, joining on keyboards the new songs they were writing really began taking shape. It wasn't all harmonious, however, as Allman's being a few years older than Marr, Rourke, and Durkin, saw him treating them as subordinates rather than equals.

Allman saw a notice in the *NME* classifieds placed by Jake Riviera, who was seeking unsigned talent for his newly-incorporated F-Beat Records. Riviera, who had co-founded Stiff Records three years earlier, was inviting acts to send in demos of the song they deemed most representative of their sound. Allman had White Dice record the song he considered to be their most accomplished composition: 'Someone Waved Goodbye'.

A couple of months passed, and Marr was returning home from school one afternoon when the phone rang. Upon answering, he heard someone with a London accent claiming to be Riviera asking for him by name. His initial reaction was that Bobby Durkin was pulling a prank, but it didn't take too long to realise that he was really speaking with Riviera. After some frenzied rehearsals and either tightening up or reworking their repertoire, White Dice were en route to London to record with F-Beat's in-house producer, Nick Lowe, at the latter's AMPRO home studio.

Lowe was away at the time of the session but his designated stand-in, one-time journeyman blues bassist Paul Riley, was certainly no slouch at the mixing desk. Their arrival at AMPRO was to prove memorable owing to Lowe's wife, Johnny Cash's step-daughter Carlene Carter, descending the stairs in a negligee that left little to the imagination. Another added bonus, at least as far as Marr was concerned, came with Riley handing him Elvis Costello's Sixties Rickenbacker to use during the session. Nothing would come of their time at AMPRO, alas, but their recording in a professional studio with a bona fide producer was to leave a lasting impression on Marr. He'd loved every minute of his time at AMPRO and returned to Manchester determined to repeat the experience.

Rourke understood Marr's drive and shared his hunger, whereas Allman and Durkin were acting as though they'd reached the pinnacle of their musical aspirations with the AMPRO session, seemingly content to plot their future through the prism of an empty beer mug. Durkin would soon announce his departure in the time-honoured fashion of simply stopping turning up for rehearsals. A replacement was soon found, but Marr and Rourke were becoming increasingly frustrated at Allman's lack of ambition. When Allman took to the stage drunk at a Students' Union event that Marr had organised, the guitarist knew the time had come for him and Rourke to move on. Playing with Allman did at least provide one important lesson – it was better to lead than follow.

Marr had grown equally bored with playing the same old 4/4 balls-to-the-floor rock. If Paris Valentinos were to make any kind of mark on the local scene, they were going to have to try something different. He hit upon the idea of putting a band together that had a rock sound yet didn't play traditional rock. Despite his having recently treated himself to a second-hand Gibson Les Paul with the money he'd earned from appearing on a long-forgotten Granada TV series called *Devil's Advocate*, which was aimed at Britain's unemployed 'youth'. It was broadcast in the wake of the recent summer riots in Toxteth, Brixton, Birmingham,

Bristol, and, of course, Manchester's Moss Side. Marr had been in gainful employment at the time but was selected simply because the producers thought he would look good in front of the cameras. The equally unknown (at the time) Terry Christian would also appear in *Devil's Advocate*. but whereas Marr would have to settle for the £30 per episode fee, Christian would be offered his own radio show (*Barbed Wireless* on BBC Radio Derby).

Marr was looking to put a band together along the lines of Talking Heads or Manchester's own A Certain Ratio. He knew Rourke's playing style would fit what he had in mind, but they were going to need a good drummer if they were to put theory into practice. As luck would have it, a schoolfriend tipped-off Marr about an Altrincham-based drummer called Funky Si, whose mere nickname was enough to galvanise the guitarist into making the call. Funky Si's full name was Simon Wolstencroft. Not only was he the same age as Marr and Rourke, his drumming hero was Topper Headon, whose versatility had enabled The Clash to experiment with funk-rock on their latest album, Sandinista! and in particular on the opening track, 'The Magnificent Seven'.

"He'd escaped a custodial sentence, was basking in his new-found reputation as a 'Jack-the-lad' and was playing music that sounded both exciting and fresh."

Despite his having sung for a time with Paris Valentinos, Marr had no intention of taking the mic in this latest venture. While the search for a singer continued, the trio initially set up rehearsals in the cellar of a carpet shop before relocating to Decibelle Studios in Ancoats. The studio was some way from completion, and the owner had only agreed to their rehearsing in return for some free labour to help complete remodelling work. Coming up with a cool-sounding band name is almost as important as finding like-minded musicians, but Wolstencroft solved that potential bugbear by suggesting they call themselves after a new song they were working on called 'Freak Party'.

The trio hadn't long been at Decibelle when some uninvited guests burst in on the party. Marr had naively agreed to put some chancer he'd encountered in the shop where he was working in touch with a guy he knew that was known to take moody merchandise off of people's hands. The chancer was looking to shift some "art" that a friend was looking to unload. Unbeknown to Marr, the sketches were by L.S. Lowry and had been stolen while on display in a city centre restaurant. All three were arrested, but Marr was the only one to go before the magistrates. The cops teased him endlessly that he was Strangeways-bound, and even his solicitor warned him he faced the possibility of anywhere between six to twelve months in a youth detention centre. Thankfully, Marr found the presiding magistrate in lenient mood and came away with a £300 fine.

Marr was in his element in more ways than one. He'd escaped a custodial sentence, was basking in his new-found reputation as a 'Jack-the-lad' and was playing music that sounded both exciting and fresh. He sensed Freak Party was on the cusp of something special if they could just find a singer. They'd auditioned a couple of people, but neither had lived up to expectations. Wolstencroft thought he'd solved the situation by inviting the singer from a Clash-influenced outfit called Patrol they'd both played in. The singer in question was Ian Brown, the future Stone Roses frontman, who was duly invited to come along for an audition but would graciously decline as he was in the process of putting his own band together.

Rather than sit on their thumbs while awaiting a frontman the trio decided to put their time at Decibelle to good use in recording an instrumental demo titled 'Crak Therapy'. Away from Decibel, however, the situation wasn't quite so harmonious. Though happy to partake in recreational drugs, Rourke's house was now party central with heroin having long-since replaced weed as the drug de jour. Whereas he'd once regarded chez Rourke a "creative refuge", Marr now saw it as a flop-house filled with reprobates whose only interest was getting high.

With Rourke and Wolstencroft insisting they only smoked heroin, Marr was willing to turn a blind eye to their chasing the dragon so long as their shenanigans didn't interfere with Freak Party. Arriving at Rourke's house one evening after rehearsals to find two of their mates shooting up in the kitchen was to prove the final straw. Marr gathered up his belongings and walked out of the door and Freak Party – without so much as a backward glance. Indeed, it would be several months before he even spoke to Rourke and Wolstencroft again.

Experimenting with Freak Party had been like stepping into the unknown. Marr had enjoyed the sensation and desperately wanted it to continue. He knew he would end up forming a new band at some point, but in the interim – having gone back to live with his parents – he retreated to his bedroom. He spent endless hours listening to his collection of Motown and Phil Spectre records working out how they were put together and applying what he learned to help construct songs from the stockpile of riffs and melodies he'd amassed.

Morrissey had been a familiar face on Manchester's burgeoning punk scene yet had been left to watch from the sidelines as any number of punk-enthused musicians came together and fell by the wayside. Such was his frustration at being "the undiscovered genius" lurking within everyone else's midst that he even resigned himself to joining the 9-5 world by taking a clerical post with the Inland Revenue. For someone bursting with creativity, this was monotony personified, and at the end of each day, he'd trudge home with the black dog of depression silently padding at his heel. Salvation of sorts came in early 1978 when he was befriended by a gang of Wythenshawe-based New York Dolls aficionados, several of whom – including Stephen Pomfret and Billy Duffy – were already acquainted with Marr or at least knew him by sight.

The invitation to join their Wythenshawe clique came via Phil Fletcher, one of the few amongst their number that hadn't thought to try his hand at playing guitar. Fletcher knew Morrissey from afar, having recognised him from the Pistols' second Lesser Free Trade Hall show. He'd also followed Morrissey's music paper musings with avid interest. Upon seeing Morrissey loitering in Virgin Records on Lever Street one Saturday afternoon he'd wandered over and introduced himself. Morrissey was understandably flattered that someone was taking such an interest in his writings. Before parting, an arrangement was made to meet up at a forthcoming Wayne County show at Rafters on March 3. Morrissey would fail to show on the night but Fletcher's perseverance eventually paid off. Fletcher would also be present at Morrissey and Marr's meeting at Patti Smith's Manchester Apollo show the following August.

Morrissey was the proverbial chalk to the Wythenshawe posse's cheese, and yet he genuinely appeared to enjoy hanging out with his new friends and hearing tales of their roguish antics – especially on discovering Pomfret, Duffy, and a couple of the others were keen to start their own punk band.

Pomfret had already started writing songs and Morrissey, sensing his boat might yet still come in after all, readily put himself forward as frontman. During an early band summit it was decided to bolster the line-up of their as yet unnamed outfit by inviting Rob Allman to join. Allman was initially enthusiastic and went so far as to meet up with his prospective bandmates. Being a singer/songwriter himself, Allman had anticipated wannabe frontman Morrissey to be the loudest and most animated one in the room. Yet Morrissey hadn't uttered a solitary word – not even to introduce himself. Ultimately, Morrissey's sole contribution came in naming Pomfret's ad hoc outfit the Tee Shirts. He also attended one of their shows but left before the end without deigning to offer comment on their worth.

Billy Duffy had never really committed himself to the Tee Shirts' cause. Indeed, it seemed to Pomfret and the rest of the Wythenshawe posse that their friend was content to kill time honing his craft jamming with one local band or another until mainstream success fell into his lap. One such outfit was The Nosebleeds, and it just so happened they were on the lookout for a singer.

The Nosebleeds, or Ed Banger and the Nosebleeds as they were originally known, had originally started out as Wild Ram. Edmund 'Ed' Garrity and Phillip 'Toby' Toman had started out jamming Beatles covers in each other's bedroom before evolving into a heavy metal act of sorts with future Durutti Column guitarist, Vini Reilly, and bassist Pete Crookes completing the line-up. The subsequent name-change to Ed Banger and the Nosebleeds was inadvertently due to the Sex Pistols. Gerrity had been co-opted to serve as a roadie for Slaughter & The Dogs at the Pistols' second Lesser Free Trade Hall outing. As previously mentioned, the show was marred by crowd violence and Gerrity and one of his mates ended up in the thick of the fighting. Once order had been restored inside the hall, a wag reportedly passed comment saying something along the lines of, "You're a right bloody mob aren't you? Headbanger here and him with a nosebleed."

The newly-christened Ed Banger and the Nosebleeds had readily adopted a punk image and set about writing songs in line with their new direction. Having inked a deal with local record label, Rabid Records, they released their debut single 'I Ain't Bin to No Music School' b/w 'Fascist Pigs'. A subsequent outing at The Roxy in London's Covent Garden would become memorable owing to their playing these same two songs over and over until the audience "went absolutely berserk" as Reilly remarked. "Consequently, we were asked to play [The Roxy] again and again because that was what was required." The single shifted upwards of 10,000 copies, but arguments over money were to bring about Garrity and Reilly's departures.

It can only be assumed that Billy Duffy was absent from those early Tee Shirts band gatherings, as Morrissey says their introduction came via a card the guitarist had placed on the "musicians wall" at Virgin Records. "I no longer wanted to watch others do what I felt sure I could do so much better," he wrote, "so I present myself to Billy as 'a singer.'"

The Morrissey/Duffy version of The Nosebleeds would make just two live appearances before juddering to a halt. The first came shoring up a four-band billing featuring Gyro, Jilted John, and the headlining Slaughter & The Dogs at Manchester Polytechnic on Saturday, April 15, 1978. The second and final outing came in supporting ex-Buzzcock Howard Devoto's band Magazine at The Ritz (where The

Smiths would of course make their live debut some four years hence) on May 8, 1978. Bootleggers are only interested in recording the main draw, so all that is known about The Nosebleeds' set that night is that it included original Morrissey/Duffy numbers such as 'I Get Nervous', 'Toytown Massacre', 'The Living Jukebox', '(I Think) I'm Ready for the Electric Chair', and 'Peppermint Heaven', along with covers of the Shangri-Las' 'Give Him a Great Big Kiss', and an unreleased New York Dolls' ditty called 'Teenage News'.

Rob Allman, Stephen Pomfret and Phil Fletcher were in the crowd that night. Although Fletcher readily confesses to having had no idea who the support act was when handing over his cash at the box office. "The Nosebleeds were quite good but got a bit of a poor reception because everybody was waiting for Devoto to come on," he recalled for Johnny Rogan's Morrissey & Marr: A Severed Alliance. "That was the first time I saw him sing 'Teenage News' by Syl Sylvain. At the time he hadn't learned to sing and had a very high-pitched scream. I kept wishing he'd bring his voice down a notch because I really wanted to hear the words. He looked very nervous and not at all at ease."

Morrissey took to the Ritz's compact stage looking like a David Johansen wannabe with his hair covering most of his face. But his debut didn't go unnoticed by the NME's young gunslinger, Paul Morley. Morley, who would go on to enjoy a career in journalism, as well as found ZTT Records with Trevor Horn, had also been in attendance at the Pistols' second Lesser Free Trade Hall show, and, according to apocryphal local folklore, was a leading instigator of the sporadic fighting that provided Garrity with the idea for the name-change. Though he was there primarily to review Magazine as part of a concert-review round-up of four Manchester acts for the NME. Morley trills about how The Nosebleeds had resurfaced "boasting a front man With charisma . . . always an advantage." While erring in the spelling of the surname of this "new minor local legend" (calling him Steve Morrison), Morley singled Morrissey out for "at least being aware that rock 'n' roll is about magic and inspiration."

Morrissey, perhaps unsurprisingly, would be in complete agreement with Morley's over-the-top assessment: "We were monstrously good and went down very well," he opined.

Morrissey would also temporarily stand in for Wayne Barrett in Slaughter & The Dogs following the latter's departure in the wake of the band's being dropped by Decca Records. Just as he had with The Nosebleeds, Billy Duffy believed Morrissey was the man to help the Dogs' ailing fortunes.

In October 1978, Morrissey accompanied Mick Rossi and the rest of Slaughter & The Dogs down to London for an unsuccessful record company audition. Although he got as far as recording with the band, he wouldn't feature in Rossi's plans while instigating a move to London.

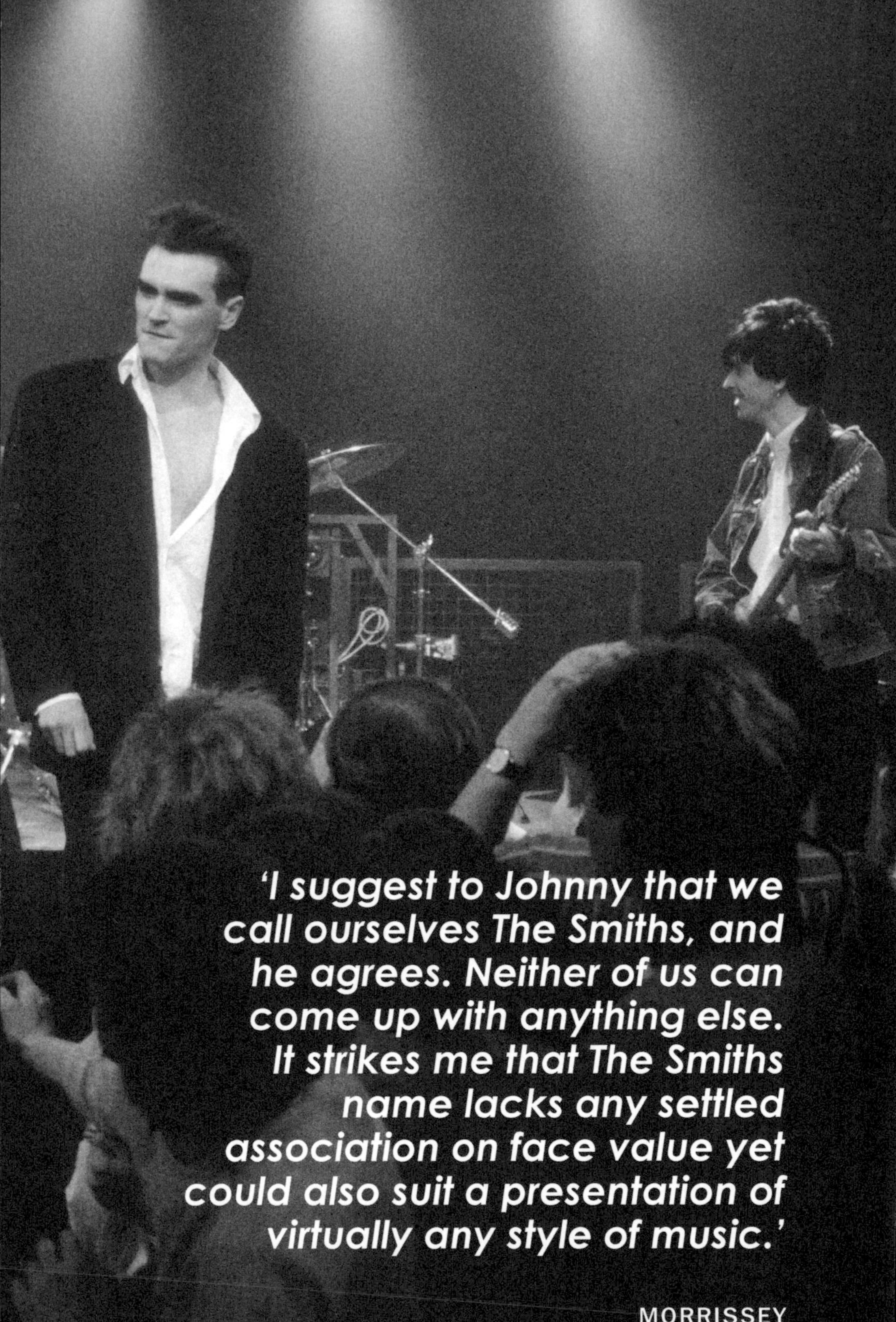

'I suggest to Johnny that we call ourselves The Smiths, and he agrees. Neither of us can come up with anything else. It strikes me that The Smiths name lacks any settled association on face value yet could also suit a presentation of virtually any style of music.'

MORRISSEY

CHAPTER TWO

WAVERING SHADOWS LOOM

Unless one of the musicians in question has a 'eureka moment' – coming up with a name for one's band can prove frustrating in the extreme. Indeed, it's not unusual for bands to undergo several name changes before hitting on the one that suits their modus operandi. The Clash are a perfect case in point as Psychotic Negatives and Weak Heartdrops were a couple of the names under consideration before Paul Simonon came up with the goods. Marr says he was taking his leave after another afternoon holed up in Morrissey's bedroom mapping out a strategy for their as yet unnamed band when the latter presented him with a piece of white card upon which were scrawled three potential band names: 'The Walking Wounded', 'The Smith Family', and 'The Smiths'. He remembers taking a moment to peruse the names, unsure as to whether he liked any of the three before jabbing a finger at 'The Smiths', if only because it was the one he disliked the least. Morrissey had responded with an affirming nod before retreating back to the sanctity of his lair. While en route to Old Trafford train station Marr mouthed The Smiths over and over, most likely envisaging what it might look like on a flyer or even an album cover. 'It sounded like a family,' he reflected, 'and I liked how simple it was. Then I thought about it some more and decided that it was great. The Smiths – it fitted. The Smiths it was.'

The Smiths was now a living entity but no nearer to becoming an actual band. Now that they had a name, however, the strategy now – at least as far as Marr was concerned – was to find the necessary musicians so he and Morrissey could set about working up the song ideas they'd been working on into proper arrangements and record a demo. Stephen Pomfret was invited to early rehearsals, but this was most likely simply down to Marr and Morrissey acknowledging his part in bringing them together – even if the latter would subsequently erase him from the picture when it came to penning his memoir. Paris Valentinos and White Dice had both featured two guitarists in the line-up, but Marr wasn't up for trading licks this time around. It quickly became apparent to Marr that Pomfret wasn't ever going to make it as a guitar player as he was struggling to play anything other than barre chords. Pomfret, however, says Marr

purposely played intricate pieces to test his own virtuosity.

Morrissey was already showing complete indifference as to whether Pomfret was in the room or not. Knowing he would never be able to hold a candle to Marr's playing, Pomfret sensed it was only a matter of time before he was shown the door. Deciding it was better to seize the initiative, he arrived at Shelley Rohde's one evening to give the Marr the news he was quitting. Marr did at least have the grace to insist his friend was a part of things, but Pomfret was under no illusion that it was nothing more than lip service. Sure enough, Marr called a couple of days later asking for the tape on which Morrissey had sung acapella on the songs they'd been working on – one of which was believed to be the long-lost 'Don't Blow Your Own Horn'. Marr's excuse was that he wanted to add some guitar pieces and said that he'd return the tape once he'd finished with them. It was the last Pomfret was to see of the tape, but his offering to accompany Marr to Morrissey's home that fateful afternoon has at least earned him a footnote in the history of The Smiths.

The Smiths' standard Morrissey/Marr/Rourke/Joyce line-up the world come to know (and love) wouldn't come into being for several months. Both Rob Allman and Pomfret have gone on record saying Paul Whittall was briefly involved, but Marr makes no mention of it in *Set the Boy Free*. According to the guitarist's sequence of events, his first port of call was Si Wolstencroft. Yet while Marr admits to a willingness to overlook Wolstencroft's drug proclivities, he wasn't as yet willing to extend the same courtesy to Rourke... for the time being, at least. When Marr called on Wolstencroft to see if he was interested in their working together again, he reportedly burst out laughing on hearing the new band's moniker but did at least agree to come along to a rehearsal to check them out.

Marr's next port of call was Phillippe Delcloque, owner of Decibelle Studios (a renovated cotton mill situated near the Rochdale Canal in Ancoats), to see about the possibility of their 'borrowing' the facilities to record a demo once the studio had closed for the day. Freak Party had been allowed to rehearse at the studio free gratis but only because of Marr's pitching in and helping with the renovations. Delcloque was happy to have his arm twisted – but only on the condition that the studio's in-house engineer, Dale Hibbert, be on hand to keep an eye on things.

20-year-old Hibbert was already known to Marr, of course, as he'd engineered Freak Party's Crak Therapy demo. "I first met Johnny at Decibelle," says Hibbert. "We became friends quite quickly. Johnny was introduced to me by my drummer, Bill Anstee, who had been in a band with Johnny called 'Sister Ray'. I was a huge Velvets fan so clearly the name resonated with me. Johnny was just another guitarist to my mind. I didn't have a lot of time for guitarists as all my bands had two bass players and no conventional guitarists. In fact, I'd never played in a group with a guitarist before."

In his 2015 memoir, *Boy Interrupted,* Hibbert says his first impression of Marr was one of self-assured cockiness; a trait he readily recognised in himself. *Coronation Street* would have the world believe Mancunians – or northerners in general – live out of each other's pockets; their doors always open, their lives an open book. 'Corrie' is a soap opera, of course, and while there are always exceptions to every rule, the northern way of life – especially back in the early-Eighties – isn't quite so candid. As such, most of their chit-chat centred around music and what each had going on at that particular time. There was no need to share familial anecdotes, and neither sought to intrude into the other's personal life. Though only two years older than Marr, Hibbert had been married, become a father, and was in the process of getting divorced.

Born in December 1961, Hibbert's had grown up in Didsbury, another of Manchester's southern suburbs, within a working-class setting not too dissimilar to those Marr and Morrissey had enjoyed. However, losing his mother within days of his entering the world had shaped his life in ways Marr and Morrissey could never hope to understand.

Hibbert's dad, Eric (who was possessed of a matinee idol look that Morrissey would undoubtedly have appreciated), struggled holding down a job and raising a child singlehandedly and shipped him off to live with paternal grandparents. It was perhaps only natural that having been cruelly denied a mother's love that he would attach himself to his dotting gran. Less understandable, however, was his grandfather's unbridled resentment at what he saw as an unwarranted intrusion. His own chicks had fled the nest long ago, and he saw no need to take a cuckoo under his wing – regardless of the circumstances. Though too young to fully comprehend the old man's antipathy, his dad's later condoning his new lady friend's open hostility towards him brought an anguish no child should have to endure; his subsequently being misdiagnosed as a paranoid schizophrenic – by the same GP that had misdiagnosed his mother's illness – merely adding to his melancholy.

It's little surprise that Hibbert grew up wearing his introversion like a badge of honour, but Marr had no agenda other than to further his musicality at the hands of anyone willing to give him the time. "Johnny made me feel important, asking my opinion, seeking approval," Hibbert enthused. "I sensed he looked up to me because I had played in more established bands and worked at a studio. This was how it worked in music; everyone always wants to know

"This was how it worked in music; everyone always wants to know how the person that little bit further down the road has got there."

how the person that little bit further down the road has got there."

Hibbert also happened to be a bass player and had honed his craft playing in a plethora of local acts. His latest band being The Adorables, an unassuming quartet that had steadily built up a decent following on the local circuit. Marr was quick to see the benefits, and co-opted Hibbert's services on both sides of the mixing desk. Hibbert says he doesn't remember Marr delivering a persuasive speech about how The Smiths were going to be the biggest thing to come out of Manchester, but he nonetheless allowed himself to be convinced to quit The Adorables and focus his energies on the demo. "I didn't take a lot of persuading really. Something had happened within The Adorables. I can't remember what that 'something' was now. All I remember is that I was disillusioned with my band and a little bored. The Adorables had a reasonable fanbase, playing in venues with a capacity of 200 or so. But on listening to a rehearsal session soon after I left, I realised they'd moved towards a 'funkier sound. A little like ACR (A Certain Ratio)." Though happy to allow himself to be cajoled into joining The Smiths, Hibbert says he wasn't looking at it being an all-or-nothing opportunity. He was proud of his musicianship, yet still saw himself carving out a career as a studio engineer.

Just as Marr was giving himself a congratulatory pat on the back for his recent endeavours, Wolstencroft called to say he was having second thoughts. Marr and Morrissey's mandate for The Smiths called for 100 per cent commitment, but Wolstencroft was reluctant to give up his day job. He was also hesitant about playing rock again. His nickname was Funky Si, after all. Marr was disappointed but remained undeterred. Such was his determination to get The Smiths up and running that he sounded out Bill Anstee. Anstee was initially sceptical but agreed to come along to a rehearsal. Marr was initially ecstatic, but the smile would slip from his face as it was apparent from the get-go that Anstee wasn't feeling the groove. The guitarist found himself at square one but had no intention of staying there. He bought the biggest bag of weed he could lay his hands on and gave Wolstencroft another call. Skunky Si was in.

With Wolstencroft on board, he and Hibbert were each given a cassette tape that Morrissey and Marr had produced of the two songs they would be recording: 'The Hand That Rocks the Cradle', and 'Suffer Little Children'. (It was still known as 'Over the Moors' but we'll refer to it 'Suffer Little Children' for simplicity's sake).

Of the two compositions, Hibbert preferred 'Suffer Little Children' as he thought 'The Hand That Rocks the Cradle' a 'bit bluesy and country and western' for his tastes. Another tape Morrissey and Marr presented to Hibbert (which he still has in his possession), featured a version of The Cookies' 'I Want a Boy for my Birthday' (the flip side to their 1963 single 'Will Power'), which Marr had recorded on his TEAC three-track Portastudio. Given what we now know of Morrissey and Marr's shared passion for sixties all-girl groups, their recording the song doesn't come as much of a surprise. Nor does Morrissey's vocal

remaining faithful to the song's saccharine-sweet girl-dreaming-about-finding-a-boy-to-love lyric.

"'Birthday' was actually the first tape, not the second," says Hibbert. "It was recorded for me in Bowden. I sat there while they recorded it. The idea being that I was to add bass to it over the next few days. One of the statements I have always found to defy all logic is that I couldn't play (bass). Johnny had heard me play many times. Style-wise I was opposite to Andy Rourke, as I came from a punk heritage while he reminded me of someone who really wanted to front Level 42. Anyhow, they gave me the tape to compose a bass line to, which I did over the next few days.

"The Decibelle demo was fast and dirty, an overnighter on stolen time. I didn't have any attachments to the songs as Johnny insisted on writing the bass parts, I made it clear that I would play them, but I had to have input on further songs. This has to be seen in the context of the time. I was a sound engineer, I had heard hundreds of bands, all of whom were convinced they were the 'next big thing'. And as with every other band, Johnny and Steven believed that this was the demo that would secure them a deal. I wasn't overawed with the songs, but I didn't dislike them either."

There are instances where male singers have changed the gender of a lyric for fear of appearing less masculine – The Beatles' amending The Donays' 1962 single 'Devil in His Heart' to 'Devil in Her Heart' on *With the Beatles* for example. It's unlikely Morrissey gave such implications a thought, but a guy singing about wanting a girl for his birthday nonetheless conjures up certain unsavoury images. Morrissey and Marr also intended to play 'I Want a Boy for my Birthday' in their live set. In *Set the Boy Free,* Marr says that he realised the song would send out a message that not only didn't bother him in the slightest, but actually left him 'fairly amused by and quite excited about'.

Hibbert probably wouldn't have given Morrissey and Marr's wanting to incorporate 'I Want a Boy for my Birthday' into the set a second thought had he not been blithely informed The Smiths were to be presented to the world as a gay band – though not in a Tom Robinson 'Glad to be Gay' kind of way, Marr had apparently been quick to stress. 'It was fine with me,' says Hibbert. 'Peoples' sexuality have no interest to me. It doesn't define them. I took Johnny's remarks to mean that their band wouldn't be so earnest or sloganeering but more oblique and enigmatic. I knew Johnny wasn't gay but had noticed immediately that Steven definitely wasn't your typical Stretford lad; a bit of an understatement.' Indeed . . .

Morrissey's sexuality was always something of a hot topic throughout his time with The Smiths and beyond. Indeed, it was only in the wake of the publication of *Autobiography* in 2013 (in which he opens up about his relationship with Jake Owen Walters) that he felt compelled to set the record straight. 'Unfortunately, I am not homosexual. In technical fact, I am humasexual,' he posted on the Morrissey fan-site True to You on October 19, 2013. 'I am attracted to humans. But, of course . . . not many.'

In an October 1986 interview with

Rolling Stone the man who once declared himself 'celibate' explained how the gender ambiguity in certain Smiths songs was intentional. 'It was very important for me to try and write for everybody. I find when people and things are entirely revealed in an obvious way, it freezes the imagination of the observer. There is nothing to probe for, nothing to dwell on or try and unravel.'

In his memoir, Morrissey also dwells on his teenage indifference to the opposite sex: 'Girls remained mysteriously attracted to me and I had no idea why, since although each fumbling foray hit the target, nothing electrifying took place, and I turned a thousand corners without caring ... Far more exciting were the array of stylish racing bikes that my father would bring home.'

The idea to push The Smiths as a gay band came from Marr's hitting the gay bars with a couple of his mates once his usual haunts had closed. 'The notion of the Smiths as a gay band was just because a lot of my mates were gay guys who liked rock music,' he explained. 'I liked the idea of us being a band that were saying things for the gay community.'

Marr's fashion sense might have brought howls of derision in certain quarters, but no one who knew him around this time would think to question his sexuality as he and Angie were now practically joined at the hip. Morrissey, like Marr, was frequenting gay bars – both in Manchester's gay village as well as in London – with his best friend, a James Dean look-a-like called James Maker, who would come to feature in The Smiths' nascent history.

Declaring themselves a gay band wasn't the only attention-grabbing gimmick Marr and Morrissey intended for The Smiths, however. According to Hibbert, each member was to adopt the name of a mass murderer with whom they shared their Christian name as an alter-ego. Hibbert says he duly became Dale Nelson.

Dale Merle Nelson was a Canadian mass murderer who killed eight people - including five young children – in September 1970 following a drink and LSD binge. Nelson used several weapons during his killing spree, including a hammer and fire extinguisher. He also reportedly attempted to eat the organs on one of his victims. Despite a plea of criminal insanity brought about by his heavy drinking and use of LSD, Nelson was sentenced to life imprisonment. He died of throat cancer in 1999 aged 60 while still in prison.

In today's internet age, information on Nelson is but a mouse-click away. It wasn't so easy back in 1982, however. There was very little coverage of Nelson's crimes on British television or in the media. The only other means open to them would have been Larry Still's 1973 book *The Limits of Sanity*.

The idea obviously came to nought, however. Hibbert says neither Marr nor Morrissey got around to choosing their own 'nom de noir'. Interestingly, neither makes mention of adopting serial killer names in their respective memoirs. 'It was merely a suggestion by Steven to prevent us having the suffix of 'Smith',' Hibbert explains. "It was only mentioned once or twice before being dropped."

Another short-lived notion was to adopt a retro-Americana look by sporting

American bowling shirts and a specific utility trousers onstage. One trend that would be adopted, however, was the official Smiths flat-top haircut, as provided by Marr's hairdresser friend Andrew Berry. Berry was becoming something of a cause célèbre on the Manchester music scene, having secured a DJ slot at the newly-opened Haçienda.

"You can't underestimate the importance of Andrew Berry," Marr told on-line magazine, *The Quietus,* in September 2009. 'He was one of the DJs at the early Haçienda and he knew everybody. He still does. He furnished Bernard Sumner with his haircut, which was very important, and then he would do mine and eventually Morrissey's. He decided that his salon was going to be in the dressing room of The Haçienda...

"One of the crucial things Andrew brought in was that he played absolutely up-to-the-minute electro at The Haçienda – up-to-date, early electro. That's why in 'How Soon Is Now' the harmonic lick is from Lovebug Starski (New York-based electro/hip-hop pioneer): that was me getting one up on the journalists, putting a lick from a hip-hop record into a Smiths song.'

Prior to switching rehearsals to Decibelle, the quartet crammed into Marr's upstairs room at Shelley Rohde's place to work on 'The Hand that Rocks the Cradle' and 'Suffer Little Children' to get them as tight as possible. Hibbert made the journey to Altrincham on his motorbike and seeing as passed close to King's Road on his route he offered to stop off and collect Morrissey. Hibbert says his kindness didn't serve to bring him and Morrissey any closer. He'd knock on the door, Morrissey would don the spare helmet Hibbert handed him, they'd get on the bike and set off with nary a word spoken. "I think Steven saw silence as enigmatic," says Hibbert. "We had a lot in common but didn't share a lot."

The Decibelle version of 'The Hand That Rocks the Cradle' isn't all that far removed from the one that appears on The Smiths – Morrissey's mournful delivery floating over what we would come to know as Marr's trademark chiming guitar. While Morrissey would come into his own as a frontman, he was still finding his range and Marr would be forced to tune up his Les Paul a full step (from the standard E/A/D/G/B/E to F#/B/E/A/C#/F#) Marr also provides backing vocals on the track – something he would surprisingly soon abandon.

'Suffer Little Children' differs from the album version but only because of Marr and Morrissey's kids-in-a-candy-store heavy-handed use of echo and reverb. Their experimentation on the song extended to splicing in Marr's pre recorded waltz-like piano. A student friend of Morrissey's called Annalisa Jablonska was called upon to provide the Myra Hindley-esque cackling, while the equally questionable sound of children at play came courtesy of Marr's living within close proximity of a primary school.

It is thanks to Hibbert's reflections that we can peel away some of the mystique surrounding the enigmatic Jablonska. "She was pretty, slim, had her dark hair cut into a bob, [and] was dressed trendily, much in the vogue of how most students were at the

time," he revealed. "I couldn't quite work out the nature of their relationship, not that I was particularly bothered. She was very enamoured of Steven, clinging to his every word and laughing at his jokes. They appeared to share the same personal space, and he was very comfortable with this. I should stress, however, that it's only ever been confirmed second-hand that Anna was the girl at Decibelle that day."

Marr says he and Morrissey stayed behind at the studio well into the early hours mixing each track. Hibbert, however, vehemently contests this. "Absolute rubbish! I didn't let anyone touch the desk, and I wouldn't leave the studio in anyone else's hands. There was a lot of valuable equipment at Decibelle. It was entrusted to me and was, therefore, my responsibility. Neither Johnny nor Steven had any idea how to use a mixing desk, effects panel, or multi-track tape machine. Johnny saying he and Steven mixed the demos is as ridiculous as him saying he visited someone in hospital and was then left to carry out brain surgery.

"The sound they were getting from the big speakers [at Decibelle] wasn't the same sound that'd come out of a radio or a cassette player. I just let Johnny mess about with the faders until he was happy with it. Then he and Steven went home with their version and I carried on with the mixing."

A second prerequisite laid down by Delcloque was that Hibbert restrict the band to using eight tracks otherwise he would charge them the studio's going daily rate. They would end up using eleven tracks during the recording but Hibbert was happy to keep that particular detail between himself and the band.

Hibbert says he was led to believe that he'd be allowed to write his own bass lines, and certainly wouldn't have walked away from The Adorables had he anticipated his being regarded by Marr and Morrissey as little more than a gun for hire. "I was brought into the group on what amounted to a false pretence," he reflected. "I was putting forward bass lines at rehearsals, but they were rejected in favour of Johnny's. He (Marr) said once or twice that mine were better, but his 'fitted the song'. I had no comeback to this assertion. He was stating clearly that the overall sound of the group was the one he decided, and he alone.

"Needless to say, I wasn't happy. I was used to being the one in charge, the realisation that I was to become a session musician came slowly. Again, context is everything. I was with the band for over six months. During this time, I left Decibelle to become a partner in Spirit (Studios), which needed to be designed and built. This took a lot of time and energy. It wasn't just the studio as there were rehearsal rooms. I was also engineering and producing for New Hormones, and there was live OB (Outside Broadcast) work for the BBC and engineering at the Band on the Wall. The Smiths were the lowest priority in all my ventures."

Marr doesn't say anything about Hibbert's engineering in Set the Boy Free but doesn't hold back about the latter's bass playing. Andy Rourke had set the bass bar pretty high, and Marr was harbouring doubts as to whether Hibbert would deliver on the songs. The guitarist's fears appeared unfounded as the initial run through of

'Suffer Little Children' went well enough and Morrissey and Marr were buzzing at hearing one of their compositions in a professional studio. It seemed a validation of their hard work to date. The euphoria soon wore off, however. Hibbert says how he 'played the bass, and it was quite easy', but Marr's version of events has him repeatedly fluffing his part on 'The Hand That Rocks the Cradle' – despite it being a rather pedestrian six-note riff.

Hibbert contests Marr's version of events. "I haven't read Johnny's book, but I would ask if I was so bad why they then wanted me to play at The Ritz? From memory, I was adding to it, and maybe he didn't like the extras. Let's be candid. We played three or four songs at the Ritz, Andy could easily have stepped in. He used to hang around the band like a lost puppy. What was the reason they didn't use him? It has gone down in history that I was 'used' for a free session. My answer has always been that many bands had free sessions, and they didn't ask me to join. And more importantly, once the session was recorded, why did they keep me to play The Ritz?"

There are no set rules to recording a demo, of course, but most bands would block-book a full day – usually a 24-hour session – in a studio to ensure enough time should things go awry. Given the rigid time restraints they were working under, the two songs were of a decent enough quality. Marr has obviously since come to realise the demo's deficiencies, but at the time he was cock-a-hoop. Not content with driving his mates and X Clothes colleagues crazy with repeated airings, he went from shop to shop with his Portastudio badgering staff and customers alike into listening to the tape.

Aside from the Factory bands, other local musos and creative types, X Clothes' clientele primarily consisted of students enrolled at Manchester University – many of whom would most likely come to champion The Smiths within the not-too-distant future. Marr's friendship with Moss would have proved sufficient to ensure the demo received an enthusiastic reception in Crazy Face and Tupelo Honey, but mournful laments – especially one relating to a harrowing series of child murders that happened on their doorstep – had some disgruntled shoppers heading for the door. Marr remained undaunted, however.

"It has gone down in history that I was 'used' for a free session."

Hibbert readily admits that the demo was 'above the usual standard' of the bands he'd engineered and produced at Decibelle yet says he didn't consider the songs anything special. "I already felt to be an old hand and had seen what had happened to many similarly promising groups and their demo tapes. Passing a small bundle [of tapes] to Johnny, I imagined they might help secure a concert or two around town or become mementos for family and friends."

Marr was hardly the first muso to think his demo tape was the best thing since Otto Rohwedder's single loaf bread

slicer, but after suffering setbacks and disappointments with Paris Valentinos, White Dice, and Freak Party, he was becoming more and more convinced that he was onto a winner with The Smiths. Funky Si Wolstencroft didn't share his belief, however, and gave notice that he would need to find another drummer. Marr was disappointed but took the view that it was better to let Wolstencroft go rather than continue with a drummer that didn't see any worth in what they were doing.

Morrissey thought he'd found a replacement for Wolstencroft after coming into possession of a demo tape featuring fellow Stretford resident, Gary Farrell, on drums. Morrissey knew Farrell and having played Marr the demo, the two made their approach. Farrell was enthused by Morrissey's vision for The Smiths but decided to pass as he didn't think much of his singing on the Decibelle demo. Aside from mooting Bill Anstee's name, Hibbert put forward his erstwhile fellow Adorable, Tony Elmsley. He'd argued neither drummer's case as he didn't want it to appear that he was furtively bringing about a power share within the band. "Bill and Tony would have been perceived as primarily friends of mine, and this 'two versus two' potential power base might have made Johnny and Steven uncomfortable. Obviously, the rhythm-section, whatever the strength of the personalities involved, only ever has a limited influence on a group where the singer and guitarist co-write the material, so it was a largely groundless concern."

Hibbert's theorising isn't without president, of course, as Johnny Rotten had affected a similar coup in the Sex Pistols. Though his growing animosity towards Glen Matlock undoubtedly played its part, Rotten viewed Steve Jones and Paul Cook as being a 'block vote' when it came to band policy and so instigated Matlock's ousting in favour of his pal Sid Vicious in early 1977. Whereas Hibbert was of secondary consideration in Marr and Morrissey's game plan for The Smiths, Rotten was glorifying in his being perceived as the focal point of the Pistols – by fans and media alike – and could hold the band to ransom.

The Smiths were still no nearer to finding a replacement for Wolstencroft when Andrew Berry called Marr to say that, along with their mutual friend John 'JK' Kennedy, he was staging a fashion showcase at the Ritz on Whitworth Street West (currently the O2 Ritz) on October 4. John Kennedy ran the Exit Club at the time which was situated just off Deansgate.

Headlining the event at the Ritz – billed as 'An Evening of Pure Pleasure' - were Blue Rondo à la Turk, a London-based salsa-loving sextet that were signed to Virgin Records. (Blue Rondo were fronted by Chris Sullivan, an early punk aficionado who had made regular forays to London with his mates from their native Merthyr Tydfil during the spring/summer of 1976 to SEX, and to see the Sex Pistols play the 100 Club as well as other venues within the capital. Chris can also boast of catching The Clash's live debut at London's 100 Club at the end of August 1976)

Blue Rondo's second single, the nonsensical-sounding 'Klactoveesedstein', had proved a favourite in nightclubs across

THE
QUEEN
IS
DEAD

the country yet had surprisingly stalled at #50 on the chart. Their debut album, *Chewing the Fat*, was set for imminent release and it was hoped their debut single 'Me and Mr Sanchez', having been selected as the theme tune for ITV's coverage of the recent World Cup Finals in Spain, would bring about an upturn in their fortunes.

The Smiths had their name in print on a poster, but Marr and Morrissey were no nearer to unearthing a drummer. Just when the duo were thinking they might have to pull out of the event, however, a friend of Marr's called Pete Hunt, who owned Discount Records in Altrincham, called in at Shelley Rohde's to put the guitarist onto a drummer he knew named Mike Joyce who was living in neighbouring Fallowfield.

All Hunt could tell Marr about Joyce – other than the two of them would get on at least – was that he'd played in The Hoax, a local punk band that had released a couple of singles on their own Hologram Music label. Marr prided himself on knowing the names of all the local bands, yet The Hoax meant nothing to him. Marr trusted Hunt's judgement and was happy to let his friend set up a meeting with Joyce that night at Legend – or 'Legends' as the Princess Street nightclub was more commonly known.

Marr did indeed click with Joyce and readily laid out his and Morrissey's blueprint for The Smiths before enquiring if the 19-year-old would be amenable to coming along to a rehearsal with Morrissey and Hibbert. Imagine his confusion when Joyce announced that he was playing in a band called Victim that was contemplating returning to their native Belfast. Did that mean Joyce was soon to be a free agent, or that he was relocating to Belfast? Joyce did at least agree to have a listen to the songs on the Decibelle demo. A couple of days later Joyce arrived at X Clothes to say that while he was unsure about the songs on the demo his flatmate had thought it worth agreeing to a rehearsal at least.

Said rehearsal took place at Hibbert's new place of employment: the newly-opened Spirit Studios. Situated on Tariff Street, a short walk from Piccadilly Station, Spirit was two years away from becoming the School of Sound Recording (the first dedicated Audio Engineering School in the UK). At the time of its opening for business it was a grimy, half-finished subterranean cinder block room; its feeble lighting serving to heighten the bunker mentality.

Hibbert was at Decibelle when a guy came through the door and introduced himself. John Breakell had recently returned from Australia with £12,000 burning a hole in his wallet coupled with a searing desire to open a studio and rehearsal complex. He'd taken possession of the Tariff Street basement premises and having been tipped the wink that Hibbert was the 'man in the know' on the Manchester music scene, he'd arrived at Decibelle determined to get his man.

Hibbert had been at Decibelle for going on 12 months and in that time Delcloque hadn't increased his weekly £20 cash-in-hand wages. But it was more the fact that he'd never truly felt appreciated by Delcloque that saw him accept Breakell's offer. Hibbert was involved with every aspect of the new studio's inception, from its design,

to overseeing the renovations, to help choosing its name. "The part that interested me most was that I would be an equal partner,' says Hibbert. 'I worked, without payment for this reason for over a year. I brought bands in and lent him (Breakell) money to make it look like the studio was earning. I was incredibly naïve; nothing was written down. John has apologised and wanted to 'build bridges', I told him to 'fuck off'. What he did to a younger version of me really has no effect 30 years down the line. But there's no forgiveness."

Marr remembers Joyce appearing apprehensive while making the introductions on the pavement outside Spirit, but this doesn't hold water given the latter having enjoyed a modicum of success during his time with The Hoax. The drummer had recognised Marr readily enough at their Legends get-together, but for his being a face on the Manchester scene rather than his guitaring prowess. Joyce's supposed nervousness was in fact down to his having taken magic mushrooms earlier in the day. That he would choose to take mushrooms before setting off for the studios suggests he wasn't expecting anything to come of the rehearsal – despite his subsequent claims that he could function well enough while in a psychedelic state.

Hibbert has no recollections as to Joyce's state. Nor was he overly impressed on seeing him that day. "Mike likes to pretend he didn't know me and was maybe the fifth or sixth drummer (one of them being Bill Anstee who'd played with Johnny and me previously). The Adorables had played with The Hoax and Victim many, many times as we were active at the same time. We'd both appeared on the Ten from the Madhouse compilation album. The compilation included a lot of bands from the Manchester Musicians Collective. So I knew Mike but didn't particularly like him. I'd no idea about his drug use and can't honestly remember whether he was stoned that day or not."

The first song the quartet played at Spirit was 'The Hand That Rocked the Cradle'. Despite his playing in a semi-hallucinogenic state, Joyce was surprisingly able to pick up the beat, but Marr sensed something was awry. He knew it wasn't his playing or Morrissey's singing which meant it had to be Joyce or Hibbert's playing that was off kilter. He decided to hold his tongue until they'd run through the rest of the songs which included 'Suffer Little Children', and new compositions 'What Difference Does It Make' and 'Handsome Devil'; the latter being built around a rockabilly riff that Marr had come up with while with Paris Valentinos.

Marr still couldn't put his finger on which of the two was at fault, however, and Joyce's admitting to his being off his head didn't exactly endear him to the guitarist. Indeed, Joyce's total disregard for the audition should have resulted in his being sent packing with his ears ringing. Marr was willing to overlook such blatant unprofessionalism, however. He decided Joyce was worth giving a shot.

Joyce continued dragging his feet, however. It wasn't that he was unsure about The Smiths' musical direction, or the band's chances of gaining a foothold on the local scene, but rather a reluctance to leave

Victim in the lurch. One day he'd be in only to reverse his decision the next. Joyce's vacillating left Marr in a quandary. He really enjoyed Joyce's company but knew Morrissey was still holding out hope that Wolstencroft would have a change of heart. With the clock ticking, Marr cajoled Joyce into doing the Ritz show and seeing where things went from there.

It's only once a band achieves success that a debut gig takes on any significance. Even then, the importance is usually the reserve of fans gaining one-upmanship in swearing they were there. Depending on the timespan involved, most bands struggle to remember their first live outing, but this is understandable given everything that has happened to them in-between. Marr, thankfully, is an exception to the rule. Whereas Morrissey makes no mention of The Smiths' Ritz debut in his memoir, the guitarist savours every detail in Set the Boy Free. He didn't work Mondays so arrived at the Ritz well in advance of Morrissey and the others, watching from the wings smoking one cigarette after another to calm his nerves. They were setting up at the left-hand side of the stage when Chris Sullivan and the rest of Blue Rondo à la Turk came through the door in what Marr describes as a 'huge whoosh of zoot-suited magnificence'.

It's not uncommon for support acts to try cosying up to the headliners in the hope of more gigs or the passing on of a demo – especially when the headliners are a signed act. The Smiths' stripped back aesthetic couldn't have been further removed from Blue Rondo à la Turk's flamboyance. As such, there was little likelihood of The Smiths being invited onto a Blue Rondo tour but having their Decibelle demo hand-delivered to the head of Virgin's A&R department conjured up certain possibilities.

Any hope of a little band interaction was supposedly crushed by one of Blue Rondo's burly roadies threatening The Smiths with serious bodily harm should they even think about moving any of the mics. Marr says the confrontation sent him into 'an attitude overhaul of indignation' that quickly spread to others banishing whatever first-night nerves they might have been suffering. Marr would subsequently dismiss Blue Rondo and their entourage as being a bunch dicks. "[They were] really rude and aggressive," he seethed. "They were all midgets too – which probably explains the attitude. Morrissey spent most of the night crouched down at an absurd angle singing into their midget-height microphone."

Any rookie musician knows not to tamper with the headliners' equipment – especially once the soundcheck has been completed. And roadies aren't usually known for their tact. Chris Sullivan, however, strongly refutes Marr's claims. "We usually didn't arrive at any venue until 15 minutes before any gig. We always got dressed in the hotel and arrived at the venue fully kitted out. We didn't mingle with the crowd before going on as we wanted that surprise element. We didn't catch The Smiths' performance as we stayed in our dressing room. I don't remember even speaking to them that much. All this talk about our crew making threats about the

use of our gear is bollocks!. It simply just didn't happen. As for Morrissey supposedly having to crouch down to use my mic is also nonsense. I'm six foot two for starters..."

Berry and Kennedy were happy enough to add The Smiths onto the billing for their fashion extravaganza, but the band's inclusion meant some hurried amendments to the running order. There would have been precious little hope of Blue Rondo à

"I was there to drink red wine, make extraneous hand gestures and keep well within the tight, chalked circle that Morrissey had drawn around me."

la Turk truncating their set, but given The Smiths' limited repertoire it's unlikely the drag queen or dance troupe's time onstage suffered to any degree.

Despite its prominence on the Manchester social and music scenes, The Ritz's stage wasn't much bigger than that of the average working men's club function room. Once Blue Rondo's crew had finished setting up the headliners' equipment and stage accoutrements (which included palm trees according to Hibbert) were in place there was no room left for The Smiths to set up. This is probably the root of their resentment, but it's perfectly understandable as no headline act is going to put up with having their gear disassembled once the soundcheck has been completed.

Getting people that have never heard of you to give up a Monday night cosied up in front of the telly is easier said than done. But Marr's working in X Clothes – coupled with his being pally with Joe Moss – provided ample opportunity to promote the Ritz show. Indeed, one of Marr's work colleagues either brought or grabbed up an acoustic guitar and joined in with the soundcheck. Morrissey didn't have a job, of course, and had but a limited circle of friends. One of these was James Maker, mentioned earlier, who readily agreed to Morrissey's offer to come up from London to introduce the band. Despite Marr's sales pitch, the vast majority of the 300 or so punters were there for the headliners, so having Maker introduce them in French – while sporting a pair of high-heeled stilettos – could have easily blown up in their face.

Another of Morrissey's supposed ideas was to have the DJ play German countertenor performance artist Klaus Nomi's version of 'The Cold Song' from Henry Purcell's 1691 opera *King Arthur* before Maker's introduction. Hibbert contests this, however. "It's been incorrectly reported by authors over the years, but one thing I would like to put straight is that we came on to 'Montagues and Capulets' (aka 'Dance of the Knights' from Sergei Prokofiev's ballet, *Romeo and Juliet*). I am 100 per cent certain about this. It's probably the same for most people, but you remember where you were when you first heard a piece of

music. This was the first time I had heard 'Montagues and Capulets', and it struck me as one of the most powerful compositions I had ever heard.'

James Maker would surprisingly remain onstage throughout The Smiths' debut. 'I was given a pair of maracas – an optional extra – and carte blanche,' he recounted. 'There were no instructions. I think it was generally accepted I would improvise... I was there to drink red wine, make extraneous hand gestures and keep well within the tight, chalked circle that Morrissey had drawn around me.'

Things got off to a shaky start owing to Marr's accidentally catching the machine head of his Gretsch as he walked up to the stage, sending the guitar out of tune. Realising something wasn't right he casually returned the guitar while still playing. The gladioli and daffodils were as yet props for a later day, but Morrissey was equally self-assured onstage – far more than he'd been during his brief tenure with The Nosebleeds at least. That any band is only as good as its drummer has become something of a cliché over the years – yet is nonetheless a truism not to be ignored. Joyce's splitting his snare during the opening number could have brought the show to a premature and embarrassing halt but he soldiered on as best he could. Hibbert's playing was competent enough, but his 'dancing around like a four-year-old at a toddler's disco' didn't sit well with Marr: "I really hoped he would stop. But no, Dale was grooving, and what's more, he looked like he was really enjoying it. At that precise moment, I knew we'd have to part company."

Hibbert makes no excuses for moving in time to the rhythm as he was unable to play any other way. It wasn't as if there had been any instruction to remain static during the performance. And if his actions were so unsettling to Marr and Morrissey's stage aesthetic, all either man had to do was whisper in his ear at the end of the opening song.

Immediately after they came offstage Marr approached Joe Moss and asked if he'd be their manager. Moss had been blown away by what he'd seen – especially Marr's guitar playing – but had never imagined himself managing a band and politely declined. Marr, however, wasn't to be dissuaded and after much arm-twisting Moss eventually caved in.

Moss's first move as manager was to offer Marr a job at Crazy Face to allow the guitarist time to fully focus on taking The Smiths to the next level without having to worry about pissing off his employers. He also provided the band with their own rehearsal room above Tupelo Honey on Portland Street.

Hibbert says he can't place Moss during his time with The Smiths. "This is a weird one, I know, but I have no recollection of him whatsoever. If I met him I do not remember it. The odd thing is that thirty years later we opened a coffee shop in Todmorden and his niece was one of our first customers."

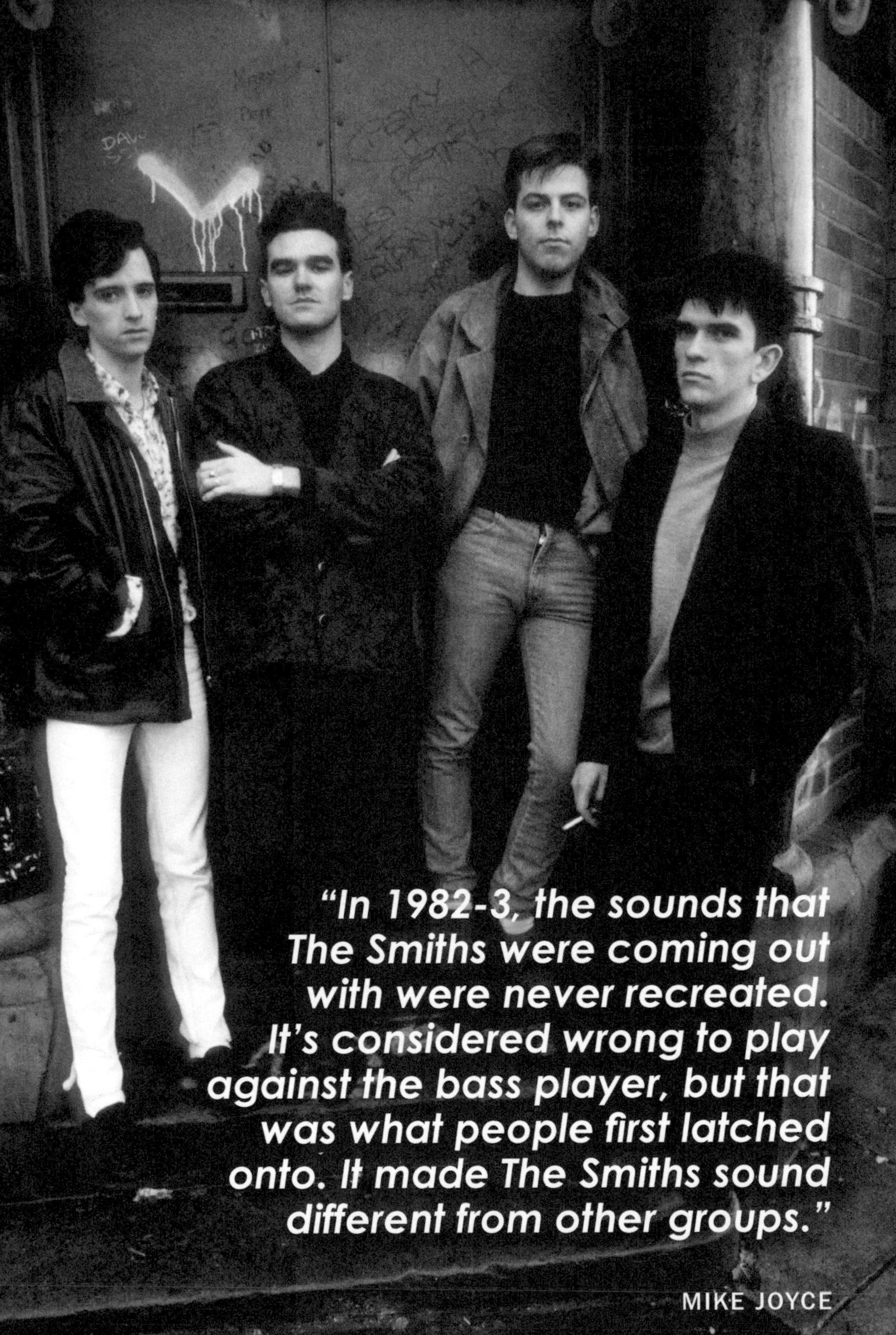

"In 1982-3, the sounds that The Smiths were coming out with were never recreated. It's considered wrong to play against the bass player, but that was what people first latched onto. It made The Smiths sound different from other groups."

MIKE JOYCE

CHAPTER THREE

THROUGH HELL & HIGH TIDE

The Smiths might still have been in a state of flux regarding establishing a stable line-up, but they'd given their first public performance and had secured a manager into the bargain. They'd also secured a first mention of sorts in the music press. The November issue of *The Face* carried a one-paragraph feature on the Ritz extravaganza and although The Smiths didn't get their name in print, the magazine's lauding An Evening of Pure Pleasure as "the kind of live music fashion show that the British don't attempt enough" provided sufficient intrigue for *i-D* magazine to approach the band for an interview. Said interview – simply titled 'The Smiths' – duly appeared in the magazine's February 1983 issue (# 11). Given that *i-D* had taken its lead from *The Face's* mention of Berry and Kennedy's fashion showcase the topics discussed centred around fashion: clothes, style etc, as well as the Manchester scene, of course. Rather than cite names the interviewees are identified simply by the first letter of their Christian names: 'S' for Steven, 'J' for Johnny, and 'D' for Dale. Joyce's absence is explained by his having yet to commit himself to The Smiths. If Hibbert no longer fitted in with Marr's game plan, one has to wonder why he was allowed to participate in the interview?

The muses were certainly smiling favourably upon Marr around this time. He was working out of Crazy Face one afternoon when Tony O'Conner, a friend from West Wythenshawe College, swung by to say that he'd recently landed a role as an A&R scout at EMI and enquired if Marr had a demo tape that he might present to his boss, Hugh Stanley-Clarke, at Manchester Square. Joe Moss had offered Marr a cushy gig at Crazy Face should such a propitious moment present itself, yet it was Morrissey that accompanied O'Conner to London the following day to meet with Stanley-Clarke. While he wasn't exactly overwhelmed by what he heard, Stanley-Clarke recognised The Smiths' potential and readily commissioned a second demo. Hibbert's days were now truly numbered.

Morrissey was already viewing his and Marr's songwriting collaboration as being the driving force behind The Smiths, so raised no objection when the latter suggested

re-establishing contact with Andy Rourke. More than a year had passed since the two had last spoken, and while Rourke was aware of Marr's latest musical venture courtesy of Si Wolstencroft, he was nonetheless caught unawares when the guitarist arrived at his door.

Marr had known deep down that he was never likely to find a bass player as good as Rourke, or certainly one that could feed off of the nuances of his own playing, but he had one non-negotiable stipulation: that Rourke keep his ongoing heroin habit away from The Smiths. Having secured such a promise, he then played Rourke a recording of the Ritz performance. Rourke liked what he heard and agreed to play on the EMI demo with a view to joining the band permanently.

Rourke had showed up with Marr on a couple of occasions – and may well have been in the Ritz crowd – but Hibbert says he didn't feel his position in the band under threat. Nor was he overly concerned that Marr and Morrissey were the only ones involved with meeting various music industry types while touting the Decibelle demo as The Smiths was fundamentally their baby. His dismissal, therefore, came completely out of the blue. He was now practically living at Spirit. The band had finished an otherwise uneventful evening of rehearsals, and he saw the others to the door when he sensed Marr was loitering with obvious intent. "I didn't understand what was happening at first as Johnny wasn't direct. It really wasn't as big a deal to me as he thought it was. I just got on with my day."

It's understandable that Hibbert took the news with good grace. After all, The Smiths had played just the one show, so there was no reason whatsoever for him to anticipate the band's subsequent meteoric rise. Indeed, his only gripe at the time was Marr – whom he'd considered a good friend – had maybe brought him into The Smiths simply to secure free recording time at Decibelle. Another enduring bugbear was his being eradicated from The Smiths' nascent history in *Autobiography*. Indeed, Morrissey's only comment about this period being: "Johnny called in Andy Rourke and Mike Joyce after a few stop-start sessions with other musicians." Hibbert was with The Smiths for four months, which might not seem any length of time given what the Morrissey/Marr/Rourke/Joyce line-up went on to achieve but certainly deserves more recognition than being a "stop-start session".

The EMI demo was recorded at the newly-established Drone Studios on Ellesmere Road in Chorlton-cum-Hardy, South-west Manchester. As with Spirit, Drone was housed in a cramped, windowless cellar. Marr, however, was buzzing at the possibilities now that he was reunited with Rourke. He'd known all along that Rourke was the missing piece to complete his vision for The Smiths and says how he knew from the moment he introduced his friend to Morrissey and Joyce outside the studio that everything else would fall effortlessly into place.

Ironically, Hibbert was at Drone that day and witnessed his former bandmates at work. He and John Breakell were at Drone

furtively checking out the studio's facilities and rates. Hibbert's only concern on seeing four familiar faces through the control booth's glass partition was his and Breakell's cover being blown. "I was embarrassed because we had gone in there under the guise of wanting to record there when really we just wanted to check out the equipment and space. I thought our cover had been blown. Drone was a similar set up to Spirit. We had an interest in their hardware, but at the time, the only way to check it out was to visit. It's often portrayed as like finding your ex-girlfriend canoodling at a table with a new lover, when in reality it was more like, worrying your ex-girlfriend is about to tell your current girlfriend about your bad habits."

Marr says he didn't spot Hibbert and probably thought Joyce was tripping out on magic mushrooms again when he pointed to the partition. With his curiosity sufficiently piqued, he made a quick recce of the studio. He supposedly found Hibbert loitering in the garden, but Hibbert insists no such encounter occurred.

Despite all the uncertainty as to who was in or out of the band, Morrissey and Marr had penned a couple of new songs that were deemed worthy of inclusion on the EMI demo: 'Miserable Lie' and 'What Difference Does It Make?'. The third track recorded that day, 'Handsome Devil', was notable for the use of saxophone courtesy of Andy Gill, a friend of one of Rourke's siblings. Seeing as Gill was something of an ever-present at Rourke's house, Marr suggested bringing him along. "We tried out a saxophone on 'Handsome Devil' because I was listening to a lot of Little Richard," he explained. "A nice man (Gill) came in and tried his best, but The Smiths and the saxophone were never meant to be and I was OK with that."

Marr was very pleased with how 'What Difference Does It Make' sounded in a studio surrounding, however. It was his and Morrissey's most-recent composition and he saw it as a positive step up. Hugh Stanley-Clarke thought otherwise and politely passed on The Smiths. EMI would come crawling back, of course. In the meantime, The Smiths had a far superior demo with which to tout around for shows.

The Smiths second live outing came towards the end of January 1983 at Manhattan (a.k.a. Manhattan Sound), an established gay club located in Spring Gardens within the heart of Manchester's city centre. According to an anonymous review of the Smiths' performance that would subsequently appear in *City Life*, the basement club wasn't so much a gay bar but rather a "club camp where crimson pile meets *Coronation Street*". (*City Life* was a Manchester-based news, arts and listings magazine that was founded in December 1983 and ran until December 2005)

It's unusual for a band to wait three months betwixt their first and second gigs, but this time The Smiths would at least be headlining. Manhattan was a disco bar rather than a club and therefore lacked a stage. It could hold around 300, which was roughly the same number of people The Smiths had played to at the Ritz. The difference this time around being that everyone was coming to see them. Marr remembers there being a lot riding on the

Manhattan show. Not only because the show sold out well in advance – a heady fillip for any new band – but rather because The Smiths had piqued the interest of what he describes as "Manchester's old guard"; the one-time punks that remembered Morrissey from his stints in The Nosebleeds and Slaughter & The Dogs.

The Smiths set up their equipment on the dancefloor playing against a backdrop

"If you were a musician in Manchester at that time, it was almost the law that you went on your hands and knees and begged Tony Wilson for his papal blessing to stick you in the studio, and I wasn't about to do that."

of Devine (the American actor, singer, and drag queen whose debut album, *My First Album,* had been released the previous year) projected on the wall beside them. Aside from three of the four songs they'd played at the Ritz (minus 'Suffer Little Children'), the extended set included 'Miserable Lie', 'What Difference Does It Make', and another new song called 'What Do You See in Him?' (which would soon be reworked into 'Wonderful Woman').

James Maker again introduced the band, and once again jiggled about in his high-heel stilettos banging a tambourine throughout the performance. While Maker's antics caused a ruffle of excitement amongst the club's regulars, others found his presence perplexing. Morrissey's long-time friend, Richard Boon, who'd been managing Buzzcocks since the band's inception, thought Maker "Dispensable". "I thought it was all spare parts, a nice joke," he added, "but it didn't add anything, and they didn't need it."

Rourke found the whole shaker-Maker scenario somewhat embarrassing, but as it was his first show as a Smith he kept his opinions to himself. Marr, however, knew they couldn't continue pandering to Morrissey.

Tony Wilson was also in attendance at Manhattan and had reportedly come away again suitably impressed by what he saw. In a near repeat of his posting the sleeve to the New York Dolls' debut album to Wilson some six years earlier, Morrissey had either posted or hand-delivered a copy of the Decibel demo to the Factory supremo. Wilson would subsequently dine out on his having turned down The Smiths, but Marr tells it differently: "Tony later went round saying that he turned down an opportunity to sign The Smiths to Factory, but he knew I would never have signed [us] to Factory. I liked Tony, but I'd already refused invitations to join a couple of his bands and I wouldn't have had my own band dressed up in khaki for anyone."

Marr's viewpoint wouldn't soften over time, either. "So much has been made of Factory apparently turning The Smiths down but that's a crock of shit," he told the *NME* in 2014. "The Smiths would have signed to Factory over my dead body. I didn't want to be assimilated into the Factory aesthetic. If you were a musician in Manchester at that time, it was almost the law that you went on your hands and knees and begged Tony Wilson for his papal blessing to stick you in the studio, and I wasn't about to do that."

According to Wilson, Morrissey invited him to his home sometime during 1980 "I sat rather uncomfortably late afternoon in this teenager's bedroom surrounded by posters of James Dean," he recalled. "He announced to me that he'd decided to become a pop star. From the very beginning he had the aura of genius, without any doubt at all, I presumed he would be a playwright or a novelist, he would be our great literary genius. I looked at this kid and I almost had to stop myself laughing. Although I was in love with his genius and I could see it in his eyes, there was no way on God's earth this strange kid was ever, ever going to be a pop star. I almost laughed in his face, but I was very polite and I said, 'Oh Steven very interesting.'"

Though happy to admit he'd realised instantly just how wrong he'd been to dismiss Morrissey's aspirations on seeing him fronting The Smiths, Wilson still maintained the decision to pass up The Smiths rested with himself: "Come 1982 we'd gone into a cold period. People in the record industry say you have to learn how to be cold, sometimes for two, three years. I'd never been cold before. I found it deeply, deeply disturbing. I was very depressed with my record label. I thought to myself, I am not going to saddle Steven and his wonderful band with a crap record label. It wasn't until the following year with Blue Monday that Factory took off again."

Wilson then went on to say that while Rob Gretton was going around telling anyone willing to listen that The Smiths were the new Beatles, he'd told the band their demo was "fucking shit", and that if they came back with a good one, then Factory would look to sign them. "Rob wanted a good demo and I wanted a good label." Wilson did at least have the grace to admit it was The Smiths' success following their signing with Rough Trade that kept the whole indie scene afloat for the remainder of the Eighties and beyond.

The City Life review lauded The Smiths as being a "standard line-up of (James) Dean-struck laddies" continu[ing] the traditions the New York Dolls and Auntie Iggy with lurid vigour," whilst singling out Morrissey as an "arresting figure whose appearance lay somewhere between Christopher Isherwood and a Foreign Office junior." The review would also questioned Maker's worth before ending with the pronouncement that The Smiths were "going to be B-I-G." This was the night that Marr says he truly realised Morrissey's potential. The Smiths "were a band with a singer who was not only a unique presence on stage. He was made for his audience, and we were made for our audience."

There was no question that a band

consisting of four "Dean-struck laddies" would appeal to Manchester's gay crowd. Yet if The Smiths were ever to be taken seriously amongst the city's cognoscenti, they would need to turn heads at Manchester's new musical bastion – The Haçienda.

The Haçienda (situated at 11-13, Whitworth Street West) has become as much of a part of Manchester folklore as any of the bands that played there. Bankrolled by Factory Records – or primarily by New Order to be more precise – the Haçienda (FAC 51) had opened the previous May to much fanfare. Working to Factory's brief of: "big bar, small bar, food, stage, dance-floor, balcony, and a cocktail bar in the basement", designer Ben Kelly (who'd overseen the renovations at 430 King's Road from SEX to Seditionaries), transformed the former Yacht builder's warehouse into a true "people's palace". The massive single space interior was painted in cool blue and grey tones with brightly clad balcony supports and diagonal stripes painted on columns. The urban theme continued with hazard markings, bollards, neon-lighting, and rounded off with cats-eyes mapping out the dancefloor.

The Smiths would be playing support to 52nd Street, a local jazz-funk five-piece that Factory had recently taken under its wing after Wilson's Factory co-director (and New Order's manager), Rob Gretton, went to check them out at The Band on the Wall. Paul Morley had made the band's debut single, 'Look into My Eyes', his single of the week at the NME, but a total lack of daytime airplay saw the record disappear without a trace.

The show wasn't particularly well attended, and the majority of those that had braved the wintry weather were jazz-funk aficionados there for the headliners. With James Maker having now been banished to the sidelines it was left to Morrissey to introduce the band as they made their way onto the stage. "Hello... We are the Smiths. We are not 'Smiths', we are the Smiths," he announced before introducing the opening number, 'These Things Take Time'.

Again, there was no place in the set for 'Suffer Little Children'. Aside from 'What Difference Does It Make,' 'The Hand That Rocks the Cradle,' 'Handsome Devil,' 'Miserable Lie', and 'What Do You See In Him?' two new songs were introduced into the set: 'Jeane,' and the aforementioned 'Hand in Glove'.

Marr came up with the riff to what would prove The Smiths' debut single while playing around with a Chic-sounding riff on an acoustic guitar at his parents' house in Wythenshawe. Like all good guitarists, he continued messing about with the riff until it sounded more in keeping with his own style of playing. There was no means of recording the riff so he had Angie rush him over to Stretford in her VW Beetle so that Morrissey could hear his latest gem; repeatedly playing the riff over and over during the drive so that he wouldn't lose it. En route, Angie had suggested he make the riff sound like something The Stooges' James Williamson might have played on *Raw Power*. Thankfully, Morrissey was at home, and Marr serenaded him up the stairwell as he rushed to grab his tape recorder.

Marr and Morrissey introduced the

finished song to Rourke and Joyce a couple of days later at their Portland Street base. All four were in agreement that 'Hand in Glove' was their best song. "The spirit in the singing was the same as the spirit in the guitar," Marr enthused. "The song defined us and described the devotion and solidarity of a powerful friendship. It was a declaration and our manifesto."

The Haçienda show was the first occasion that Morrissey introduced flowers as a stage accessory. The inspiration, according to Marr, came during an after-work pint or three with Joe Moss at Manhattan; the idea being to brighten up the Haçienda's sterile atmosphere. Morrissey would say as much during a subsequent interview with Sounds. "We introduced them as an antidote to the Haçienda when we played there [because] it was so sterile and inhuman." The flowers would also show harmony with nature, while hopefully representing a sense of optimism in Manchester. "Manchester is semi-paralysed still," Morrissey continued, "the paralysis just zips through the whole of Factory."

The Smiths came away from the Haçienda having made a few more friends that would spread the word. One of these was Jim Shelley, whose gushing review – which appeared in the *NME* several weeks later – would liken The Smiths to Magazine and Josef K.

By the time Shelley's review of the Haçienda show appeared in print The Smiths had recorded 'Hand in Glove' (b/w 'Handsome Devil' lifted from the mixing desk at the Haçienda) at Strawberry Studios in Stockport. The band felt their musicality had progressed beyond the EMI demo and didn't need asking twice when Moss offered to finance the recording costs (£213). Moss' benevolence also stretched to covering the cost of cutting and pressing the single should the Strawberry demo fail to garner any serious record company interest.

With Marr taking it upon himself to direct the recording, The Smiths set up their gear, spent 20 minutes or so working on Joyce's drum sound and nailed the finished version of 'Hand in Glove' in three takes. Marr then doubled up the electric guitar and added acoustic overdubs, while Joyce added tambourine and Morrissey rounded things off with a haunting backing vocal. Still not wholly satisfied with what he was hearing in the control booth, Marr added a harmonica intro that he worked up outside in the corridor before playing it to the others.

Morrissey contacted Richard Boone with a view to cutting a distribution deal with New Hormones, the label Boone had incorporated to release Buzzcocks' 1977 debut four-track EP, *Spiral Scratch*. Boone's vision for New Hormones to emulate Stiff Records had failed to materialise owing to the rise of Factory, and he was already winding down the label. Rather than send his friend away empty-handed, Boone suggested Morrissey try Simon Edwards, who was the then head of distribution at Rough Trade.

Edwards was suitably impressed by what he heard, going so far as to suggest the possibility of a one-off record deal. "This was something that didn't sound like 95 per cent of the bands that were coming through

the door at that time. When they said they wanted Geoff (Travis, Rough Trade's founder) to hear it, I thought it was fair and true for him to listen to it. It was good enough as far as I was concerned."

This was all Marr needed to hear, and with Rourke in tow, they arrived at Rough Trade's record store/offices on Kensington Park Road, West London, one Friday afternoon in March 1983. The duo practically laid siege to Travis' door. "I'm in a band from Manchester, we're called The Smiths," the guitarist blurted out to the bemused Travis whilst thrusting a cassette tape into his hand, "We've done a song we'd really like to put out on Rough Trade. If you don't want to put it on the label, we could put it out on our own label and you could distribute it. You won't have heard anything like it before."

In *Autobiography*, Morrissey, for some unfathomable reason, would have us believe it was he that accompanied Marr to London and devotes a half-a-page or so recounting what occurred at Rough Trade's offices. He also takes delight in pointing out that it was himself and Marr that signed with Rough Trade rather than The Smiths as a whole.

Having bands come in off the street seeking assistance of one form or another was nothing new at Rough Trade, of course. Indeed, the label's first record release, Métal Urbain's 'Paris Maquis' b/w 'Cle De Contact' (RT101), came about owing to the French punksters descending on the shop back in 1977. Rough Trade had since gone on to release Stiff Little Fingers' standard-bearer, 'Alternative Ulster', in October 1978, as well as the band's debut album *Inflammable Material* the following February (The first independently released album to sell in excess of 100,000 copies in the UK). That same year saw Rough Trade the subject of a South Bank Show documentary highlighting the label's success in going up against the majors with acts such as The Monochrome Set, Subway Sect, Swell Maps, Electric Eels, and Spizzoil.

Travis told his Mancunian interlopers that he'd listen to the tape over the weekend and get back to them sometime on the Monday with an answer. Marr remained in

Rough Trade East 1983

London over the weekend catching up with his old friend Matt Johnson, the frontman and driving force behind post-punk outfit The The, leaving Rourke to make the return journey to Manchester alone.

Recording original material for demo purposes in a professional studio usually ends with the excitement of the first listen to the finished track(s) played through a mixing console. The songs sound fantastic, so much so that it's easy to believe any record company would be insane to reject them. The magic of the mixing consul is seriously diminished once the songs are transferred onto a cassette tape, however. This is usually only realised on the journey home while listening to the tape on either a car or van's in-built cassette player. The songs won't sound much better on the average sound system, either, because the console would be state-of-the-art.

Marr could only hope that Travis hadn't skimped on Rough Trade's in-house system. Imagine his elation upon walking into

Moss's office on Monday morning to be told that Travis had already been in touch to say he loved 'Hand in Glove' and wanted to release it through Rough Trade.

Travis would get to hear 'Hand in Glove' live when The Smiths made their London debut at the Rock Garden, a subterranean punk/goth enclave situated beneath a restaurant on the Piazza in Covent Garden, on March 23. "I see Morrissey onstage as pretty much a revelation at the Rock Garden," Travis would recall. "Because he was fully formed. Dancing about, it was great. Then again, I remember some people were going, 'I'm not sure about this lot.' But you have to have that kind of ridiculous belief. If you take a consensus of opinion, you've had it. You end up signing Shed Seven."

Morrissey's opinion of Travis and Rough Trade is somewhat less fulsome. In *Autobiography*, he dubs Travis the "moral conscience of Rough Trade" and a "lugubrious historian". He then mocks Rough Trade's "hysterical intellectual spinster image that the label had considered so confrontational until 'Hand in Glove' shattered their afternoon work rotas, poetry workshops and Woman's Hour."

'Hand in Glove' (RT131) was released on May 13, 1983. The Smiths' second foray to the capital saw them supporting The Sisters of Mercy at the University of London Union on May 6. *NME*'s Barney Hoskyns lauded 'Hand in Glove' as being "one of the years few masterpieces, a thing of beauty and a joy forever," while his counterpart over at *Sounds*, Bill Black, described it as a "daunting" debut. Despite enthusiastic ravings within the music press, the single fail to crack the Top 40, yet reached a very respectable # 3 on the UK Indie Chart.

The Smiths were on their way.

The initial Rough Trade agreement was a one-off single deal, but with 'Hand in Glove' cracking the Top 3 on the Indie Chart, Travis was keen to secure The Smiths signatures to an album deal. So keen, in fact, that he travelled up to Manchester contract in hand to meet with the band and Joe Moss at the latter's Portland Street office. Virgin, Polydor, Warner Brothers, and CBS were all apparently showing interest, but while Marr and Morrissey were happy to meet with the corporate suits, they sensed their interests would be better served sticking with Rough Trade – for the time being, at least.

Upon signing with Rough Trade, The Smiths – or Marr and Morrissey to be exact (with Joyce somewhat bizarrely witnessing the document) – received a £3,000 advance with a further £3,000 being paid at the end of July. Marr has the initial amount being £4,000, but whatever the exact amount, his and Morrissey's high-handed attitude to Joyce and Rourke's standing in The Smiths would come back to haunt them.

'Hand in Glove' might not have gotten any daytime airplay at Radio One, but that didn't mean to say The Smiths weren't without their champions at the station. John Walters, the producer of John Peel's late-night show, had been in attendance at the ULU show. Such was his enthusiasm that he invited the band to record a session at the Beeb's Maida Vale studios.

Peel was to prove equally impressed and played 'Hand in Glove' every night, sometimes twice. "It was Walters who heard The Smiths before I did," Peel told Simon Goddard in the latter's *Songs That Saved Your Life: The Art of The Smiths 1982-87*. "He went to see them at ULU and it was a result of his enthusiasm that the band were initially booked for the programme.

Few subjects are considered taboo within rock music – especially in the wake of punk - but paedophilia sits right at the top of the tree.

"When I heard them I was equally impressed," Peel went on, "because unlike most bands – and I've said this before because it remains true - you couldn't immediately tell what records they'd been listening to. That's fairly unusual, very rare indeed. It made you think, 'How have they got to where they are?' and 'Where have they come from?'. It was that aspect of The Smiths that I found most impressive."

According to Morrissey, Peel didn't attend this or any other subsequent sessions The Smiths recorded for his show or even bother to check out the band live. "He (Peel) is cited as instrumental in the Smiths' success, but if not for the continued exuberance of John Walters, John Peel might never have encountered the Smiths."

Marr says he wandered about the corridors at the BBC studios feeling like a "card-carrying professional musician and a schoolboy required to show deference around the establishment." He and the rest of the band had arrived at the studios with their heads frazzled from the copious amount of weed they'd imbibed on the drive down from Manchester, yet they still managed to hit their stride from the off.

The four songs recorded that day were 'Handsome Devil', 'Miserable Lie', 'What Difference Does It Make', and a new Marr/Morrissey composition called 'Reel Around the Fountain'. After laying down the basic guitar, bass, drum, and vocal tracks, Morrissey re-recorded his vocal, while Marr was left to his own devices conjuring up various guitar overdubs to suit the mood of each song. The session was first broadcast on May 31, but such was the interest garnered amongst the Peel faithful that it would be repeated five times over the following 18 months. The Smiths would also record a four-song session for Peel's fellow Radio One DJ, David 'Kid' Jensen: 'These Things Take Time', 'What Difference Does It Make', 'Wonderful Woman', and 'You've Got Everything Now', which was broadcast on July 4, 1983.

Between juggling Radio One recording sessions and live outings, The Smiths set up base at Elephant Studios in Wapping, East London, to work on their highly-anticipated debut album – tentatively titled *The Hand That Rocks the Cradle* and set for release in

time for the Christmas market. The sessions were being overseen by former Teardrop Explodes guitarist Troy Tate, who'd recently signed to Rough Trade as a solo artist and released his debut single, 'Love Is...'.

Morrissey and Marr were both initially flattered to be working with Tate, and things seemed to be moving along nicely – even if having to run through each track over and over until Tate deemed them satisfactory drove the band to distraction. They also had to contend with working in a cramped, airless basement during a heatwave. Tate's vision for the album – as Marr remembers it – was to capture the way The Smiths sounded onstage. Marr and the rest of the band were left somewhat deflated on hearing the finished album, however.

Geoff Travis was equally underwhelmed at the "rash rumble" emanating from the speakers, yet rather than allow Tate the chance to redeem himself, the Rough Trade supremo instead called in one-time Roxy Music bassist and resident BBC producer, John Porter. Travis had initially wanted Porter to look at remixing the "Troy Tate tapes" as they've become known amongst Smiths aficionados. Porter, however, deemed all fourteen tracks "out of tune and out of time" and suggested the band re-record the album from scratch.

Morrissey and Rourke were thrilled at the news as Porter had produced Japan's *Quiet Life*, an album both greatly admired. Marr was initially reticent about starting the album afresh but soon came around to the idea. A two-week session was booked at Manchester's Pluto Studios, with further sessions coming at Strawberry Studios and Matrix Studios in South-west London. Porter would also oversee The Smiths' second David Jensen Show sessions (The songs recorded were 'Accept Yourself', 'I Don't Owe You Anything', 'Pretty Girls Make Graves', and 'Reel Around the Fountain').

The Smiths were beginning to make waves but storm clouds were nonetheless gathering on the horizon. When reviewing the ULU show in the May 14 edition of *Sounds*, Dave McCullough (who was himself a fan of the band) brought attention to what he perceived as references to "child molesting" and "more mature sexual experimentation" within the lyrics to certain songs He also singled Morrissey out for his supposedly "hat[ing] women with a vengeance." McCullough would return to the subject three weeks later noting how "child molesting crops up more than a few times in Smiths songs." Though he was careful to qualify his comments by saying the lyrics were "hilarious" because they suddenly touch on the personal."

Few subjects are considered taboo within rock music – especially in the wake of punk - but paedophilia sits right at the top of the tree. Unsurprisingly, *The Sun* was quick to pick up McCullough's cudgel to give The Smiths the full tabloid treatment by linking McCullough's references of child molesting within specific Smiths' lyrics – 'Handsome Devil' in particular – to a recent homosexual attack on a 6-year-old boy in Brighton. The band were understandably furious – both at The Sun and Sounds. "We really can't emphasise how much it upset us because obviously it was completely fabricated," an indignant Morrissey told the *NME*. When subsequently called upon to explain the meaning of the lyrics to 'Handsome Devil', Morrissey said how the message of the song was to "forget the cultivation of the brain and to concentrate on the cultivation of the body.

"'A boy in the bush' is addressed to the scholar," he continued. "There's more to life than books, you know, but not much more – that is the essence of the song so you can take it and stick it in an article about child molesting and it will make absolutely perfect sense. But you can do that with anybody. You can do that with Abba."

The Smiths, as the album was now rather unimaginatively set to be called, was rescheduled for a mid-February 1984 release with 'Reel Around the Fountain' slated as the lead single. The controversy surrounding certain of Morrissey's lyrics would bring about a rethink, however – especially when the BBC elected to pull 'Reel Around the Fountain' from the second Jensen session (set for broadcast on September 5) as a "precautionary measure".

Within days of the BBC's decision The Smiths were back at Maida Vale Studios recording a second session for John Peel. All four songs – 'Back to the Old House', 'Still Ill', 'This Night Has Opened My Eyes', and 'This Charming Man' – were brand-new compositions not set to appear on the album. When Travis heard the band running through 'This Charming Man' he knew they had a hit record on their hands.

Aztec Camera was by far the most significant act on Rough Trade's roster at that time. Their debut album, *High Land Hard Rain,* had reached an impressive # 22 on the UK chart, while its lead single 'Oblivious' had cracked the Top 20 at the second time of asking. Pondering whether the Scottish act's mainstream success stemmed from their songs being predominantly bright and breezy. Grabbing his guitar Marr set about strumming chord progressions till he hit upon a sequence that conjured up a similar feeling. When he found a second sequence that suited what he was playing he knew he had something special.

'This Charming Man' was recorded in a 10-day rush at Matrix Studios, but as with the Troy Tate sessions, the finished master was found wanting. At Travis's behest, The Smiths returned to Manchester and recorded the song afresh at Strawberry Studios. Marr says that once the session was over, he sat at the console in complete awe at what they'd achieved. 'With 'This Charming Man', John Porter had taken what I could only dream of in my bedroom and made it a reality," he enthused. "I thought my band were the best. We were eccentric and subversive, and we were about to gate-crash the mainstream."

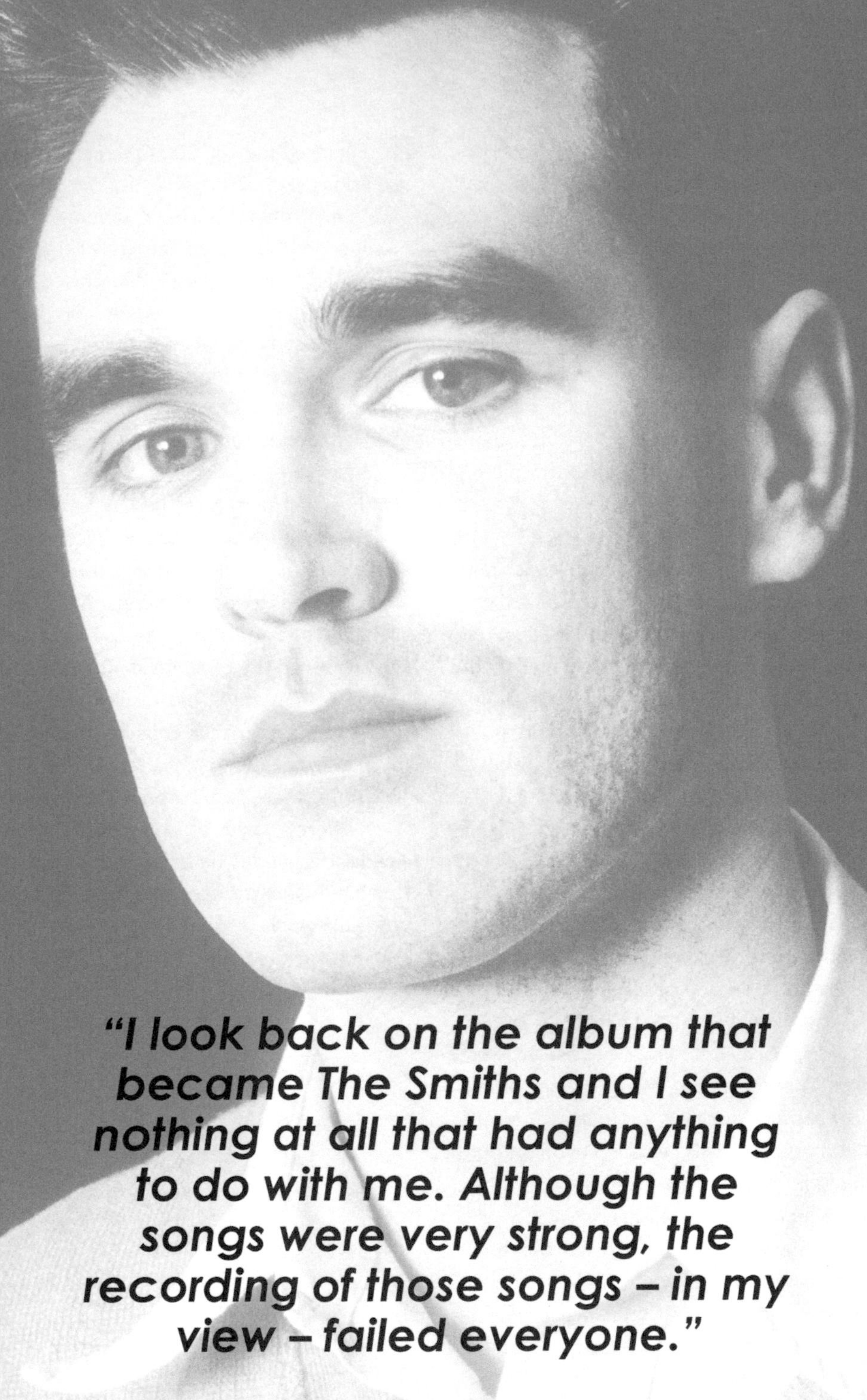

"I look back on the album that became The Smiths and I see nothing at all that had anything to do with me. Although the songs were very strong, the recording of those songs – in my view – failed everyone."

MORRISSEY

CHAPTER FOUR

GOING ABOUT THINGS THE WRONG WAY

'This Charming Man' (b/w 'Jeane') (RT136), gave The Smiths their first Top 30 hit, peaking at #22. It would be some time to come before the band received any royalties, of course, but Joe Moss thought it sensible to sound out solicitors and accountants – if only to prime the group for the financial headaches that were sure to arise once the money started rolling in. Morrissey and Marr were one step ahead of the game, however; the pair having worked out in advance who was deserving of what. "We decided that we would split the income for the group with 40 per cent each for me and Morrissey, and ten per cent each to the other[s] seeing as we ran the band," Marr explained. "However much I'd have liked to have thought that The Smiths were made up of equals, we weren't, and unlike some bands The Smiths didn't fall into being a band together."

Marr and Morrissey were already splitting the money from music publishing straight down the middle, but they also saw themselves as the driving force behind The Smiths and Rourke and Joyce had simply been recruited as a means to an end. "There wasn't an equal division of responsibility," the guitarist continued. "Morrissey and I dealt with the management and the record companies And as far as Rough Trade were concerned, The Smiths were me and Morrissey."

Any ideas that either Rourke or Joyce had been harbouring as to their worth were addressed at Pluto Studios during the recording of 'What Difference Does It Make?' (intended as the follow-up single). The duo readily accepted Marr and Morrissey could do as they saw fit with the publishing money as they wrote all the songs. While certain bands - the Sex Pistols, U2, and Echo & The Bunnymen, for example – split the publishing equally regardless of who brought what to the table, the vast majority restricted the royalties to the actual songwriter[s]. For all their swagger, however, Marr and Morrissey couldn't play the songs live or in the recording studio without a rhythm section. Joyce could have been confused over the terms of his enlistment as he'd been off his head on mushrooms at the time of his audition, but both he and Rourke had been invited to join The Smiths.

They weren't merely hired hands. What difference did being shafted make? Quite a lot as it would turn out . . .

Marr had only turned 20 and didn't want to think about financial finagling. He just wanted to play the guitar and make music. Though it was Morrissey that had insisted on the proposed 40:40:10:10 net split, he didn't want to deal with Joyce and Rourke either. One might have expected Joe Moss to be given the task of breaking the news to Joyce and Rourke. But as far as Morrissey was concerned, Moss ranked even lower in the pecking order. Regardless of it being Moss that had paid for the 'Hand in Glove' demo, and his providing the band with a rehearsal space free gratis, Morrissey couldn't accept Moss as their manager and was only putting up with him because of his friendship with Marr. Instead, Morrissey – having taken a break from recording at Pluto supposedly to grab something to eat – boarded the next available train bound for London to explain his position to Geoff Travis. The next thing Marr knew, Travis was on the phone calling an end to the Pluto session until the financial machinations were sorted.

"All me and Mike were trying to do was stop Johnny leaving the band"

Marr was understandably angry at Morrissey. To his mind, the situation should have been sorted out in-house and not through intermediaries such as Travis – regardless of Rough Trade's vested interest in The Smiths. Appearing in the BBC's 2001 documentary, *The Rise and Fall of The Smiths,* Moss said how Morrissey was unwilling to move on with the band until it had been established in terms that all would understand as to what he perceived to be each person's rightful share. "And as far as he was concerned," Moss revealed, "that was Johnny's job to do that with Mike and Andy [as] Johnny had brought them in."

Marr had every right to be pissed off with Morrissey's underhand antics. If it hadn't been for his dogged determination to track Morrissey down, the latter would still be holed up in his bedroom in Stretford instead of making powerplays from his record label's HQ. With a Top Three album on his CV, Marr could walk away from The Smiths and look to putting another band together. With Morrissey yet to return to Manchester, Moss called a band meeting where Marr told Joyce and Rourke of his intention to walk unless they both agreed to the ten per cent arrangement. Moss reportedly chipped in with a clichéd bird-in-the-hand pitch of how ten per cent of something was better than 25 per cent of nothing.

Marr came away from the meeting believing the matter resolved, and that Joyce and Rourke had accepted the arrangement. Joyce and Rourke were probably no less aggrieved but the fact that both remained with The Smiths throughout – aside from the latter's brief absence following his sacking in 1986 (which will be covered in a later chapter) – suggests they were at least content with their lot.

"All me and Mike were trying to do was stop Johnny leaving the band," Rourke explained in *The Rise and Fall of The Smiths*. "We didn't come to an agreement that we were going to get 25 per cent. [But] there was no agreement that we were going to get less."

Moss would subsequently insist that Joyce and Rourke both agreed to the designated percentages during the meeting at Pluto. If only he, Marr, or Morrissey had thought to get it confirmed in writing.

Moss, of course, would end up a genuine casualty of Morrissey's powerplay. "As soon as Geoff Travis was speaking to me, I knew that that was it for me," he revealed in the BBC documentary. "If Morrissey couldn't come to me to sort that out – which I would have sorted out for him without question because that was [my] role – that there was too much of a division then for me to be able to stay. And I realised that if I stayed, that it was going to put a strain on Morrissey's relationship with Johnny."

With 'This Charming Man' breaking into the Top 30, The Smiths were duly invited to appear on Top of the Pops. For all its cheerleading cheesiness, *Top of the Pops* was the BBC's flagship music show with a viewing audience of millions. Most musicians supposedly hated going on the show for fear of losing their street cred because they had to mime along to a pre-recorded track. Most were willing to swallow their pride, however, as an appearance usually proved sufficient to propel their latest single further up the chart. Despite their appearance, however, 'This Charming Man' was set to climb no higher than # 25. Morrissey would subsequently lay the blame at Rough Trade's door for failing to keep up with demand (a failing that often befell independent labels). "Suddenly they (Rough Trade) have a single that people want to buy and they are caught cat-napping by the radiator," he bemoaned. "'This Charming Man' spends its entire life hedging and hovering outside of the Top 20, Rough Trade unable to supply sufficient quantities when the Top 10 called out with arms wide open."

The Smiths had made their TV debut some three weeks earlier on *The Tube*, a Tyne-Tees TV production broadcast via Channel 4 on Friday evenings, that served up promo videos, interviews, live performances by renowned acts as well as the Young Turks intent on knocking them from their pedestals. The Smiths were filmed lip-synching to 'This Charming Man' at their Portland Street rehearsal space. Morrissey's penchant for floral accoutrements goes into overdrive: daffodils, gladioli, and a plethora of other blooms cover the floor, as well as being strewn over Joyce's drum kit, while Morrissey – wearing a loose shirt open to the naval and sporting several rows of love beads – brandishes a bouquet of gladioli as though aiming a slingshot at the camera. Marr has threaded chrysanthemums around the machine head and bridge of his Rickenbacker to continue the flowery theme, but for reasons known only to the director, he is only shown from the neck down. It wasn't until many years later that the director revealed he'd thought Marr's

blank-eyed gaze was due to his being on drugs and therefore too risqué for the nation's impressionable youth.

Every written account – including Marr's *Set the Boy Free* - has the band recording their slot at the BBC TV Centre in London's White City on Thursday, November 24, before hightailing it back to Manchester to play a triumphant 'homecoming' show at the Haçienda that same evening. *Top of the Pops* was always recorded the day prior to broadcast (ie a Wednesday), however, so the jury remains out on that one. Regardless of the logistics, the Haçienda would indeed prove a memorable evening for the 1500 or so fortunate souls that bore to witness it (including the author).

The excitement was palpable both inside The Haçienda as well as on the pavement outside the venue. The sheepskin-coated touts hovering on the fringes – enabling them to make a sharp getaway should the police appear unexpectedly - were making a killing charging upwards of £20 for non-member £3 tickets (inexplicably reduced from £3.50).

The Smiths' growing celebrity was evidenced by the number of people – not only girls – that were clutching either daffodils or gladioli as they made their way inside. Indeed, the cloying perfumed air within the Haçienda was mindful of a florists' shop. The support on the night was James, another up-and-coming local band that had signed with Factory the previous year and had recently released their debut three-track EP, Jimone. The night, however, belonged to the headliners.

The noise was incredible as The Smiths took to the stage. Morrissey's playful "Hello, you ugly devils!" served to presage the intro to 'Handsome Devil' and it was showtime. There would be two encores, and, except for 'Wonderful Woman', the crowd was treated to every song within the Smiths canon, with 'This Charming Man' and 'Hand in Glove' being given two airings.

The Smiths released two singles (neither of which had set the charts alight), and yet a telling indication of just how far their star was expected to rise in the ascendency came with *The Old Grey Whistle Test* spin-off, *Whistle Test: On The Road*, filming their entire performance at the Derby Assembly Rooms on December 6. The footage is available on *You Tube* (search on: The Smiths Derby"). Though the footage serves as an excellent visual document of The Smiths' circa late 1983 (with Marr sporting his short-lived Beatles-esque mop-top). The show itself is somewhat lacklustre, however – as though the band are self-conscious about having the Beeb intruding on their turf. One memorable moment comes during 'Miserable Lie' when a gladioli-swinging Morrissey is hit in the eye by a missile. He understandably flees the stage, leaving the rest of the band to soldier on without him. Marr clearly looks anxious as they're only six songs into the set. Morrissey does return, however, and other than a by now trademark stage invasion the show continues to its climax.

Following further shows in Dublin, and London, The Smiths ended what had already proved a year of unprecedented highs with a show at New York's Danceteria (although technically, they didn't play till New Year's Day seeing as they went onstage at 2 a.m.)

THE SMITHS

Danceteria, located on West 21st Street, was the first of three US dates intended to introduce The Smiths to America, but the shows in New Jersey and Boston would have to be cancelled owing to Joyce's coming down with chicken pox. The trip also allowed the band – or rather Marr and Morrissey – to seal the deal Rough Trade had arranged with Sire Records to distribute Smiths product in the US.

Sire Records had a reputation for introducing up-and-coming British acts to the American market. Founded in 1966 as Sire Productions by Seymour Stein and his fellow Brill Building habitué, Richard Gottehrer, the fledgeling label released singles by the likes of the Climax Blues Band, Barclay James Harvest, Tomorrow, Matthews Southern Comfort, and proto-punksters The Deviants, via London Records. Sire came to the fore during the mid-to-late seventies (by which time the label had been acquired by Warner Brothers) by signing The Ramones, the Dead Boys, Talking Heads, and The Undertones.

Sire would subsequently go on to achieve mainstream success on both sides of the Atlantic with British-based acts such as The Pretenders, Soft Cell, Depeche Mode, The Cure, and Echo & The Bunnymen. The label was also in the process of launching the career of a certain Madonna Louise Ciccone. Indeed, an enduring urban myth – promulgated by Marr – has Madonna opening for The Smiths at Danceteria. "Supporting us was the girl who worked on the coat-checking thing. We really didn't pay too much attention to her, but it was Madonna. She played for about 20 minutes before we went on." He then went onto say that while he'd quite liked the music, he hadn't thought much of her act.

Madonna had indeed worked as a coat-check girl at Danceteria, but by the time The Smiths were making their American debut she'd released her own eponymously-titled album back in the summer, while her latest single 'Lucky Star' was steadily climbing both the Billboard and UK charts. The flyer for the show makes no mention of Madonna whatsoever. The support acts on the night were Lovebug Starski and his fellow hip-hoppers Whodini.

Indeed, the only link Madonna has to The Smiths is in making her UK debut at The Haçienda – a live broadcast for *The Tube* - in January 1984.

The one person Marr would have dearly loved to be in attendance at Danceteria was Joe Moss. Though Moss would cite Morrissey's powerplay as making his position as manager untenable, he'd come to realise – especially in the wake of the Haçienda show - that the coming year would see The Smiths taking up more and more of his time. Indeed, he'd spent the latter part of the year living out of a holdall. Not only did he have a business to oversee, but his wife Janet had recently given birth to their second child. The realisation dawned upon his arriving home for Christmas. 'I saw this little girl,' he reflected, "I saw her and I just realised I wasn't going anywhere again."

Aside from the onset of Joyce's chicken pox, the band were jetlagged from the flight; so much so that Morrissey had no sooner stepped onto the stage then he misplaced his feet and tumbled off again – much to the rest of the band's bemusement. "I walk onstage at the Danceteria and as I do so my blindness and bewilderment lead me directly off the lip of the stage, and I crash at the feet of the assembled human spillage. Unaided, I scramble back up and onto the stage, and I limp directly off — past three blank musicians who are unable to cope with such embarrassment. My right leg is bruised from top to bottom."

When The Smiths were first introduced to Seymour Stein backstage at the London ICA (Institute of Contemporary Arts) back in early October, the Sire head had told an anecdote about his taking Brian Jones to buy a guitar from We Buy Guitars, a renowned music store located on 48th Street, just off Times Square. Quick as a flash, Marr had made Stein promise that he'd do the same for him as a condition of The Smiths signing with Sire. True to his word, following the signing (on January 2, 1984), Stein took Marr to We Buy Guitars and allowed him his pick of guitars. Marr chose a hollow-bodied, cherry-red 1959 Gibson 355. The Smiths were staying at the Iroquois Hotel on West 44th Street (the hotel favoured by James Dean whenever he was in town), and upon his return, he reeled off the tunes for two new songs that would make up the next Smiths' single. They were: 'Heaven Knows I'm Miserable Now' (A play on Sandie Shaw's 1969 hit, 'Heaven Knows I'm Missing Him Now') (RT156), and 'Girl Afraid'.

To coincide with the US jaunt, Rough Trade pressed a limited edition 12" dance version of 'This Charming Man' (remixed by François Kevorkian, a.k.a. François K) to be played in New York's clubs. Geoff Travis would fall foul of Morrissey's ire over Rough Trade's subsequent issuing the dance remix as a UK release, however. The music press were quick to side with Morrissey and lambasted Travis for his shamelessly milking of his cash cow. While Travis readily admits to it having been his idea, he vehemently denies any wrongdoing as all decisions regarding the release of Smiths product had to be first okayed by Marr and Morrissey.

"There were constant dramas with the crew, and as we had no manager, Morrissey and I were always left to sort it out."

Tony Wilson had copied Jerry Dammers 2-Tone blueprint to prove that the mountain would come to Mohammed if the bait were sufficient tempting. Yet at the beginning of 1984, The Smiths relocated to London. Though abandoning Manchester for the bright lights of the capital brought criticism from Wilson and other dyed-in-the-wool Mancunians, the move made logistical sense as more and more of their time – or certainly Marr

and Morrissey's time – was being taken up dealing with accountants, solicitors, PR people etc. Indeed, Marr's Earls Court flat quickly became the band's HQ and hangout, with people coming and going at all hours.

There was plenty of i-dotting and t-crossing to be done as The Smiths were set to embark on a 32-date nationwide UK tour to promote the release of their highly-anticipated eponymous debut album at the end of January. The tour would be marred by stage invasions by over-exuberated fans struggling to contain their excitement at being up close and personal with their heroes. Indeed, by the tour's end 'Smithsmania' would reach an extent whereby shows would be considered something of a disappointment if an invasion didn't occur. The band were by and large okay with fans mounting the stage so long as they and their equipment were left alone.

The lead single, 'What Difference Does It Make?' / 'Back to the Old House' (RT146), had been released a fortnight earlier and was rapidly climbing the charts by the time of the opening show at the University of Sheffield (Jan 31). The single's entering the chart at #26 brought a second invitation onto *Top of the Pops,* while Morrissey also gave his first TV interview (a live outside broadcast from the Haçienda) on *The Tube*. Though he'd enthused about the impending album on the show – citing it a "signal post in music" – he was somewhat less impassioned when speaking about 'What Difference Does It Make?' on Sheffield's Radio Hallam. "I get very bored with it now. It's a very old song we wrote over 18 months ago and now I realise that it didn't have the impact that some of album tracks do. It's not as strong as 'This Charming Man' and I think every record should equal, if not go beyond, the last one."

Reflecting on the tour, Marr said how Smiths fans were "looking for something that expressed their times and culture." Although there were stubborn pockets of resistance in London and elsewhere across the country, by 1984 Punk seemed a sepia-toned memory. The UK charts were clogged with the usual pop dross, there was plenty of interesting and innovative music being created during the early Eighties. Yet while bands such as Spear of Destiny, Echo & The Bunnymen, Big Country, U2, The Alarm, Icicle Works, New Order, and Aztec Camera all had their respective admirers, none came close to capturing the imagination quite like The Smiths.

"The Smiths had become known for many things: quiffs, jangly guitars, National Health specs and flowers," Marr observed. "We were associated with disaffection, discontent, and how grim it was up north too. All of it was accurate, but one thing we become synonymous with more than anything else was a thing called 'miserablism'. If you'd have asked anyone on the street about The Smiths, they'd have invariably said the word 'miserable', and regardless of the fact that much of the band's output was laced with a lot of humour, the tag spread through the media and would stay with us forever."

Morrissey was the only one of The Smiths who looked perennially miserable – as though he'd lost his wallet and found

Photo: Archive

a pound down the back of the sofa. But seeing as he was the band's public face, it was perhaps inevitable Marr, Rourke, and Joyce would find themselves tarred with the same brush.

Having to deal with legal matters and endless paperwork when they just wanted to get on with making music was anathema to Marr and Morrissey. So much so, that in the lead-up to the tour the pair tried their utmost to cajole John Porter into talking the managerial helm, if only on an ad hoc basis. Despite their repeated pleadings, however, Porter wasn't to be persuaded. Ever reluctant to bring in an outsider, Marr took it upon himself to deal with whatever problems the tour might throw their way. One such problem – the recruitment of finicky Phil Cowie as tour manager – was self-inflicted. "Phil seemed to be under stress," Marr reflected. "There were constant dramas with the crew, and as we had no manager, Morrissey and I were always left to sort it out."

"I didn't respect Phil Cowie at all and wouldn't do what he wanted," the band's sound engineer and all round factotum, Grant Showbiz (a.k.a. Grant Cunliffe) chimed in. "I refused to carry the gear. As far as I was concerned, all I had to do was the soundcheck. I wasn't being a good team player. There was resentment, because at the end of the night, I'd be swanning around getting beer, and talking to people at the front of the stage."

Soon into the tour, Marr's friend and

one-time flatmate, Ollie May, up and quit his role as driver/roadie. May had been with The Smiths from day one. His departure had nothing to do with Cowie's appointment, however, but rather because he'd grown "disillusioned and disappointed with both the band and the direction that their career has been and is doing." May had never really seen himself as a bona fide roadie. He'd simply helped out to remain close to Marr, but as The Smiths' star rode in its ascendancy, he found himself being sidelined as the band's entourage inevitably became more professional. His Jack-the-lad attitude and easy-going nature would be sorely missed in the months ahead.

Despite the swelling popularity, there was still more than a hint of "Marmite" in the air surrounding The Smiths. The *NME's* review of the University of Sheffield show is a perfect case in point as it appears to have been penned by someone still struggling to decide which side of the Morrissey divide to plant his flag. The singer is openly upbraided for being "too big for his boots," for being an "ambitious fool, a charming idiot, having a giggle, playing the fiddle while brave new pop burns in a pyre of sentimental idiocy, consumers, and cretinism. The Smiths as a whole, meantime, are deemed "bland and unsensational enough for Morrissey to shine."

The review then changes tack saying how Morrissey has channelled his "soft-centred harshness and painful integrity" to "entertain and lecture, to slam into the soft cultural soma of the south, to narrow the distance, to reject silly elitism. He is depicted as being no "Helen of Troy", yet "his is the face that has legitimised a thousand plebeian dance steps."

The tour had yet to get into full swing when the plebeian pied piper fell ill, a niggling sore throat that had rebuffed all over-the-counter remedies causing the postponement of a clutch of shows in Liverpool, Hull, Loughborough, Leicester, Sheffield, and Birmingham. "I never worried about him psychologically," Marr would later reveal, "[but] there were times that I worried about him physically when he was burned out, and you could see that he was going to be ill. And I think that happened because all of us had unhealthy lifestyles. But he had more on his plate, psychologically, in dealing with that pop world thing and being the focal point. Us three lived off nicotine, amongst other things, and Morrissey needed to eat right, and none of us did. And I think that particularly affected him."

It was obvious to all that The Smiths couldn't continue running a rudderless ship indefinitely, but no one imagined for a heartbeat that Ruth Polsky – the New York-based promoter that had arranged the Danceteria show – would take in interest. Such was her determination to play Mother Hen that she arrived unannounced in London to have a meeting with Morrisey on the day the tour was set to resume with a sell-out show at London's Lyceum Ballroom on February 12. Neither she nor Morrissey have disclosed publicly what occurred during their afternoon tête-à-tête, but Polsky arrived at the Lyceum with a

Dear Sandie,

We could never begin to emphasize the endless joy we would feel if you would care to listen to our song with a view to possibly covering it.

Obviously the song was written with you in miind. It is an absolute fact that your influence more than any other permeates all our music. Without doubt we are incurable Sandie Shaw fans. Studying all your material, as we do day and night, we felt that your future musical direction must avoid the overt icky momism trap that most of your 60's contemporaries seized.

We have strong ideas about the musical backing which should accompany your version of 'I don't owe you anything'. It should be upbeat and immediate; after all, the audience you left behind was a youthful one - the audience you must seize now must also be youthful. Ken Woodmans' arrangement on such as 'Keep in touch' or 'You've not Changed' could easily be an electric guitar. But let's leave the past behind, good as it was. We feel that your future needs an injection of high spirit and vengeance. Should you dislike 'I don't owe you anything' we can supply others with variation. You must surely realize that your name is sufficiently on the lips of young people to demand interest in new, vital product. We would be honoured to provide material for consideration. The Sandie Shaw legend cannot be over yet - there is more to be done!

Love Forever,
Morrissey (Wordsmith/voice)
Johnny (multi-instrumentalist/composer)
THE SMITHS

list of gripes aimed squarely at Rough Trade's door (the label having moved its base of operations to a warehouse on Collier Street, near King's Cross, in March 1984). She wanted to know how it was that a band being mooted as having the potential to be the biggest band of the Eighties and beyond was having to stay in second-rate hotels and travel from venue to venue in a panel van with beanbags instead of proper seating. Indeed, she was questioning what they were doing signed to Rough Trade at all.

The idea that a woman could manage an all-male rock band was hitherto unheard of. The reason for this, of course, was simply due to the music business being the staunchest of male bastions. The Smiths would surely have been rendered a laughing stock, but it's worth remembering that Polsky wouldn't have flown to London without some tacit encouragement from Morrissey.

Marr was oblivious to what was afoot, and so was utterly taken aback when she came sashaying up to him at the Lyceum during the soundcheck to announce Morrissey had given his blessing for her to assume the mantel of manager. Of course, getting Morrissey's blessing was not the same as getting a mandate in writing. Following some heated dressing room deliberations it was left to the band's road manager, Scott Piering, to tell Polsky that her overtures were unwanted.

Piering would use Polsky's failed power play as a launchpad for his own managerial aspirations. Though Marr and Morrissey tentatively allowed him to step into Joe Moss's shoes, they wilfully deferred making the appointment permanent. In *Set the Boy Free,* Marr lauds Piering as being a "good guy and had our best interests at heart" yet defines his role as being a "surrogate manager" – as though he was merely keeping the seat warm till someone with the necessary credentials entered the picture. Piering's role was so ill-defined that he wouldn't be allowed access to the purse strings and would have to run all expenditures through Marr. Yet while Marr agreed with Piering that the band needed to appoint either himself or someone capable of looking after their affairs – if only because he was tired of having to field calls from Rough Trade and elsewhere - he chose to keep the carrot dangling.

The Smiths were enjoying a rest day betwixt dates when their debut album hit the record shops on Monday, February 20 (ROUGH61). The band, as indeed did anyone else with a vested interest in their fortunes, had high hopes for the album, yet none of them would have expected it to slam onto the chart at # 2 the following week – only being denied the coveted top slot by the Thompson Twins' Into the Gap. Still, not a bad return for Travis's initial £20,000 outlay. As per their agreement with Rough Trade, the band had full artistic control over the album's artwork. In keeping with the homoerotic imagery that adorns the picture sleeves of three out of four of the singles the album's front cover features American actor Joe Dallesandro naked from the waist up in a cropped still from Andy Warhol's 1968 film *Flesh*. The single that was the exception being 'Heaven Knows I'm Miserable Now',

Sandie Shaw.

which featured ill-feted sixties pools winner Viv Nicholson from her 1977 autobiography, Spend Spend Spend). Along with Jackie Curtis and Candy darling, Dallesandro was one of Warhol's so-called 'Superstars' and is name-checked in Lou Reed's 'Walk on the Wild Side' ("Little Joe never once gave it away . . .")

History tells us the success of their eponymous debut album propelled The Smiths to another level, yet if truth be told they were already a different band by the time of the album's release. Marr and Morrissey's song-writing had certainly moved on exponentially from the songs on the album. Some would argue that this is only to be expected, but how many bands have fallen victim to "second album syndrome" over the years.

The set-list for the majority of the tour dates featured eight of the ten album tracks, which is hardly surprising seeing they were primarily promoting the album. But Marr and Morrissey were knocking out new songs such as 'Heaven Knows I'm Miserable Now', 'Barbarism Begins at Home', and 'This Night Has Opened my Eyes' with seemingly consummate ease.

Marr always ensured a guitar was within easy reach so he'd be prepared whenever inspiration struck. He was noodling with his Epiphone acoustic in the back of the van while en route to one venue or another on the UK tour when the "speed and momentum of the journey" conjured up yet a riff he deemed worthy of working into a tune for the follow-up to 'What Difference Does It Make?'

It's often said there's a fine line betwixt self-confidence and arrogance, but Marr's confidence in his ability was such that instead of giving himself a congratulatory pat on the back for coming up with a tune he felt worthy of an A-side, he wasn't satisfied till he'd conjured up tunes for the mooted single's B-side and bonus track for the 12" version. He was suffering a bout of homesickness at the time and was missing his family in particular. Remembering a mournful song that was a particular favourite of his mother's, he channelled his melancholy into a suitable chord sequence. With the A-side tune having a Buzzcocks brevity, being "short and fast", and the B-side tune being "short and waltzy", he decided the 12" bonus tune should be longer in length and feature a Gun Club-type groove as he was a long-time fan of the Californian post-punk outfit. (Coincidentally, the live photo of Morrissey on the original card inner sleeve of The Smiths was taken by Romi Mori, who would subsequently play bass for The Gun Club).

Having recorded all three tunes onto his recently-acquired four-track Tascam Portastudio, programmed in simple beats using a Roland Dramatix drum machine (another new purchase), and having got a thumbs-up from Angie, he handed Morrissey the demo tape – the individual tracks labelled simply: 'Fast', 'Irish Waltz' and 'Swampy'. Morrissey then set about working his own magic and the completed songs had been retitled 'William, It Was Really Nothing' (RT166), 'Please, Please, Please, Let Me Get What I Want', and 'How Soon Is Now?' And all three tracks would indeed feature on varying formats of The

Smiths' forthcoming follow-up single.

By the time 'William, It Was Really Nothing' was ready to go to press (August 1984), Morrissey had realised his ambition in having Sandie Shaw record one of his and Marr's compositions. The one-time Eurovision Song Contest winner had last tasted success on the UK Singles chart back in February 1969 with 'Monsieur Dupont', and Morrissey was keen to address the situation and began shamelessly petitioning Shaw to cover 'I Don't Owe You Anything'. Marr was no less of an admirer of Shaw's, of course, and had presciently told Morrissey, during an early get-together at Shelley Rohde's, they would one day pen a song for Shaw. Their introductory letter (penned in a child-like scrawl) to the sixties icon couldn't have been more gushing had they asked for a signed photo and a lock of Shaw's hair. (spelling and grammatical errors left untouched):

Shaw was initially reticent about getting involved because of the negative media attention surrounding certain other Marr and Morrissey compositions; while George O'Mara's naked form (lifted from Margaret Walter's 1978 book, *The Nude Male*) adorning the cover of the copy of 'Hand in Glove' the duo posted off to Shaw did little to ease her concerns. Having been won over by Morrissey's name-checking

her at every turn in interviews, however, Shaw acquiesced and accompanied Marr, Rourke, and Joyce into Matrix Studios in Southwest London to record 'I Don't Owe You Anything', 'Hand in Glove' and 'Jeane'.

Morrissey somewhat surprisingly elected to stay away from the studio but had already met his long-time barefooted heroine courtesy of Geoff Travis. Indeed, it was only through Travis's personal intervention that Shaw agreed to the meeting. "Gallantly, Geoff introduced me to Sandie by wheeling me round to her Harley Street flat," he revealed in *Autobiography*. "I was delighted to meet her in her own London digs – a fascinating floppy padhouse of little and dark cubby-hole rooms, with Sandie still in her pyjamas making breakfast."

The Smiths' version of 'Hand in Glove' was written in the key of E but owing to Shaw's vocal range differing to that of Morrissey the reworking at Matrix was recorded a half-step down in D minor. Though Marr and Morrissey had penned 'I Don't Owe You Anything' with Shaw in mind, the latter opted for 'Hand in Glove' as the single's A-side after altering certain of the lyrics. ('Jeane' would feature on the 12" version)

The Smiths' pulling power was such that Shaw's version of 'Hand in Glove' (RT130) scored her a Top 30 hit, and a surprise return to the Top of the Pops stage where she was again accompanied by Marr, Rourke, and Joyce (not performing barefoot as an homage to Shaw as reported elsewhere). Morrissey again deigned to stay away, but Shaw's joining The Smiths onstage both at the Hammersmith Palais on March 12, to sing 'I Don't Owe You Anything' was surely another tick on Mozzer's bucket-list.

Rough Trade would subsequently release two further Sandie Shaw singles: 'Please Help the Cause Against Loneliness' b/w 'Steven (You Don't Eat Meat') (RT220) in September 1988, and 'Nothing Less Than Brilliant' b/w 'Love Peace' (RT230) in November that same year.

It doesn't take too much of a stretch of the imagination to guess the subject matter of the B-side to 'Please Help the Cause Against Loneliness'. "'Steven, (You Don't Eat Meat)' [was] a song I had just then written about Morrissey [and] has the lines: 'You dressed me in my glad rags, you in your gladioli,'" Shaw revealed in her 1991 memoir, *The World at My Feet*. "It refers to the first time, in 1984, that he asked me to join him and The Smiths on stage, at the Hammersmith Palais. I hadn't a clue what to wear then, either. Luckily, Morrissey relished the task of dressing me up. Before the performance, I turned up at his flat with a huge pile of clothes and did an hour-long fashion parade in the kitchen while he scoffed tubs of vegetarian goodies from Marks and Sparks. "Finally he proclaimed, 'I want you to walk on stage as if you've just walked in off the street' and dismissed all the outfits with a theatrical wave of his teaspoon. He insisted I wore the jeans I arrived in, and a fresh Smiths T-shirt. He lent me his belt to hold my jeans up and then took great pains over selecting a blue plastic popper-bead necklace from his bag of jewellery. Something old, something new, something borrowed, something blue . . ."

THE SMITHS

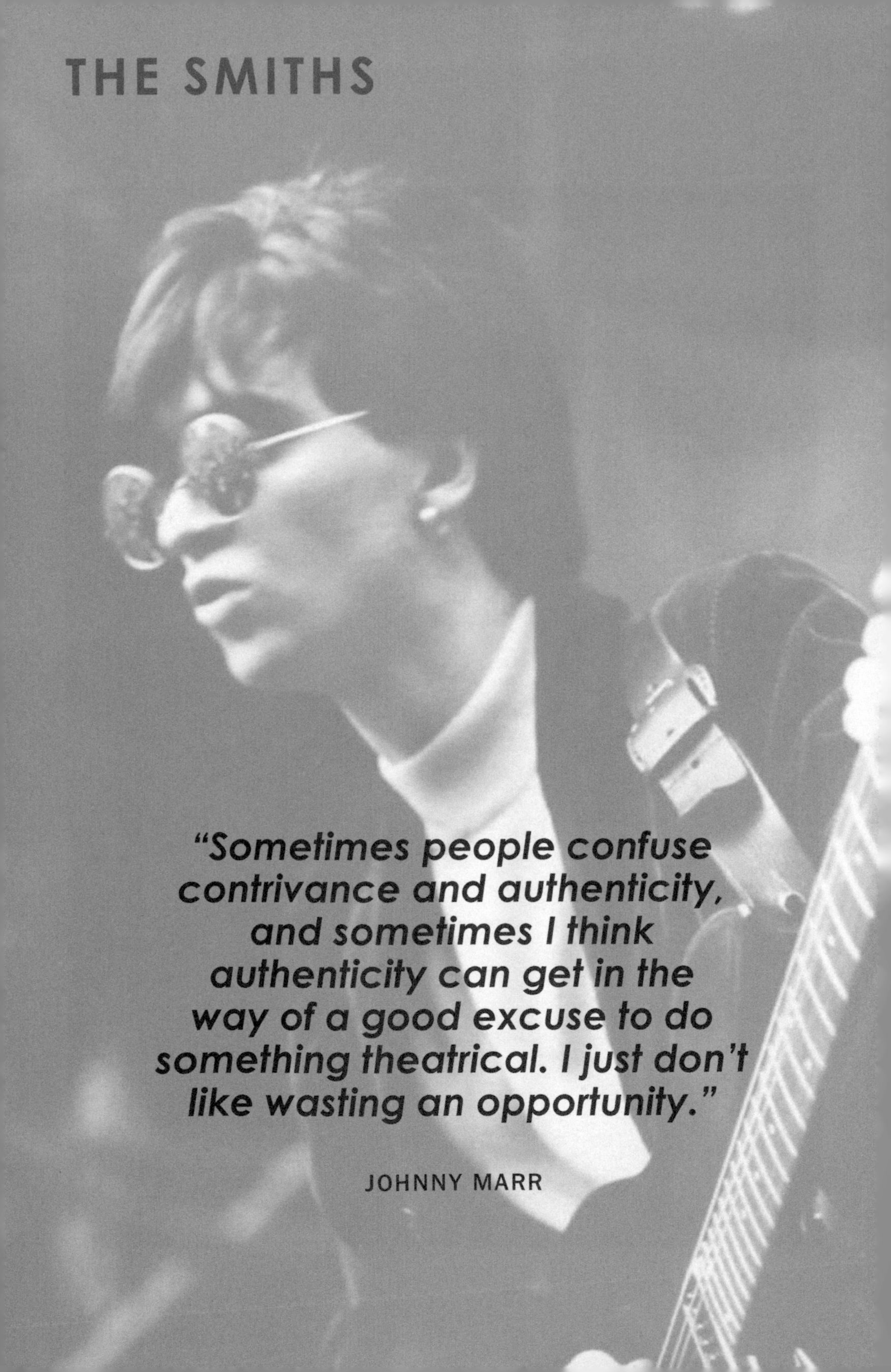

"Sometimes people confuse contrivance and authenticity, and sometimes I think authenticity can get in the way of a good excuse to do something theatrical. I just don't like wasting an opportunity."

JOHNNY MARR

CHAPTER FIVE

BLOOD ON THE TURNTABLE

The Smiths had slipped out of the Top 10 on the album chart by the time of the rearranged final UK tour date on March 20 at Birmingham's Tower Ballroom. But still, the album was holding its own in the Top 20 when The Smiths arrived in Amsterdam to participate in *Vinyl* magazine's fifth-anniversary celebrations at the Theater de Meervaart at the start of a 10-date European jaunt. The Theater de Meervaart show was a landmark of sorts as it was the first occasion The Smiths had played to an audience where English wasn't the audience's first language. The UK tour set-list had featured eight songs from the debut album. While the European dates were intended to boost sales of The Smiths on the continent, the sets didn't reflect this. Only six of the 13 songs played at the *Vinyl* party were from the album, while the following day's showing at the Breekend Festival in Bree, Belgium, featured four out of the 11 played. The compliment was back to six – with 'Hand in Glove' serving as both set-opener and closer – at Zurich's Rote Fabrik two nights later.

The original tour itinerary was for 15 dates, but shows in Vienna, Munich, Frankfurt, Koln, and Bremen (all scheduled for late April) ended up being pulled. The band were scheduled to fly back to London so that Marr, Rourke, and Joyce could appear alongside Sandie Shaw during the recording 'Hand in Glove' for that week's *Top of the Pops*, then return to the continent. No sooner were they in the air when Morrissey threw a hissy fit saying the tour was over because he couldn't "handle it". Instead of accompanying the rest of the band to the BBC studios, he headed for Stretford and the cosy sanctuary of his old bedroom where Scott Piering tracked him down several days later.

The tour resumed with a show at Hamburg's Markthalle on May 4, which went out on the long-running West German TV music show, *Rockpalast*. It's ironic that someone who considered himself "cosmopolitan" would toss his toys out of the pram simply because Europe's outlook on vegetarianism didn't match his own. Marr had also recently turned vegetarian, of course, but according to Piering's recollections, Rourke and Joyce

had proved equally dismissive of European fare. In Paris five days later, other than play the show (at L'Eldorado on Rue Petit Pont), the band didn't set foot out of their hotel, preferring to remain holed up in their rooms grumbling endlessly about the absence of egg and chips from the room service menu. It just goes to show that taking a boy from Manchester doesn't necessarily mean one can so easily prise Manchester from the boy.

From Paris, The Smiths flew to Belfast where food constraints and language barriers were thankfully less taxing. Since the Sixties, the Ulster Hall, on Bedford Street, has been Northern Ireland's spiritual home of rock music, playing host to the likes of the Rolling Stones, Led Zeppelin, The Who, Thin Lizzy, AC/DC, and The Clash.

Few bands were willing to venture to Belfast because of the ongoing sectarian conflict, and The Smiths could be sure of a thunderous reception. Because of his Irish roots, Marr had been looking forward to the Ulster Hall show from the moment the European dates were confirmed – "it wasn't just another town on the calendar," he told the Belfast Telegraph in October 2015. He was all too aware of the sectarian strife that was tearing the ailing city apart, of course, but having seen and read about the 'troubles' from afar, he was relishing the opportunity to see the situation for himself. "I got used to the image of Belfast from the news," he continued. "It gave it an air of unpredictability and a strangeness that it was so close, but there was a tension that I hadn't experienced anywhere else. I was very young, but to be honest, it made it really exciting for me. There was a working-class street culture, I think. And, of course, you couldn't have grown up in Manchester in the Sixties and Seventies and go to Belfast and not think about George Best. It'd be like going to Hong Kong and not thinking about Bruce Lee. For young Manchester lads with Irish descent, and me in particular, I had an interest in going to Belfast."

From Belfast, The Smiths headed for Dublin for two shows over consecutive evenings at the Irish capital's SFX Centre. It was their second visit to the venue, having played there the previous December. Following a fourth and final Irish date at the Savoy in Cork 's – where, according to local legend, they "burned the house down" – the band flew out to Finland for an appearance at the Provinssirock Festival.

Rough Trade had released 'Heaven Knows I'm Miserable Now' / 'Suffer Little Children' (RT156) while The Smiths were on their European travels. The single entered the UK chart at # 19 and would end up giving the band their first Top 10 hit. Indeed, the single was lodged at #10 for the second week in a row when The Smiths kicked off another string of promotional dates. These started with a headline appearance at the GLC's inaugural 'Jobs for a Change' Festival in Jubilee Gardens on London's South Bank on Sunday, June 10, alongside Billy Bragg, The Redskins, Mari Wilson, Aswad, and a host of other acts.

The Jobs for a Change Festival – named after the title of a GLC newspaper – was a free outdoor concert devised in the main due to the GLC's Industry and Employment committee's ongoing disquiet that its initiatives to combat unemployment and help create and fund jobs were not getting across to a wider public. The event took place over 12 hours along a stretch of the South Bank, taking in County Hall, the Royal Festival Hall, Queen Elizabeth Hall, the National Film Theatre, the National Theatre, the GLC car park, and Jubilee Gardens. An estimated 50,000 people turned out for the festival, and other than a contingent of National Front causing unrest during The Redskins' performance, the day passed without incident.

The event's organiser, Tony Hollingsworth had booked The Smiths to headline "before they had had a hit, but I was sure they would have one. By the time of the festival they were No.3 (sic) in the charts and rising. It was a gamble that paid off handsomely. We were right on it in terms of the music." The Smiths were introduced onstage by The GLC's larger-than-life leader, Ken Livingstone.

"The turn out for the GLC concert was huge, by far the biggest audience The Smiths had played to," Marr reflected in *Set the Boy Free*. "I was so nervous that I threw up before going on. We went out to 10,000 people, some of whom were hanging off balconies and screaming out of windows around the square behind the GLC building, and during the set I could see people climbing on the outside of the buildings and dangling from the roof."

> *One fan was trying to climb on stage, I helped pull him up, and then a few more people followed, and all of a sudden we'd managed to turn it into a Smiths gig."*

The Smiths would end up in hot water after the show owing to Rourke and Joyce tossing flowers to fans from the GLC windows. In the frenzy to grab the floral tributes, fans trampled over the bonnets of the vehicles belonging to the backstage caterers. With the fans having dispersed - and having no one else to blame – the disgruntled caterers came gunning for the band, and it was only their being given a police escort from the building that prevented the scene turning uglier.

Sandwiched betwixt shows at Carlisle's Market Hall on June 12, and the Blackpool Opera House eight days later The Smiths undertook a five-date mini Scottish tour with shows in Glasgow, Edinburgh, Dundee, Aberdeen, and Inverness. At the Blackpool gig Morrissey was introduced to Viv Nicholson and spent some much time chatting with her, both at the band's hotel as well as during a stroll along the promenade.

The Smiths rounded off their Summer excursions with an appearance at Glastonbury on June 23. These days, the Glastonbury Festival is regarded as the must-see outdoor musical extravaganza of the year, with audiences well in excess

of 100,000 and extensive TV coverage courtesy of the BBC. Back in 1984, it was a different story. The first Glastonbury festivals, including in 1984, were run in conjunction with the Campaign for Nuclear Disarmament (CND).

"What people don't realise is how mellow and low-key Glastonbury used to be," Marr reflected in *The Guardian* in June 2010. "It wasn't televised, and it wasn't a career-defining moment back then. You'd turn up to find just three fields – and they would be by no means full. You had a choice between the shit field, the field no one cares about, or the muddy one. Today's video screens would have seemed like an utter abomination."

Speaking about the event in his memoir, Marr says The Smiths were browbeaten into playing Glastonbury by Geoff Travis because of the festival's musical legacy, coupled with the importance of its political agenda and allegiance to the CND campaign. While speaking with *The Guardian*, the guitarist admitted The Smiths were "slightly out of our element" at Glastonbury that day. "Previously, we'd always played to manic, devoted audiences who were more like supporters at a cup final, but at Glastonbury, we were playing to people who largely hadn't seen us before. It wasn't like when Jay-Z played (2008), but we were very 'urban' compared to the other acts (The Waterboys, Elvis Costello, Joan Baez, and Ian Dury). Our songs were so fast that we got through our first four in about the time it took for the other bands to finish their intro. Eventually, I did manage to instigate a stage invasion, which raised a few eyebrows. One fan was trying to climb on stage, I helped pull him up, and then a few more people followed, and all of a sudden we'd managed to turn it into a Smiths gig."

The Glastonbury Festival was an experience Morrissey would prove in no particular hurry to repeat. "It wasn't the best of our performances and there was animosity from certain sections of the crowd," he said in an interview soon after the event. "I didn't think The Smiths really worked at Glastonbury. I'm not exactly sure why... perhaps because we built our following in smaller clubs and now we've advanced to larger halls. We're very much a live group and it was always very intimate and personal, which is something we couldn't capture at Glastonbury."

Seymour Stein (cutting a somewhat bizarre spectacle dressed head-to-toe in white) had accompanied Travis to Glastonbury with the express desire of getting Marr and Morrissey to consent to bring The Smiths over to America in the not-too-distant future – despite *The Smiths* having barely scraped into the Billboard 200. Though plans were set in motion for a US tour later in the year – and would get as far as the band playing a trio of warm-up shows in Gloucester, Cardiff, and Swansea towards the end of September – Marr and Morrissey ultimately set word they were in favour of starting work on a second Smiths studio album.

It was seen as being the norm for bands or solo artists to include all their A-sides

– regardless of whether they were a hit – on their studio albums. The Smiths, like The Beatles and The Clash, were a band happy to buck the trend. 'This Charming Man' hadn't appeared on The Smiths, and as far as Marr and Morrissey were concerned, there would be no place on the follow-up album for either. Nor for 'Heaven Knows I'm Miserable Now', or their latest offering, 'William, It Was Really Nothing' (RT166), which although failing to emulate the giddy heights of the former, did at least score the band their second consecutive Top 20 hit (peaking at #17).

Despite their ravings at the time *The Smiths* was released, Marr and Morrissey had come to realise the album's obvious shortcomings – particularly with the 'flatness' of the production. Indeed, such was Morrissey's dislike of the debut by the autumn of 1984 that he mooted the idea to Travis of releasing an interim compilation album consisting of all four Peel and Jensen sessions along with selected B-sides and 12" bonus tracks. The singer had been moved by the number of letters he'd received from fans beseeching the band for an official release. Though fans had had ample opportunity to record the sessions owing to repeat airings due to popular demand, said recordings ultimately suffered from what can best be described as "DJ interference".

Defending his 180 degree about face in the music media about the record he'd been "ready to be burned at the stake in total defence of" soon after the release of *Hatful of Hollow*, Morrissey said how the situation the band had found themselves in had left them with no option but to release the album. "At the time we were behind it completely and that LP means a great deal to many people who weren't even aware of the Peel sessions... *Hatful of Hollow* was there because I absolutely felt that the first LP was an inaccurate representation of our skills, which is embarrassing, but I think we can survive the embarrassment."

Releasing a compilation album so soon into their career undoubtedly raised eyebrows amongst purists and had *Hatful of Hollow* stiffed on the chart the naysayers might have had a case. However, *Hatful of Hollow* containing nearly an hour's worth of Smiths treasures (16 tracks in total packaged in a gatefold sleeve featuring a photo of Jean Cocteau aficionado Fabrice Collette). It retiled at a budget-price of £3.99 and attracted a fair number of buyers who were aware of The Smiths from hearing them on the radio but had thus far passed on purchasing any of their records.

Hatful of Hollow entered the UK chart at # 7 following its November 12 release, and remained on the chart for an impressive 46 weeks. (In 2000, *Q* magazine placed *Hatful of Hollow* at # 44 on its 100 Greatest British Albums Ever.) The album was Rough Trade's biggest-selling album to date, and yet Geoff Travis would churlishly insist that it didn't count as a contractual album.

Had it not been for the decision to carry over 'Barbarism Begins at Home'

and 'Rusholme Ruffians' onto the new album, it could be construed that by book-ending *Hatful of Hollow* with both sides of the 'William, It Was Really Nothing' The Smiths were signing off the first chapter of their story. This was further evidenced by Rough Trade's decision to release 'Still Ill' b/w 'Reel Around the Fountain' and 'Please, Please, Please, Let Me Get What I Want' (RTD018T) as a 12" West German release only.

Hatful of Hollow was deemed to be a tad too rough around the edges for the mainstream American market and wouldn't be released in the US till 1993. Stein would go into raptures about 'How Soon Is Now?', however, going so far as to proclaim the song the "Stairway to Heaven of the Eighties". Warner Brothers, however, were to prove less enthused. As a result of lacklustre promotion, the ensuing 12" single (Sire 0-20284) wasted what might have proved a gilt-edged opportunity to break The Smiths in the US. With 'How Soon Is Now?' already featuring on *Hatful of Hollow*, the UK 7" version (RT176) would stall at a desultory #24 on the chart much to everyone's disappointment.

The fabled British Invasion of the mid-Sixties – spearheaded by The Beatles, Stones, Animals, Herman's Hermits, The Kinks et al – certainly opened the door for British acts but relatively few enjoyed similar success – especially those bands deemed to be quintessentially-English in their song-writing. The Jam probably being the best example of a band that achieved "God-like" status in Britain yet struggled to make any impact across the pond. Sire had previous experience with both Madness and The Specials, of course, but neither band made much of an impact anywhere outside of Anglophile enclaves such as New York, Boston, Philadelphia, and Los Angeles. So whether 'How Soon Is Now?' would have helped boost The Smiths' profile in the US is a matter of conjecture.

By the time The Smiths headed into Amazon Studios in Kirkby, Merseyside (currently trading at Parr Street Studios), Morrissey was the member of the band still living in London, though King's Road was still serving as a surrogate abode. Rather than call upon John Porter's services (the band would work with him again in the future), it was decided that Marr would oversee production on the as-yet-untitled new album with Stephen Street. The latter, an up-and-coming engineer who had worked alongside Porter on 'Heaven Knows I'm Miserable Now' and had built up a rapport with the band, especially Marr. Like most people, the 24-year-old's introduction to The Smiths had come seeing them performing – or miming along to – 'This Charming Man' on *Top of the Pops* and was "really excited" by what he heard. "I was working at Island as an in-house engineer," he explained. "There was a session booked for the weekend, so they wanted someone who was prepared to come in. Once I heard it was The Smiths, I said, 'I'd definitely like to do that.' You could tell the band were excited. They were very together. They'd done a lot of touring so

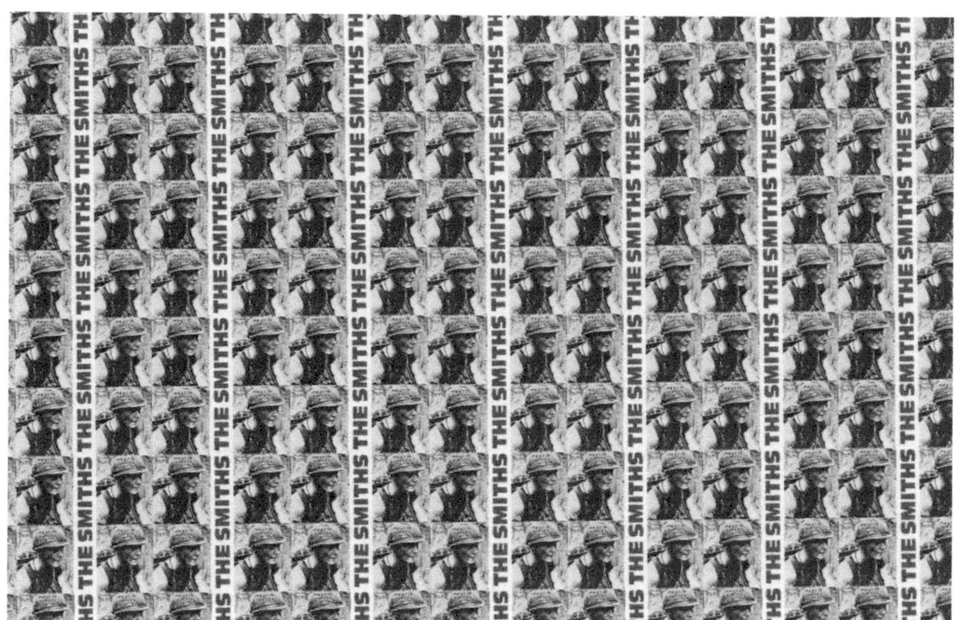

they were in good shape... really hot."

The session to which Street is referring was the recording of 'Heaven Knows I'm Miserable Now' back in March. The band had been impressed by Street's know-how and unbridled enthusiasm. When Geoff Travis called to see if he was free to work on The Smiths new album, there was only one answer. "He (Travis) said the band want to do a record where they want to produce it themselves and they want to work with an engineer they like and trust – would I be up for it?" he continued "So we started sessions at Amazon. You could tell that the feeling in the band was very positive. They knew they were onto something good. Everything was flying. We would get picked up at 9.30-10 in the morning in Manchester. Get to Amazon at about 11, work through to about eight o'clock at night, perhaps nine, and then get driven back."

The Smiths might have been unhappy with how their debut turned out but setting to work on the follow-up without an established producer to lean on was an audacious move on their part as they would have had no one else to blame should things go awry. "I had to follow my own instincts," Marr reflected. "There were never any arguments or disagreements in the studio between the band members about the direction of the record or the way anything was going. I was inspired by the songs we were writing, and the return to the north was definitely the right move as it inspired me to follow a sound with a northern spirit. We were firing on all cylinders and doing it ourselves."

Speaking with *Guitar* magazine in

January 1997, the guitarist said that it was because the Peel and Jensen sessions had been "banged out and ended up sounding great" that he'd first thought why bother using a name producer on the new album. It was a very exciting period for me - realising I could hijack 16 tracks all for myself... In hindsight, I wasn't happy with the overall sound. I think it's too thin. And artistically, I think *Meat Is Murder* is the least successful of all The Smiths' albums. Some of the songs are just played too fast. That's me – I'm terrible for just speeding things up. Super hyper!"

The band had rented a white limo to ferry them to and from the studio. The car had two sets of seats in the rear, one facing the other as in the rear of a black cab. Morrissey and Marr would always sit in the one facing forward with Rourke and Joyce in the other. Any disagreements as such were usually about the heating, which Morrissey would complain wasn't turned up high enough. "Amazon was on an industrial estate in the middle of nowhere," Rourke told Uncut magazine in September 2015 to mark the album's thirtieth anniversary. "It was the freezing winter. We'd stop for a cup of tea at this mobile café and carry that into the studio. That was our routine for two or three weeks."

Amazon, which Morrissey grumbles about being a "predictably cheap studio", was indeed situated on an industrial estate some six miles from Liverpool's city centre. Yet while Kirkby was hardly the most auspicious setting from which The Smiths would storm the citadel, their working far from the usual distractions on offer in Manchester allowed for a freewheeling and stimulating atmosphere. "It was very exciting," Street acknowledged. "It felt like all the stars were in alignment... everything seemed to be working."

The new album quickly began to take shape with songs 'The Headmaster Ritual', 'That Joke Isn't Funny Anymore', and 'What She Said' joining 'Barbarism Begins at Home' and 'Rusholme Ruffians' in the can. It was only towards the end of the sessions that the album gained an identity. "Morrissey and I were sitting in the control room when he asked me what I thought about calling the album *Meat Is Murder*." Marr loved the title as it was in perfect keeping with their perception of what the Smiths were about and by the end of the conversation they'd decided to pen a title track.

"We had about 80 per cent of the songs in hand," says Rourke. "We always worked in the same way. Johnny, myself and Mike would put down a rough track with Johnny playing live guitar, just so we had that as a reference. We'd go all the way back and Mike would lay down the drums proper, listening to Johnny's guitar, and then I'd put the bass on top. Then Johnny would layer all his guitars. Lastly, Morrissey would do his magic over the top. He would come into the recording room with his notebook and his lyrics. He wouldn't show them to anybody beforehand. That was always an exciting part! You'd hear the lyrics for the first time when he was singing them over the track."

Morrissey found the relief of their making the album free from Porter's "schoolmasterly ear" near palpable. Marr,

Rourke and Joyce had practically been told what to play on The Smiths, while Porter's insistence that Morrissey record his vocals line by line had done little to enamour him to the producer. "With *Meat is Murder* we thrashed through all of the new songs back-to-back in order to see – just for the hell of it – where everything would land.

"Out poured the signature Smiths' powerhouse full-tilt that had been lost on the debut. Straight away the hard Ardwick aria spits out as the 'Headmaster Ritual'; a live-wire spitfire guitar sound that takes on all-comers; bass domination instant on 'Rusholme Ruffians', weighty and bruiser drums on 'I Want the One I Can't Have'. The Smiths begin to stand upright."

'The Headmaster Ritual' was in fact a left-over from The Smiths' recording sessions as Marr explains: "The nuts and bolts of 'The Headmaster Ritual' came together during the first album, and I just carried on playing around with it. It started off as a very sublime sort of Joni Mitchell-esque chord figure; I played it to Morrissey but we never took it further. Then, as my life got more and more intense, so did the song. The bridge and the chorus part were originally for another song, but I put them together with the first part. That was unusual for me; normally I just hammer away at an idea until I've got a song."

Putting references to the Sheila Delany's plays and the Moors Murders to one side, Morrissey's lyrical themes on *The Smiths* were either introspective, self-deprecative, or of lost innocence. *Meat Is Murder* was to present a different, highly politicised side to The Smiths; the song addressing powerful and (then) contemporary themes - domestic and institutionalised violence, and of course, animal rights. Of all the political topics to be scrutinised people are still disturbingly vague about the treatment of animals," Morrissey explained in an interview with the *NME* towards the end of December 1984. "People still seem to believe that meat is a particular substance not at all connected to animals playing in the field over there. People don't realise how gruesomely and frighteningly the animal gets to the plate..."

"The Smiths were out there on their own," Paul Weller said in the same *Uncut* feature. "I thought they were similar to The Jam, really. It wasn't a party line thing, and the lyrics weren't always overly political. But they still seemed to reflect what was going on in people's lives."

"The politics of the day had a big effect on the music and Morrissey's lyrics," Rourke added. "That's what we wrote songs about: our experiences. That comes across in the music, also."

Billy Bragg, whose own lyrics were somewhat left-of-centre, echoed Weller's comments about the issues The Smiths were addressing on *Meat Is Murder* being socio-political. "My politics were more ideological, but The Smiths were more involved in broader issues; we lived in a time when those issues were right to the forefront of debate.

"There was something in the air in that period, 1984 -1985," he continued. "It was incredibly intense. You have to see Live Aid in some ways as a reflection of that, because they were all the bands who didn't want to get their hands dirty with the miners. But as me and The Smiths broke in 1984, we were very much of those times. We weren't there alone, but in terms of addressing issues, The Smiths were at the forefront."

It's interesting that given The Smiths burgeoning popularity as 1984 drew to a close was their being overlooked while Bob Geldof and Midge Ure were assembling their star-studded celebrity ensemble at Basing Street Studios to record 'Do They Know It's Christmas?' If Geldof and Ure were intent on bringing the cream of British musical talent together to give the song as broad an appeal as possible to the record-buying public, then including The Smiths – if only Marr and Morrissey – could only have proved beneficial. The Smiths weren't the only ones to be overlooked, of course, as on the day of the recording Geldof would churlishly ignore Joe Strummer, leaving the Clash frontman standing outside in the cold. For reasons known only to themselves, Geldof and Ure would decide against inviting The Smiths onto the Live Aid bill the following July.

With the majority of the nine tracks in the can, The Smiths relocated to Ridge Farm, a residential recording studio outside of Horsham in Surrey. The white limo had been returned to its owners, but the band was still keen to be seen to travel in style. "They would travel to press engagements and meetings in a black limousine," their designated driver, Dave Harper, recalled. "It didn't appear to have a key for the ignition. It was all a bit dodgy. You put a large screwdriver in the ignition and that's how you started it. The boot didn't have a thing to hold it up, so you had to use a broomstick. It was originally a funeral cortege car from Holland. Morrissey once asked me about the history of the vehicle. He was sitting behind me. He was in one of his chatty moods. I said, 'It used to be a funeral cortege car from Holland.' He said, 'I wish you hadn't told me that.' He didn't talk to me for the rest of the journey."

It was at Ridge Farm that the album's title track was knocked into shape. "It was me, Mike and Johnny jamming out this very mellow, repetitive riff," said Rourke. "It just happened organically. Morrissey already had the lyrics."

According to Street, the band didn't even have a rough demo to work from. "The chords are quite strange with that song and they wanted to create an atmosphere. So Johnny sketched out the chords, then we marked it out with a click track, put some piano down, and reversed the first notes to creative this oppressive kind of darkness. Morrissey handed me a *BBC Sound Effects* album and said, 'I want you to try and create the sound of an abattoir.'

"So there's me with a *BBC Sound Effects* album of cows mooing happily in a field. It was a challenge, but I really enjoyed it. I found some machine noises and put them through a harmoniser and turned the pitch down so they sounded darker and deeper. I did the same things with the cows, to make it sound spooky. It was like a sound collage. The band learnt how to play it live after we'd recorded it."

The artwork for *Meat Is Murder* saw The Smiths venture away from homoerotic and sixties icon imagery. Instead, they borrowed the promo poster for Emile de Antonio's 1968

film, *In the Year of the Pig* (which documents America's ongoing involvement in Vietnam), replacing the slogan on the GI's helmet to read Meat Is Murder. The GI caught for posterity on the album is 20-year-old Marine Cpl. Michael Wynn, of Columbus, Ohio, who was snapped while taking a breather during Operation Ballistic Charge in the Da Nang Valley, South Vietnam, on September 21, 1967. It was Wynn's having daubed "Make War Not Love" (a play on the counter-cultural anti-war slogan: "Make Love, Not War") on his helmet that most likely caught de Antonio's attention.

When questioned about the artwork's deliberate link between war and animal rights, Morrissey said that to his mind, animal rights groups weren't making sufficient headway because by and large their methods were quite peaceable. "It seems to me now that when you try to change things in a peaceable manner you're actually wasting your time and you're laughed out of court. And it seems to me now that as the image of the LP hopefully illustrates, the only way that we can get rid of such things as the meat industry, and other things like nuclear weapons, is by really giving people a taste of their own medicine."

Something else Morrissey was keen to see the back of was the Tory government – and its leader, Margaret Thatcher, in particular. Speaking with *Rolling Stone* back in June he said how "The entire history of Margaret Thatcher is one of violence and oppression and horror," and that he "pray[ed] there is a Sirhan Sirhan [Robert Kennedy's supposed assassin in June 1968] somewhere. It's the only remedy for this country at the moment."

The Smiths had only just moved into Amazon to begin work on *Meat Is Murder* when Thatcher narrowly escaped assassination at the hands of the IRA at the Grand Brighton Hotel in Brighton where the Conservatives were holding their annual conference. Morrissey would express his "sorrow" in an interview with *Melody Maker* that "Thatcher escaped unscathed".

Speaking about Morrissey's antipathy towards Thatcher in *Uncut*, Rourke said that while his singer was "always very outspoken in interviews about Thatcher and the royal family," he'd never felt uneasy

"There was something in the air in that period, 1984 -1985"

about such comments. "I was 18, 19, I used to panic about what my dad might read [but] I was OK with it," he explained. "As a band, we showed a great deal of solidarity and stood behind Morrissey with all his beliefs. We all had to have the same beliefs."

By this juncture, the band's shared beliefs had extended to all four members sharing Marr and Morrissey's dietary regime. "You can't record an album called *Meat Is Murder* and slip out for a burger," Rourke continued. "One time, we stopped at a service station to get some breakfast. Everyone ordered scrambled eggs or fried eggs or whatever. I ordered the full English breakfast. When it arrived, Morrissey left the table. Then Johnny left the table. Then Mike left the table. So I was sat on my own with this English breakfast feeling very

uncomfortable. I went vegetarian after that."

Harper would also find himself in Morrissey's crosshairs over his eating habits. "On one of our many trips we stopped at a service station with a Little Chef," he revealed. "In those days, if you ordered an all-day breakfast it came on a plate decorated with a farmyard scene. So you had the joy of eating bacon and sausages off a plate with pictures of pigs on it. I thought it was quite funny, particularly eating it in front of Morrissey.

"He didn't make a scene, he just said, 'Why have you done that?' I replied, 'I don't know what you're talking about. Done what?' He didn't harangue me, or never forgive me for eating meat. It wasn't the right environment for him to start sounding off about politics. It never came up. But it was a big thing: what does Morrissey eat? Biscuits, cake, ice cream..."

Meat Is Murder (ROUGH81) was released on February 11, 1985 and slammed onto the UK album chart at #1 the following week (achieving a BPI gold certification for sales of 100,000 and dislodging Bruce Springsteen's *Born In The USA* in the process). The album would only hold onto the top spot for one week before slipping to #3, but it nonetheless cemented their standing as Britain's hippest band.

"Morrissey went up to the microphone and got an electric shock. We said, 'Look, we're not even gonna play this gig."

MIKE JOYCE

CHAPTER SIX

TIME'S SMOTHERING TIDE

The first six months of 1985 were taken up promoting *Meat Is Murder* with tours in the UK, Europe, and the US. The 24-date UK tour commenced with a show at Golddiggers in Chippenham on February 27, included all the usual customary stop-offs for a band of The Smiths' standing, culminating with a sell-out finale at London's Royal Albert Hall on April 6. The show scheduled for March 10 at the Cliffs Pavilion in Southend would be cancelled at the eleventh hour owing to the venue being deemed unsafe. Fellow Mancunians, James, were once again providing support.

The majority of the venues on the tour would be put to the test owing to fans' overexuberance spilling over into the by now customary stage invasions. The band had come to regard stage invasions during the encores as part of the evening's itinerary, even going so far as to encourage the crowd to storm the stage. In hindsight, this was somewhat foolhardy on Morrissey's part. While a stray elbow might cause Marr or Rourke to hit a bum note, the same could send the mic slamming into Morrissey's mouth and that would have surely brought the tour to a premature halt. The fans were only reacting to what they'd read about stage invasions in the *NME* or *Sounds*. It was shades of 1977 where kids thought that to be a true punk they had to gob at the bands. The Smiths had long-since abandoned the idea to promote themselves as a gay band, but with the vast majority of the stage invaders being teenage males, homoeroticism was still very much flavour of the day.

The venues' respective security tended to take a far dimmer view, however. With over-zealous bouncers rigidly adhering to a zero-tolerance approach to unruly behaviour, the band were forced into having their road crew manning the front of the stage.

Golddiggers was something of a strange choice of venue to kickstart a national tour. Although the club had staged a number of raucous rock concerts since opening its doors some four years earlier, its glitterball interior was more suited for staging discos – and would subsequently become a regular haunt of the Hitman & Her travelling roadshow.

Except for 'Well I Wonder', the set-list at Golddiggers featured every song on *Meat*

Is Murder. An even newer composition, the band's soon-to-be-released latest single 'Shakespeare's Sister' (RT181), was also unveiled that evening. Despite its being a stand-alone offering, the single would rise no higher than # 26 on the UK chart, while 'That Joke Isn't Funny Anymore' / 'Meat Is Murder' (live Oxford 18/3/85) (RT186) – the first song culled for the album for UK release – would give an even worse showing by only just breaking into the Top 50 following its early-July release. Morrissey, rather uncharitably, laid the blame squarely at Rough Trade's door – much to Geoff Travis' annoyance. "There was a problem with Morrissey thinking he had a divine right to a higher chart position," the latter fumed. "We did as well as anyone in the world could have done with those records. Morrissey would have liked us to advertise every single on television, as though it was the event of the decade. But you can't do that. It's not logical. If you're selling 20 million records worldwide, you can afford to spend the kind of money you'd splash out on Michael Jackson, but The Smiths were not a major group internationally."

Rough Trade had never made any secret of their having to work within a finite budget, but Marr and Morrissey must have known as much when they signed with the label. Indeed, the band were as much to blame as anyone for their relatively poor showing internationally – especially on the continent. Their previous European outing in support of The Smiths had been a token affair compared to the tours undertaken by most of their peers – and several of those dates were cancelled owing to Morrissey throwing a hissy fit. This time around, the European promotion of *Meat Is Murder* consisted of just four dates – one in Italy, and three in Spain (one of which would be cancelled). No one has said as much, but the band's reluctance to venture across the Channel is the only viable explanation.

The UK tour ended on April 6, and the US tour wasn't set to get underway until June 7. Controversy would raise its ugly head again with Morrissey very much at the forefront. When Scott Piering arrived at the singer's Kensington flat to ferry him to Heathrow there was no answer. Suspecting Morrissey at home, the quick-thinking Piering roused Morrissey's next-door neighbours and cajoled them into allowing him to scramble over their balcony. He found the pyjama-clad Morrissey hiding in his bedroom.

There would be further drama at Heathrow. Morrissey was griping about Rough Trade having lined up what they considered a prestigious appearance on the Italian TV network RAI (Radiotelevisione Italiana). Travis and Co. were already smarting at The Smiths pulling out of performing 'That Joke Isn't Funny Anymore' on the BBC's early evening show, *Wogan*, and so sent a delegation to the airport to plead their case. Despite some prima-diva behaviour in switching hotels until finding one to the band's liking, the previous evening's show at Rome's Teatro Tendastrisce (which was instead staged within a red and white-striped circus-like tent) on May 14 proceeded as scheduled. It was, however, to prove an illusory dawn.

Though the band would get as far as going through rehearsals at the TV studios,

Morrissey felt their having to perform amid fake Roman ruins beneath him and sent word from the dressing room. The producers were understandably furious and vented their spleen at Virgin Italy, who were licensing Smiths product in Italy and had arranged the appearance, threatening that no other Virgin acts would ever again be invited onto the show. The Smiths remained unmoved, however. "The easy option would have been to do it," Marr reflected. "It took some real insight and perception to go, 'I don't want to be seen doing this.' I'm really glad he (Morrissey) saved my bacon. Sometimes he took one for the team."

Jo Slee, Rough Trade's European licensing rep, had accompanied the band to Rome to ensure they honoured their RAI commitments. While the band were sat about the Sheraton Hotel's lobby awaiting transport to the nearby airport, Slee cornered Mike Joyce and vented her own frustrations, telling the bemused drummer that she might as well quit if she wasn't allowed to carry out her duties. All Joyce had to say on the matter was that if she carried out her threat, Rough Trade would simply appoint someone else. "Coming

from the drummer, that told me everything I needed to know," Slee bemoaned. "Dealing with them was like going up and down escalators all the time and they seemed to take every excuse to sabotage what Rough Trade were doing." On returning to London, Slee would indeed quit her post in licensing to work alongside Richard Boon in the label's production department.

Following on from Rome the band flew to Barcelona for a show at the Catalan capital's Studio 54. The show was filmed, with seven of the 18 songs – 'Hand In Glove', 'Handsome Devil', 'Barbarism Begins At Home', 'Heaven Knows I'm Miserable Now', 'Rusholme Ruffians', 'The Headmaster Ritual' and 'Miserable Lie' – featuring in a Spanish TV one-hour special on The Smiths titled *Arsenal*. The special also included interviews with Marr and Morrissey. Two days later, The Smiths were again filmed playing an outdoor show at Madrid's Paseo de Camoens Festival.

Owing to something getting lost in translation, The Smiths arrived in the Spanish coastal town of San Sebastián to find the venue – the local sports hall – had been supplied with the wrong equipment rider. After a frustrating soundcheck, The Smiths announced the show was off and returned to their hotel, leaving their hapless tour manager, Stuart James, to deal with the promoters and disgruntled fans. The scene turned ugly, with local police arriving to quell disturbances. The officers then descended on the band's hotel, threatening to confiscate their passports until the show went ahead. "It all got very nasty," said James. "We weren't being blackmailed into doing the gig, but we weren't really being given any assistance. All the band wanted to do was get the hell out."

While The Smiths were in Spain, Piering received a letter from an Alexis Grower of Seifert, Sedley Williams solicitors. In the letter, Grower informed Piering that The Smiths had retained his services to contend the band's Rough Trade contract and had telexed both Rough Trade and Sire as per his instructions. Grower's missive also informed Piering that he was in negotiations with an unnamed third party to assume control of The Smiths' American merchandising deals. Piering flew out to Madrid to confront the band. The Smiths arrived at their hotel to find Piering asleep in the lobby, yet rather than hold a meeting to discuss Grower's letter, they went out of their way to avoid him.

Piering had long-since come to recognise that his role as surrogate manager was primarily to serve as a buffer between Morrissey and the rest of the world. "I had to make excuses for whatever fucked up thing he did," he explained. "I would rationalise it and try to sell it to whomever he offended and keep things sweet. A lot of things were focused on giving Morrissey what he wanted.

"It was my own weakness," he continued. "A serious manager has to tell the band what to do in certain instances and have enough input to make a decision, otherwise you're a mere functionary. I had no control over the money and couldn't make any creative or business decisions. I lasted until things became so big that, without any power or authority, I could not handle it. I couldn't do business on their behalf because I was never authorised to make any decisions. It was impossible."

The previous March, Marr and Morrissey had set up Smithdom as a limited company, with themselves listed as the company's sole directors. Though Rourke and Joyce were partners in Smithdom, it was Marr and Morrissey that retained sole control of the band's purse strings.

Piering's standing within The Smiths' hierarchy was such that he found himself in a near-constant struggle with Mike Hinc of All Trade Booking, who'd overseen The Smiths' touring to date. In a last desperate roll of the dice, Piering thought to expose All Trade Booking's perceived shortcomings by providing alternative plans for the impending US tour. He recruited high-powered American promoter, Hector Lazarides, to put together a budget proposal that would ensure The Smiths a profit margin between $60,00-$80,000. Marr was happy to stand in Piering's corner, but with Morrissey siding with Hinc, Piering's fate was all but sealed from that point on.

Stuart James was to prove another casualty. Finding his position untenable in the wake of the San Sebastián debacle, he called Hinc to serve notice that he was quitting after the US tour. Hinc blithely informed James that the band had already decided to dispense with his services after the tour.

By the time the US tour kicked-off with an opening show at Chicago's 5000-capacity Aragon Ballroom, The Smiths had hired one-time Madness road manager, Matthew Sztumpf. Sztumpf, who sadly succumbed to a brain aneurism in March 2010, was put forward for the role of tour manager by All Trade Booking. He'd actually been interviewed by Morrissey earlier in the year as a potential manager. Though not a Smiths fan himself, Sztumpf was happy to take the reins and see what, if anything, developed. He would also find himself questioning his eating habits and climbing aboard the vegetarian bandwagon.

Morrissey's insistence on having drag acts support them on the tour was to backfire badly in Chicago, with the hapless transvestite being pelted with beer cans – not all of which were empty. Although Dainty Adore O'Hara, a 300-pound drag queen with a penchant for frilly yellow dresses, would open for The Smiths at one or both LA shows, Billy Bragg was flown out to open the remainder of the dates.

Seymour Stein would put in an appearance when The Smiths played Toronto's open-air Kingswood Theatre on June 9. Evidence that The Smiths were on an upward curve stateside came with 12,000 turning out to see them when the band had only sold around 10,000 albums in Canada to date. Rather than watch from the safety of the wings, Stein elected to rough it out at the front of the stage. "Seymour was right down the front squashed against a barrier for the entire show," Sztumpf explained. "He was really into it. That's the great thing about Seymour. He always has been a music fan and always will be. What MD of a record company would spend an entire evening squashed up against a crash barrier

at the front of a gig?" The Sire head was also intent on attending both of The Smiths' appearances at New York's Beacon Theatre on June 17/18. Morrissey had other ideas, however, and had Stuart James call Stein at his hotel to say his presence wouldn't be welcomed.

The Smiths were making their way through to the stage for the opening show when Marr was introduced to a rather imposing individual dressed head-to-toe in white; a white fedora rounding off his incongruous ensemble. The band had already been subjected to a lot of backstage banter from concerned New Yorkers about how the Mafia were overrunning the city, so his being "pointedly introduced" to a guy looking as though he'd just stepped out of central casting was to leave an indelible impression on the guitarist. Marr, in turn, would leave a Rickenbacker-shaped impression on one of the theatre's more tactile security staff. On seeing the guy in question being overly heavy-handed with a fan during the encore, he rushed across and kicked him from the stage. When this failed to subdue the guy, Marr unslung his guitar and clubbed him with it. Though his frustrations were wholly understandable, getting into an altercation with a venue's security isn't the smartest move a musician can make. Marr admits to keeping his eyes riveted to his guitar the following night so as to avoid making eye contact with any of the security staff.

"He was really into it. That's the great thing about Seymour. He always has been a music fan and always will be."

The remainder of the tour would be thrown into jeopardy by Morrissey's fear of flying. The singer wasn't overly thrilled at playing the West Coast anyway, and James feared he was using his chronic aviophobia as an excuse to cancel the five Californian shows. According to James, the band and their entourage were taxi-ing down the runway at JFK when Morrissey announced he wanted to get off the plane.

The opening West Coast date was at the H. J. Kaiser Auditorium in Oakland. Exploring San Francisco featured on both Marr and Angie's bucket-list. Upon arrival in the city, Angie set about circling the tourist haunts on her pocket guide. Marr, however, had other designs on how to utilise their free time. Getting hitched anywhere in the US other than Las Vegas can prove problematic – especially when the wedding is spur-of-the-moment. Help was at hand, however. The Oakland show was being promoted by legendary Bay Area promoter, Bill Graham. Upon learning about Marr's intentions, Graham offered any assistance they might need. Marr says he and Angie were required to undertake blood tests, but blood tests weren't (and never have been) a requirement under Californian law. Perhaps it was simply their giving blood at a doctor's office in Height-Ashbury, the epicentre of Sixties counter-

culture, providing added allure.

The ceremony was witnessed by the band, road crew, and a handful of fans that got wind of the location. "It was a timeless moment and one that I felt was serious and significant in my life," the guitarist reflected. "It didn't matter that our families weren't there. Angie and I had been living an unconventional life for a few years now, and our families were used to our lifestyle."

Immediately after the service, the newlyweds jumped in a cab and headed over to the Golden Gate Bridge. Rough Trade had got in on the act booking a local photographer to take some photos. The photographer was a Smiths fan and offered his services for free. In return for his show of generosity, Marr promised him guest passes for the show. The passes failed to materialise, however. With everything that was going on, Marr could hardly be held accountable for the oversight. The guitarist was making his way out of the venue after the show when the irate photographer called out saying he could forget about the photos.

Awkwardness would soon turn to anger, however, when *Rolling Stone* contacted Rough Trade to say the photographer was offering the wedding photos for $5,000. Marr wasn't about to be held to ransom and told the magazine they could shove the photos where the sun don't shine.

The US tour had proved an unqualified success, even with *Rolling Stone* refusing each and every one of Seymour Stein's entreaties to promote either The Smiths or their records. The majority of the shows were sold out – including two dates at the 5,000-capacity LA Palladium.

While the rest of the world's attention was focused on the impending global jukebox extravaganza, all four Smiths busied themselves with moving house. Marr and Angie moved into a three-storey Victorian town house, Morrissey and Joyce secured leases on houses in neighbouring villages, while Rourke was content with a new flat. Marr remembers the summer of 1985 as being a "good period" for The Smiths, but. "We'd made some money and were the most popular guitar band in the country." The lyric to 'What Difference Does It Make?' references the idiom about the devil making work for idle hands to do. Loosely translated, this means one should always occupy one's time so the devil won't spare a glance in his quest to make mischief. Mike Joyce might have been living in an upmarket neighbourhood, but the distribution of moneys within the band still rankled him. Finding himself with nothing to otherwise occupy his thoughts, he called the band's booking agent, Mike Hinc, requesting an up-to-date set of accounts. Said accounts would fail to materialise, however.

Within days of his contacting Hinc, Joyce received an irate call from Morrissey. Joyce tried explaining that he simply wanted to satisfy his curiosity but came away sensing Morrissey regarded his request as a personal slight. Although wary of further antagonising Morrissey and Marr, Joyce elected to continue picking at the scab. Both he and Rourke were willing to accept they were never going to be viewed as equal partners in The Smiths, but both felt they were worthy of a bigger slice of the spoils.

Marr and Morrissey remained unmoved, however. To their thinking, they were responsible for the creativity and rhythm-sections were easily replaceable. "The attitude was 'If you don't like it, you can get out,'" Rourke explained. "I think they knew me and Mike really loved what we were doing, so they knew we never would. We were made to feel like second-class citizens – even by the record company."

Marr and Morrissey's refusal to alter their stance left Rourke and Joyce well-and-truly wedged betwixt the axiomatic rock and hard place. Though unhappy with their lot, they knew there were hundreds

"The attitude was 'If you don't like it, you can get out'"

of drummers and bass players that would happily take their place for an even smaller slice of the pie. Insult was soon to be heaped on top of injury, however. On discovering Morrissey was intent on slashing their share of the moneys the band received from touring and recording from 25 per cent to 15 per cent, Joyce called his singer to vent his frustrations. Morrissey would subsequently deny all knowledge of both the phone call and the alleged pruning of Joyce and Rourke's touring and recording income. Indeed, during the 1996 royalties dispute Morrissey insisted that at the time of Rourke and Joyce's grumblings, he'd been under the impression that the pair had received a 10 per cent share from the Rough Trade signing onwards – even though accounts up to 1985 revealed a 25 per cent split.

Morrissey was to also find himself at the centre of a managerial storm. Matthew Sztumpf had approached Marr on the day the band were set to return to the UK following on from the final US tour to voice his concerns about his standing. Marr had assured him that his concerns were unfounded and that his position as manager would soon be finalised. Sztumpf was happy to take Marr at his word and continued with his duties. It was to prove an illusory dawn, however. Sztumpf, in conjunction with Rough Trade's marketing department, secured The Smiths an appearance on the BBC's then flagship talk show, *Wogan*, on Friday, July 19, to promote their latest single, 'That Joke Isn't Funny Anymore.'

As with *Top of the Pops*, every artist booked to appear on *Wogan* was required to pre-record their performance in advance of the 7pm broadcast. One of Michael Grade's first edicts on taking over as Controller of BBC1 was to move *Wogan* to weekday evenings because he believed the series "would bring a much needed element of surprise and unpredictability to BBC Television." Morrissey's unpredictability was such, however, that he made the unilateral decision that The Smiths were above appearing on shows such as *Wogan* – despite its seven-figure viewing figures. Therefore, while Marr, Rourke and Joyce made the journey to London, Morrissey remained holed up in Hale Barns. Sztumpf was accustomed to Morrissey's autocratic antics, of course, but being left to shoulder

the blame for the singer's no-show proved too much to bear.

'That Joke Isn't Funny Anymore' would stall at a derisory # 49 on the UK chart following its July 1 release. There were other mitigating factors for the single's poor chart showing – such as its inclusion on *Meat is Murder* and live recordings of already released songs featuring on the B-side of both the 7" and 12" version – but Morrissey's refusal to appear on *Wogan* undoubtedly played its part.

The Smiths brought their 1985 touring commitments to a close with a seven-date foray in Scotland. Aside from the usual stop-offs of Glasgow, Edinburgh, Aberdeen, and Dundee, the tour featured off-the radar dates in Irvine, Lerwick, and Inverness. "The Smiths had a strong connection with Scotland because we played places that a lot of bands didn't play," Marr told the *Daily Record* in 2013. "That's the kind of band we were, the kind of people we were."

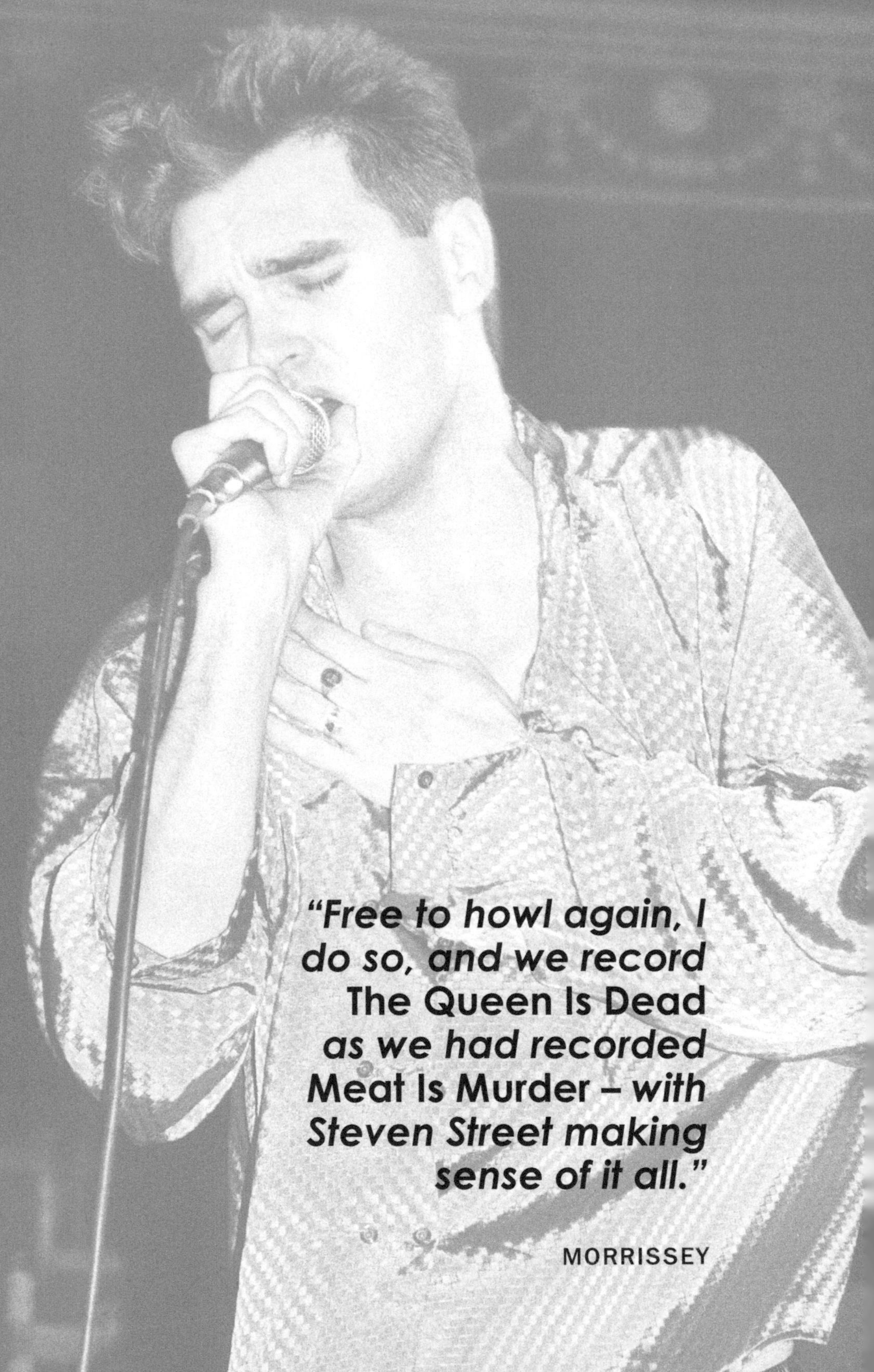

"Free to howl again, I do so, and we record The Queen Is Dead *as we had recorded* Meat Is Murder *– with Steven Street making sense of it all."*

MORRISSEY

CHAPTER SEVEN

LAST EXIT TO REASON

Meat Is Murder was always going to be a tough act to follow. Indeed, how does one go about topping a UK No. 1 album? Geoff Travis' response, should the question have been put to him, would have been for The Smiths' follow-up album to top the chart in both the UK and the US. Given *Meat Is Murder's* failure to break into the upper half of the Billboard 200, Travis would have most likely settled for the next Smiths long-player at least emulating its predecessor in the UK. 'The Boy with the Thorn in His Side' / 'Asleep' (RT191) had stalled at #23 following its mid-September 1985 release, yet it was nonetheless viewed as a return to winning ways of sorts. Marr and Morrissey were unquestionably the most accomplished English songwriting duo since Joe Strummer and Mick Jones. Indeed, the music press were going so far as to compare The Smiths to The Who and The Kinks in their respective swinging-sixties heyday. Such heady praise wasn't without its caveats, of course, and Marr, for one, was all too aware how quickly adulation would turn to antipathy should The Smiths fall short of expectations. "I knew the next album had to be the best I could possibly do," he revealed. "The stakes had got higher, and greatness was a possibility for the band if we were prepared to go for it."

Marr had been busy working up several new songs intended for the new album, of course. The first of these was a waltzy ballad with tentative verses and dramatic choruses that built up momentum as the tune progressed. The other idea was built around a breezy minor chord progression into which the guitarist had cheekily added a rhythmic skip from the Velvet Underground's 'There She Goes Again'. He wasn't too abashed at such a blatant display of plagiarism as the Velvets had, in turn, lifted it from the Stones' version of Marvin Gaye's debut US Top 40 hit, 'Hitch Hike'. "There's a little in-joke in there just to illustrate how intellectual I was getting," the guitarist told *Select* magazine in1993. "At the time everyone was into the Velvet Underground and they stole the intro to 'There She Goes Again' - da-da-da-da, da-da! - from the Stones' version of 'Hitch Hike'. I just wanted to put that in to see whether the press would say, 'Oh it's the

Velvet Underground!' Cos I knew that I was smarter than that. I was listening to what the Velvet Underground was listening to."

Lifting the intro to 'There She Goes Again' wouldn't be Marr's only pilfering from the Velvets' canon, however. Having purchased a copy of *VU*, a recently-released compilation of outtakes, Marr incorporated Sterling Morrison's scratchy guitar style on 'I Can't Stand It' into a chord progression he'd been working on. The end result being six-and-a-half-minutes of howling wipe-out that would become 'The Queen Is Dead'

The third and final tune Marr would present to Morrissey was, by his own admission, in stark contrast to the others and "sounded like Sandie Shaw or a vaudevillian romp." Morrissey duly retreated to Hale Barns and set about putting lyrics to the new tunes. The finished results are 'I Know It's Over', 'There Is a Light That Never Goes Out', and 'Frankly, Mr Shankly'.

With the creative juices well and truly flowing again, The Smiths booked themselves into RAK Studios in St. John's Wood, northwest London. The first song recorded that day was 'Big Mouth Strikes Again', featuring Kirsty MacColl on backing vocals. Having been dropped by her label, Polydor, two years earlier, MacColl had returned to Stiff Records and scored a UK Top 10 with a cover of Billy Bragg's 'A New England'. Her bubbly personality proved a hit with the band – especially with Marr.

Indeed, the two stayed behind at RAK long after everyone else had left; their playing and singing together into the early hours serving to cement a friendship that would last until MacColl's tragic death in December 2000.

MacColl's vocals would ultimately be scrubbed in favour of a speeded-up vocal by Morrissey (for which he is credited as 'Ann Coates' – a play on Ancoats – on the album). MacColl and Marr's subsequent working relationship would result in several memorable collaborations, however, such as 'Walking Down Madison', which reached the UK Top 30 in 1991.

The majority of the songs slated for *Margarite on the Guillotine* – as the new album was tentatively titled – were recorded at Jacobs Studios (named in honour of a breed of sheep that were farmed in the area), a converted Georgian farmhouse set in 13 acres of lush Surrey countryside in Dippenhall, near Farnham. Upon their arrival, Marr set up his four-track and a couple of amps in a small cottage away from the main house where he could work on the new songs to his heart's content. He'd also procured an E-mu Emulator, a digital synthesiser that reproduced a plethora of high-quality orchestral sounds. Status Quo were recording *In The Army Now* in the second studio. According to Jacobs' co-owner, Andy Fernbach, The Smiths had considered calling on Rick Parfitt to play on *The Queen is Dead*.

Away from the music things weren't quite so harmonious, however. The Smiths' contract with Rough Trade was about to expire and Morrissey, for one, had serious reservations about the band remaining with the label – especially when the band's new solicitor, Alexis Grower, (whom Marr would describe as being "an absolute shark of a lawyer") revealed he was in furtive negotiations with EMI. While the irony of EMI having rejected the demo to 'What Difference Does It Make?' out of hand three years earlier wasn't lost on The Smiths, there was an overriding feeling within the band that they'd outgrown Rough Trade and needed to sign with a major label if they were to advance to the next level. The music business was so incestuous that secrets rarely remained a secret for long.

With the grapevine attune to rumours that The Smiths were contemplating jumping ship, Rough Trade set about securing a High Court injunction restraining the band from releasing new product via EMI or any other label. Grower arrived at Jacobs soon after that to inform Marr and Morrissey that Rough Trade had been notified that *The Queen Is Dead*, as the new album was now titled, would be the final Smiths album before their moving to EMI. In *Autobiography*, Morrissey says the writ – which was served to him at his newly-acquired abode in Cadogan Square, Chelsea – prohibited the release of *The Queen Is Dead* until the courts sat to decide whether *Hatful of Hollow* counted as a contractual album.

A malaise would descend on Jacobs when the news filtered through that Rough Trade had succeeded in securing the writ. What was the point in completing the album when there was a genuine risk of it's never seeing the light of day?

Leaving the lawyers to their wrangling, The Smiths, in varying capacities, added their weight to Billy Bragg's Red Wedge musicians collective. It took its name from a 1919 poster by Russian constructivist artist, El Lissitzky: "Beat the Whites with the Red Wedge". Bragg had launched it to help enhance the Labour Party's public profile in the run-up to the 1987 General Election. Alongside Bragg, The Style Council, The Communards, and Jerry Dammers had added their weight to the Red Wedge collective, with the likes of Madness, Prefab Sprout, Elvis Costello, Tom Robinson, The Beat, and The Blow Monkeys making guest appearances. Marr had appeared alongside Bragg at the opening Red Wedge date at the Manchester Apollo, while he and Rourke had then performed together in Birmingham on January 30. The solidarity Bragg was hoping far amongst the Red Wedge collective was strangely absent, however. "Andy and I got treated with pretty short shrift in Birmingham by some of the other bands and their crews and we took off straight after we'd played," Marr explained. "The next day the rest of The Smiths were all at my house. I was talking about what had happened, and then someone suggested that we all turn up at the Red Wedge show that night and play as a band."

With Angie at the wheel, The Smiths headed for Newcastle without so much as a plectrum between them. Upon arriving at the Newcastle City Hall, they strode through to the stage and informed the bemused stage manager that The Smiths were adding themselves to the billing. "The word went around that The Smiths were playing, and Paul Weller offered to loan us his gear," Marr continued. "When the time came for us to go on, Billy introduced us. When he said 'The Smiths' there were a few seconds of silence and then an enormous eruption of hysteria. The audience were still in disbelief as we grabbed up borrowed guitars and roared into 'Shakespeare's Sister'."

Without let-up, The Smiths tore through 'I Want the One I Can't Have' and 'The Boy With the Thorn in His Side' before storming into 'Bigmouth Strikes Again', which, current legalities depending, Rough Trade were intent on releasing as the lead single from *The Queen Is Dead*. It was the first time the song had been aired outside of a rehearsal room or recording studio, and Marr describes the Red Wedge crowd's reaction as being "hit by a tornado". He's since described the moment The Smiths took to the City Hall stage that night as being the "peak" of their career.

"When the time came for us to go on, Billy introduced us. When he said 'The Smiths' there were a few seconds of silence and then an enormous eruption of hysteria."

A week on from the Newcastle date, The Smiths joined forces with fellow Mancunian acts New Order, The Fall, and John Cooper-Clarke for "From Manchester With Love". This was a benefit concert staged at Liverpool's Royal Court Theatre to raise funds towards the estimated £100,000 legal costs facing the city's 49 councillors in their ongoing fight against the District Auditor's decision to surcharge them for their delay in setting a rate the previous year. The councillors were also facing being disqualified from holding public office.

'Vicar in a Tutu', 'Cemetry Gates', and 'There is A Light That Never Goes Out' would all receive their first public airings at the benefit. When reviewing the benefit show, the *NME* pithily commented how The Smiths "lean towards their live predilection for fast and perishable rock songs with only occasional relief in the dwindling ways they manage to juggle the clichés". Having highlighted the debt 'Rusholme Ruffians' owes to Elvis' '(Marie's the Name) His Latest Flame', the review cites the humour within the "cleverly-twisted" lyric to 'Frankly, Mr Shankly' as being The Smiths' "most redeeming feature" before dismissing their efforts as a whole as "a foolish waste".

Having put those within the Red Wedge collective that were harbouring an inflated view of their importance firmly in their place, Marr was determined to cock a similar snook at Rough Trade. Cajoling roadie Phil Powell into joining him in the madcap venture, Marr set off for Farnham determined to steal the master tapes for *The Queen Is Dead*. Dawn was breaking by the time the pair arrived at the lane leading to Jacobs Studios. Leaving Phil at the wheel, Marr tiptoed through the snow to the farmhouse. As luck would have it, the kitchen door was unlocked. He made his way through to the studio and was rummaging through the cupboards where the master tapes were kept when the lights flicked on. Marr wheeled round to find either Andy Fernbach or his brother Fran – standing in the doorway. Fernbach was obviously curious as to what the guitarist was doing. "I've come for our tapes," said Marr, before then explaining about Rough Trade's injunction. Though sympathetic, Fernbach wasn't about to let Marr walk off with the masters. Not so much because of a reluctance to get embroiled in a legal dispute, but rather because the studio bill remained outstanding. Marr gave up the ghost and returned to Manchester empty-handed.

After much lawyering and deliberating, an agreement was reached between the warring parties whereby The Smiths would deliver one more studio album as a means of fulfilling their contractual obligations in return for Rough Trade's releasing *The Queen Is Dead*. With Morrissey having selected a shot of French sex symbol Alain Delon from the latter's 1964 film *L'nsoumis (The Unvanquished)* for the album's front cover, Rough Trade arranged a photo session in Salford with up-and-coming photographer Stephen Wright. It was during this session that the iconic shot of The Smiths standing outside Salford Lads Club that appears on the inner sleeve was taken. The cover of this book is a shot from the same session.

"I barely slept the night before but the band were all amiable," Wright told *The Guardian* in June 2011. "The setting was Morrissey's idea. He wanted an iconic Manchester location. We also tried Victoria Station but it was too dark, so we ended up at Salford Lads Club in the winter cold. You can see Johnny Marr shivering in some shots. I like the casual, staggered way they are standing, and they're nicely framed by the arches. However, I always say it's the band, not the photo, that is classic. Morrissey has a Mona Lisa expression: it's neither a smile nor a smirk, but he's very much in command. If you look at the body language, you can tell he was king of the pack."

Wright was in his mid-twenties at the time and a big Smiths fan. He'd first shot the band onstage at Manchester's Free Trade Hall in March 1984. Wright says on his website. "The first live show I shot was in 1984 at the Free Trade Hall. By his own admission, he'd had to walk all the way home after the show as he'd spent the last of his cash on a reel of film. "From this show I caught the shot of dead flowers hanging from his jeans, but my favourite now is of Morrissey waving flowers above his head, shot from the side of the stage," he says on his website. "More live shows followed and then Rough Trade asked me to shoot a session The Lads Club photo was shot on a cold, dark, winter day in Salford, yet somehow it is the darkness that sets the mood. My friend George Pace and I went to the session in mid-December with a pocketful of film and a bit of taxi fare. It seems so casual and un-posed and in a way that's just how it came together. Apparently, it's the most famous photo of The Smiths, and that makes me smile."

The famous shot didn't meet with everyone's approval, however. While looking through Wright's proof-sheets from the shoot, Marr crossed off the ones he wasn't keen on so was understandably irked that it somehow made its way onto the album's artwork. What was proving infinitely more exasperating was Rourke's inability to wean himself off of heroin.

The Smiths were set to return to Ireland in February 1986 for a brace of shows in the republic – Dublin and Dundalk – with

"Morrissey has a Mona Lisa expression: it's neither a smile nor a smirk, but he's very much in command."

a third and final show in Belfast. Rather than risk getting caught in possession at a customs check, Rourke visited his doctor. But imbibing a cocktail of prescription drugs – primarily methadone, anti-depressants, and sleeping tablets – ended up affecting his playing more than the heroin; the nadir coming at the opening Irish date at Dublin's National Stadium on February 10. Rourke's playing was integral to The Smiths' sound. So much so, that the two basses he used onstage had alternate tunings (One in the standard E tuning, the other in F#). His guitar tech, being a

local hired hand, couldn't be expected to know such intricacies, but Rourke was too stoned to realise the error until it was too late. Even when he was playing the correct bass, however, he missed more notes than he played.

No band can afford to carry passengers, and Marr and Morrissey weren't about to start setting precedents. One of the enduring myths surrounding The Smiths is Morrissey's callously leaving a note (tucked inside an envelope) pinned under the windscreen wiper of Rourke's car upon which was written: "Andy, you have left the Smiths. Good luck and goodbye, Morrissey". Although he makes no mention of either the note or Rourke's dismissal in Autobiography, Morrissey strenuously denies being the note's author – even though Rourke readily recognised the singer's familiar scrawl. "Andy's 'dismissal' from The Smiths would not be a decision solely made by me and would not be announced by me on a note bearing only my name," he said via a sanctioned website missive in 2009. "It would also not be executed by a handwritten note carelessly thrown on to the hood of a car (or window-wipers, as has often been reported). Doesn't anyone have the wit to work this one out?"

Although Morrissey, and Joyce, were in agreement that the situation had to be addressed sooner rather than later, it was left to Marr to break the news to Rourke. In Set the Boy Free, he describes the moment as being "the worst I've ever had to go through."

Given The Smiths' need to keep things "in the family" so to speak it's a wonder Marr didn't think to approach Dale Hibbert about the now-vacant Bass slot. Hibbert says he wouldn't have accepted even if such an eventuality had come to pass. "No, I had no interest in The Smiths by then. I think it's a pity that friendship counts for so little, that loyalty has a price. I'm still naïve in that respect. I want friendships and love to be eternal, rather than to fracture through greed and materialism. I've been asked to join quite high profile Smiths tribute bands, but it would bring me nothing but unhappiness. I'm older and wiser, I can't run away from or avoid the things in my head. But I don't need anything apart from the love of my partner, and good coffee."

There would have been no shortage of takers had The Smiths gone public in their search for Rourke's replacement, but according to Marr, there was only ever one name in the frame. Marr says he first became aware of the Salford-born guitarist, Craig Gannon, while the latter was playing in Aztec Camera. Simon Wolstencroft had also sung Gannon's praises from their short stint together touring in The Colourfield. Indeed, it was Funky Si that reportedly suggested Gannon for the role. "I was aware that Si and Johnny had been speaking about me with the view to us meeting up," says Gannon, who was 19 at the time. "I knew Johnny had been asking Si about me as he knew we were friends and had played in The Colourfield together. The general idea was that there was a possibility of me being asked to join The Smiths. It soon became apparent that Johnny knew of me from being in Aztec Camera whom he liked, so

Si was our mutual friend and in the right position to link us up."

By his admission, Gannon had something of an eclectic taste in music during his formative years – said tastes ranging from The Beatles, Burt Bacharach and Pink Floyd, through to The Clash, Buzzcocks, XTC, Talking Heads and Television, to Echo and the Bunnymen, The Monochrome Set and The Pale Fountains. "I was basically into the more musical of the punk and so-called 'new wave' and indie bands. My main influence from the start, however, was The Beatles. They were an obsession for me as soon as I started listening to music and I'm still obsessed with them today. Along with all these bands I really got into the Postcard Records scene – especially Orange Juice and Aztec Camera. At the same time as listening to guitar bands, I also really loved film music although obviously compared to being able to learn an instrument and play in bands, film music seemed like a completely different world which seemed less attainable to hope to be a part of."

Gannon started learning the guitar while still at school, jamming with like-minded mates at every available opportunity to try out the riffs he'd picked out from his favourite bands. Whereas his mates saw this as little more than a passing hobby, he was determined to master the guitar. "At the same time as learning guitar, I was also learning how to write music and songs.

THE SMITHS

I pretty much practised constantly and would learn all the guitar parts and even the bass parts of all my records. I always took practising and playing really seriously, but it never entered my mind to get really good in the hope that I could audition for a band. I planned to do it the way The Beatles did it – form a band with mates, write my own music, get signed and release records that way. It's just fascinating that it went in another direction – which I'm eternally grateful for."

Auditioning for bands might not have entered Gannon's thinking, but his brother thankfully thought otherwise and alerted him to an ad he'd seen in the *Melody Maker* classifieds announcing that Aztec Camera were on the lookout for a new guitarist. After much deliberation, Gannon put pen to paper and fired off his missive to Roddy Frame via Rough Trade's offices. To his astonishment, he received a return letter from the Aztec Camera frontman inviting him to attend an audition. "I was late down to London having been stuck in traffic, so I was late for the audition and was the last guitar player in. Roddy told me recently that until I turned up they were really disappointed and depressed about not being able to find the right person as some were great players but didn't look right or didn't have the right attitude. However, once I turned up, chatted and played with them, I ticked all the boxes so they were really happy." Heady praise, indeed!

Though not a bass player per se, Gannon acquitted himself to Marr's satisfaction when the two jammed together during their initial meeting. "Johnny came around to my house to pick me up and we then drove over to his place in Bowdon. The roadie, Phil Powell, always drove Johnny around in those days and he did that night. When I got to Johnny's, Mike was already there and the three of us just sat around in the living room chatting and eating. As I've always said, we all got on really well and did so right up until a couple of weeks before the end of my time in the band. After a while, Johnny took me up to his studio which was a spare room in his house where he played me various things including the next single which was 'Bigmouth Strikes Again', which straight away I thought was fantastic. Johnny and I then sat down on our own with guitars and started playing together, jamming and playing some Smiths' songs which he showed me there and then.

"Of course one person missing – apart from Morrissey, – was Andy, and it eventually became apparent as to why. As we were chatting, Johnny got around to the fact that they were getting rid of Andy and if I wanted to replace him the job was mine there and then. As I didn't show any interest in joining as a bass player he carried on the conversation saying that it was possible I could join as a guitar player instead. He always knew I was a guitarist and not a bass player anyway. That was basically the end of any conversation regarding me as a bass player as shortly after that Johnny called me telling me that he wanted me to join The Smiths as a guitar player. The following meeting with Morrissey at his new place in London was just to make sure that he liked me too.

"In the car journey the mood was really

up and Johnny and Mike were really buzzing and excited about me joining the band. I can't remember being nervous, but I think I probably was once we arrived at Morrissey's flat. It was myself, Johnny, Mike, Morrissey and his friend, James Maker, so at that point I was in a room full of strangers and obviously all eyes and ears were on me as joining The Smiths was what the meeting was all about. After we'd chatted for a while Johnny and Morrissey went off into another room to chat about me and that was it, they wanted me to join the band.

"I've heard I said that I wasn't much of a Smiths fan prior to joining but it's not so much that I wasn't a fan, it's more the fact that until I joined I didn't really know that much about The Smiths. As I've mentioned before, I think that was just because I'd been so busy with Aztec Camera and The Bluebells and others. Also, at that time I suppose I was quite closed-minded with regards to listening to new bands as I was generally underwhelmed by most new music I heard at that time. My brother actually had a couple of Smiths records so I'd probably heard them through him, but I can't remember which songs. I never owned a record by The Smiths until I was given them all by Johnny when I joined the band and that's when I really started getting into them and realising what a great band they were. Up until that point, I'd only heard The Smiths singles on the radio and I'd seen the odd appearance on TV. I also remember reading a few interviews and features in the music press at the time. Having said that, Aztec Camera were signed to Rough Trade in 1983 when The Smiths first signed and when I'd go to their offices I remember there were copies of 'Hand in Glove' hanging around and I remember Geoff Travis talking to me about them."

As excited as he was at the prospect of joining The Smiths, Gannon says he wouldn't have responded had Marr got as far as advertising the position as second guitarist. "If that had been the case I'm pretty sure I wouldn't have looked into auditioning as apart from auditioning for Aztec camera when I was 16, auditioning for any band never really entered my mind. I've only ever auditioned once for anything and that was for Aztec Camera. Also, at that time I was playing with The Colourfield so it wasn't like I was looking for something else at that point either. Although I've worked with a lot of bands and singers over the years I was never a 'session guitarist' per se, I was either a member of the bands I played in or I worked with singers and bands who asked me rather than being a 'hired hand' guitar player. Throughout my time in bands before and after The Smiths I'd occasionally hear of some famous or well-known bands or artists who were looking for a guitar player but I wouldn't look into it or ask to audition which is what you would do if you're a session player. These days it'd be a different matter if it was for someone like Paul McCartney though."

Rather than seek professional help to try and get some semblance of order in his life, Rourke spiralled ever deeper into his heroin mire. His shambolic state was such that a simple hair-bleaching went awry to the point of his locks turning a ridiculous

shade of orange. If he was thinking his life couldn't get any worse, he was in for a rude awakening, however. He'd no way of knowing the house in Oldham from which his new supplier was operating was under 24-hour police observation. But in the back of his mind he must have known it was only a matter of time before his luck ran out. The Smiths' standing was such that Rourke's arrest featured on that evening's edition of Granada Reports. Marr had made a point of staying on friendly terms with Rourke, even going so far as to provide a psychological shoulder to cry on so it was, perhaps, only to be expected when Rourke showed up at Marr's door the morning following his arrest. Marr remembers his friend being "strangely calm", as though his being busted was indeed merely the eventuality he'd always known would come to pass. Unlike most junkies, however, Rourke never looked beyond the mirror for someone to blame.

Rourke did at least have the wherewithal to seek sanctuary, albeit a temporary one, at his mother's home in Majorca. While the errant bassist was taking stock of his life amid sun, sangria, and sympathy, his erstwhile bandmates were busy doing a little soul-searching of their own. Marr was convinced his friend would either end up in prison or dead. And he wasn't on his own in that respect. "When he (Rourke) left he became even more depressed than when he was with the group," Morrissey revealed. "It was getting quite serious so he really had to come back . . . it seemed very unnatural and ridiculous to even consider such things as session musicians and people from other parts of the country."

Offering the olive branch to Rourke left Craig Gannon dangling on a limb, of course. But Marr again did the honourable thing by inviting Gannon to come onboard as second guitarist.

Joyce was quick to second the motion but rather than pick up the phone and seek Morrissey's approval, Marr had Phil Powell drive himself, Joyce, and Gannon to the singer's Cadogan Square flat. Morrissey wasn't at home when they arrived and so they had to camp at the kerb till his return. "I still didn't know what was happening with Andy," says Gannon, "but I got the feeling they were having serious thoughts about sacking him – even though we'd just driven 250 miles to meet with Morrissey. We chatted about this and that and then Johnny and Morrissey went into another room to discuss the situation privately. I knew they were talking about me, but nothing was said when they emerged. We said our goodbyes to Morrissey, got back in the car, and set off for the M1. I was sat in the back with Mike. We hadn't gone far when Johnny spun round in his seat and said, 'Well, that's it then. We like you. You're in The Smiths playing guitar.'"

"When Rourke left he became even more depressed than when he was with the group,"

The insular "us-against-the-world" mentality remained as strong as ever, but

Gannon's inclusion undoubtedly brought an added dynamic to The Smiths. Aside from both appreciating Gannon's playing and liking him as a person, Marr's primary reason for bringing him in as second guitarist stemmed from the realisation he couldn't hope to recreate the multi-layered, wall-of-sound guitar that made up the majority of the songs making up The Queen Is Dead. The album was still in limbo but The Smiths were set to embark on a 24-date promotional US tour following four UK "warm-up" dates, and Marr was anxious about their new sound translating to the live arena – especially big American venues.

Following on from a handful of rehearsals at Joyce's house, Gannon accompanied The Smiths into the studio to record brand-new Marr/Morrissey compositions 'Panic', 'Sweet and Tender Hooligan', and 'The Draize Train'. "Johnny told me that I was to be put on wages once the PAYE system had been sorted," says Gannon. "In the meantime, I was handed a cheque for £500 which was signed by both Johnny and Morrissey. Being the newcomer I wasn't about to start questioning how much I would be getting. I hadn't recorded a note with them prior to the 'Panic' sessions so I was hardly in a position to pester them about money. It wasn't even about money. I was just delighted to be in The Smiths and determined to be the best I could."

Money was never far from the forefront of Mike Joyce's thinking, however – especially when he received a letter from Inland Revenue demanding outstanding taxes a week or so prior to *The Queen Is Dead's* June 16 release. With many of the impending US dates having already sold out, Joyce had already approached Mike Hinc asking to see the band's latest accounts. It was only due to his badgering that the accounts finally dropped through his letterbox. Once in possession of the accounts Joyce was able to complete his tax return. His only concern had been to get the returns back to the Inland Revenue to keep the taxmen at bay for another year.

By his own admission, he'd plucked the cheque from the envelope before stashing the accounts in a drawer. Had he studied them more closely, however, he would have surely realised the significance of the 40:40:10:10 split of net profits in favour of Marr and Morrissey. Each of the band's names were listed next to the appropriation of said net profits. Whereas Joyce and Rourke received four-figure sums, Marr and Morrissey's comprised an extra digit.

The Queen Is Dead (ROUGH96) was released to critical acclaim in mid-June 1986. Despite Genesis' *Invisible Touch* denying it the coveted top spot, the album would spend 22 weeks on the UK chart. It also gave The Smiths their highest stateside placing to date, peaking at #70 on the Billboard 200. Perhaps unsurprisingly, the album's provocative title drew comparisons with the Sex Pistols' 1977 single, 'God Save the Queen'. "It didn't really occur to me ever that people would consider the title offensive," Morrissey said during an interview with Dutch magazine, *Oor*, the following February. "The song existed, and I thought it was so strong it deserved special attention, which it was given by being the

THE SMITHS

FROM THE MAKERS OF NME & UNCUT

THE SMITHS

SPECIAL COLLECTORS' MAGAZINE

£4.99 LIMITED-EDITION PUBLICATION

THE FULL STORY OF THE ULTIMATE INDIE BAND!

FEATURING

CLASSIC MORRISSEY AND MARR INTERVIEWS

EVERY ALBUM REVISITED

RARE PHOTOGRAPHS

THE STORIES BEHIND THE SLEEVES

PLUS

WHAT THEY ALL DID NEXT

AND THEIR PRE-SMITHS BANDS!

NME ICONS

UK £4.99

11

5 010791 129007

title track. Another aspect was that no Top 10 groups, or any English group with a high status, were trying to compile a thoughtful language. And I thought 'The Queen Is Dead', as a title between 'Invisible Touch' and 'A Kind Of Magic' (Queen), and 'Picture Book' (Simply Red), was something one would pause over."

Defending the album elsewhere, Morrissey said the title didn't necessarily mean Queen Elizabeth II. "There's a safety net in the song... that the old queen in the lyrics is actually me," he explained. "So when they lynch me or nail me to the cross, I have that trapdoor to slide through. But, having said that, the song is certainly a kind of general observation on the state of the nation."

In hindsight, the musicality and lyrical prowess on The Queen is Dead shows The Smiths at the peak of their game. Indeed, in 2013 the *NME* would proclaim it "the greatest album of all time". Marr and Joyce have both gone on record stating it their favourite Smiths album, while Morrissey would wax lyrical about their not being "one second of any track which does not delight me" in a letter to Stephen Street.

While the success and critical acclaim accompanying *The Queen Is Dead* undoubtedly propelled The Smiths onto a higher plane, it also brought attendant complications. With Morrissey camping it up in Cadogan Square, the band of brothers' camaraderie that had forged The Smiths' identity was once again splintering. Owing to increased demands on their time for interviews, photo sessions, and other promo activities, Marr was obliged to move into the Portobello Hotel in Notting Hill. Angie's having to remain at their Cheshire town house wouldn't come even remotely close to straining their relationship, but it nonetheless saw Marr realise the differences in his and Morrissey's visions for The Smiths.

Marr's self-imposed relocation to the capital did throw up the occasional "once-in-a-lifetime" moment. Having tired of his living-out-of-a-suitcase existence, Marr had moved into Kirsty MacColl's one-bedroom flat in Shepherd's Bush which she'd vacated upon marrying Steve Lillywhite. He hadn't long moved in when his landlady rang to say someone wanted to speak with him. He immediately identified the gravelly voice on the other end of the line as being that of Keith Richards, one of his all-time heroes. Within the hour he, along with a couple of acoustics, was being ferried over to Kirsty's pad in Richards' chauffeured vintage Bentley for an evening of jamming and joints.

Craig Gannon's live debut came on the opening night of a four-date mini UK tour at the Barrowland Ballroom in Glasgow on July 16. It was to prove something of a baptism of fire for the 18-year-old. The Barrowlands faithful had taken The Smiths to their hearts from the get-go, but a mindless minority pelted the stage with plastic beer glasses throughout. Worse still, some of the morons thought it amusing to celebrate punk's tenth anniversary by "gobbing" at the band.

Worse was to follow at Newcastle's long-since demolished Mayfair Ballroom

the following evening. Being the hottest ticket in town counted for naught amongst the drunken louts gathered en masse at the front who subjected The Smiths to a hail of beer and phlegm from the moment they kicked into – ironically enough – 'Bigmouth Strikes Again'.

Being spat on is perhaps the worst insult one can suffer and it's a testament to the band's resolve that they remained onstage. When Morrissey was caught in the eye during the encore (the band were performing 'Hand in Glove'), however, he deemed enough was enough and departed the stage. Marr and the others carried on playing, unsure as to whether their singer might return. On receiving a signal from the wings that Morrissey wouldn't be returning, Marr brought the song to a premature close, unslung his guitar, and stepped up to the mic. With perfect comic timing he shouted out, "And if the people spit, then the people spit . . ." before strolling off into the wings followed by Rourke, Joyce, and Gannon.

Support during the mini-tour was provided by Stockholm Monsters, a Burnage-based post-punk Factory act that would inadvertently prove an inspiration to a certain Noel Gallagher.

The Smiths dried themselves off and headed back to Manchester for an appearance on the final day of the week-long "Festival of the Tenth Summer" at the city's newly-opened GMex centre. Factory Records were staging the festival as a celebration commemorating Manchester's role as punk's second city. Almost ten years to the day, the Sex Pistols made their second of two now-legendary appearances at the Lesser Free Trade with Slaughter and the Dogs and Buzzcocks in support. Playing alongside The Smiths on the night were co-headliners New Order, as well as The Fall, John Cooper-Clarke, A Certain Ratio, OMD, Pete Shelley, Howard Devoto's Luxuria, and Sandie Shaw to name but a few. The event was co-compared by Bill Grundy, whose laissez-faire attitude to on-screen swearing propelled the Pistols onto the nations' front pages.

Punk had totally revolutionised the UK music scene, yet with the Pistols and every other band from the much-vaunted 'class of '76' having either split or been assimilated into rock's mainstream, it had retreated back into the shadows. Indeed, from 1981 onwards punk had become an embarrassing cliché – hilariously lampooned by Everett's onscreen character Sid Snot. Suddenly, however, punk was cool again. But whereas the music press promulgated the positives that had made punk so exciting first time around to a new audience, tabloids such as The Sun sought only to dredge up the negatives as were evidenced in both Glasgow and Newcastle.

The fourth and final UK date at the University of Salford was to prove an equally rambunctious affair. This time, however, for all the right reasons. The crowd, already in ebullient mood before The Smiths even arrived onstage, went into frenzied overdrive from the off. So much so, the stage collapsed midway through the show forcing a temporary halt while the necessary repairs were hurriedly carried out. The restart was greeted with a stage invasion, forcing Marr, Rourke, and Gannon

to retreat to Joyce's drum riser for the remainder of the show. When asked to name the best gig he'd ever played during a 2007 interview, Marr didn't hesitate: "Salford University in 1986 with The Smiths. The PA had to be tied down because the floor was bouncing up so high that the stage was practically falling to pieces."

The US tour was set to get underway at the 1625-capacity Centennial Hall in London, Canada on July 30. It was The Smiths' biggest tour to date. Given the dim view US authorities tended to take in regard to drug-related offences when it came to issuing the all-important visas, Rourke's reinstatement presented the band with something of a problem. The unwritten rule – at least according to Sex Pistols' one-time US representative Rory Johnston – is that the management of any band or artist with a drug conviction should proceed on the basis that the first visa application will always be refused (which is exactly what happened with the Pistols, of course – albeit with a $1 million surety proviso). Providing said management has secured the services of an above average lawyer, the second application is more often than not successful. The Smiths didn't have any management, of course, but it stands to reason that Seymour Stein could have greased the necessary palms. Marr wasn't for taking chances, however, and called upon Guy Pratt, a 24-year-old multi-instrumentalist whom he'd befriended whilst the two were adding their respective magic to Bryan Ferry's latest solo album, *Bête Noire*. (Angie's hitting it off with Pratt's then girlfriend Caroline, helping cement their bromance).

Pratt, whose late father Mike, an accomplished guitarist and pianist, was something of a regular on the 2i's coffee bar scene before going on to find fame playing as Jeff Randall in the late Sixties ITC detective series *Randall and Hopkirk (Deceased)*, was cut from the same impish cloth as Marr. Pratt readily jumped at the chance to join The Smiths at their temporary Stanbridge Farm rehearsal space (situated close to Gatwick Airport) to rehearse the songs the band intended to play during the impending US tour. But then again, how could he have refused Marr's offer to "[Come] to the States to play punk rock and fall over."

There was never any danger of Rourke's being ousted from the band so soon after being brought in from the cold, but to his credit he magnanimously offered to show Pratt his bass-lines. If he wasn't going to be playing them on the tour, he was determined they be played correctly. Pratt reciprocated by offering Rourke the use of his one-and-only suit for the latter's impending court appearance in Mold, Flintshire.

Though willing to suffer the torments of Marr and Pratt's drug and booze-fuelled antics at Stanbridge Farm, Morrissey was concerned about their temporary bassist's non-Smiths image – particularly his shoulder-length tresses. With Pratt proving amenable to his undergoing a makeshift makeover, Andrew Berry was flown down from Manchester to restyle his hair into a Smiths-esque quiff. He was also willing to agree to a temporary conversion to vegetarianism while taking The Smiths' shilling. Both provisos would ultimately prove superfluous, however, owing to the US authorities showing unforeseen leniency in granting Rourke's visa application.

Prior to the band's departure to the US, Rough Trade released 'Panic' / 'Vicar in a Tutu" (RT193). 'Panic' was a brand-new song the band had recorded at Livingston Studios in Wood Green, north London with John Porter sometime during May. Marr and Morrissey had reportedly penned the lyric in response to Radio One's callously following up a Newsbeat report on the Chernobyl disaster (April 25/26) with Wham's latest hit 'I'm Your Man'. For all their more obvious shortcomings, Radio One's daytime DJs adhered to the station's playlists, but Morrissey was so outraged by what he perceived to be a total lack of sensitivity that he immediately put pen to paper – hence the song's otherwise nonsensical spiteful refrain "Hang the DJ". 'Panic' would peak at # 11 on the UK Chart, giving The Smiths their best chart placing since 'Heaven Knows I'm Miserable Now' some two years earlier. Morrissey is said to have taken great delight in the song being aired betwixt the daytime radio pap it openly criticised.

Porter, who coincidently had last worked with The Smiths on 'Heaven Knows I'm Miserable Now', was concerned about the song's running time of 2: 20. He set about splicing a repetition of the first verse from the band's original recording and tagging it onto the end. Marr and Morrissey remained unimpressed with his efforts, however, and insisted the song be released as was.

Whatever Morrissey's intentions, 'Panic' received largely negative press owing to the lyric being construed as having racist connotations. The *NME*'s Paolo Hewitt had no truck with Morrissey having a pop at Radio One in general and Steve Wright in particular – but thought his "use of words like disco and DJ, and all the attendant imagery that brings up for what is a predominantly white audience, he is being imprecise and offensive."

The *NME*'s readership disagreed, however, and voted 'Panic' their Single of the Year in the paper's annual readers' poll.

Thanks to a May 2014 post from a Twitter user known only as @VivaHate72, The Smiths' rider for the 1986 28-date US tour has since accrued much interest for certain Spinal Tap-esque absurdities. These included the need for six carrier bags with identifying names written on them, or Morrissey's cheese sandwiches having to be 'thinly cut' (Whether it's the cheese or bread that needed to be cut sparingly isn't specified), a selection of nuts, a bottle of red wine and a quart of gin. Marr's prerequisites include cheese and tomato sandwiches sans either butter or margarine, two packets of fags and a couple of cans of beer (brand not specified). The non-veggies stipulations extend to tuna sarnies sans mayo, beer, fag, and biscuits, while the 15-man crew get to avail themselves of unspecified rolls or sandwiches washed down with domestic beers, orange juice, and Jack Daniels.

Morrissey, by all accounts preferred the sanctity of his hotel room on the tour. With Angie accompanying Marr, it was left to Rourke, Joyce, and new boy Gannon to paint each town they visited in turn varying shades of red.

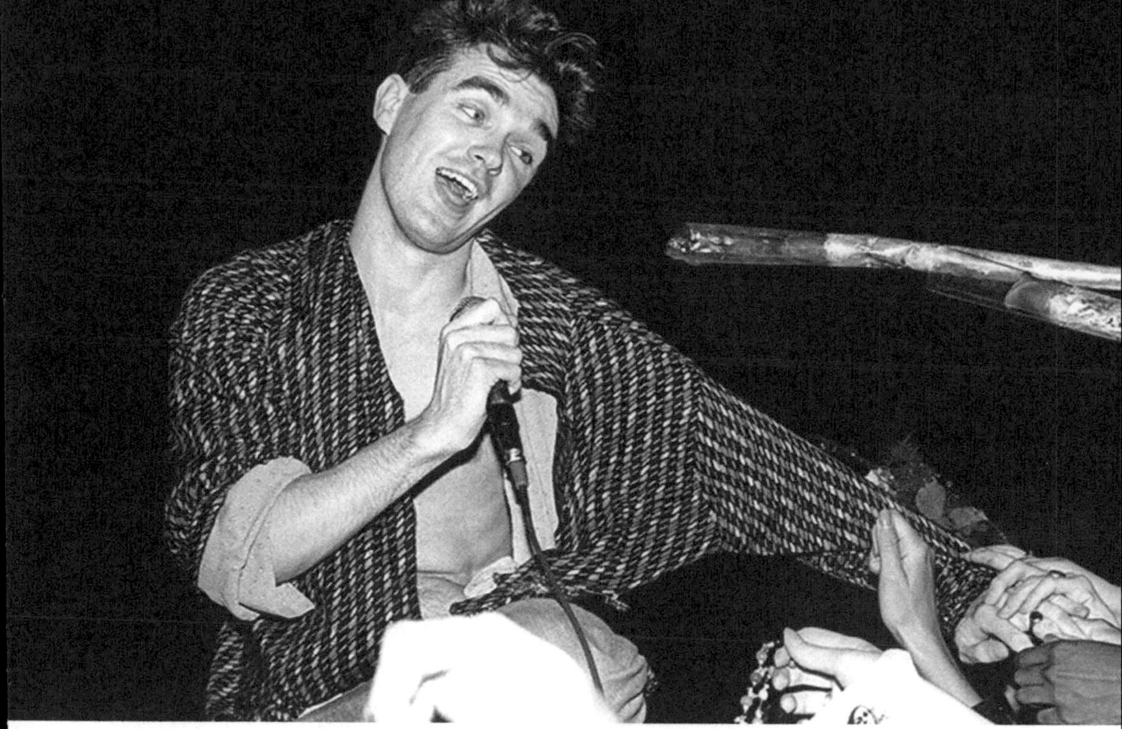

The Smiths arrived in London, Ontario, several days in advance of the opening show, reportedly filling the time either rehearsing or hanging out with fans in the parking lot behind the Centennial Hall. The band opened the show with 'Panic', which, given that it was only released in the US in gold-stamped 12" format, coupled with Sire's insistence on holding off release until a couple of weeks before the Stateside release of follow-up single 'Ask' in October, failed to register on the Billboard chart.

During the next song, 'Still Ill', a fan presented Morrissey with a book on Oscar Wilde which he proceeded to jig about the stage with. Nigh on a century earlier, Morrissey's literary hero had undertaken a lecture tour of Canada and the US. The tour came early in Wilde's career, long before he set to penning his one and only novel, *The Picture of Dorian Gray*, plays, essays and short stories. He was, however, already known to his Stateside audiences owing to his notoriety back home in England and his philosophising whilst parading about the stage in velvet knickers, lace shirt and comic opera cape had his audiences in fits of laughter. When the Centennial Hall crowd erupted into similar bouts of laughter owing to Morrissey's announcing, 'Hand In Glove' as the final song of the evening, only for the rest of the band to kick into 'Bigmouth Strikes Again', he fled the stage in obvious embarrassment leaving the others to perform the latter song as an instrumental. He would, however, return to the stage for 'Hand In Glove'.

Following on from the fourth and final Canadian date at the Centre Sportif de l'Université de Montréal on August 3,

The Smiths crossed the border into the contiguous USA. Since the much-vaunted 'British Invasion' of the mid-sixties, few quintessentially-English acts had made much of an impact on America and yet here were The Smiths playing to massive sell-out crowds. The Great Woods Center for the Performing Arts (since renamed The Xfinity Center) outdoor amphitheatre in Mansfield, Massachusetts for example, had a capacity of 19,900. Of course, with it being The Smiths, the opening US date wasn't without its attendant problems. Marr remembers relaxing in his hotel room when a delegation from amongst the road crew arrived at his door threatening to quit as they had yet to receive any wages. To quell the mutiny the guitarist was forced to make a quick call to the record company to get the situation sorted to everyone's satisfaction. When they arrived at the venue they discovered a batch of old promo photos in the dressing room. They'd been left there by Warner Brothers staffers for the band to sign. Had the staffers bothered to ask in person they might have had better luck. As it was, the photos were torn up and dumped in the nearest bin.

Come the following evening's show at New York's Pier 54 (Where the survivors from ill-feted RMS Titanic arrived in April 1912 aboard the RMA Carpathia, and from where the equally doomed RMS Lusitania had set sail for Liverpool three years later), it wasn't so much a case of quantity but rather the calibre of certain members of the audience. "In New York, Mick Jagger arrives backstage and extends the hand of friendship," Morrissey would subsequently observe. "It is a big moment for Johnny, but I, of course, am I nightmare of judgement, and it takes me years to understand the genius secret of the Rolling Stones."

Jagger, according to Morrissey's recollections at any rate, stayed for just four numbers, but his bopping away with Anita Pallenberg was akin to a royal seal of approval from His Satanic Majesty.

Following a show in Washington D.C., the tour wended its way through America's rust belt. These shows were rather more subdued affairs, particularly at the Cleveland Music Hall on August 11. The 3,000-capacity venue had an orchestra pit directly in front of the stage lined with security. There was also a barrier to keep the fans at bay. During 'Bigmouth Strikes Again' Morrissey, ignoring the venue's strict policy, attempted to get close and personal with those in the front row, only to lose his balance and tumble into the orchestra pit. Screaming fans promptly mobbed him and it was by no mean effort that the security managed to get him back on stage while fending off the fans. Even when

"We stormed the audience, and Morrissey took things to a new level by holding up a giant sign that read, The Queen Is Dead."

they succeeded getting him back onstage, Morrissey fled to the dressing room much to Marr's obvious amusement.

A somewhat less humorous episode during their Cleveland stopover came with Morrissey's encountering one-time Manicured Noise frontman, Owen Gavin, who was now writing for *Melody Maker* under his real name Frank Gavin. Manicured Noise were another of Manchester's here-today-gone-tomorrow post-punk acts that featured former Flowers of Romance's Steve Walsh on guitar. (Walsh, of course, also wrote articles for *Sniffin' Glue*).

Morrissey was already acquainted with Owen and the two were reminiscing about the current Manchester music and scenes, pop music in general when the latter said the lyric to 'Panic' suggested the singer was leading a "black pop conspiracy" owing to his dislike of disco music. Morrissey was quick to denounce Owen's line of questioning only to then offer an opinion that reggae was "the most racist music in the entire world." Marr was said to be beside himself when the interview appeared in *Melody Maker* some six weeks later (the same week Hewitt's review of 'Panic' appeared in the *NME*). Indeed, in a 1987 interview with the *NME* he would threaten to "kick the living shit" out of Owen if the two ever came face-to-face.

The promotor had warned the Smiths prior to their arrival in Los Angeles that any disruptive crowd behaviour – notably stage invasions - could result in the band being banned from appearing again anywhere in California. As it transpired, the two sell-out shows at LA's Universal Amphitheater would prove the most raucous of the entire tour. Despite the promotor's warnings, Morrissey openly encouraged the fans to mount the stage. "The first night in LA they brought in the police, [and] the second night they had to bring in the army," Morrissey subsequently revealed. "People were so responsive. I had to be dragged off the stage several times. It was really insane."

"The amphitheatre (sic) was totally charged when we started the set," says Marr. "We stormed the audience, and Morrissey took things to a new level by holding up a giant sign that read, The Queen Is Dead. Having Craig with us as a five-piece made a difference: we were a new incarnation of the band, with a more expansive sound and a more powerful presence."

It was at the Universal Amphitheater that Marr realised the futility of the band's attempt to keep secret their signing to EMI. The band came offstage to be informed by security that an irate Warner Bros. executive was demanding to see them. It was the label's vice-president, Steven Baker. Ironically, Baker was one of the few people at Warner Bros. the band could actually relate to. Marr told security to show Baker through to the dressing room while he went to change his shirt. On his return, Morrissey and the rest of the band were nowhere to be seen. Baker didn't bother with pleasantries and demanded to know what the hell was going on; his frustration spilling over to punching a hole in the dressing room's plasterboard wall.

In *Set The Boy Free,* he says he and the rest of the band were at Heathrow awaiting

their flight when the EMI contracts were "rushed to us at the airport". With nothing to go on other than their solicitor's word, they signed the contract, slipped it in the return addressed envelope, and stuck it in the nearest post box. It was far from the end of The Smiths' working relationship with Rough Trade, however, as the band still needed to deliver a brand new studio album in order to fulfil their contractual obligations.

On a lighter note, it was at the first of the two LA dates that The Smiths had the opportunity to meet with Joe Dallesandro. The Universal Amphitheater's backstage area would also prove the setting for Morrissey's encounter with Richard Davalos, the American film, stage, and TV actor whose debut came with playing James Dean's onscreen brother in *East of Eden*. Apparently without saying a word, Davalos had slipped a square-faced silver ring onto Morrissey's wedding finger. It was the start of a beautiful friendship that presumably continued up to Davalos' death in March 2016. A publicity still of Davalos from *East of Eden* graces the sleeve of *Strangeways, Here We Come*.

Morrissey's antipathy towards Rough Trade meant a parting of the ways was inevitable at some juncture, and yet Geoff Travis admits to feeling a certain sense of betrayal. "I think we learned the lesson that if musicians always think the grass is greener on the other side, they need to go and experience it," he explained. "'Why aren't we riding around in our own Boeing 747 with our name emblazoned on the side?' It's all that kind of mentality. 'We want to be riding around in limousines and if we're so great, why aren't these things happening?'

"That's a very easy way of displacing underlying problems, by focusing on that kind of rubbish. I think we did a good job with The Smiths and I don't have any regrets about that. I wish them nothing but well, but I don't think they could really say that they underachieved while they were with Rough Trade. In a conventional sense, they did very little, in that they [only] toured America one and a half times. They still sold about half a million copies of every record, which is pretty decent." The irony surely wasn't lost on Travis that The Smiths would implode before their final Rough Trade album, *Strangeways, Here We Come*, had even hit the shops.

The craziness of the LA dates didn't extend to the remaining Californian dates in Laguna Hills and San Diego. Visits to Arizona, Colorado, and Texas would also prove lacklustre affairs, but things were to spice up again in New Orleans. As it transpired, the Norwegian trio A-ha (who were midway through their own North American jaunt in support of their soon-to-be released second album, *Scoundrel Days*) were appearing at the Saenger Performing Arts Theater the same night The Smiths were set to play the McAlister Auditorium. As luck would have it, both bands were booked into the same upmarket jazz quarter hotel. Whilst conducting a recce of the hotel's bar facilities, Rourke had spotted A-ha's pin-up singer, Morten Harket, sitting at one of the tables. The bassist had no interest in introducing himself but did casually make mention of it to Morrissey.

Though Morrissey makes no mention of encountering Harket in *Autobiography*, the two frontmen reportedly spent a considerable amount of downtime in each other's company.

With Marr off sightseeing with Angie and Craig Gannon preferring to hang out with the crew, it was left to Rourke and Joyce to sample what the "Big Easy" had to offer. The band's security officer, James Connelly, wasn't about to leave two already tipsy Mancunians to their own devices and insisted on accompanying them.

The trio happened on a bar where some local Smiths fans that had attended the gig were congregated. Assuming his charges would be in safe hands, Connelly retreated back to the hotel. While Joyce was outside having a cigarette he espied a commotion further along the street. Two police officers were questioning a girl who was becoming increasingly agitated by their line of questioning. Joyce, somewhat misguidedly it has to be said, decided to see if he might save this damsel in obvious distress. It's doubtful his celebrity would have counted for much with the cops back in Manchester in a similar situation. To the two cops, Joyce was just a drunken Limey shooting his mouth off and he soon found himself in the back of the patrol car with the girl. To add to the farce, when he did identify himself as being a member of The Smiths, the girl told the cops she'd been at the show and that he was lying.

By the time Rourke noticed his friend's absence, Joyce was en route to the local precinct where he was unceremoniously deposited in the drunk tank. Rourke didn't know what had happened but knew enough that something was amiss and rushed back to the hotel to rouse Connelly from his slumber. Though shaken, Joyce was otherwise unhurt and at the very least came away from New Orleans with a not-so-run-of-the-mill tour anecdote.

The next stop-off was St. Petersburg, Florida, where, somewhat Ironically, it was Rourke who found himself the centre of attention – this time of the medical variety. The show itself, at the 8,600-capacity Bayfront Arena, was unremarkable other than for a one-girl stage invasion towards the end of the set. Before moving onto Miami the band were enjoying a rest day at the beach. The barefooted Rourke was larking about in the surf when he felt a stabbing pain in his heel. Assuming he'd stepped on a piece of discarded broken glass he'd retreated to the shore to inspect the wound. To his surprise, the wound was bite-shaped. He'd stepped on a stingray. "The pain went up my leg, then both legs," the bassist recalled. "Then it hit my balls, and it felt like I'd been punched in the balls. Then it went up, and my heart started beating fast and when it hit my head . . . I thought I was going to die."

Stingrays aren't usually aggressive and only attack humans if provoked or in this instance, accidentally stepped upon. As Rourke was discovering, stingray venom causes swelling and severe muscle cramps. The bite itself can also prove mightily discomforting. And if the barb breaks off in the wound then surgery may be required to remove the fragments. Rourke was duly whisked off to the nearest hospital where,

having neglected to ensure someone was in possession of the band's medical insurance policy, he was forced to endure further agonies until the paperwork arrived and he was given the all-important tetanus shot. The bassist wasn't quite home and dry, however, as he was still required to keep the injured heel submerged in hot soapy water.

The prospect of having to take to the stage in Miami with one foot plonked in a bowl of water was the stuff of hallucinatory nightmares, but thankfully Morrissey's coming down with laryngitis while still in St. Petersburg spared Rourke's potential embarrassment. Though the tour party still travelled onto Miami, it was for R&R purposes only. Indeed, Morrissey's condition was such that the other remaining dates in Atlanta, Nashville, and New York were also cancelled.

Following a month-long recuperation, The Smiths embarked on a 13-date UK tour in support of their latest single, 'Ask' / 'Cemetry Gates' (RT194), commencing with a show at Carlisle's Sands Centre on October 13. For the majority of the dates, the support act was Raymonde, a four-piece featuring James Maker on lead vocals. The band appear relaxed and in good spirits throughout the 21-song set, which included live unveilings of both 'London' and 'The Draize Train', yet away from the stage things were rather less harmonious.

'Ask' was an up tempo rocker in the 'Panic' vein (with Kirsty MacColl providing backing vocals), which would give The Smiths another Top 20 hit, even if it fell three places short of its predecessor. The song had been recorded back in June at Jam Studios with John Porter once again at the production helm. Other new material recorded during the session included a second Marr/Morrissey original called 'Is It Really So Strange?' and a reviving of Twinkle's 1965 hit, 'Golden Lights' (which features on the 12" version of 'Ask'), with Porter's involvement on the latter track extended to his standing in for Rourke on bass.

According to Porter's recollections, Morrissey had wanted their version to stand out and suggested they record the track with the guitars out of tune. He remembers the mix having a Mexican feel owing to the inclusion of mandolins, and of it sounding fantastic. Morrissey, however, was somewhat less exuberant with the mix and contrived to have it remixed elsewhere. The singer's disillusion with Porter would extend to his calling upon Steve Lillywhite to remix 'Ask'. In typical Morrissey fashion, he chose to largely ignore Porter during the session, leaving Marr to act as a go-between.

Excessive touring and grumblings over producers undoubtedly played their respective part in destabilising the band, yet the overriding bugbear within The Smiths camp appeared to be Craig Gannon's supposed antipathy. Despite his being instrumental in bringing about Gannon's introduction into the band, Marr was harbouring serious misgivings about continuing The Smiths as a five-piece. In *Set the Boy Free*, the guitarist cites Gannon's remoteness and lack of enthusiasm. While admitting Gannon had "walked into an intense situation with a tightly-knit group

of people who had an unconventional way of going about things," Marr lays the blame for the latter's perceived reticence to fit in with the in-house craziness within The Smiths.

Gannon had found himself in a no-win situation through no real fault of his own. Though he admits to keeping his own counsel in the studio when he might have been better served speaking his mind, the general vibe surrounding the band was distinctly unpleasurable. "I may not have given much input after a put a couple of guitar tracks down, but they never made me feel that I was in a situation where I could start taking most of the control myself. I started to feel that this is how The Smiths work, so they can't slag me off for forcing me into that situation."

An ongoing lack of clarity regarding the financial arrangements surrounding his tenure in The Smiths was beginning to grate – especially since their returning from the US. More galling, however, was Marr's wilful refusal to acknowledge his contribution on "Ask".

"Me and Johnny were sat in the library playing acoustic guitars and they must have been miked up as we were probably putting down the acoustic tracks for 'Panic'. I just started playing the chord sequence which would later become 'Ask' in exactly the way it appears on the record... The only section of the chord structure that I didn't come up with was the middle-eight section with the chords E-minor, D and C. That was actually what Johnny came up with. Up until the release of 'Ask' I still thought I'd be given a writing credit."

The second show of the tour at Middlesboro Town Hall was marred somewhat by a handful of morons spitting at Morrissey, forcing him to leave the stage temporarily. This, however, was small potatoes compared to what occurred during the show at Newport's Leisure Centre five days later. The Smiths were in buoyant mood, particularly Morrissey who was happily glad-handing those fans gathered at the front of the stage. During 'The Boy With the Thorn in His Side', however, he was leaning out to reach the hands of those further back when he was pulled into the crowd. The rest of the band continued playing while Morrissey was carried backstage by anxious security staff. With the exuberant crowd repeatedly chanting Morrissey's name the band burst into 'The Draize Train'. When the instrumental came to a close, Grant Showbiz walked out onto the stage to announce that Morrissey was "getting his breath back at the moment" and would be returning to the stage in ten minutes or so. But a doctor's concerns over the concussion Morrissey had suffered from his fall was serious enough to warrant a dash to the nearest hospital. When Showbiz returned to announce the show would have to be cancelled owing to the doctor's instructions he was struck by a flying bottle. The mood quickly turned ugly, the disgruntlement at the show's curtailment spilling over into violence. Six fans would be arrested during the ensuing melee.

The riot featured in the following day's edition of *The Sun*, with Gary Bushell claiming Morrissey's injuries were due to monarchists protesting about the opening song, 'The Queen is Dead'. This was patently untrue, of course, but why let the truth get in the way of a good story. Morrissey was sufficiently recovered by the time of the next show in Nottingham two days later.

Next up was the first of three London dates at the National Ballroom, Kilburn, which was recorded and subsequently broadcast (in part) via Radio One. Many of the songs from that night would make up The Smiths' sole live album, *Rank*, released in September 1988.

The second London show at the Brixton Academy the following evening would prove memorable for The Smiths inviting Fred Hood, the one-time drummer with the Impossible Dreamers, whose debut RCA single, 'Spin' was produced by Marr, to add Burundi-style drumming to 'The Draize Train'. Following on from the third and final London date at the Palladium, The Smiths returned northwards for a show at the Preston Guild Hall. The band were late taking to the stage, but the show was over before it even began owing to Morrissey being struck in the face by a drum stick thrown from the crowd soon into the opening number, 'The Queen Is Dead'. Somewhat ironically, it was the same drum stick Marr had tossed into the crowd as a keepsake after accompanying Joyce during the song's intro. Morrissey immediately stopped singing and fled the stage leaving the rest of the band to soldier on as they had in Newport. It was initially announced that the show would be delayed five minutes while Morrissey received treatment. Soon afterwards, however, a second announcement informed the crowd that the singer had been taken to Preston Royal Infirmary and that the show would have to be cancelled. Thankfully, the Preston crowd proved slightly more stoical than their Newport counterparts, but the rest of the band were nonetheless glad to make their escape. Marr, in particular, remembers being pretty rattled. "I finished the song and got off [stage]. The gutter press created the

"I finished the song and got off [stage]. The gutter press created the whole incident but the fact that a Smiths gig could be so ugly left me incredibly depressed."

whole incident but the fact that a Smiths gig could be so ugly left me incredibly depressed."

Morrissey's injuries brought about the cancellation of the penultimate date in Llandudno, but the security was ramped up for obvious reasons at the hometown finale at Manchester's Free Trade Hall, there was never any danger of its being pulled. The band were greeted onstage with a banner reading "Welcome Home" which would remain at Morrissey's feet throughout the show. What neither the banner's creator, nor

anyone else in the Free Trade Hall realised, for that matter, was that this would prove The Smiths' final Manchester outing.

The Free Trade Hall show was to prove Craig Gannon's final outing as a Smith. He would have had to have been in a coma not to pick up the "bad vibes" emanating from Marr whenever they were in close proximity, but he had no inkling as to what was afoot. Had The Smiths had any form of third-party management it stands to reason they would have been called upon to deliver the news that he was now surplus to the band's requirements. Failing that, a simple press statement explaining the situation and thanking Gannon for his contribution would have sufficed. Given that Marr was largely responsible for bringing Gannon into the band, and was now the driving force behind his expulsion, he should have stepped up to the plate. Yet rather than do the decent thing and tell Gannon to his face, Marr elected to leave him to learn of his fate elsewhere. In the end, Gannon was given the news by his pal Gary Rostock, the drummer in fellow Rough Trade act, Easterhouse. "I received no word from the band or anyone connected to The Smiths," he says. "When I first heard the news from Gary that I was no longer in the band I did feel kinda relieved that it was all over because of all the bad vibes going round. I'm not saying I would have quit, but I was definitely relieved. I also felt a certain disappointment that it hadn't worked out as everyone had intended. For the majority of the time I was with Johnny – on a personal level, at least – it was a disaster."

Marr would prove less tactful in his reflections. "Craig really threw it away! We weren't closing doors; we were opening them for him and he just screwed it up for himself. I felt Craig was lazy. Morrissey felt the same. We could have picked a thousand people from our audience who would have made us feel that they were pleased to be in the group.

"Trying to have a conversation with Craig was just impossible after five minutes. He had nothing to say and little to contribute. When he did come up with his own parts, others said it was like something I'd played on the last single. It wasn't exactly his style. Musically, he fitted in, in that respect, but he was a lazy bastard and that's all there is to it." Morrissey was to prove equally scathing as to Gannon's worth in *Autobiography*. Though he accepts Marr's need to be "released of basic rhythm patterns to then be free for more complicated lead riffs", he says he saw no intrinsic value to The Smiths' sound following Gannon's inclusion. The guitarist's supposed indifference to adhering to the band's touring schedule coupled with his predilection for causing chaos in his hotel room, had also gone against the grain.

To heap insult on top of injury, Marr and Morrissey dragged their feet in paying Gannon what he felt was his due. The reason being they felt Gannon was asking for more than they believed he was owed. The resulting stalemate saw Gannon forced to seek legal redress. Following several years of legal wrangling the guitarist came away with an out-of-court settlement of £44,000.

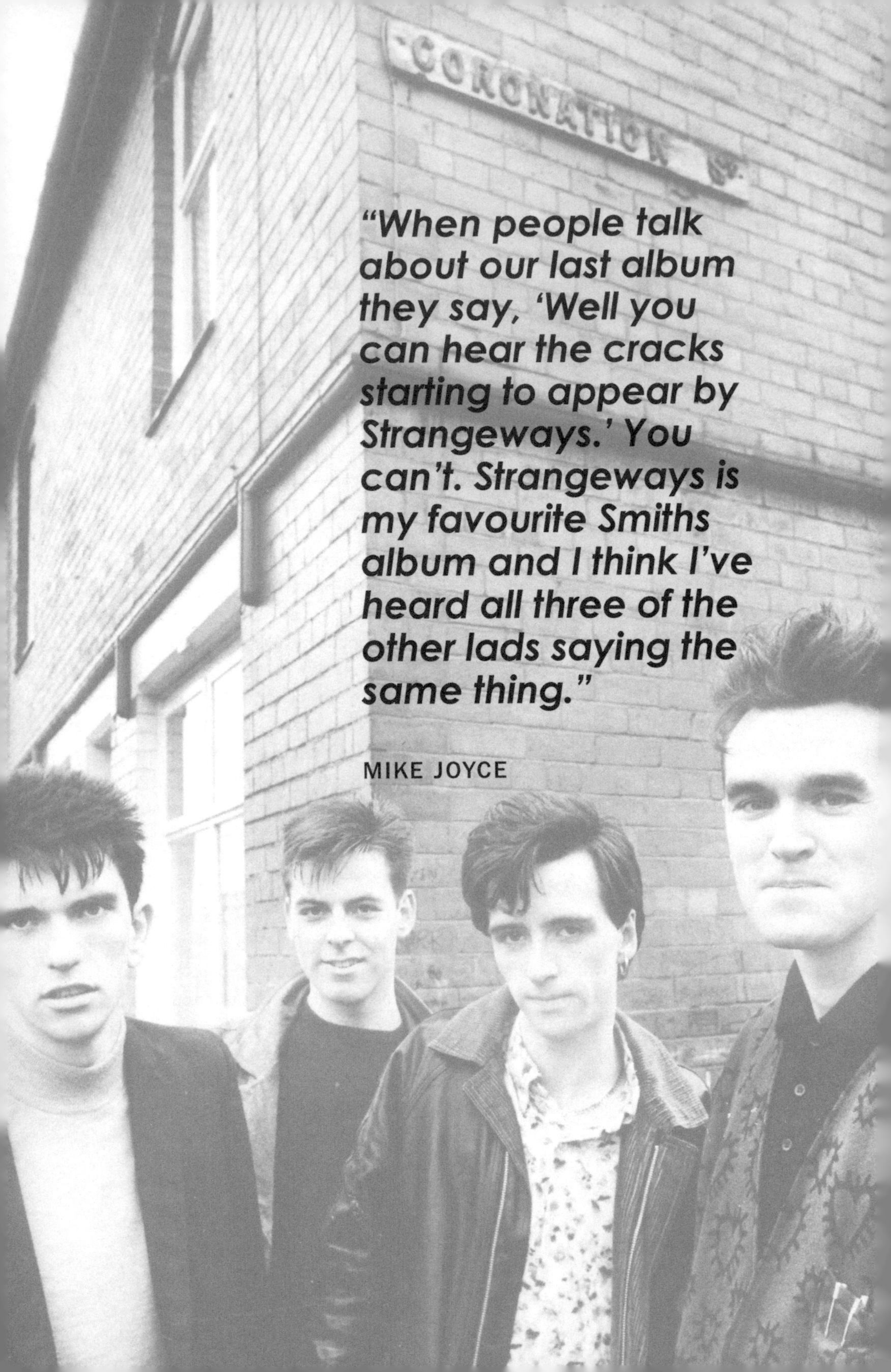

"When people talk about our last album they say, 'Well you can hear the cracks starting to appear by Strangeways.' You can't. Strangeways is my favourite Smiths album and I think I've heard all three of the other lads saying the same thing."

MIKE JOYCE

CHAPTER EIGHT

CRASHING DOWN ON THE CROSSBAR

The newly-truncated Smiths were set to play a benefit show for Artists Against Apartheid at the Royal Albert Hall on November 14 with fellow Mancunians The Fall in support. Both the date and venue would have to be hastily rescheduled, however, owing to Marr smashing his BMW into a solid stone wall close to his home three days before the show. He'd been drunk at the wheel and fortunate to walk away from the crash with minor injuries.

Aside from a bruised ego, he'd suffered whiplash and had to be fitted with a neck brace. A minor injury to his arm would also require a temporary splint. In the subsequent press statement it was erroneously claimed Angie had also been in the car. It would have only taken a passing glance at the BMW's accordioned bonnet to know that anyone sitting in the passenger seat most likely wouldn't have survived the impact. Lady luck was still smiling on Marr when he presented himself at his local police station the following day. Instead of having the book thrown at him, as he fully deserved, the duty officer happened to be a huge Smiths fan and he was let off with a mild caution.

The crash was to serve as a wake-up call in more ways than one. He'd been dancing close to the line for some time now and knew the time had come to re-evaluate his lifestyle. As with many others who undergo a near-death experience, Marr found himself imbued with a renewed sense of purpose. Aside from curbing his excesses, he was keen to move away from what he'd been doing onstage. The Smiths were already being accused of losing touch with reality and of believing their own hype.

The Smiths still owed Rough Trade one studio album in order to fulfil their contractual obligations before moving over to EMI's perceived greener pastures. Whereas most bands would have cobbled together whatever songs were to hand, Marr was intent on moving away from what he calls "hallmark Smiths". "I was sick of the way the band was were being perceived. We were starting to be defined by all the things we supposedly hated – as if all we were about was negativity, which I didn't feel."

Marr's injuries were fully healed by the

time of the rescheduled Artists Against Apartheid show on December 12. The 15-song set that night saw the debut of 'Some Girls Are Bigger Than Others' (replete with additional verse), and a dusting off of 'This Night Has Opened My Eyes'. Also featured was The Smiths' forthcoming new single, 'Shoplifters of the World Unite' / 'Half a Person' (RT195), which the band had recorded at Trident Studios in Soho soon after Gannon's departure. ('London' features on the 12" version.)

As was perhaps to be expected, the crowd proved as blasé to Gannon's departure as either Marr or Morrissey. Yet his absence was felt onstage that night, however. "It was difficult going back to being a four-piece again," says Rourke. "It sounded a lot weaker. Craig would play brilliantly whatever Johnny wanted him to play [so] I was surprised when [he] was asked to leave."

"At the time there was a bit of friction between Johnny and Morrissey, but it was kept really quiet."

As they had done on numerous other occasions, The Smiths brought the evening to a close with 'Hand in Glove'. The fans no doubt spilled out into the street with the song's familiar "I'll probably never see you again" refrain ringing in their ears. Yet other than for a handful of promotional TV appearances, their heroes would never again share the same stage.

When speaking with Piccadilly Radio a couple of weeks prior to the Brixton show, Morrissey said that he couldn't envisage collaborating with anyone other than Marr and hinted that The Smiths could only go from strength to strength in the coming years. Rourke, however, paints a gloomier picture. "It had all changed a lot. At the time there was a bit of friction between Johnny and Morrissey, but it was kept really quiet. I didn't really know what the problem was . . . and I still don't know to this day"

'Shoplifters of the World Unite' would peak two places higher on the UK chart (#12), giving The Smiths another Top 20 single following its late January 1987 release. Another brand-new composition, 'You Just Haven't Earned It Yet, Baby', was originally earmarked as the new single. The idea getting as far as the white label test pressing stage.

Speaking with playwright and self-confessed Smiths fan Sean Duggan about the new single on The Tube, Morrissey said the lyric to 'Shoplifters . . .' supposedly represented a cultural shoplifting and taking things and using them to your own advantage rather than wandering into your local supermarket and pocketing a loaf of bread. Speaking about this in *Autobiography*, Morrissey says his going before the camera on The Tube to explain the song's meaning had come at Rough Trade's insistence. The label going so far as to summon him to their offices to say unless he was willing to clarify the matter then the band wouldn't be

allowed to perform on the show.

"Around the table everybody looks at me as if I've just eaten a small child, and the Rough Trade faces seem newly traditionalist in the mid-afternoon light. Like a bull in a Spanish bullring, I look left and right for clarity. 'But the song IS about shoplifting!' I wheeze out."

Morrissey's acquiescence would allow The Smiths' appearance on *The Tube* to proceed as scheduled.

Speaking with renowned LA radio station KROQ-FM in 1997, Morrissey said he penned "Shoplifters of the World Unite during what he believed to be The Smiths' high water mark: "Very, very witty single and a great moment for The Smiths in England. I think it was probably the best days of our career. It was just a very funny time and a time of very sparky rebellion, and this song, more than any, I think, exemplifies that. I like it." Indeed, he did. So much so, that 'Shoplifters . . .' has featured on many a Morrissey set list over the years.

Another bugbear causing some friction between Marr and Morrissey was the recent appointment of Ken Friedman as the band's manager. The San Franciscan-born Friedman had cut his teeth working for Bill Graham before setting up his own company. Ironically, it was Morrissey that had introduced Marr to Friedman. Whereas Marr was relieved to be free from the pressures of dealing with the band's business affairs, Morrissey was unhappy about ceding responsibility to an outsider.

In early February The Smiths flew out to Liguria in north-western Italy for the San

Photo by Paul Slattery.

Remo Festival where they mimed along to 'Shoplifters of the World Unite', 'There Is a Light That Never Goes Out', 'The Boy With the Thorn in His Side', 'Panic', and 'Ask' from a revolving stage. They then flew to Ireland for the usual round of promotional appearances on various radio and TV shows.

That same month saw the release of a second Smiths compilation album, *The World Won't Listen*; the track-listing consisting of the varying mixes of the band's singles and B-sides from 1985 to 1987. The album narrowly missed out on the top slot on the UK album chart – denied by *The Phantom of the Opera* musical soundtrack – but would remain on the chart for 14 weeks. Indeed, *The World Won't Listen* was still able to hold its own on the chart despite Rough Trade's releasing the similar but extended US-intended compilation *Louder Than Bombs* domestically. The decision was purportedly made to release *Louder Than Bombs* in the UK to save British fans from paying US import tax on the album. As it transpired, it was largely only the die-hard fans that cared one way or the other as the album would stall at #38.

The World Won't Listen and *Louder Than Bombs* were both still on the chart when The Smiths set up at The Wool Hall, a residential recording studio in the village of Beckington, near Bath in Somerset which, at the time, was owned by Roland Orzabal and Curt Smith of Tears for Fears, to record their final studio album for Rough Trade. Stephen Street would once again co-produce. With the teetotalling Morrissey not set to arrive until the following day, Marr, Rourke, and Joyce were free to carouse the night away without fear of reprimand. The revelry continued after Morrissey's arrival, of course, but only after he'd gone to bed. "It wasn't really his bag," says Street. "We'd carry on finishing overdubs and then the records would come out. We'd be partying all hours."

Despite ever-present temptations such as a fully-stocked wine cellar, The Smiths worked as hard as they partied with each session lasting ten-to-twelve hours. "It wasn't all one *Spinal Tap* mongo fest!" says Marr.

Street, however, remembers the conviviality being tinged with tension, however, owing to Marr's sizeable brandy intake. Street was "bashing away" at a DX-7 synth keyboard with Rourke and Joyce adding haphazard accompaniment when Marr playfully shouted: "Hey, Streety, you don't like this, do you? You want us to sound jingly-jangly, like the good old Smiths days.'"

Street is quick to stress the sessions themselves were free of tension with the four Smiths knuckling down to laying down the basic tracks. It was a sentiment subsequently echoed by Joyce. "The sessions were positive. Speaking first and foremost as a player, the relationship between the four of us at that time was the healthiest it ever was. We were all getting out of it with the ales. Things were getting quite crazy at times, but that was the beauty of The Smiths – the craziness."

Marr disputes Joyce's rose-tinted recollections, however, saying the inter-band harmony was no longer extending outside the studio. Nor was his seemingly throwaway comment to Street about The

Smiths moving away from their trademark jingly-jangly sound. "I went into the making of *Strangeways, Here We Come* with an agenda to use fewer overdubs and not fill up all the space in the sound. I made the decision that the first track on the album would be all keyboards and no guitars ("A Rush and a Push and the Land Is Ours"). Even if no one else cared, it was important for me to do something different, to feel like we were going forward."

Ironically, in the run-up to their entering The Wool Hall, Marr sought to take The Smiths to the next level by taking inspiration from The Beatles' *White Album* and *Let It Be*, as well as early Walker Brothers albums. Bowie's 1977 album, *Low*, gave rise to 'Last Night I Dreamt That Somebody Loved Me', which he's since cited as epitomising the uniqueness of The Smiths. A more up-to-date inspiration came from his pal Matt Johnson's latest The The offering, Infected, (a Matt Johnson solo album in all but name) To Marr's mind, the songs on Infected were "innovative, with great guitars and strong songwriting, and managed to be a new kind of pop while still being socio-political."

It was during the Strangeways sessions, of course, that the first chinks began to appear in Marr and Morrissey's hitherto fore seemingly unassailable relationship. Marr and Street had spent an afternoon working on a glam rock-esque guitar line reminiscent of T. Rex on 'I Started Something I Couldn't Finish' and were understandably pleased with their endeavours. Upon hearing the end result, however, Morrissey expressed his dislike. Marr happened to be absent from the studio at the time. When Street reported Morrissey's comments to Marr, the latter reportedly yelled, "Well, let Morrissey fuckin' think of something!"

The Smiths were still holed up at The Wool Hall when Rough Trade released 'Sheila Take a Bow' / 'Is It Really So Strange' (RT196). Despite several of the tracks intended for *Strangeways, Here We Come*, still requiring lyrics – a situation that would see Morrissey return to Hale Barns to come up with the goods – in typical Smiths fashion, 'Sheila Take a Bow' was released as a stand-alone single.

Morrissey had originally wanted Sandie Shaw to duet with him on the song. Come the day of the recording session with John Porter at Matrix Studios back in December, however, he was too ill to attend. Given that it was he who'd suggested inviting Shaw to the session, it beggars belief that he didn't think to extend her the courtesy of making her aware of the situation. Shaw would later recall how Marr bore the haggard countenance of someone "tired of making excuses for his ill-mannered friend" that day. A second session was duly arranged with Porter again at the helm. Though Shaw recorded her vocal second time around, Morrissey's pitch was so high that her own harmony was superfluous and the version was scrapped. The revised version of 'Sheila Take a Bow' would reach #10, giving The Smiths their highest placing on the UK Singles Chart during the band's lifetime.

Not everybody that had worked on the 'Sheila . . .' session was pleased with the single's success, however. Whilst awaiting the band's arrival at the studio John Porter had added a snazzy slide guitar riff to one of Marr's chord progressions. He'd simply been amusing himself in the band's absence, but Marr was happy with the effect. When Porter heard the single on the radio, however, his ear told him something was awry. His suspicions were confirmed on scanning the label and seeing Stephen Street's name where his own should be on the label. Porter has since accused Morrissey of sampling the guitars from his recording – including the slide guitar part – on the Street mix.

While Porter's ire was aimed solely at Morrissey, the amended version was recorded by all four Smiths. Perhaps unsurprisingly, Marr makes no mention of their re-recording 'Sheila Takes a Bow' with Street in *Set the Boy Free*. Speaking with Johnny Rogan, Street – rather disingenuously, it has to be said - comes to the band's defence saying how they were running out of time at the studio and Marr couldn't remember who was responsible for the slide guitar part. "I thought it was just a piece of work that Johnny had done and couldn't be bothered to re-create. It was a guitar line and sounded good, so why bother doing it again?"

Marr and Morrissey had been working cheek-by-jowl for four years by this juncture, and as with many another songwriting partnership of note, the strain of operating within each other's shadow was beginning to show. Morrissey was still sulking over Ken Friedman's appointment – regardless of the arrangement allowing him and Morrissey to concentrate on making music. For the first time since Joe Moss's departure, the band's affairs were being tended to with efficiency and enthusiasm. In a fit of pique, at what he saw as obduracy on Marr's part, he failed to show for a promo video shoot that Sire would use to promote *Louder Than Bombs* in the US.

By the mid-Eighties making a promo video was a prerequisite for any band – especially since the advent of MTV. Indeed, the music station's recently-launched 120 Minutes, a weekly Sunday evening two-hour show dedicated to alternative acts, was tailor-made for The Smiths. Sire's marketing strategy came with a caveat from Warner Bros' Burbank HQ, however: the band had to give their full support to the video. Any messing up on their part, and they could expect the cost of the production being deducted from future US royalties.

The Smiths were a popular draw amongst America's college and university fraternities but they had yet to make any real impact on the mainstream US market. The 24-track *Louder Than Bombs* might have been a compilation album, but it was an almost complete body of work in terms of singles and B-sides and Sire believed having the promo video on heavy rotation on 120 Minutes and MTV's regular playlist would help expose The Smiths to a wider audience. All four Smiths believe *Strangeways, Here We Come* to be the zenith of the band's creativity – their "masterpiece", if you will. But while the album would give The Smiths their fourth Top 3 album at home, it would fail to crack the Billboard 200 Top 50.

Sire had recommended 25-year-old up-and-coming female director, Tamra Davis, who just also happened to be a huge fan of The Smiths. Having liaised with Friedman before leaving LA, she arrived at The Wool Hall with the understanding she would spend several days getting acquainted with

> *"Things were getting quite crazy at times, but that was the beauty of The Smiths – the craziness."*

the band before then beginning filming. She and Friedman having taken a temporary lease on a nearby house. While Marr, Rourke, and Joyce proved genial hosts, Morrissey retreated into his shell. Davis was to spend many frustrating hours in the singer's company before finally finding common ground with their shared passion for old Hollywood films. It was as if the clouds had parted and betwixt their celluloid musings an agreement was soon reached. Davis would capture the band at work and play at The Wool Hall on her handheld camera before heading for London and filming them performing 'Shoplifters of the World Unite' and "Sheila Take a Bow" on a soundstage.

Friedman obviously wasn't a film buff or he might also have enjoyed a happier relationship with Morrissey. Indeed, it appeared there was nothing – other than tender his resignation, of course – that might meet with Morrissey's approval. Every attempt to pin Morrissey down to discuss plans for a world tour in support of *Strangeways, Here We Come* was met with utter indifference. Indeed, one such occasion saw Morrissey order Friedman from the room for daring to interrupt his creativity with talk of business.

The handheld footage was soon collated. Leaving Street at The Wool Hall to crack on with mixing the album, Friedman booked a soundstage in Battersea. Though Marr, Rourke, and Joyce arrived at the appointed hour, there was no sign of Morrissey. With London traffic being what it was, no one thought anything untoward was afoot. It was only when the minutes started to roll by with a full crew standing about twiddling their thumbs racking up untold thousands of pounds – money that Warner Bros had every intention of recouping. Rather than hang out wondering when or even if Morrissey would show, Marr and Friedman, with a distraught Davis in tow, set off for Cadogan Squire.

According to Davis' recollections, it didn't come as much of a surprise to either of her companions that Morrissey was home but refusing to come to the door. Sensing Morrissey was lurking behind the door, Friedman immediately went into conciliatory mode. Marr was beside himself, however, and didn't bother pulling any punches. He told Morrissey that he couldn't see how they could continue with The Smiths if he was going to pull a "Diva" every time the band was required to something he didn't want to do. The video shoot was aimed at promoting the band in the US and would also no doubt be shown on terrestrial TV. It was a win-win situation for The Smiths, yet Morrissey remained entrenched behind the door. The door remained closed even though he could hardly have failed to hear Marr announce to Friedman that The Smiths were finished before storming off. Seeing as there was little point in returning to the Battersea soundstage, Marr, Friedman, and Davis retreated to the Portobello Hotel to drown their frustrations.

Morrissey's no-show for the video shoot didn't bring about the immediate dissolution of The Smiths, of course, but from this juncture on the writing was on the wall for all to see. Indeed, when the band subsequently appeared on the Friday, April 10 edition of The Tube languidly miming live to 'Shoplifters of the World Unite' and 'Sheila Take a Bow', Marr and Morrissey's body language says it all.

With the ten tracks making up the new album were now in the can a further session was booked at The Wool Hall three weeks hence to work on songs intended as B-sides for the songs earmarked as singles. Come the day of the session, however, neither Marr nor Morrissey bothered to show up leaving Rourke, Joyce, and Street kicking their heels and pondering what was going on. At some point in the day, Marr finally returned one of their many calls, but only to enquire if Morrissey was there. On being informed in the negative, Marr announced he wouldn't be coming either and the session was cancelled.

Rather than arrange a clear-the-air meeting with Morrissey to iron out their widening differences, Marr instead flew over to Paris (with Angie) to add some guitar parts to Talking Heads' latest album, *Naked*, which was being produced by Steve Lillywhite. (The tracks Marr played on were 'Ruby Dear', '(Nothing But) Flowers', 'Mommy Daddy You and I', and 'Cool Water').

It wasn't until returning to London that Marr finally got together with Morrissey at the latter's flat. Their peace pow-pow soon ground to a halt with the two at loggerheads over Friedman's appointment. Morrissey wanted Friedman gone and have things go back to how they were. This was anathema to Marr, however. He was still only 23, and readily admits he was woefully ill-equipped to deal with all the lawyers and accountants. Separating themselves from Rough Trade was still far from cut and dried, and to add to the confusion Seymour Stein was insisting Sire would have a claim on all future Smiths albums. With Friedman on board, it was as though the proverbial weight had shifted. It was of little interest to the suits at EMI that their advance had long-since been swallowed-up by solicitors fees. Therefore, the label was well within its rights in making noises about new product from their latest acquisition. With *Strangeways, Here We Come* being readied for release, Marr felt the band should maybe take time away from each other before reconvening to work on the mooted debut EMI album.

Though the conversation moved onto other matters, the impasse over Friedman remained. Realising the futility of ignoring the elephant in the room, Marr broached the subject of their disbanding The Smiths. He still loved being the guitarist in The Smiths but felt that unless he and Morrissey could formulate a forward-thinking strategy they ran a serious risk of becoming as anachronistic as the Beach Boys.

He and Angie were set to fly out to LA on a belated honeymoon. They would be gone for a fortnight. Rather than wait till their return he called a full band meeting for later that same evening at Geales Fish Restaurant in Kensington. With Morrissey seemingly happy to remain a passive observer, Marr gave Rourke and Joyce an overview of his and Morrissey's musings from earlier, while repeating his assertion about their needing to get some perspective as to how they might take the band forward once they moved to EMI. His version of events has Rourke and Joyce's response being both unresponsive and unfriendly. He was already sensing that he was in a minority of one on band policy. His suspicions that the other three had been colluding behind his back came with Joyce announcing they were going back into the studio to work on songs for a new album.

Strangeways, Here We Come hadn't even been mixed yet and Joyce was talking about writing songs for a new album? The only song ideas that needed working on as far as Marr was concerned were those the band had earmarked for potential B-sides at the

aborted Wool Hall session. Though he felt he was being railroaded, he nonetheless agreed to return to the studio.

Joyce remembers things somewhat differently, however. He says he was left dumbfounded when Marr repeated his and Morrissey's broaching breaking up the band. In hindsight, he says he maybe wasn't as attuned to the strain Marr was under owing to his deteriorating relationship with Morrissey. "Maybe I wasn't sympathetic enough to the way Johnny was feeling. He would express his dissatisfaction and anger about something more so than Morrissey. But I don't think he did on this occasion and, because nobody saw the signs, he got a bit upset. He wanted everyone to rally round him and say, 'Don't worry, have some time [off].' It was all a massive shock and I just remember it being surreal. I thought he really meant it (to quit). That's why I wanted to sort it there and then. I thought, 'If we leave this, then that's it really.'"

A session was duly set up sometime in early May at The Cathouse, a home studio in Streatham run by Grant Showbiz and James Hood who was a mutual friend of the band. The overriding reason it's being cheap and cheerful. Marr arrived at the studio with no real understanding of what they were hoping to achieve other than work on a couple of songs to serve as B-sides for the 7" and 12" versions of 'Girlfriend in a Coma' (RT197); the first single to be culled from the new album. He and Showbiz got everything in readiness for when the others arrived.

The atmosphere was comfortable from the off, with Marr and Morrissey each acting as if the other wasn't in the room. And even when they did communicate it was with monosyllabic grunts. Even had the atmosphere been harmonious, it was difficult for anyone to grasp their reason for being there as all they had in the locker was sketches for songs. When Morrissey suggested covering an obscure 1968 Cilla Black B-side and film theme called 'Work Is a Four Letter Word', Marr thought it simply an off-the-cuff remark to try and lighten the mood. The smile soon slipped from his face on realising Morrissey was serious. He had no interest in recording any Cilla Black song and certainly didn't appreciate his being the last to find out about it.

Despite his mounting anger, Marr gritted his teeth and went through the motions. A half-hearted rendition of Elvis' 'A Fool Such As I' was attempted but abandoned after a couple of takes. The other song recorded that fateful spring afternoon, 'I Keep Mine Hidden' which features on the 12inch version of "Girlfriend in a Coma" was, alas, to prove the final Marr/Morrissey composition. For as legal documents have since confirmed, their partnership was effectively dissolved on May 31, 1987.

Marr says in *Set the Boy Free* that he spent the next two days at The Cathouse mixing the two tracks; his determination to get them in the can before he and Angie flew out to LA extending to his grabbing snatches of sleep under the mixing desk. Once in LA, Marr tried pushing all thoughts of The Smiths, and the ongoing ructions that were tearing the band apart from within, to the back of his mind. This was easier said than done, of course. He'd boarded the flight to LA half-expecting one of the others to call at

some point during the next fortnight. As the days rolled by with nary a word, however, he began to realise maybe the situation was beyond saving. Unbeknown to Marr, at the time at least, Morrissey flew out to LA while he and Angie were enjoying their belated honeymoon.

Upon his return to Manchester, Marr settled into his home studio to work on several instrumental tracks he'd amassed. He thought it odd that his none of his fellow Smiths called – if only to enquire how the holiday went yet was nonetheless enjoying writing away from the pressures of being in The Smiths. Though he made no effort to pick up the phone himself, he was awaiting his bandmates to break radio silence. When the phone did finally ring, however, it was the band's publicity agent, Pat Bellis, calling to say the media had gotten hold of a rumour that he'd quit The Smiths and wanted to know how he'd like to respond? He declined the sensible option was to decline making a comment. After all, even if Bellis hadn't contacted the rest of the band, the *NME* or one of the other music weeklies would surely do so. Two days later, however, a story - replete with a Rough Trade publicity photo that had caught him scowling in contrast to the other three Smiths smiling for the camera - appeared in the *NME* stating that he had indeed left The Smiths.

Contrary to customary PR practice, Bellis took it upon herself to offer her own

THE SMITHS

observations on the Marr/Morrissey rift to the music papers. Having attempted to cover herself by saying that it was no secret that the differences between Marr and Morrissey's lifestyles had caused several arguments in the past, she then proceeded to say how the latest spat wasn't over a single issue and that Marr simply wanted to "move in a completely different direction" – presumably different to the one Morrissey was intent on taking The Smiths? When asked if Morrissey's ire stemmed from the company Marr had been keeping of late, she said it was unlikely Morrissey was even aware of who Marr might be hanging out with as the guitarist tended to keep his private life exactly that.

Marr understandably felt honour-bound to offer a response to the *NME*'s "Smiths Split" article. Needless to say, the *NME*'s editor, Danny Kelly, could hardly believe his luck on answering the phone to find an emotional Marr on the other end of the line. Convinced that it was Morrissey that had leaked the story to the paper, Marr was determined to give his version of events: "First of all, it's very important to me to clear up some of the inaccuracies that were in your story last week. There is nothing even approaching acrimony between myself and the other members of the band. I've known them all a long time and I love 'em. Nor was there any truth in the idea that Morrissey has any problem with the company I keep, personally or workwise; we're different people and lead different kind of lives, but that stuff is patently untrue. And lastly, the stuff about me using record company funds to pay for a trip to America is totally wrong. I'm not denying that there weren't certain problems involving the band, and it's also very true that a group like The Smiths can begin to take over your whole life and all your energy. That's certainly happened to me, but the major reason for me going was simply that there are things I want to do, musically, that there is just not scope for in The Smiths. I've got absolutely no problem with what The Smiths are doing. The stuff we've just done for the new album is great, the best we've ever done. I'm really proud of it. But there are things I want to do that can only happen outside The Smiths. In the final analysis, the thing that used to make me happy was making me miserable and so I just had to get out." He then signed off by stating he'd never wanted The Smiths to turn into the Rolling Stones; that was just more lazy, journalistic bullshit."

The Smiths would issue a statement saying they wished Marr good luck in his future musical ventures and that they were already considering other named guitarists to replace him. In Autobiography, Morrissey says Geoff Travis mooted Roddy Frame as a possible contender: "As quick as lightening, Frame proudly issues a 'Morrissey asked me to join The Smiths, but I refused' badge of honour to the press." This was to prove a non-story as Frame was busy with his own solo commitments at the time. One cannot help but wonder what Frame's reaction might have been had Morrissey rather than Travis had made the call?

A three-day session with one-time Easterhouse guitarist, Ivor Perry, did indeed take place at the Power Plant in Chelsea. The Manchester-born Perry was currently

playing alongside Craig Gannon in The Cradle when Travis made the call. Having once lived a few hundred yards further along King's Road from Morrissey, the two were well-acquainted. The opportunity to work with a singer of Morrissey's prestige – either with The Smiths or in any other capacity – was one Perry simply couldn't afford to spurn. Settling himself in front of a cassette recorder he laid down a collection of riffs chord sequences and posted them off to Cadogan Square. Morrissey obviously saw sufficient potential in the tape as on August 5, Perry accompanied The Smiths and Stephen Street into the studio.

The opening session would be blighted somewhat owing to the obvious antagonism between Perry and Street stemming from the latter having worked with Easterhouse but would nonetheless result in two new "Smiths" tracks. The first of these was a souped-up version of 'Bengali in Platforms', which contrasts starkly from the version that appears on Morrissey's solo debut, *Viva Hate*. While impressed with Morrissey's musical knowhow, Perry couldn't help but ponder the singer's motives for wanting to keep The Smiths a going concern. He'd assumed Morrissey had invited him into the studio to maybe help out with song ideas for the B-sides The Smiths still required should further singles by culled from *Strangeways, Here We Come*. He'd certainly no intention of even attempting to fill Marr's shoes. Prior to the session Perry visited with Morrissey at Cadogan Square where the latter had broached the idea of continuing The Smiths. Perry, however, thought otherwise and said as much. To his mind, the idea of his trying to replicate Marr's trademark style was a non-starter.

When reflecting on that fateful session in *Autobiography*, Morrissey says the session was "de trop" (unwanted) as if to indicate his heart wasn't in it – regardless of Rourke and Joyce's "pledging allegiance, aware of the impending precipice." To Perry's mind, the "precipice" to which Morrissey alludes is his furtively planning for a solo career but was as yet unwilling to break the news to Rourke and Joyce. The drummer, himself, had come to realise the futility of the exercise. The new songs sounded okay but lacked the Johnny Marr magic. Throughout the session Joyce's eyes kept wandering to the door as if in anticipation of Marr's arrival. His eyes were certainly riveted on the door when Morrissey bolted from the room. His bid to escape the exasperation hanging over The Smiths like a winding sheet continued until he was safely ensconced back in Hale Barns. Joyce would spend a fruitless couple of weeks calling Morrissey on the phone leaving one unanswered message after another. Realising there was little point continuing with the pretence, Joyce released a statement to the music press announcing he'd "fulfilled his role" with The Smiths.

Marr had initially thought the comment about other guitarists being lined up to replace him in The Smiths couldn't be anything other than a hoax. When a friend called to say the rumour was in fact true and that the others had indeed gone into the studio with another guitarist, he knew he'd reached the end of the line. Even had he wanted to kiss and make up his pride

wouldn't let him. "I was really hurt. To be replaced so quickly by your friends, before you've even had a chance to change your mind, was the end of it."

From the moment Marr confirmed he was no longer in The Smiths the media circus went into hyperdrive. He opted to refrain from making any public comment. He wasn't only walking away from The Smiths he was also calling time on three very close friendships. "It (the split) was hard enough to deal with as it was, and too painful for me to put a spin on in public. I had to stand back and let people say what they wanted, whether it was true or not.

With obvious exceptions such as the Stones and The Who, few band last beyond five years. And even if they do, their most productive body of work comes within the first five years. As stressful as leaving The Smiths was for Marr, the rupture nonetheless came with an overwhelming sense of relief. It also presented a new lease of life. He was still only 23 years old, and one of the most respected guitarists of his generation. He admits to having to idea what he wanted to do other than continue playing guitar. "It was a time of rejuvenation, pro-future, pro-music . . ."

After all the bruhaha surrounding the split, the summer of 1987 passed with hardly a word as to whether Marr and Morrissey would come together to try and resolve their differences for the greater good of The Smiths. Indeed, Morrissey was now collaborating with Stephen Street on song ideas the latter had presented him. Rourke and Joyce were asked for whatever insight they might provide on the situation, of course, but they appeared just as much in the dark as anyone else. No one was in any position to provide a definitive answer as to whether The Smiths would take to a stage again other than the two main protagonists, of course, and they were keeping tight-lipped. Indeed, it wouldn't be until mid-September that Morrissey finally With the weeks slipping by with the situation seemingly no nearer to being resolved, EMI grew ever more frantic. They had signed The Smiths in anticipation of taking the band to levels Rough Trade could only dream of. The Smiths were now a band in name only but EMI were intent on recouping their advance by all means necessary and issued writs to Morrissey insisting he was their artist and legally bound to "fulfil what are known as 'the Smiths contracts'." Sire were equally determined to accrue as much meat as they could from The Smiths' rotting carcass. As for Rough Trade, they had the luxury of retaining the band's back catalogue for future cash ins. The Smiths were dead, but there were so many ways to dress up the corpse. Indeed, one can almost imagine the marketing mantra within the lyric to 'Paint a Vulgar Picture' – "Re-issue! Re-package! Re-package! Re-evaluate the songs. Double-pack with a photograph. Extra Track (and a tacky badge) –ringing about Rough Trade's offices.

In the meantime, of course, *Strangeways, Here We Come* (ROUGH106) was pressed and ready for release. Given that all four previous Smiths studio albums had gone Top 3 in the UK, it was only to be expected that *Strangeways, Here we Come* would follow

suit. As it was set to serve as The Smiths' epitaph, it stands to reason that Geoff Travis and everyone else at Rough Trade would surely have been anticipating a second No. 1 Smiths album. If so, they were in for a surprise as The Smiths were once again left to play bridesmaid. This time to Michael Jackson's *Bad*. A consolation of sorts came with the album remaining on the chart for 17 weeks.

Strangeways... would also give The Smiths their highest US chart placing peaking at # 55 on the Billboard 200. It's purely a matter of conjecture, of course, but the album might have achieved a higher showing had Morrissey not thrown his mic out of the pram over Ken Friedman's appointment and participated in the promo video for *Louder Than Bombs*.

Given they were now talking about The Smiths in the past tense, the reviews for Strangeways . . . were inevitably coloured with melancholy at what might have been with *Uncut*'s Simon Goddard going so far as to proclaim the album "cursed with the adverse status of a bitter, cryptic postscript to a brief but glorious career."

Marr and Morrissey could no longer see eye-to-eye, but once the dust had settled both would cite *Strangeways, Here We Come* as being their favourite Smiths album. "Strangeways . . . suffers because it was our last record so people think there were arguments and horrors in making it, but there weren't," Marr told Select magazine in December 1993. "Morrissey and I both think it's possibly our best album. [It] has its moments, like 'Last Night I Dreamt That Somebody Love Me'. Last time I met Morrissey he said it was his favourite Smiths song. He might be right. Over the last few years I've heard 'Girlfriend in a Coma' in shops and people's cars, and I'm always surprised by how good it sounds. 'Unhappy Birthday' I really like."

Speaking with Q magazine the following year, Morrissey opined: "*Strangeways Here We Come* is the Smiths best album. Well it is. We're in absolute accordance on that. We say it quite often. At the same time. In our sleep. But in different beds (. . .) Strangeways... said everything eloquently, perfectly at the right time and put the tin hat on it basically."

Mike Joyce perhaps best sums up the situation within The Smiths at the time they were recording the album in highlighting the pressure that Marr and Morrissey put themselves under to write the best possible Smiths album. "And that's why Strangeways... to me sounds like a total white-knuckle ride. We were very tense. But we were playing together really well, better than we'd ever played before. I wish we'd toured Strangeways..." Two further UK singles would be culled from *Strangeways, Here We Come* over the proceeding months. 'I Started Something I Couldn't Finish' (RT198) would peak at # 23, while 'Last Night I Dreamt That Somebody Loved Me' (RT200) came in seven places lower at # 30. The primary reason for the lacklustre showings, of course, is due to the absence of a hitherto previously unreleased B-side owing to the Record Plant sessions being aborted.

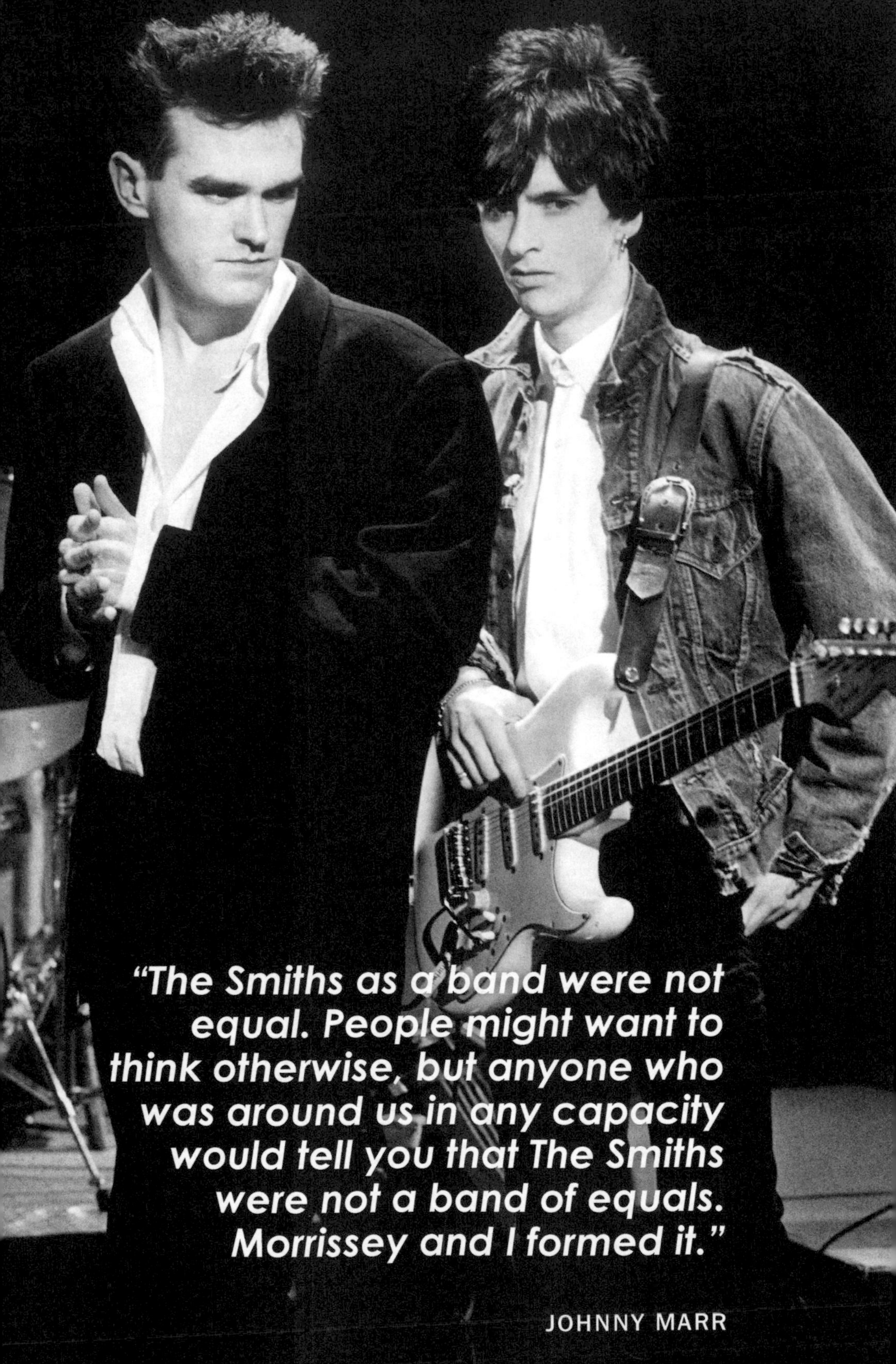

"The Smiths as a band were not equal. People might want to think otherwise, but anyone who was around us in any capacity would tell you that The Smiths were not a band of equals. Morrissey and I formed it."

JOHNNY MARR

CHAPTER NINE

WE DON'T OWE YOU ANYTHING

AS IT TRANSPIRED, *Strangeways, Here We Come* didn't quite fulfil The Smiths' contractual obligations to Rough Trade after all. Morrissey was now signed to HMV, and with his debut solo album, *Viva Hate* (HMV CSD3787), having topped the UK chart and its attendant singles – 'Suedehead'/ 'I Know Very Well How I Got My Name' (HMV POP1618) and 'Everyday is Like Sunday' / 'Disappointed' (HMV POP1619) both breaking into the Top 10 (at # 5 and # 9 respectively), the only realistic option available to Rough Trade was to release another retrospective package. Rather than brazenly rip the fans off with another compilation offering, the label instead chose to close the book on its dealings with The Smiths with a live album. Bootleg recordings of Smiths live outings had been doing the rounds since early 1983, but, unless the recording came via the mixing desk, the sound quality often left much to be desired. Official live albums can also prove hit and miss affairs owing to a venue's acoustics. Most acts have the sound engineer record the shows – if only to look for imperfections in the performance. Rough Trade most likely had scores of Smiths mixing desk recordings stashed in desk drawers and elsewhere. Fortunately, they also had the masters of the band's October 23, 1986, performance at the National Ballroom in Kilburn which Radio One had recorded for transmission.

The full set-list from the Kilburn show was 21 songs, but Morrissey culled this to a more manageable 14 tracks, which, having first gained Marr's approval, were delivered to Rough Trade. He was magnanimous in his selections as the inclusion of 'The Draize Train' would see Marr receive a larger slice of the royalties then himself. He's also reported to have wanted to call the live album *The Smiths in Heat*. When Rough Trade objected to the title, he instead playfully proposed *Rank*, as in "J. Arthur Rank" (Cockney rhyming slang for wank) To his bemusement, the label offered no resistance.

Rank (ROUGH126) was released in early-September 1988. It may have been going on two years since The Smiths last shared a stage, and a full year on from their official dissolution. Their appeal was showing no sign of diminishing, however, and the album entered the UK chart at – yes, you've guessed it – #2. (This time being pipped to the post by Kylie Minogue's eponymous debut).

The success of *Rank* provided The Smiths with a gilt-edged opportunity to come together one last time and bow out with a bang. Morrissey would go as far as calling Marr to mull over the idea of a farewell outing at the Royal Albert Hall. Indeed, he'd let his feelings be known about a potential full-blown Smiths reunion as far back as February while speaking with the *NME*. Though he was basking in the first flush of solo success with 'Suedehead' nestled in the UK Top 10, Morrissey said how he'd be totally in favour of a reunion, and

that he'd be first through the door should anybody wish to return to the Smiths fold to make records. For 'anybody' one might as well read Johnny Marr, but the sentiment was genuine all the same. With Marr happy playing "Rickenbacker for hire" with the likes of Paul McCartney and The Pretenders, the proposal was sadly left withering on the bough.

Morrissey couldn't quite let go of the reunion idea, however. Such was his determination to reward Smiths fans for their unwavering dedication that he drafted in Rourke, Joyce, along with a somewhat bemused Craig Gannon filling in for Marr, for his debut solo outing at Wolverhampton Civic Hall on Thursday, December 22, 1988. Needless to say, once news broke of the "unofficial Smiths farewell show" fans from all corners of the UK descended on Wolverhampton. An added bonus came with free admission being offered to those sporting Smiths or Morrissey T-shirts. However, with the Hall's capacity standing at just 1,700, only half of those gathered outside made it through the door.

The show was fundamentally Morrissey's solo live debut, but he cleverly sandwiched his solo material betwixt tracks from *Strangeways, Here We Come* – 'Stop Me If You Think You've Heard This One Before' and 'Death at One's Elbow' that hadn't been played live by The Smiths, of course, with 'Sweet and Tender Hooligan' serving as the encore. With stage invasions a plenty, it did indeed seem like the glory days of old.

Gannon's bemusement at his being invited to participate in the proceedings stemmed from the fact that his legal dispute for unpaid earnings against Morrissey (and Marr) was still ongoing. Even more bizarrely, he'd also worked with Morrissey in the recording studio on many of the solo songs featuring in the set-list that night (and would subsequently appear on the 1990 Morrissey compilation album, *Bona Drag*. Rourke and Joyce had also served as hired hands in the studio – with the three ex-Smiths collaborating on songs such as 'Interesting Drug', 'Such a Little Thing Makes Such a Big Difference', 'The Last of the Famous International Playboys', and 'Lucky Lisp'.

Morrissey no doubt viewed his munificence as a means of sustaining a healthy relationship with his erstwhile rhythm-section. What few people knew as the quartet took their final bow at the Wolverhampton Civil Hall, however, was that Morrissey (and Marr) was now ensnared in legal wranglings with Rourke and Joyce.

In his memoir, Morrissey says how he received a letter from Joyce's solicitors stating their client was intent on seeking "legal action in search of Smiths royalties" but was amenable to dropping his lawsuit should he be made a "permanent member of the Morrissey Band". With the exception of Stephen Street (bass), there was no "Morrissey Band" to speak of. Morrissey, therefore, saw Joyce's actions as little more than an empty threat and treated it accordingly. But Joyce's actions were far from hollow, however. Back in September 1987, he'd given the set of accounts he'd been holding onto from 1986 to a friend of his girlfriend's called Gill Smith who worked for an accountancy firm. Though only a junior accountant, Smith had little difficulty confirming that Joyce and Rourke were both receiving just 10 per cent of The Smiths' non-songwriting income.

Joyce's solicitors duly wrote to Rough Trade and Sire requesting they account for royalties based on 25 per cent, with copies of said letter being sent to Marr and Morrissey's London-based solicitors, Harbottle & Lewis. This was in accordance with the near-century-old Partnership Act of 1890, which stipulates that in the absence of an otherwise clear agreement, all partnerships are deemed equal. In other words, a partnership is defined in the Act as being the relation which subsists between persons carrying on a business in common with a view of making a profit. In turn, Harbottle & Lewis wrote to Joyce's solicitors informing them that their client, being deemed a "subsidiary member" of The Smiths, was in

fact only entitled to ten per cent of the band's non-songwriting income. The same, of course, applied to Rourke.

In *Set the Boy Free,* Marr argues that Joyce (and Rourke) had readily agreed to the 40:40:10:10 split back in 1983 during what he describes as being a "very emotional day at Pluto Studios." Joyce, unsurprisingly, begs to differ: He argues that while he might have agreed to a 10 per cent share that day at Pluto, no such proposal was ever put forward. He and Rourke had no truck with Marr and Morrissey each taking 40 per cent of the Smiths publishing – estimated at £3 – 4 million - as they'd written the songs. They just couldn't swallow the duo creaming the same amount in performance royalties. (Performance royalties are the fees music users pay when music is performed publicly. Music played over the radio, in a restaurant or bar, or via online services such as Spotify or Pandora is considered a public performance.)

Joyce v Morrissey & Others (case citation [1999] E.M.L.R. 233), would take some nine years to bring about a conclusion in the plaintiff's favour. Though Rourke was initially party to the litigation, the bassist soon lost heart and instead settled for an upfront payment of £83,000 "in full and final settlement" of outstanding income through to December 31, 1988, and a 10 per cent share of all future non-songwriting royalties. Though there were mitigating circumstances for his volte face, it was a decision he would come to regret. For when the case finally reached its conclusion at the High Court of Justice (Chancery Division) in November 1998, the judge found in Joyce's favour, ordering that he receive approximately £1 million in back-payments and 25 per cent henceforth.

Much to everyone's surprise, Morrissey elected to appeal the decision. Though he hadn't exactly covered himself in glory when taking the stand, going to far as to challenge the judge on occasion. Indeed, his combative attitude in the witness box lead the judge to subsequently describe the singer as being "devious, truculent and unreliable where his own interests were at stake." Morrissey viewed the judge's comments as an "unjust and scurrilous attack". The three appeal judges thought otherwise, however, and upheld the original ruling. His application for leave to appeal to the House of Lords was also refused.

Speaking with *The Guardian* in October 2016, Marr said that while Joyce was within his rights to bring his case to court, he still harked back to the supposed 40:40:10:10 verbal agreement. "Looking back, I would have done things differently," he went on. "I'd make sure you don't move a muscle without a contract –

> *"Being in a court room with three guys I'd spent five years with and for it to end up like that. It was difficult for us all."*

for everybody's benefit. Young people aren't good at doing that kind of thing, and we had to pay the price for it." Though admitting he would be more generous second time around, he remained adamant that The Smiths had never been "a band of equals".

Speaking with the same newspaper some two years on, Joyce expressed his remorse at his having to resort to seeking legal redress against his one-times friends and bandmates: "I regret that it had to happen [but] don't regret that I went through with it. I was hoping to have dealt with it prior to going into court, but that wasn't the case, unfortunately. But obviously I felt vindicated. Of course it hurt, being in a court room with three guys I'd spent

five years with and for it to end up like that. It was difficult for us all."

While Marr devotes several pages to the court case in *Set the Boy Free*, Morrissey, perhaps unsurprisingly, waxes lyrical on the subject for 50 pages or more in his own memoir. Joyce bears the sledgehammer brunt of his ire, but Marr also comes under fire for his failing to support him in the appeal.

Joyce's January 2018 interview with *The Guardian* wasn't due to it being 20 years since his high court victory, but rather because he, Rourke, and Gannon were coming together again under The Smiths standard some three decades on from their taking the stage with Morrissey at the Wolverhampton Civic Hall in December 1988. There was no Morrissey or Marr, of course, but the news that three-fifths of one of the most influential bands in British pop history were coming together with the Manchester Camerata Orchestra for a series of classical concerts reinterpreting the Smiths' hits nonetheless caused something of a stir.

With Rourke residing in New York (where he'd been collaborating with Dolores O'Riordan who would tragically die as a result of "accidental drowning in a bathtub, following sedation by alcohol intoxication" that same month), Joyce and Gannon got together in the basement of the drummer's Altrincham house a week or so prior to the announcement being made to jam through 'There Is a Light That Never Goes Out' and 'How Soon Is Now'. "It just sounded absolutely fantastic," Joyce told *The Guardian*. "And if it sounds that good with two of us ..."

Although a press release would quote Rourke as being "thrilled and excited" at the prospect of setting Smiths classics to symphonic strings, within hours of *The Guardian* going to press, the bassist underwent a change of heart issuing a second press statement in which he stated his participation in the tour had been "erroneously reported". He then went on to say that at no time had he given his consent "for anyone in connection with this Classically Smiths project" to act on his behalf or in name, and that nothing was ever confirmed, approved or contracted by himself or his representatives.

Rourke's publicly extracting himself from the project would bring about Joyce's own withdrawal. His press statement intimated he was already aware of Rourke's stance at the time of the press conference, which explains his and Gannon's attempts to skirt around the issue of the latter's involvement in subsequent interviews. "After much deliberation and soul-searching," the statement continued, "I have decided that without Andy, an integral part of why I agreed to take part in the first place, I have come to this difficult decision. I still believe the shows and concept to be a fantastic idea and wish them all the success they deserve."

Within days of Joyce's statement the Classically Smiths tour was cancelled – "with regret" – via Gannon's Facebook page. According to Gannon, he, Joyce, and Rourke had each confirmed their involvement during the autumn of 2017, but that Rourke's alleged last-minute withdrawal had come too late to amend the marketing materials. "It also meant that we were under obligation to go ahead with the press launch, which Mike and myself did, but were told we couldn't mention anything about the situation with Andy. That's unfortunate as the last thing we wanted was to mislead anyone."

There can be no true Smiths reunion without Morrissey or Marr, of course, and with their respective solo endeavours showing little indication of taking a downward turn anytime soon, the likelihood of said reunion remains as chimerical an illusion as ever.

That doesn't mean to say the two haven't discussed such a scenario. In September 2008, Marr and Morrissey met in a south Manchester pub, the first occasion they'd come to face-to-face since the court case. According to Marr, the conversation turning towards a Smiths

Photo by Andre Csillag.

reunion came totally out of the blue. "I didn't go there with that in mind, but there had been quite a few rumours about it so naturally we discussed it," he revealed. "'It could happen...' 'How d'you feel about it?' 'What if?' And off we went. I think we were both as keen as each other. It was great – a really nice meeting."

At the time of their get-together, Morrissey was busy recording his ninth studio album Marr was working with The Cribs on their fourth album, *Ignore the Ignorant*, but the two parted company at the end of the evening with the notion of a Smiths reunion very much alive. So much so, in fact, that they continued weighing up the pros and cons during several lengthy phone conversations. However, when Marr headed off on tour with The Cribs in support of the new album soon into 2009 he didn't hear from Morrissey again.

On being asked the all-important question as to whether his and Morrissey's friendship could be rekindled, Marr opted for diplomacy: "I think it's run its course. I don't feel unfriendly in any way towards Morrissey – there's just no need for it. One of the things we had in common was that we lived for work, and we're too busy doing what we're doing now."

And what better place to leave things . . .

"NME scribe Nick Kent proclaimed The Smiths to be the greatest rock band of the Eighties because they 'seemed to function on sixteen cylinders when everybody was tootling on four.'"

JOHNNY MARR

PART TWO

THE SMITHS DISCOGRAPHY

STUDIO ALBUMS

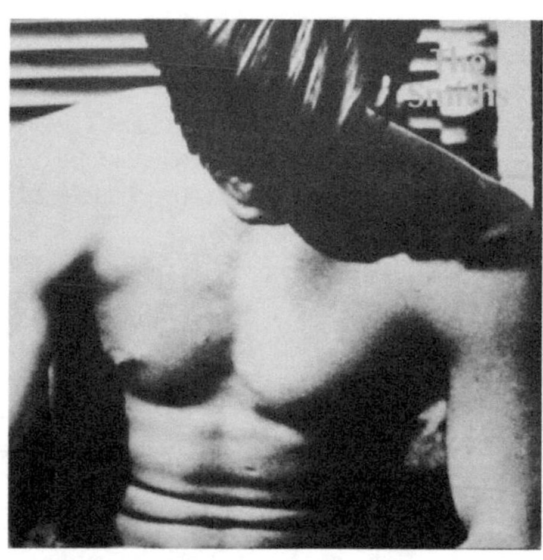

THE SMITHS

Highest Chart Position: UK #2; US #150
UK, Rough Trade, February 20, 1984; US, Sire Records, April 1984.

Reel Around the Fountain / You've Got Everything Now / Miserable Lie / Pretty Girls Make Graves / The Hand That Rocks the Cradle / Still Ill / Hand in Glove / What Difference Does It Make? / I Don't Owe You Anything / Suffer Little Children

Despite 'Hand in Glove' and 'This Charming Man' both having failed to crack the UK Top 20, the media buzz surrounding The Smiths over the winter of 1983 grew to such a crescendo there was a very realistic sense of "overkill" by the time the band's eponymous debut album hit the record shops in late-February 1984. Morrissey's doleful lyrics and falsetto wailings weren't everyone's cup of tea, of course, but Marr's Rickenbacker riffs nonetheless gave the songs a poetic majesty that elevated *The Smiths* above the generic pap clogging up the charts and airwaves during the early-to-mid-eighties. Indeed, it's been suggested Morrissey forwarded the proposal to Marr that they opt for a bland name such as The Smiths so as to separate themselves from exotically-named acts of the day such as Teardrop Explodes, Spandau Ballet, A Flock Of Seagulls, and Orchestral Manoeuvres in the Dark. It's also worth pointing out, however, that Fred Smith, Fred "Sonic" Smith, and the latter's then punk poet spouse, Patti Smith, had all featured to varying degrees in Morrissey's musical education.

The Smiths' debut is the album most associated with what's since come to be regarded as the band's "signature sound". Somewhat remarkably, there are virtually no audible guitar solos on any Smiths records. Instead, Marr opts to show his virtuosity by working up a different sound and technique for nearly every song within the band's repertoire. If formulating a trademark sound was Marr's remit, then Morrissey's half of their Faustian pact, of course, undoubtedly came in calling upon his consummate English wit to craft lyrics that were evocative and enigmatic in equal measure.

Marr and Morrissey had already proved they knew a thing or two about crafting the consummate pop single, and yet conversely they choose to lead off *The Smiths* with 'Reel Around the Fountain', a meandering, six-minute elegy which sees Morrissey purportedly alluding to child abuse was a particularly audacious move; his low vocal floating over Marr's haunting riff serves to give the song an even more morose feel. Then again, *The Smiths* was peppered with couplets alluding to wicked goings on involving adults and children - most notably with the album closer "Suffer Little Children".

The pace cranks up a notch or three on occasion with tracks such as 'You've Got Everything Now','Still Ill', 'Hand in Glove', and 'What Difference Does It Make?', but it's the mournful lyrics that people have come to associate with The Smiths – and Morrissey in particular – but nobody conveys misery in song, of course, quite like Mozzer.

Despite Rough Trade's limited budget, and an overall lack of daytime radio play, *The Smiths* entered the UK album chart at #2 – an unprecedented achievement. Whether the album would have toppled the Thompson Twins' *Into the Gap* from the top slot had The Smiths been signed to a major is a moot point. Equally debatable, of course, is whether *The Smiths* suffered as a result of the entire album being re-recorded from scratch once John Porter replaced Troy Tate in the producer's chair? Both band and record label were dissatisfied with Tate's efforts, but was there really any need to record the album a second time? Especially given Porter's insistence on constructing each track around a Johnny Marr arpeggio regardless of whether they benefited the song or not.

Morrissey is on record stating his disillusion with Porter's version, but, then again, his mistrust of the one-time Roxy Music man extended far beyond *The Smiths*. With the advantage of hindsight it would surely have made sense to let Porter have free reign with the Tate masters until reaching a level of production that everybody was happy with. With many of tracks on *The Smiths* having been recorded with the emotion they reserved for John Peel; the evidence of the album's production shortcomings was there for all to see.

Though ultimately less than the sum of its parts, *The Smiths* is nonetheless a terrific debut from a band that was still finding its feet in the recording studio. It's not The Smiths as the world come to know them, yet their aesthetic is already wholly formed; the albums sexual candour, and situational uncertainty merely a reaction against the early-to-mid-eighties pop landscape. And hands up who assumed the topless guy adorning the front cover was Fergal Sharkey?

MEAT IS MURDER

Highest Chart Position: UK #1; US #110
UK, Rough Trade, February 11, 1985; US, Sire Records, February 1985.

The Headmaster Ritual / Rusholme Ruffians / I Want the One I Can't Have / What She Said / That Joke Isn't Funny Anymore / Nowhere Fast / Well I Wonder / Barbarism Begins at Home / Meat Is Murder

By the time The Smiths headed into Amazon Studios in Kirkby (situated some six miles to the north-east of Liverpool city centre) to begin work on their highly-anticipated second album, Morrissey was already being lauded as the spokesman of his generation. Punk had primarily been about personal politics, but by the mid-eighties bands were picking up the

> *"People still seem to believe that meat is a particular substance not at all connected to animals playing in the field."*

protest cudgels left over from the sixties and making records that prodded the listener into awareness of whatever issues close to their own heart. Bono was still some way from having audiences with the pope, but U2 were writing songs about the then ongoing Troubles in Northern Ireland; Billy Bragg was railing against Thatcherism, while Bob Geldof was gearing himself up for his one-man crusade against famine in Ethiopia. The cause closest to Morrissey's heart was animal rights, of course. He'd been a vegetarian since the age of 11. Marr's girlfriend – and future wife – Angie also happened to be vegetarian, but the guitarist himself was a card-carrying meat-eater. The moment Morrissey suggested calling the new album *Meat Is Murder*, however, he readily turned a lettuce leaf and gave up meat in a show of solidarity for his song-writing partner. Speaking with the *NME* in December 1984, Morrissey said that of all the political topics open to scrutiny, people were "disturbingly vague" about the treatment of animals. "People still seem to believe that meat is a particular substance not at all connected to animals playing in the field," he continued. "People don't realise how gruesomely and frighteningly the animal gets to the plate."

What gave The Smiths the capacity to change people's thinking was their songs speaking about real issues with a sincerity early-to-mid-eighties pop tended to shy away from. They weren't interested in providing escapist entertainment – the characters Morrissey wrote about were possessed of traits you recognised in yourself and those around you. Who didn't have the name of the teacher who'd made their schooldays a misery etched on their brain? ('The Headmaster Ritual'), had run with a gang ('Rusholme Ruffians'), or knew someone suffering physical abuse at the hands of a slap-happy parent? ('Barbarism Begins at Home')

That isn't to say *Meat Is Murder* is devoid of humour, of course, as the lyrics to songs such as 'Shakespeare's Sister' and 'What She Said' readily testify. Marr's fascination with opting for off-key chords isn't merely to provoke attention but also to raise a smile.

The Smiths had narrowly missed out on giving The Smiths a number one album at the first time of asking, yet their dissatisfaction with the production on the debut had left a sour taste in the mouth. So much so, the band decided they would produce the new album themselves with Stephen Street helping out with the engineering. To put it more succinctly, Morrissey, Rourke, and Joyce were content to let Marr don the producer's cap. This was a bold move that could have so easily blown up in their faces.

Whatever blame the band attached to John Porter's production on The Smiths, his subsequent work on stand-alone singles

such as 'Heaven Knows I'm Miserable Now', 'William, It Was Really Nothing', and 'How Soon Is Now?' should have gone some way to making amends. Marr is on record saying he'd have been happy having Porter installed as producer every time The Smiths entered a studio, so his removal was obviously at Morrissey's behest. In an attempt to bring Morrissey round, the hapless Porter had invited the singer to his home for a lavish vegetarian feast. Morrissey not only failed to show on the night, he didn't even have the decency to let his hosts know he wouldn't be coming.

Geoff Travis certainly deserves credit for according The Smiths free rein with the new album. It's one thing to allow a band creative control, but few label bosses would have countenanced letting their charges twiddle and diddle to their hearts content.

Producing the album in-house was to prove inspired, of course. For what Marr and Morrissey may have lacked in studio experience they more than made up for in self-belief and an unshakable assuredness in what they were doing, and how the songs should sound. "The whole idea was to control it totally," Morrissey would opine. "Without a producer, things were better. We saw things clearer." The 24-year-old Street's involvement with The Smiths up to this juncture consisted solely of his engineering credit on 'Heaven Knows I'm Miserable Now', but his hiring was to prove another inspired decision.

Working without an established producer allowed Marr to follow his instincts free from having said instincts second-guessed. The guitarist also remembers the sessions being harmonious affairs with no arguments or disagreement about the direction the album was taking.

Meat Is Murder entered the UK album chart at #1 following its February 1985 release, and yet both its attendant single 'Barbarism Begins at Home' and 'That Joke Isn't Funny Anymore' surprisingly failed to crack the Top 30. Indeed 'That Joke Isn't Funny Anymore' just about scraped into the Top 50

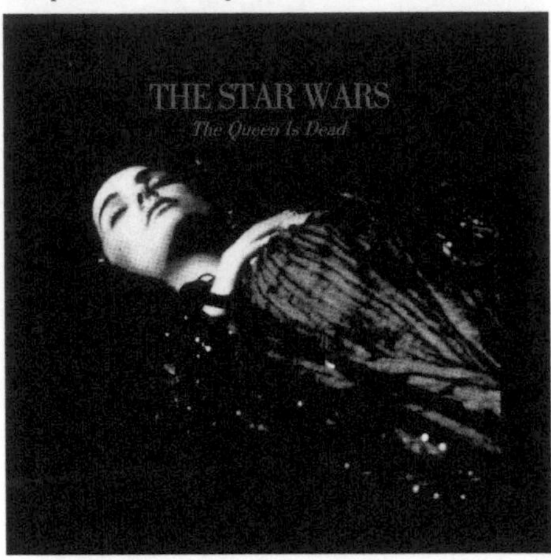

THE QUEEN IS DEAD

Highest Chart Position: UK #2; US #70
UK, Rough Trade, June 16, 1986; US, Sire Records, June 16, 1986.

The Queen Is Dead / Frankly, Mr Shankly / I Know It's Over / Never Had No One Ever / Cemetry Gates / Bigmouth Strikes Again / The Boy with the Thorn in His Side / Vicar in a Tutu / There Is a Light That Never Goes Out / Some Girls are Bigger Than Others

The Queen Is Dead has come to be regarded amongst Smiths aficionados as being the best of the band's four studio albums. Indeed, the *NME* would go so far as to proclaim it the greatest album of all time in 2013. Setting such obvious hyperbole aside, *The Queen Is Dead* did indeed see Morrissey and Marr at the zenith of their creativity. The Smiths may have avoided succumbing to the fabled "second album syndrome" with consummate ease yet would have entered Amazon Studios in the late-autumn of 1985 only too aware that it's any band or solo artist's third album that is viewed as being the music industry yardstick for longevity. Think Primal Scream (*Screamadelica*), Blur (*Parklife*), Radiohead (*OK Computer*), and of course, The Clash (*London*

Calling).

Britain's morality metronome had clearly altered tempo since the Sex Pistols' 'God Save the Queen' caused such outrage during the summer of 1977. As John Lydon has repeatedly pointed out over the years, 'God Save the Queen' was a sonic assault on the British Establishment rather than Queen Elizabeth II, and it's worth remembering the song was originally called "No Future". Penning a song with such an incendiary title as 'The Queen Is Dead' was risky enough in itself, but then utilising it as the title for the new album was courting controversy. When asked to explain his reasoning behind the song around the time of the album's release, Morrissey said that the "old queen" in the lyric was actually himself before going on to admit the song was a "kind of general observation on the state of the nation." The reference to Charles craving "to appear on the front of the *Daily Mail* in [his] mother's bridal veil leaves little to the imagination, however.

Marr was also of the opinion the album would "undoubtedly shock a lot of people", but he was referring to its musicality. Speaking to the *Melody Maker* the previous summer, the guitarist gave forewarning to Smiths fans that the songs he and Morrissey were working on for the album were "very much in the R & B groove," but would nonetheless be a "move away from the old jingly-jangly guitars of old."

It's now 33 years and counting since the release of *The Queen Is Dead*, and yet the album sounds no less fresh and exciting – from the lead track's raucous Max Miller-esque sing-along intro through to the closing refrain of 'Some Girls Are Bigger Than Others', The Smiths do indeed break new ground while retaining their distinctive identity throughout. Marr weaves an intricate web of guitar lines, deftly alternating from acoustic pop ('Cemetry Gates'), melancholic lilt ('I Know It's Over' and 'There Is a Light That Never Goes Out') and faux rockabilly romp ('Vicar in a Tutu').

What tends to get overlooked when people reminisce about The Smiths' brilliance, is that while Marr's fretwork and Morrissey's seemingly-effortless ease at turning a phrase were deserving of every accolade that came their way, it was Rourke and Joyce's rhythmic musicianship that got those same people off their arses and onto the dance floor.

'Frankly, Mr Shankly' isn't an ode to Liverpool FC's dour-faced manager, Bill (and how could it possibly be with all four Smiths being dyed-in-the-wool Mancunians), but rather a thinly-veiled attack on Geoff Travis. Rough Trade's head honcho has since acknowledged as much. Speaking with *Mojo* in April 2011, Travis said how he'd viewed

> *"A move away from the old jingly-jangly guitars of old."*

the lyric as part of Morrissey's burning desire to remove The Smiths from Rough Trade's clutches. And they almost made it as well.

It's solely my personal observation, of course, but if there is a weak link on *The Queen Is Dead* then it's the album closer 'Some Girls Are Bigger Than Others'. For although it's indeed true that the female form comes in all shapes and sizes, it was nonetheless an observation best kept for pub banter – and was certainly beneath a songsmith of his calibre. Speaking with the *NME*, Morrissey muddied the waters of his sexuality by saying how the whole idea of womanhood was something that had passed him by, and that his having "scuttled through 26 years of life without ever noticing that the contours of the body are different is an outrageous farce" Marr certainly thought the highlighting of the vagaries of the female form an unconventional theme to set to music, but then again, has

there been an artist less conventional than Morrissey? It's just as Joyce succinctly observed: Only Morrissey could get away with lyrics centring around vegetarianism, sexism, and children being murdered.

And it's interesting to note that 'Some Girls Are Bigger Than Others' received just the one live airing – at what proved to be The Smiths' final show at the Brixton Academy on December 12, 1986.

THE QUEEN IS DEAD 2017 COLLECTOR'S EDITION:

(Disc One) The Queen Is Dead / Frankly, Mr. Shankly / I Know It's Over / Never Had No One Ever / Cemetry Gates / Bigmouth Strikes Again / The Boy with the Thorn in His Side / Vicar in a Tutu / There Is a Light That Never Goes Out / Some Girls Are Bigger Than Others

(Disc Two) The Queen Is Dead (full version) / Frankly, Mr. Shankly (demo) / I Know It's Over (demo) / Never Had No One Ever (demo) / Cemetry Gates (demo) /Bigmouth Strikes Again (demo / Some Girls Are Bigger Than Others (demo) / The Boy with the Thorn in His Side (demo) / There Is a Light That Never Goes Out (outtake) / Rubber Ring / Asleep / Money Changes Everything / Unloveable

(Disc Three) Live in Boston (Great Woods Amphitheatre – 5 August 1986): How Soon Is Now? / Hand in Glove / I Want the One I Can't Have / Never Had No One Ever / Stretch Out and Wait / The Boy with the Thorn in His Side / Cemetry Gates / Rubber Ring / What She Said / Rubber Ring / Is It Really So Strange? / There Is a Light That Never Goes Out / That Joke Isn't Funny Anymore /The Queen Is Dead / I Know It's Over

(Disc Four) DVD: The Queen Is Dead – A Film by Derek Jarman / The Queen Is Dead / There Is a Light That Never Goes Out / Panic

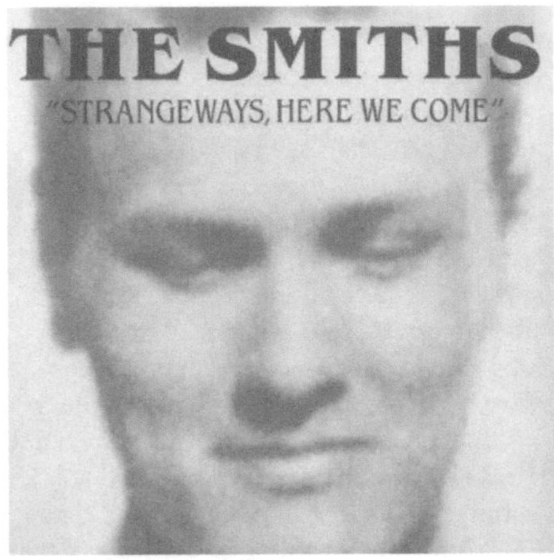

STRANGEWAYS, HERE WE COME

Highest Chart Position: UK #2; US #55
UK, Rough Trade, September 28, 1987;
US, Sire Records, September 28, 1987.

A Rush and a Push and the Land Is Ours / I Started Something I Couldn't Finish / Death of a Disco Dancer / Girlfriend in a Coma / Stop Me If You Think You've Heard This One Before / Last Night I Dreamt That Somebody Loved Me / Unhappy Birthday / Paint a Vulgar Picture / Death at One's Elbow / I Won't Share You

While Marr and Morrissey offer differing – and oft-contradictory – accounts as to what brought about a parting of the ways in their respective memoirs, and yet the one-time musical soulmates both readily cite *Strangeways, Here we Come* as The Smiths' finest hour – or finest 37 or so minutes to be precise. This, perhaps, is only to be expected. To say otherwise would suggest The Smiths were on a downward trajectory at the time of the rift.

Morrissey even goes so far as to proclaim the album a "masterpiece, with everything in its perfect place." Though rather less effusive in *Set the Boy Free*, Marr nonetheless talks favourably about the album elsewhere. During a Q & A with *www.theartsdesk.com* in August 2013, he said that Strangeways . . . was always his favourite Smiths album, if only because he'd succeeded in capturing the atmosphere while leaving space to allow other elements to breathe. "The production doesn't have tons of overdubs, and the songs breathe a little bit, and it has a slightly unresolved atmosphere. There is space in it, and that was a conscious thing. I knew that the record was good at that time."

Another reason for swimming against the tide with their continuing affection for *Strangeways . . .* over *The Queen Is Dead*, of course, is that it presents The Smiths at their least jingly-jangly. "Every combination of chords has been done, but Johnny somehow manages the most imaginative bursts of sound on these final sessions, and the three other Smiths follow," Morrissey gushes in *Autobiography*. Marr readily admits to his having an agenda upon arriving at the Wool Hall, and the "most imaginative bursts of sound" Morrissey alludes to were in the main due to his burning desire to shake things up. And this is evident from the get-go as 'A Rush and A Push and This Land Is Ours' hasn't got a single guitar part in the mix.

"Every combination of chords has been done, but Johnny somehow manages the most imaginative bursts of sound on these final sessions, and the three other Smiths follow."

Speaking with the *Melody Maker* around the time of the album's release in September 1987, Morrissey said how *Strangeways . . .* perfected every lyrical and musical notion The Smiths had ever had. "It isn't dramatically, obsessively different in any way and I'm quite glad it isn't because I've been happy with the structure we've had until now. It's far and away the best record we've ever made. I expect when the dust has settled after *Strangeways . . .* there will have to be some degree of rethinking, because we can't go on forever in our present form. Inevitably certain aspects of the band would become tarnished, so a slight readjustment will have to be made. I think now is absolutely the right time to do it. When something becomes too easy and it's all laid out for you, one is robbed of the joy of achievement. When there's no need to fight any more, it'll be time to pull up the shutters on the Smiths."

Marr, of course, had already pulled the shutters down on The Smiths by the time of "Every combination of chords has been done, but Johnny somehow manages the most imaginative bursts of sound on these final sessions, and the three other Smiths follow."Morrissey's aforementioned *MM* interview, which suggests he was still hoping for a reconciliation. The dust has long-since settled on The Smiths, of course, and listening to *Strangeways . . .* some three decades on, one can appreciate Morrissey and Marr's drive and determination to craft a subtly-shaded album that would stand the test of time.

Given Morrissey's penchant for penning angst-ridden vignettes, it comes as no surprise to find *Strangeways . . .* peppered with recurring themes of death, separation, and unrequited love set to Marr's sublime melodies – 'I Won't Share You', 'Death at One's Elbow', 'Unhappy Birthday,' and 'Paint a Vulgar Picture'. But then again, love, sex, and death are constants in many an artist's canon.

Just as he had with 'Frankly, Mr Shankly" on *The Queen Is Dead*, Rough Trade and Geoff Travis come under fire in 'Paint a Vulgar Picture', a rancorous assault on the label's exploitation of the band's success. Morrissey would assure us that was impossible for any record company to get the better of him, and yet he practically wet himself at the prospect of shackling The Smiths to the faceless and utterly nonconforming EMI. Whether The Smiths would have thrived in such hothouse conditions is, alas, a matter of conjecture.

There's also been plenty of speculation over the years as to the hidden meaning behind the lyric to the album's closing track,'I Won't Share You'. Was this a caustic missive subliminally aimed at Marr over his recent Rickenbacker-for-hire dalliances with Bryan Ferry and Talking Heads? Although the song's protagonist is clearly female, Rourke has always believed Morrissey was committing his frustrations over Marr's wanderlust to verse.

Joyce has admitted the lyric's poignancy reduced him to tears in the studio. Marr, however, remains ambivalent as to the song's meaning: "The lyrics were brought to my attention by somebody before we got out of the studio. There were raised eyebrows and, 'Whaddya think of that, then?' But it was all in a day's work for me really, still is. If that sentiment was directed towards me, then I feel quite good about it. It's nice."

LIVE ALBUMS

RANK

Highest Chart Position: UK #2; US #77
UK, Rough Trade, September 5, 1988; US, Sire Records, September 5, 1988

Intro: "Montagues and Capulets": Philadelphia Orchestra) / The Queen Is Dead / Panic / Vicar in a Tutu / Ask / Rusholme Ruffians/(Marie's the Name)/ His Latest Flame / The Boy with the Thorn in His Side / What She Said / Rubber Ring / Is It Really So Strange? / Cemetry Gates / London / I Know It's Over / The Draize Train / Still Ill / Bigmouth Strikes Again
Exitus: "You'll Never Walk Alone": Shirley Bassey)

Several bootleg recordings of The Smiths' October 23, 1986 outing at the National Ballroom in Kilburn (of varying sound quality) had long been doing the rounds by the time Rough Trade decided upon releasing it as a live album so as to fulfil the band's contractual obligations. Live albums can prove hit-and-miss affairs, of course, but with the BBC having recorded the Kilburn show for transmission, Rough Trade could rest assured as to the sound quality – regardless of Morrissey's conjuring up ever-more bizarre animal-like noises to mask his near-breathless vocal throughout the performance.

With The Smiths being an augmented five-

piece at the time of the Kilburn show, *Rank* captures the band at their rockiest with Craig Gannon aiding and abetting Marr in a twin guitar attack through an adrenaline infused 20-song-set featuring crowd-pleasures 'The Queen Is Dead', 'Panic', 'How Soon Is Now?' and 'Bigmouth Strikes Again', through to less familiar numbers 'London' and 'The Draize Train'. Rather than release the entire show, which has a running time of around 82 minutes, however, Morrissey (with Marr's tacit approval) pared down the track-listing to 14 songs. (The omitted tracks being: 'I Want the One I Can't Have','There Is a Light That Never Goes Out', 'Frankly, Mr Shankly', 'Never Had No One Ever','Meat Is Murder', and 'How Soon Is Now?')

> *"He had little doubt that Rank would top the UK album charts."*

It's fair to say the vast majority of those that rushed out to grab a copy of *Rank* on release day had one or two ticket stubs tucked away in a drawer from when The Smiths had swung by their respective cities and towns. For those that had missed out, the artwork featured a photo of fans frenziedly jostling for a piece of Morrissey's shirt at Manchester's G-Mex on 19 July 1986. The photo adorning the album's front cover is of sultry British actress, Alexandra Bastedo, lifted from John D. Green's 1967 tome *Birds Of Britain*. Bastedo is best known for her role as secret agent Sharron Macready in ITV's late-sixties espionage/science-fiction series, *The Champions*. Morrissey's fascination with Bastedo no doubt stems from her being a vegetarian and animal welfare advocate.

Rank was never intended as a contender for all-time best Smiths album, of course. It was simply a contractual means to an end. Indeed, with all the protagonists talking about The Smiths in the past tense by the time of its release in early September 1988, the album has an almost eulogistic feel rather than one of celebration. Having said that, *Rank* nonetheless serves as a fascinating testament to a band at the top of their game – even if said game was deep into the second half and rapidly approaching denouement with no hope of extra-time or penalties. Marr's wah-wah-meets-feedback smeared riff into to 'The Queen Is Dead' propels the listener headlong into the pandemonium that was The Smiths live experience.

'The Draize Train' served to provide Morrissey a much-needed breather in readiness for the encores, but why he would favour an instrumental interlude over heart-rending versions of 'There Is a Light That Never Goes Out' or 'How Soon Is Now?' is anyone's guess.

When reviewing the album for *The Catalogue*, one-time *NME* scribe Nick Kent proclaimed The Smiths to be the greatest rock band of the Eighties because they "seemed to function on 16 cylinders when everybody was tootling along on four." He had little doubt that *Rank* would top the UK album charts and was also happy to wager the album would succeed where previous Smiths offerings had failed in finally breaking them in the US if only because at the time he was penning his missive there was nothing musically in the air to remotely threaten the album's worth.

Neither prediction would come to pass, of course, but as live albums go, *Rank* can still hold its head high.

COMPILATION ALBUMS

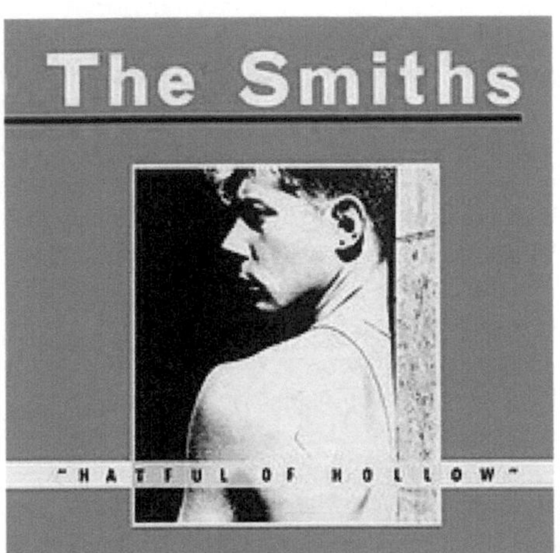

HATFUL OF HOLLOW

Highest Chart Position: UK # 7
UK, Rough Trade, November 12, 1984; US, Sire, November 9, 1993

William, It Was Really Nothing / What Difference Does It Make? (Peel session 31/5/83) / These Things Take Time (Jensen session 4/7/83) / This Charming Man (Peel session 21/9/83) / How Soon Is Now? / Handsome Devil (Peel session 31/5/83) / Hand In Glove / Still Ill (Peel session 21/9/83) / Heaven Knows I'm Miserable Now / This Night Has Opened My Eyes (Peel session 21/9/83) / You've Got Everything Now (Jensen session 4/7/83) / Accept Yourself (Jensen session 5/9/83) / Girl Afraid / Back To The Old House (Peel session 21/9/83) / Reel Around The Fountain (Peel session 31/5/83) / Please, Please, Please, Let Me Get What I Want

It was unheard of for a band to release a compilation album within nine months of their debut album but *Hatful of Hollow* is so much more than the hastily thrown-together assortment of Radio One sessions interspliced with the A and B-sides to 'William, It Was Really Nothing', and 'Heaven Knows I'm Miserable Now'. It was to prove something of a masterstroke on Morrissey's part as *Hatful of Hollow* served to silence the naysayers that were beginning to question whether The Smiths could live up to the hype. Indeed, it could be argued that *Hatful . . . is* The Smiths' true debut in all but name.

Concerned about the "flatness" of the debut album, Morrissey approached Geoff Travis of releasing the BBC session tracks as an interim collection that would hopefully "detain those scared off by the blunted thud" of the band's debut. "We wanted it released on purely selfish terms because we liked all those tracks and those versions," he told *Jamming* magazine around the time of the album's release. "I wanted to present those songs again in the most flattering form. Those sessions almost caught the very heart of what we did - there was something positively messy about them, which was very positive. People are so nervous and desperate when they do those sessions, so it seems to bring the best out of them."

Smiths fans up and down the country had been left bemused by the radio session versions sounding infinitely more alluring than they do on *The Smiths*, with many of them venting their frustrations via fan mail. "A good portion of our [fan] mail contains imploring demands that we release versions of our songs that we recorded for Radio One sessions," Morrissey explained in another interview at this time. "The band and I suddenly realised that we hadn't even proper-sounding tapes of them ourselves - except for a few dire bootlegs that we bought at our concerts. As far as we're concerned, those were the sessions that got us

excited in the first place, and apparently it was how a lot of other people discovered us also. We decided to include the extra tracks from our 12inch singles for people who didn't have all of those, and to make it completely affordable."

Marr had also come to realise that some of the versions of the songs on *The Smiths* weren't as good as the Radio One sessions yet was initially unsure as to the validity of *Hatful Of Hollow* during a January 1997 interview with *Guitar* magazine. "Although the radio sessions were great, I was keen for them to remain just being that. In hindsight, I realised there were certain tracks - particularly 'Handsome Devil' - that had something the produced version just didn't. It's a very valid record."

Indeed, it is as the radio session tracks on *Hatful*... have a spark found wanting in *The Smiths*, with 'Hand in Glove', 'Reel Around the Fountain', and 'What Difference Does It Make?' suddenly resembling the live crowd-pleasers that had won them so many plaudits. *And Hatful*..., of course, also contains the first appearance of what many Smiths aficionados believe to be the band's finest moment, 'How Soon Is Now?'

THE WORLD WON'T LISTEN

Highest Chart Position: UK # 2

UK, Rough Trade, February 23, 1987

Panic / Ask (Remix) / London / Bigmouth Strikes Again / Shakespeare's Sister / There Is a Light That Never Goes Out / Shoplifters of the World Unite / The Boy with the Thorn in His Side / Money Changes Everything / Asleep / Unloveable / Half a Person / Stretch Out and Wait / That Joke Isn't Funny Anymore / Oscillate Wildly / You Just Haven't Earned It Yet, Baby / Rubber Ring

Compilation albums are by and large viewed as being little more than a record label's attempt to cash in on an act's popularity. The Smiths determination to give their fans added bang for their buck by continually releasing non-album singles would spare both themselves and Rough Trade from such accusatory indignation, however. *The World Won't Listen* (the title apparently reflecting Morrissey's mounting frustration to the lack of interest The Smiths were garnering amongst the general record-buying public and mainstream radio) was conceived as a collection of the band's singles and attendant B-sides from 1985 to 1987. Aside from the original Drone Studios version of 'The Boy with the Thorn in His Side' (sans synth strings), an alternate version of 'Stretch Out and Wait', and an edited version of 'That Joke Isn't Funny Anymore', the track-listing also included the aborted single, 'You Just Haven't Earned It Yet, Baby', and the near-single 'There Is a Light That Never Goes Out' were also included.

The British Phonographic Industry's anti-copyright infringement campaign was in full swing while The Smiths were in their pomp, and the dust sleeves of their albums most likely bore the slogan "Home Taping Is Killing Music" (replete with a cassette-shaped skull and crossbones). As such, the cassette versions of *The World Won't Listen* included Marr's atmospheric instrumental 'Money Changes Everything'.

The World Won't Listen was a worthy sequel to *Hatful of Hollow* and proved a hit with the fans. Surprisingly, however, the album would come in for criticism at the hands of certain music journos – one going so far as to dismiss it as being "Inessential". Morrissey was also believed to be unhappy about the project. The Smiths were in the studio recording *Strangeways, Here We Come*, and the delicious irony of The Smiths running through ;'Paint a Vulgar Picture' and Morrissey singing "reissue, reissue, repackage, repackage — extra bonus track!" – while Rough Trade were doing that very thing.

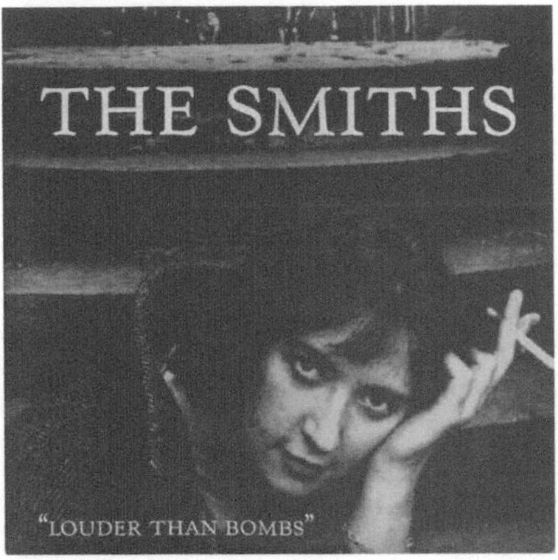

LOUDER THAN BOMBS

US, Sire Records, March 30, 1987; UK, Rough Trade, May 1987

Is It Really So Strange? (John Peel session, 12/2/86) / Sheila Take a Bow / Shoplifters of the World Unite / Sweet and Tender Hooligan (John Peel session, 12/2/86) / Half a Person / London / Panic / Girl Afraid / Shakespeare's Sister / William, It Was Really Nothing / You Just Haven't Earned It Yet, Baby / Heaven Knows I'm Miserable Now / Ask / Golden Lights / Oscillate Wildly / These Things Take Time / Rubber Ring / Back to the Old House / Hand in Glove / Stretch Out and Wait / Please, Please, Please, Let Me Get What I Want / This Night Has Opened My Eyes (John Peel session, 9/14/83) / Unloveable / Asleep

Sire had been issuing Smiths product in the US from the band's debut album onwards yet *Louder Than Bombs* was the first – and indeed, only - album the label would release under its own volition. Borrowing a line from Elizabeth Smart's poem, *By Grand Central Station I Sat Down and Wept, Louder Than Bombs* was a 24-track double album intended as a US-only counterpart to *The World Won't Listen*. The album consisted of all the singles (and the majority of the attendant B-sides) that as yet remained unreleased in the US, as well as a few tracks from *Hatful of Hollow* which also remained unreleased in the US.

The front cover features a photograph of Morrissey's beloved Shelagh Delaney, the Salford-born dramatist and screenwriter whose May 1958 literary debut, *A Taste of Honey*, would provide the inspiration behind many of his early lyrics. (The photo of the then 22-year-old Delaney was originally published in the October 21, 1961 edition of the long-defunct US magazine, *The Saturday Evening Post*).

As is previously mentioned elsewhere in the book, Sire believed having a promo video of The Smiths on heavy rotation on MTV's *120 Minutes* as well as the music station's regular daytime playlist would expose The Smiths to a wider demographic, which, in turn, would help secure *Louder Than Bombs* a higher placing on the *Billboard* 200. Morrissey's histrionics over Ken Friedman's appointment as the band's manager would put paid to Sire's aspirations, of course, and as a result the album would reach no higher than #62 on the *Billboard* chart. The clamour for import copies of *Louder Than Bombs* amongst the band's UK fan base would result in Rough Trade subsequently releasing the album domestically where it would peak at # 38.

Reflecting on the album with *Guitar Player* magazine in January 1990, Marr said that while it had been his and Morrissey's love of the classic 7inch pop format that had brought them together, because singles culture was largely ineffectual in the US compared to the UK, a "huge facet of what we were about was missed out on but I thought *Louder Than Bombs* was great."

SUBSEQUENT COMPILATION ALBUMS

BEST... 1

WEA. Released 17 August 1992. UK
Peak UK Chart Position: 1,.No. 139 (US)

This Charming Man / William, It Was Really Nothing / What Difference Does It Make? / Stop Me If You Think You've Heard This One Before / Girlfriend in a Coma /Half a Person / Rubber Ring / How Soon Is Now? / Hand in Glove / Shoplifters of the World Unite / Sheila Take a Bow / Some Girls Are Bigger Than Others / Panic / Please, Please, Please, Let Me Get What I Want

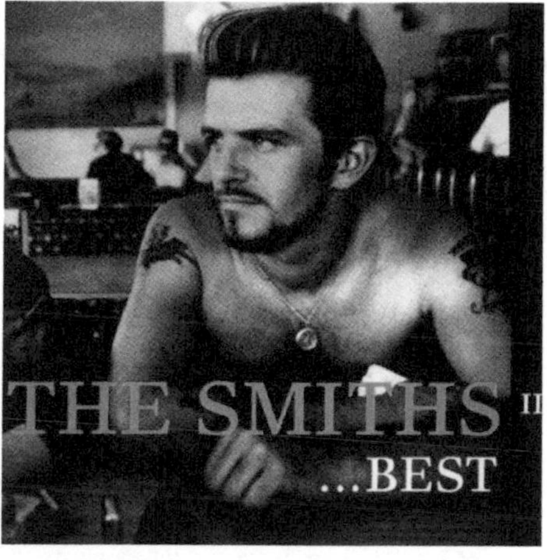

...BEST II

WEA. Released 2 November 1992. UK
Peak UK Chart Position: 29

The Boy with the Thorn in His Side / The Headmaster Ritual / Heaven Knows I'm Miserable Now / Ask /Oscillate Wildly / Nowhere Fast / Still Ill / Bigmouth Strikes Again / That Joke Isn't Funny Anymore /Shakespeare's Sister / Girl Afraid / Heaven Knows I'm Miserable Now / Reel Around the Fountain / Last Night I Dreamt That Somebody Loved Me / There Is a Light That Never Goes Out

THE SMITHS

SINGLES

Warner Music Group. Released 20 February 1995. UK
Peak UK Chart Position: 5

Hand in Glove/This Charming Man/What Difference Does It Make?/Heaven Knows I'm Miserable Now/William, It Was Really Nothing/How Soon Is Now?/Shakespeare's Sister/That Joke Isn't Funny Anymore/The Boy with the Thorn in His Side/Bigmouth Strikes Again/Panic/Ask/Shoplifters of the World Unite/Sheila Take a Bow/Girlfriend in a Coma/I Started Something I Couldn't Finish/Last Night I Dreamt That Somebody Loved Me/There Is a Light That Never Goes Out

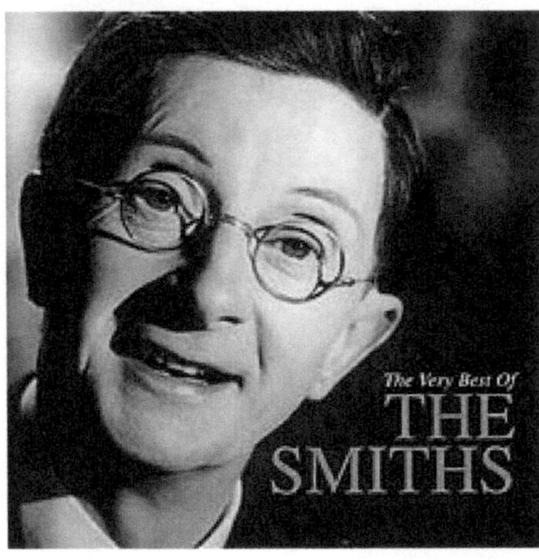

THE VERY BEST OF THE SMITHS

WEA. Released 4 June 2001. UK
Peak UK Chart Position: 30

Hand in Glove/This Charming Man/What Difference Does It Make?/Heaven Knows I'm Miserable Now/William, It Was Really Nothing/How Soon Is Now?/Shakespeare's Sister/That Joke Isn't Funny Anymore/The Boy with the Thorn in His Side/Bigmouth Strikes Again/Panic/Ask/Shoplifters of the World Unite/Sheila Take a Bow/Girlfriend in a Coma/I Started Something I Couldn't Finish/Last Night I Dreamt That Somebody Loved Me/There Is a Light That Never Goes Out

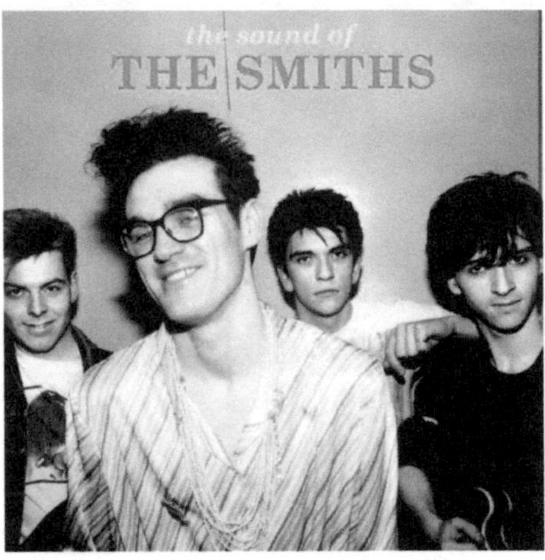

THE SOUND OF THE SMITHS

Rhino Records. Released 10 November 2008. UK
Peak UK Chart Position: 21. No. 98 (US)

(CD 1): Hand in Glove/This Charming Man/What Difference Does It Make?/Still Ill/Heaven Knows I'm Miserable Now/William, It Was Really Nothing/How Soon Is Now?/Nowhere Fast/Shakespeare's Sister/Barbarism Begins at Home/That Joke Isn't Funny Anymore/The Headmaster Ritual/The Boy with the Thorn in His Side/Bigmouth Strikes Again/There Is a Light That Never Goes Out/Panic/Ask/You Just Haven't Earned It Yet, Baby/Shoplifters of the World Unite/Sheila Take a Bow/Girlfriend in a Coma/I Started Something I Couldn't Finish/Last Night I Dreamt That Somebody Loved Me*
(CD 2 Deluxe version): Jeane/Handsome Devil (Live at The Haçienda, Manchester 4/2/83)/This Charming Man (Promo)/Wonderful Woman/Back to the Old House/These*

Things Take Time/Girl Afraid/Please, Please, Please, Let Me Get What I Want/Stretch Out and Wait/Oscillate Wildly/ Meat Is Murder (Live at Oxford Apollo 18/3/85)/Asleep/ Money Changes Everything/The Queen Is Dead/Vicar in a Tutu/Cemetry Gates/Half a Person/Sweet and Tender Hooligan/Pretty Girls Make Graves/Stop Me If You Think You've Heard This One Before/What's the World? (Live at The Barrowlands, Glasgow 25/9/85)London (Live at National Ballroom, Kilburn)

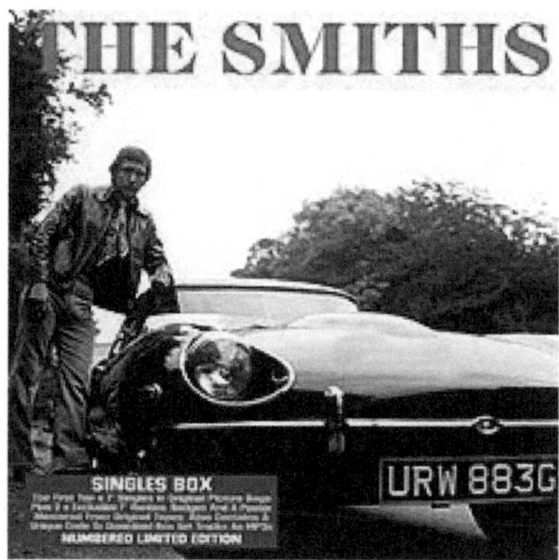

THE SMITHS SINGLES BOX

Rhino Records. Released 8 December 2008. UK
Peak UK Chart Position: N/A

Hand in Glove/Handsome Devil (live)/This Charming Man/ Jeane/What Difference Does It Make?/Back to the Old House/Still Ill/You've Got Everything Now/Heaven Knows I'm Miserable Now/Suffer Little Children/William, It Was Really Nothing/Please, Please, Please, Let Me Get What I Want/How Soon Is Now?/Well I Wonder/Shakespeare's Sister/What She Said/The Headmaster Ritual/Oscillate Wildly/That Joke Isn't Funny Anymore/Meat Is Murder (live)/The Boy with the Thorn in His Side/Asleep/Bigmouth Strikes Again/Money Changes Everything

COMPLETE

Rhino Entertainment. Released 26 September 2011. UK
Peak UK Chart Position: 63

(CD1/LP1) (The Smiths): Reel Around the Fountain/You've Got Everything Now/Miserable Lie/Pretty Girls Make Graves/The Hand That Rocks the Cradle/This Charming Man/Still Ill/Hand in Glove/What Difference Does It Make?/I Don't Owe You Anything/Suffer Little Children
(CD2/LP2) (Meat Is Murder): The Headmaster Ritual/ Rusholme Ruffians/I Want the One I Can't Have/What She Said/That Joke Isn't Funny Anymore/Nowhere Fast/Well I Wonder/Barbarism Begins at Home/Meat Is Murder
(CD3/LP3) (The Queen Is Dead): The Queen Is Dead/ Frankly, Mr. Shankly/I Know It's Over/Never Had No One Ever/Cemetry Gates/Bigmouth Strikes Again/The Boy with the Thorn in His Side/Vicar in a Tutu/There Is a Light That Never Goes Out/Some Girls Are Bigger Than Others
(CD4/LP4) (Strangeways, Here We Come): A Rush and a Push and the Land Is Ours/I Started Something I Couldn't Finish/Death of a Disco Dancer/Girlfriend in a Coma/Stop Me If You Think You've Heard This One Before/Last Night I Dreamt That Somebody Loved Me/Unhappy Birthday/ Paint a Vulgar Picture/Death at One's Elbow/I Won't Share You
(CD5/LP5) (Rank): The Queen Is Dead/Panic/Vicar in a Tutu/Ask/His Latest Flame/Rusholme Ruffians (Medley)/ The Boy with the Thorn in His Side/Rubber Ring/What She Said (Medley)/Is It Really So Strange?/Cemetry Gates/London/I Know It's Over/The Draize Train/Still Ill/ Bigmouth Strikes Again
(CD6/LP6) (Hatful of Hollow): William, It Was Really Nothing/What Difference Does It Make?/These Things Take Time/This Charming Man/How Soon Is Now?/ Handsome Devil/Hand in Glove/Still Ill/Heaven Knows I'm

Miserable Now/This Night Has Opened My Eyes/You've Got Everything Now/Accept Yourself/Girl Afraid/Back to the Old House/Reel Around the Fountain
Please, Please, Please, Let Me Get What I Want (CD7/LP7) (The World Won't Listen): Panic/Ask/London/ Bigmouth Strikes Again/Shakespeare's Sister/There Is a Light That Never Goes Out/Shoplifters of the World Unite/ The Boy with the Thorn in His Side/Money Changes Everything/Asleep/Unloveable/Half a Person/Stretch Out and Wait/That Joke Isn't Funny Anymore/Oscillate Wildly/ You Just Haven't Earned It Yet, Baby/Rubber Ring (CD8/LP8) (Louder Than Bombs): Is It Really So Strange?/ Sheila Take a Bow/Shoplifters of the World Unite/Sweet and Tender Hooligan/Half a Person/London/Panic/Girl Afraid/Shakespeare's Sister/William, It Was Really Nothing/ You Just Haven't Earned It Yet, Baby/Heaven Knows I'm Miserable Now/Ask/Golden Lights/Oscillate Wildly/These Things Take Time/Rubber Ring/Back to the Old House/ Hand in Glove/Stretch Out and Wait/Please, Please, Please, Let Me Get What I Want/This Night Has Opened My Eyes/ Unlovable/Asleep

(DELUXE EDITION 7" SINGLES)

Hand in Glove/Handsome Devil/Reel Around The Fountain/ Jeane/This Charming Man/Jeane/What Difference Does It Make?/ Back to the Old House/Heaven Knows I'm Miserable Now/Suffer Little Children/William, It Was Really Nothing/Please, Please, Please Let Me Get What I Want/How Soon Is Now?/Well I Wonder/Shakespeare's Sister/What She Said/Barbarism Begins at Home/ Shakespeare's Sister/The Headmaster Ritual/Oscillate Wildly/That Joke Isn't Funny Anymore/Meat Is Murder/ The Boy with the Thorn in His Side/Asleep/Bigmouth Strikes Again/Money Changes Everything/Panic/Vicar in a Tutu/Ask/Cemetry Gates/Shoplifters of the World Unite/ Half A Person/Sheila Take A Bow/Is It Really So Strange?/ Girlfriend in a Coma/Work Is A Four-Letter Word/I Started Something I Couldn't Finish/Pretty Girls Make Graves/ Last Night I Dreamt That Somebody Loved Me/Rusholme Ruffians/Sweet And Tender Hooligan/I Keep Mine Hidden/ There Is A Light That Never Goes Out/Half A Person/Some Girls Are Bigger Than Others/The Draize Train/Stop Me If You Think You've Heard This One Before/Girlfriend in a Coma/William, It Was Really Nothing/How Soon Is Now? (Deluxe Edition DVD): This Charming Man/What Difference Does It Make?/Panic/Heaven Knows I'm Miserable Now/Ask/The Boy with the Thorn in His Side/How Soon Is Now?/Shoplifters of the World Unite/ Girlfriend in a Coma/Sheila Take A Bow/Stop Me If You Think You've Heard This One Before

VIDEO ALBUMS

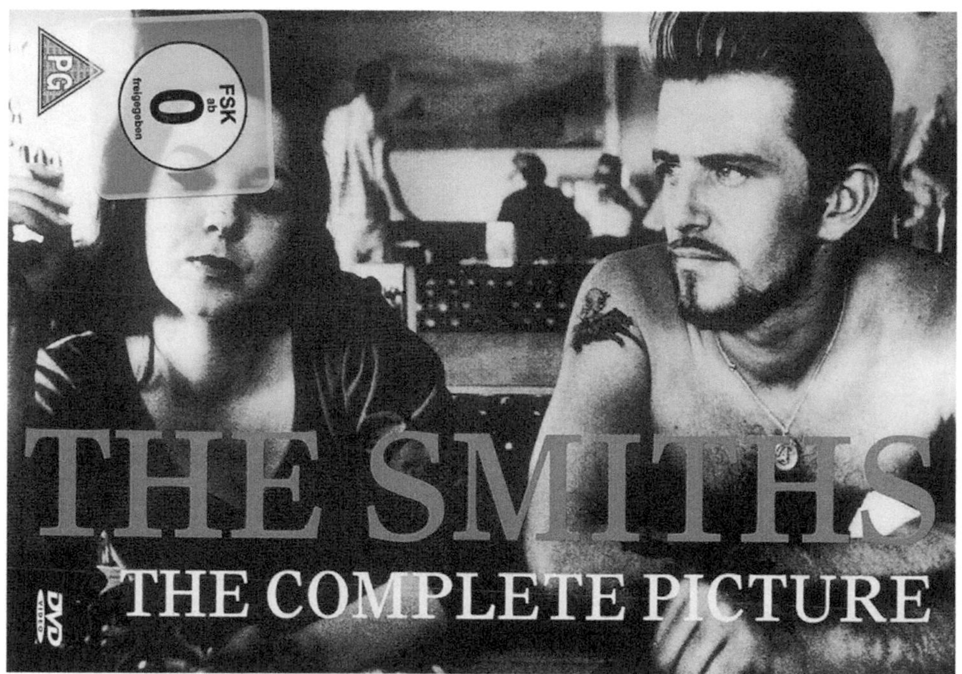

WEA. Released November 1992. UK

This Charming Man / What Difference Does It Make? / Panic / Heaven Knows I'm Miserable Now / Ask / The Boy With The Thorn In His Side / How Soon Is Now? /Shoplifters Of The World Unite / Girlfriend In A Coma /Sheila Take A Bow / Stop Me If You Think You've Heard This One Before / The Queen Is Dead (A Film By Derek Jarman)

THE SMITHS

SINGLES

HAND IN GLOVE/HANDSOME DEVIL (LIVE)

Rough Trade. Released 13 May 1983. UK Chart Position: 124

REEL AROUND THE FOUNTAIN (JOHN PEEL SESSION 18/5/83)/JEANE

Rough Trade. (Unreleased, scheduled for 23 September 1983)

THIS CHARMING MAN/JEANE
12" SINGLE: **THIS CHARMING MAN (MANCHESTER)/THIS CHARMING MAN (LONDON)/ACCEPT YOURSELF/WONDERFUL WOMAN**

Rough Trade. Released 31 October 1983. UK Chart Position: 25

WHAT DIFFERENCE DOES IT MAKE?/BACK TO THE OLD HOUSE
12" SINGLE: **WHAT DIFFERENCE DOES IT MAKE?/BACK TO THE OLD HOUSE/THESE THINGS TAKE TIME**

Rough Trade. Released 16 January 1984. UK Chart Position: 12

HEAVEN KNOWS I'M MISERABLE NOW/SUFFER LITTLE CHILDREN
12" SINGLE: **HEAVEN KNOWS I'M MISERABLE NOW/GIRL AFRAID/SUFFER LITTLE CHILDREN**

Rough Trade. Released 21 May 1984. UK Chart Position: 10

WILLIAM, IT WAS REALLY NOTHING/PLEASE, PLEASE, PLEASE, LET ME GET WHAT I WANT
12" SINGLE: **WILLIAM, IT WAS REALLY NOTHING/HOW SOON IS NOW?/PLEASE, PLEASE, PLEASE LET ME GET WHAT I WANT**

Rough Trade. Released 20 August 1984. UK Chart Position: 17

STILL ILL/REEL AROUND THE FOUNTAIN (JOHN PEEL SESSION 31/5/83)/PLEASE, PLEASE, PLEASE, LET ME GET WHAT I WANT

Rough Trade: Released November 1984 German 12" only

HOW SOON IS NOW?/WELL I WONDER
12" SINGLE: **HOW SOON IS NOW?/WELL I WONDER/OSCILLATE WILDLY**

Rough Trade. Released 28 January 1985. UK
Chart Position: 24

SHAKESPEARE'S SISTER/WHAT SHE SAID
12" SINGLE & CD VERSION: **SHAKESPEARE'S SISTER/WHAT SHE SAID/STRETCH OUT AND WAIT**

Rough Trade. Released 18 March 1985. UK Chart Position: 26

BARBARISM BEGINS AT HOME/SHAKESPEARE'S SISTER
12" SINGLE: **BARBARISM BEGINS AT HOME/SHAKESPEARE'S SISTER/STRETCH OUT AND WAIT**

Rough Trade. Released April 1985. Germany

THE HEADMASTER RITUAL/OSCILLATE WILDLY
12" SINGLE: **THE HEADMASTER RITUAL/ NOWHERE FAST** (LIVE OXFORD 18/3/85)/ **STRETCH OUT AND WAIT** (LIVE OXFORD 18/3/85)/**SHAKESPEARE'S SISTER** (LIVE OXFORD 18/3/85)/**MEAT IS MURDER** (LIVE OXFORD 18/3/85)

Rough Trade. Released Summer 1985. Netherlands

THAT JOKE ISN'T FUNNY ANYMORE/MEAT IS MURDER (LIVE)
12" SINGLE: **THAT JOKE ISN'T FUNNY ANYMORE/ NOWHERE FAST** (LIVE)/**STRETCH OUT AND WAIT** (LIVE)/**SHAKESPEARE'S SISTER** (LIVE)/**MEAT IS MURDER** (LIVE)

Rough Trade. Released 1 July 1985. UK
Chart Position: 49

THE BOY WITH THE THORN IN HIS SIDE/ASLEEP
12" SINGLE: **THE BOY WITH THE THORN IN HIS SIDE/RUBBER RING/ASLEEP**

Rough Trade. Released 16 Sept 1985. UK
Chart Position: 23

BIGMOUTH STRIKES AGAIN/MONEY CHANGES EVERYTHING
12" SINGLE: **BIGMOUTH STRIKES AGAIN/MONEY CHANGES EVERYTHING/UNLOVEABLE**

Rough Trade. Released 22 May 1986. UK
Chart Position: 26

PANIC/VICAR IN A TUTU
12" SINGLE & CD VERSION: **PANIC/VICAR IN A TUTU/THE DRAIZE TRAIN**

Rough Trade. Released 21 July 1986. UK
Chart Position: 11

SOME GIRLS ARE BIGGER THAN OTHERS/THE DRAIZE TRAIN
12" SINGLE: **SOME GIRLS ARE BIGGER THAN OTHERS/FRANKLY, MR. SHANKLY/THE DRAIZE TRAIN**

Rough Trade. Autumn 1986. Germany

ASK/CEMETRY GATES
12" SINGLE & CD VERSION: **ASK/CEMETRY GATES/GOLDEN LIGHTS**

Rough Trade. Released 20 October 1986. UK
Chart Position: 14

YOU JUST HAVEN'T EARNED IT YET BABY/ LONDON/HALF A PERSON

Rough Trade. (Unreleased, scheduled for 31 January 1987)

SHOPLIFTERS OF THE WORLD UNITE/HALF A PERSON
12" SINGLE: **SHOPLIFTERS OF THE WORLD UNITE/LONDON/HALF A PERSON**

Rough Trade. Released 26 January 1987. UK
Chart Position: 12

THERE IS A LIGHT THAT NEVER GOES OUT/ HALF A PERSON

Rough Trade. Released January 1987. France

SHEILA TAKE A BOW/IS IT REALLY SO STRANGE? (PEEL SESSION, 17/12/86)
12" SINGLE: SHEILA TAKE A BOW/IS IT REALLY SO STRANGE? (PEEL SESSION, 17/12/86)/

THE SMITHS

SWEET AND TENDER HOOLIGAN (PEEL SESSION 17/12/86)

Rough Trade. Released 13 April 1987. UK Chart Position: 10

GIRLFRIEND IN A COMA/WORK IS A FOUR-LETTER WORD
12" SINGLE: **GIRLFRIEND IN A COMA/WORK IS A FOUR-LETTER WORD/I KEEP MINE HIDDEN**

Rough Trade. Released 10 August 1987. UK Chart Position: 13

I STARTED SOMETHING I COULDN'T FINISH/ PRETTY GIRLS MAKE GRAVES (TROY TATE VERSION)
12" SINGLE: **I STARTED SOMETHING I COULDN'T FINISH/PRETTY GIRLS MAKE GRAVES (TROY TATE VERSION)/SOME GIRLS ARE BIGGER THAN OTHERS** (LIVE LONDON 12/12/86)
CASSETTE: **I STARTED SOMETHING I COULDN'T FINISH/PRETTY GIRLS MAKE GRAVES** (TROY TATE VERSION)**/SOME GIRLS ARE BIGGER THAN OTHERS** (LIVE LONDON 12/12/86)**/WHAT'S THE WORLD** (LIVE)

Rough Trade. Released 6 November 1987. UK Chart Position: 23

STOP ME IF YOU THINK YOU'VE HEARD THIS ONE BEFORE/GIRLFRIEND IN A COMA

Rough Trade. Released November 1987. Germany

LAST NIGHT I DREAMT THAT SOMEBODY LOVED ME/RUSHOLME RUFFIANS (JOHN PEEL SESSION 9/8/84)
12" SINGLE: **LAST NIGHT I DREAMT THAT SOMEBODY LOVED ME/RUSHOLME RUFFIANS** (JOHN PEEL SESSION 9/8/84)**/ NOWHERE FAST** (JOHN PEEL SESSION 9/8/84)
CD SINGLE: **LAST NIGHT I DREAMT THAT SOMEBODY LOVED ME/RUSHOLME RUFFIANS** (JOHN PEEL SESSION 9/8/84)**/NOWHERE FAST** (JOHN PEEL SESSION 9/8/84)**/WILLIAM, IT WAS REALLY NOTHING** (JOHN PEEL SESSION 9/8/84)

Rough Trade. Released 7 December 1987. UK Chart Position: 30

THIS CHARMING MAN/JEANE (REISSUE)

Rough Trade. Released August 1992. UK Chart Position: 8

HOW SOON IS NOW? (ALBUM VERSION)**/HAND IN GLOVE** (ORIGINAL SINGLE VERSION) (REISSUE)
CD SINGLE 1: **HOW SOON IS NOW?/THE QUEEN IS DEAD/HANDSOME DEVIL** (JOHN PEEL SESSION 31/5/83)**/I STARTED SOMETHING I COULDN'T FINISH**
CD SINGLE 2: **I KNOW IT'S OVER/SUFFER LITTLE CHILDREN/BACK TO THE OLD HOUSE/HOW SOON IS NOW?** (ALBUM VERSION)

Rough Trade. Released Aug/Sep 1992. UK Chart Position: 16

Handsome Devil (live Manchester Hacienda 4/2/83)/Jeane/Some Girls Are Bigger Than Others (live London 12/12/86)/Money Changes Everything/ Work Is A Four-Letter Word/I Keep Mine Hidden/I Know It's Over

Rough Trade. Released October 1992.

France

THERE IS A LIGHT THAT NEVER GOES OUT/ HANDSOME DEVIL (LIVE MANCHESTER HACIENDA 4/2/83) (REISSUE)
CD SINGLE 1: **THERE IS A LIGHT THAT NEVER GOES OUT/HAND IN GLOVE** (LIVE LONDON 29/6/83)**/SOME GIRLS ARE BIGGER THAN**

OTHERS (LIVE LONDON 12/12/86)/**MONEY CHANGES EVERYTHING**
CD SINGLE 2: **THERE IS A LIGHT THAT NEVER GOES OUT/HAND IN GLOVE** (WITH SANDIE SHAW ON VOCALS)/**I DON'T OWE YOU ANYTHING** (SANDIE SHAW ON VOCALS)/**JEANE** (WITH SANDIE SHAW
ON VOCALS)

Rough Trade. Released 12-19 October 1992. UK
Chart Position: 25

ASK/CEMETRY GATES (REISSUE)

Rough Trade. Released 6 February 1995
Chart Position: 62

SWEET AND TENDER HOOLIGAN (PEEL SESSION 17/12/86)/**I KEEP MINE HIDDEN/WORK IS A FOUR-LETTER WORD/WHAT'S THE WORLD** (LIVE GLASGOW 25/9/85)

Sire Records. Released 23 May 1995. US

THE SMITHS

EXTENDED PLAYS

GIV 1
(NME READERS' POLL WINNERS' '84)
WHAT SHE SAID (LIVE)

THE PEEL SESSIONS
WHAT DIFFERENCE DOES IT MAKE?/MISERABLE LIE/REEL AROUND THE FOUNTAIN/HANDSOME DEVIL

Strange Fruit. Released October 1988. UK

MORRISSEY

ALBUMS

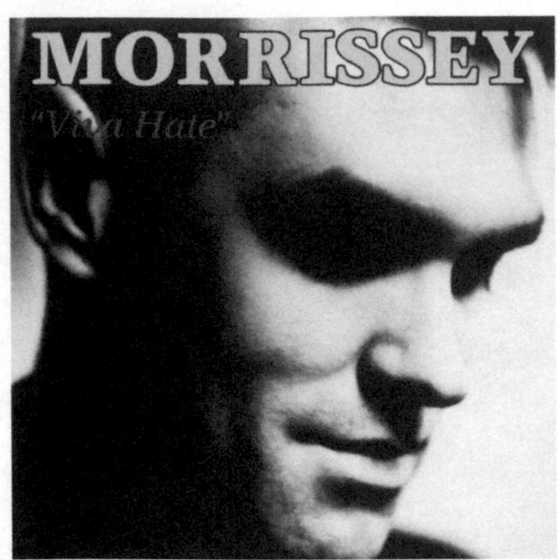

VIVA HATE

HMV. Released 14 March 1988. UK
Peak UK Chart Position: 1. No. 48 (US)

Track-listing: ***Alsatian Cousin/Little Man, What Now?/ Everyday Is Like Sunday/Bengali in Platforms/Angel, Angel Down We Go Together/Late Night, Maudlin Street/ Suedehead/Break Up the Family/The Ordinary Boys/I Don't Mind If You Forget Me/Dial-a-Cliché/Margaret on the Guillotine***

US bonus track: ***"Hairdresser on Fire"***

1997 EMI Centenary Special Edition bonus tracks: ***Let the Right One Slip In/Pashernate Love/At Amber/Disappointed (live)/Girl Least Likely To/I'd Love To/Michael's Bones/I've Changed My Plea to Guilty***

2012 Remastered Special Edition bonus track: ***Treat Me Like a Human Being***

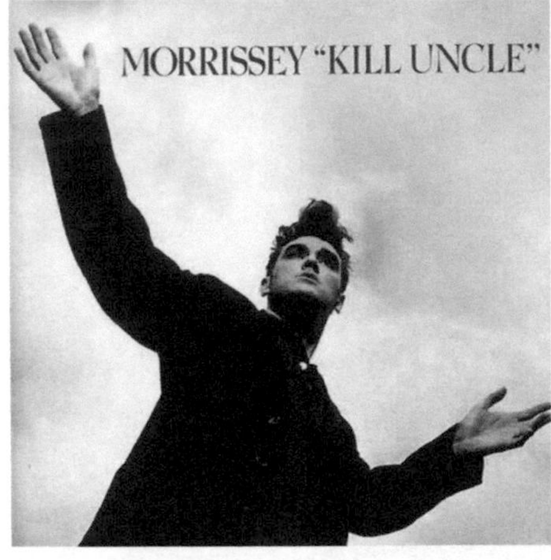

KILL UNCLE

HMV, EMI. Released 4 March 1991. UK
Peak UK Chart Position: 8

Track-listing: ***Our Frank/Asian Rut/Sing Your Life/Mute Witness/King Leer/Found Found/Driving Your Girlfriend Home/The Harsh Truth of the Camera Eye/(I'm) The End of the Family Line/There's a Place in Hell for Me and My Friends***

US bonus track: ***Tony the Pony***

2013 expanded edition version
Track-listing: ***Our Frank/Sing Your Life/Mute Witness/King Leer/Asian Rut/Pashernate Love/East West/Found Found Found/Driving Your Girlfriend Home/The Harsh Truth of the Camera Eye/There's a Place in Hell for Me and My Friends*** *(Live in the Studio Version)/* ***(I'm) The End of the Family Line***

YOUR ARSENAL

HMV. Released 27 July 1992. UK
Peak UK Chart Position: 4. No. 21 (US)

Track-listing: ***You're Gonna Need Someone on Your Side/ Glamorous Glue/We'll Let You Know/The National Front Disco/Certain People I Know/We Hate It When Our Friends Become Successful/You're the One for Me, Fatty/Seasick, Yet Still Docked/I Know It's Gonna Happen Someday/ Tomorrow***

VAUXHALL AND I

Parlophone (UK), Sire Records (US).
Released 14 March 1994. UK
Peak UK Chart Position: 1

Track-listing: ***Now My Heart Is Full/Spring-Heeled Jim/ Billy Budd/Hold On to Your Friends/The More You Ignore Me, the Closer I Get/Why Don't You Find Out for Yourself/I Am Hated for Loving/Lifeguard Sleeping, Girl Drowning/ Used to Be a Sweet Boy/The Lazy Sunbathers/Speedway***

SOUTHPAW GRAMMAR

RCA. Released 28 August 1995. UK
Peak UK Chart Position: 4

Track-listing: ***The Teachers Are Afraid of the Pupils/Reader Meet Author/The Boy Racer/The Operation/Dagenham Dave/Do Your Best and Don't Worry/Best Friend on the Payroll/Southpaw***

MALADJUSTED

Island Records. Released 11 August 1997. UK

Track-listing: ***Maladjusted/Alma Matters/Ambitious Outsiders/Trouble Loves Me/Papa Jack/Ammunition/Wide to Receive/Roy's Keen/He Cried/Sorrow Will Come in the End*/Satan Rejected My Soul***

** Not included on UK pressings, in any format, until the 2009 reissue*

2009 reissue track-listing: ***Maladjusted/Ambitious Outsiders/Trouble Loves Me/Lost/He Cried/Alma Matters/Heir Apparent/Ammunition/The Edges Are No Longer Parallel/This Is Not Your Country/Wide to Receive/I Can Have Both/Now I Am a Was/Satan Rejected My Soul/Sorrow Will Come in the End***

YOU ARE THE QUARRY

Sanctuary/Attack. Released 17 May 2004. UK
Peak UK Chart Position: 2. No. 11 (US)

Track-listing: ***America Is Not the World/Irish Blood, English Heart/I Have Forgiven Jesus/Come Back to Camden/I'm Not Sorry/The World Is Full of Crashing Bores/How Can Anybody Possibly Know How I Feel?/First of the Gang to Die/Let Me Kiss You/All the Lazy Dykes/I Like You/You Know I Couldn't Last***

Deluxe Edition bonus disc
Track-listing: ***Don't Make Fun of Daddy's Voice/It's Hard to Walk Tall When You're Small/Teenage Dad on His Estate/Munich Air Disaster 1958/Friday Mourning/The Never-Played Symphonies/My Life Is a Succession of People Saying Goodbye/I Am Two People/Mexico***
Deluxe Edition bonus DVD: ***Irish Blood, English Heart*** *(promo video)/* ***First of the Gang to Die*** *(promotional video)/* ***First of the Gang to Die*** *(from The Late Late Show, 22 July 2004)/* ***I Have Forgiven Jesus*** *(from The Late Late Show,*

RINGLEADER OF THE TORMENTORS

Sanctuary/Attack. Released 3 April 2006. UK
Peak UK Chart Position: 1. No. 27 (US)

Track-listing: ***I Will See You in Far-Off Places/Dear God Please Help Me/You Have Killed Me/The Youngest Was the Most Loved/In the Future When All's Well/The Father Who Must Be Killed/Life Is a Pigsty/I'll Never Be Anybody's Hero Now/On the Streets I Ran/To Me You Are a Work of Art/I Just Want to See the Boy Happy/At Last I Am Born***

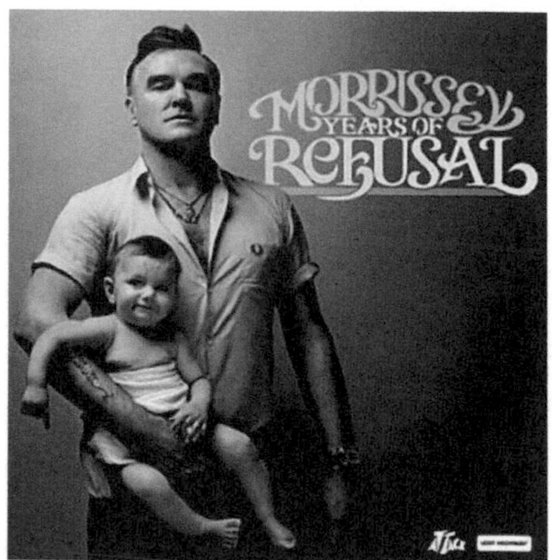

YEARS OF REFUSAL

Decca/Polydor (UK); Attack/Lost Highway (US). Released 16 February 2009.
Peak UK Chart Position: 3. No. 11 (US)

Track-listing: Something Is Squeezing My Skull/Mama Lay Softly on the Riverbed/Black Cloud/I'm Throwing My Arms Around Paris/All You Need Is Me//I spoke to Carol/That's How People Grow Up/One Day Goodbye Will Be Farewell/ It's Not Your Birthday Anymore/You Were Good in Your Time/Sorry Doesn't Help/I'm OK by Myself

iTunes U.S. bonus tracks: Because of My Poor Education/ Shame Is the Name

WORLD PEACE IS NONE OF YOUR BUSINESS

Harvest (UK); Capitol (US). Released 15 July 2014.
Peak UK Chart Position: 2. No. 14 (US)

Track-listing: World Peace Is None of Your Business/Neal Cassady Drops Dead/I'm Not a Man/Istanbul/Earth Is the

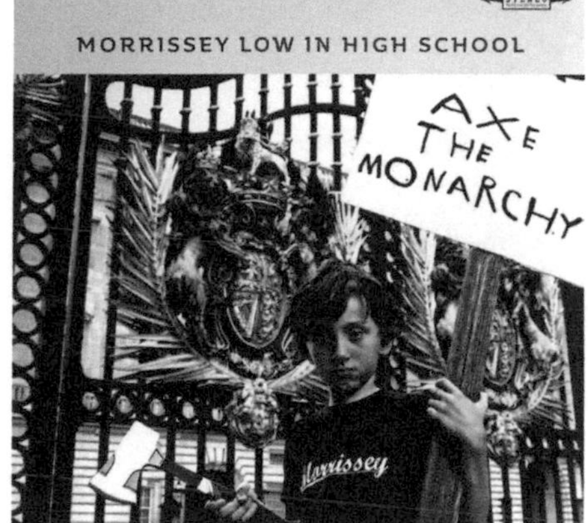

LOW IN HIGH SCHOOL

BMG. Released 17 November 2017. UK
Peak UK Chart Position: 5. No. 20 (US)

Track-listing: My Love, I'd Do Anything for You/I Wish You Lonely/Jacky's Only Happy When She's Up on the Stage/ Home Is a Question Mark/Spent the Day in Bed/I Bury the Living/In Your Lap/The Girl from Tel-Aviv Who Wouldn't Kneel/All the Young People Must Fall in Love/When You Open Your Legs/Who Will Protect Us from the Police?/Israel

LIVE ALBUMS

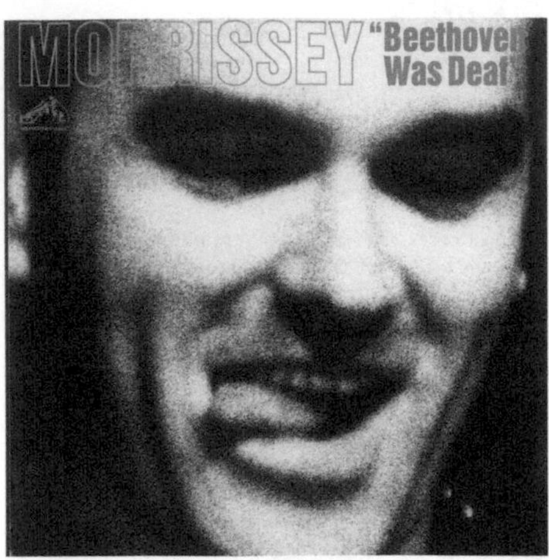

BEETHOVEN WAS DEAF

HMV. Released 10 May 1993. UK
Peak UK Chart Position: 13

Track-listing: You're the One for Me, Fatty/Certain People I Know*/National Front Disco*/November Spawned a Monster/Seasick, Yet Still Docked/The Loop/Sister I'm a Poet/Jack the Ripper/Such a Little Thing Makes Such a Big Difference/I Know It's Gonna Happen Someday/We'll Let You Know*/Suedehead/He Knows I'd Love to See Him*/You're Gonna Need Someone on Your Side*/Glamorous Glue*/We Hate It When Our Friends Become Successful*

Recorded live at Paris Zenith on December 22, 1992, except for the titles followed by an asterisk which were recorded live at London's Alexandra Palace two days earlier.

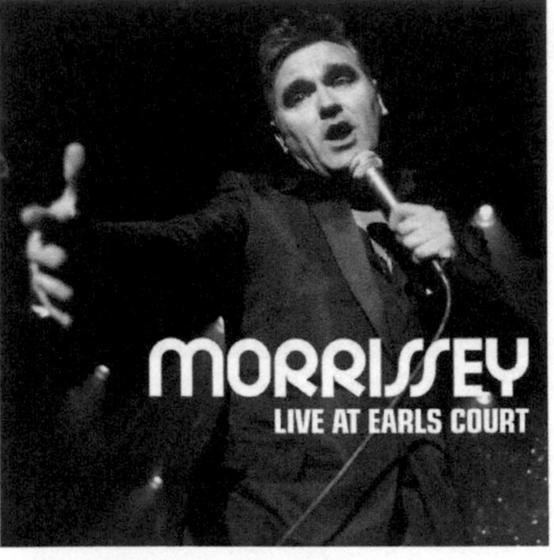

LIVE AT EARLS COURT

Sanctuary. 29 March 2005. UK
Peak UK Chart Position: 18. No. 119 (US)

Track-listing: How Soon Is Now?/First of the Gang to Die/November Spawned a Monster/Don't Make Fun of Daddy's Voice/Bigmouth Strikes Again/I Like You/Redondo Beach/Let Me Kiss You/Subway Train – Munich Air Disaster 1958/There Is a Light That Never Goes Out/The More You Ignore Me, the Closer I Get/Friday Mourning/I Have Forgiven Jesus/The World Is Full of Crashing Bores/Shoplifters of the World Unite/Irish Blood, English Heart/You Know I Couldn't Last/Last Night I Dreamt That Somebody Loved Me

Recorded live at Earls Court, London. on 18 December 2004.

COMPILATION ALBUMS

BONA DRAG

HMV (UK); Sire Records (US). Released 15 October 1990.
Peak UK Chart Position: 9. No. 59 (US)

Track-listing: Piccadilly Palare/Interesting Drug/ November Spawned a Monster/Will Never Marry/Such a Little Thing Makes Such a Big Difference/The Last of the Famous International Playboys/Ouija Board, Ouija Board/ Hairdresser on Fire/Everyday Is Like Sunday/He Knows I'd Love to See Him" (Morrissey/Armstrong)
B-side of "November Spawned a Monster/Yes, I Am Blind/ Lucky Lisp/Suedehead/Disappointed

Bonus tracks on 2010 reissue: Happy Lovers at Last United/Lifeguard on Duty/Please Help the Cause Against Loneliness/Oh Phoney/The Bed Took Fire/Let the Right One Slip In

WORLD OF MORRISSEY

Parlophone (UK; Sire Records (US).
Released 6 February 1995.
UK Peak Chart Position: 15. No. 154 (US)

Track-listing: Whatever Happens, I Love You/Billy Budd/ Jack the Ripper/Have-a-Go Merchant/The Loop/Sister I'm a Poet/You're the One for Me, Fatty/Boxers/Moonriver/My Love Life/Certain People I Know/The Last of the Famous International Playboys/We'll Let You Know/Spring-Heeled Jim

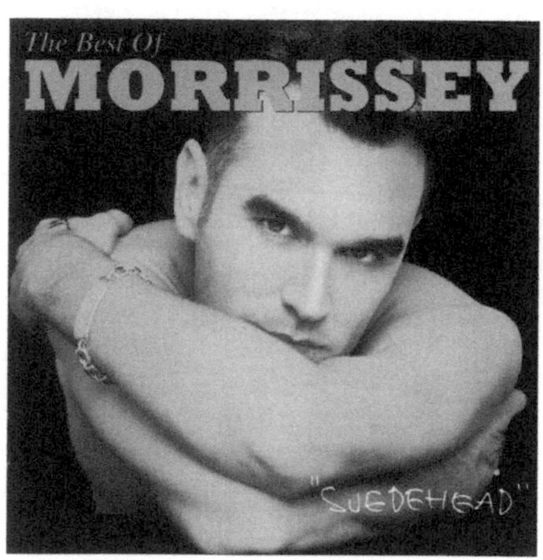

SUEDEHEAD: THE BEST OF MORRISSEY

EMI. Released 8 September 1997. UK
Peak UK Chart Position: 25

Track-listing: Suedehead/Sunny/Boxers/Tomorrow/Interlude/Everyday Is Like Sunday/That's Entertainment/Hold on to Your Friends/My Love Life/Interesting Drug/Our Frank/Piccadilly Palare/Ouija Board, Ouija Board/You're the One for Me, Fatty/We Hate It When Our Friends Become Successful/The Last of the Famous International Playboys/Pregnant for the Last Time/November Spawned a Monster/The More You Ignore Me, the Closer I Get

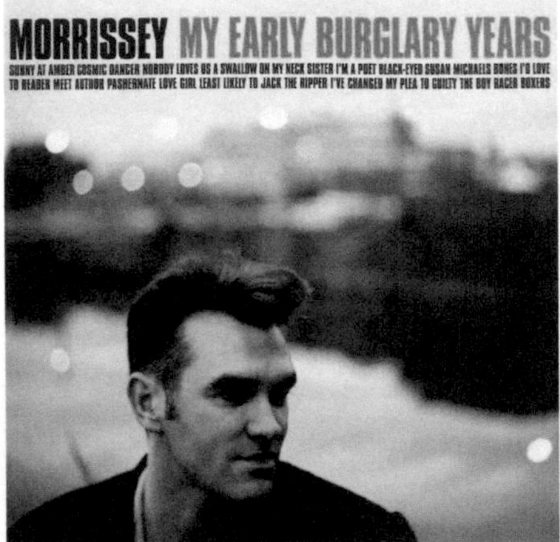

MY EARLY BURGLARY YEARS

Reprise. Released September 1998. UK
Peak UK Chart Position: N/A

Track-listing: Sunny/At Amber/Cosmic Dancer (live Costa Mesa 1/6/91)/Nobody Loves Us/A Swallow on My Neck/Sister I'm a Poet/Black-Eyed Susan/Michael's Bones/I'd Love To/Reader Meet Author/Pashernate Love/Girl Least Likely To/Jack the Ripper (live Paris 22/12/92)/I've Changed My Plea to Guilty/The Boy Racer/Boxers

THE CD SINGLES '88-91'

EMI. Released 19 June 2000. UK
Peak UK Chart Position: N/A

Track-listing: (CD 1) Suedehead/I Know Very Well How I Got My Name/Hairdresser on Fire/Oh Well, I'll Never Learn
(CD 2) Everyday Is Like Sunday/Sister I'm a Poet/

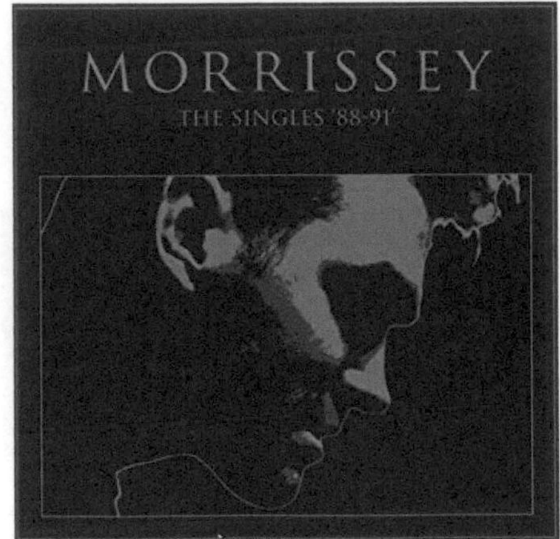

Disappointed/Will Never Marry
(CD 3) The Last of the Famous International Playboys/Lucky Lisp/Michael's Bones
(CD 4) Interesting Drug/Such a Little Thing Makes Such a Big Difference/Sweet and Tender Hooligan (live)
(CD 5) Ouija Board, Ouija Board/Yes I Am Blind/East West
(CD 6) November Spawned a Monster/He Knows I'd Love to See Him/Girl Least Likely To
(CD 7) Piccadilly Palare/Get Off the Stage/At Amber
(CD 8) Our Frank/Journalists Who Lie/Tony the Pony
(CD 9) Sing Your Life/That's Entertainment/The Loop
(CD 10) Pregnant for the Last Time/Skin Storm/Cosmic Dancer (live)/Disappointed (live)

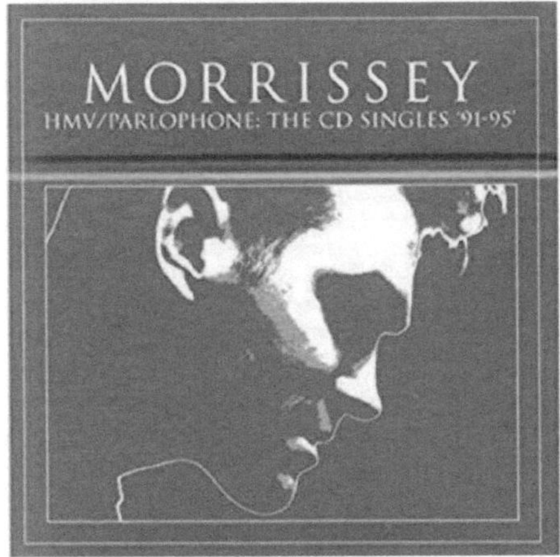

THE SINGLES '91-'95

EMI. Released 17 September 2000. UK
Peak UK Chart Position: N/A
Track-listing: (CD 1) My Love Life/I've Changed My Plea to

Guilty/There's a Place in Hell for Me and My Friends
(CD 2) We Hate It When Our Friends Become Successful/ Suedehead (live London 4/10/91)/I've Changed My Plea to Guilty (live London 4/10/91)/Pregnant for the Last Time (live London 4/10/91)/Alsatian Cousin (live London 4/10/91)
(CD 3) You're the One for Me, Fatty/Pashernate Love/There Speaks a True Friend
(CD 4) Certain People I Know/You've Had Her/Jack the Ripper
(CD 5) The More You Ignore Me, the Closer I Get/Used to Be a Sweet Boy/I'd Love To
(CD 6) Hold on to Your Friends/Moonriver/Moonriver (extended version)
(CD 7) Interlude/Interlude (extended)/Interlude (instrumental)
(CD 8) Boxers/Have-a-Go Merchant/Whatever Happens, I Love You
(CD 9) Sunny/Black-Eyed Susan/A Swallow on My Neck

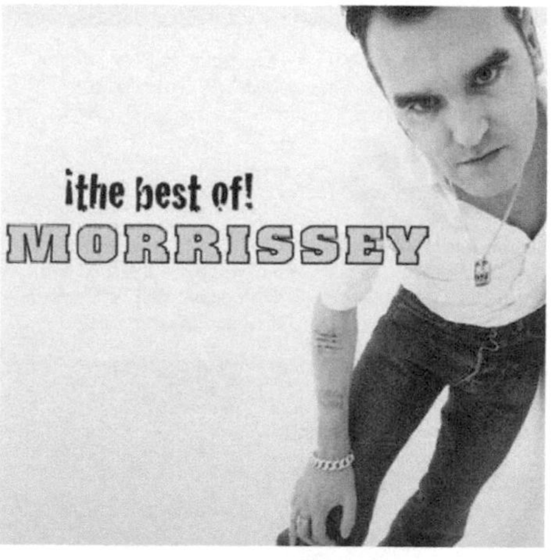

THE BEST OF MORRISSEY

Rhino Records. Released 6 Nov 2001. UK
Peak UK Chart Position: N/A

Track-listing: The More You Ignore Me, the Closer I Get/ Suedehead/Everyday Is Like Sunday/Glamorous Glue/Do Your Best and Don't Worry/November Spawned a Monster/ The Last of the Famous International Playboys/Sing Your Life/Hairdresser on Fire/Interesting Drug/We Hate It When Our Friends Become Successful/Certain People I Know/Now My Heart Is Full/I Know It's Gonna Happen Someday/Sunny/Alma Matters/Hold on to Your Friends/ Sister I'm a Poet/Disappointed/Tomorrow/Lost

GREATEST HITS

Decca. Released 11 February 2008. UK
Peak UK Chart Position: 5. No. 178 (US)

Track-listing: First of the Gang to Die/In the Future When All's Well/I Just Want to See the Boy Happy/Irish Blood, English Heart/You Have Killed Me/That's How People Grow Up/Everyday Is Like Sunday/Redondo Beach (live) Suedehead/The Youngest Was the Most Loved/The Last of the Famous International Playboys/The More You Ignore Me, the Closer I Get/All You Need Is Me/Let Me Kiss You/I Have Forgiven Jesus
Bonus live CD (Hollywood Bowl 8/6/2007)
Track listing: The Last of the Famous International Playboys/The National Front Disco/Let Me Kiss You/Irish Blood, English Heart/I Will See You in Far-Off Places/First of the Gang to Die/I Just Want to See the Boy Happy/Life Is a Pigsty

THE HMV/PARLOPHONE SINGLES '88-'95

EMI. 12 October 2009. UK
Peak UK Chart Position: N/A

Track-listing: (Disc 1) Suedehead/I Know Very Well How I Got My Name/Hairdresser On Fire/Oh Well I'll Never Learn/Everyday Is Like Sunday/Sister I'm A Poet/Disappointed/Will Never Marry/The Last Of The Famous International Playboys/Lucky Lisp/Michael's

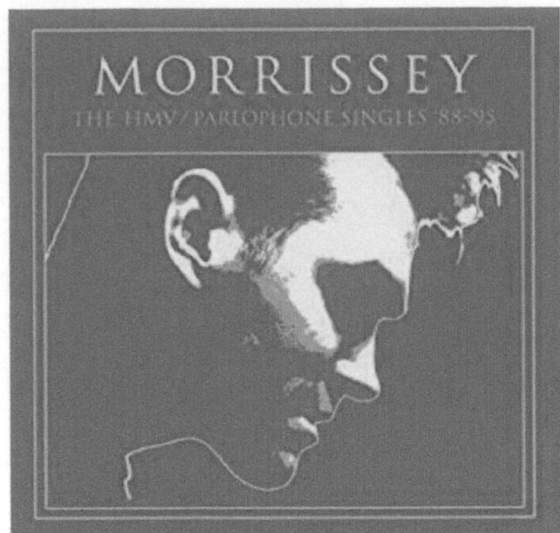

Bones/Interesting Drug/Such A Little Thing Makes Such A Big Difference/Sweet And Tender Hooligan (live Wolverhampton Civic Hall 22/12/88)/Ouija Board, Ouija Board/Yes, I Am Blind , East West/November Spawned A Monster/He Knows I'd Love To See Him/Girl Least Likely To/Piccadilly Palare/Get Off The Stage/At Amber (Disc 2) Our Frank/Journalists Who Lie/Tony The Pony/ Sing Your Life/That's Entertainment/The Loop/Pregnant For The Last Time/Skin Storm/Cosmic Dancer (live Utrecht 1/5/91)/Disappointed (live MCV, Utrecht 1/5/91)/My Love Life/I've Changed My Plea To Guilty/There's A Place In Hell For Me and My Friends (KROQ radio session)/We Hate It When Our Friends Become Successful/Suedehead (live Hammersmith Odeon, London 4/10/91)/I've Changed My Plea To Guilty (live Hammersmith Odeon, London 4/10/91)/ Pregnant For The Last Time (live Hammersmith Odeon, London 4/10/91)/Alsatian Cousin (live Hammersmith Odeon, London 4/10/91)/You're The One For Me, Fatty/ Pashernate Love/There Speaks A True Friend (Disc 3) Certain People I Know/Jack The Ripper/You've Had Her/The More You Ignore Me The Closer I Get/Used To Be A Sweet Boy/I'd Love To/Hold On To Your Friends/Moonriver/ Moonriver (extended)/Interlude/Interlude (extended)/ Interlude (instrumental)/Boxers/Have-A-Go Merchant/ Whatever Happens, I Love You/Sunny/Black-Eyed Susan/ Swallow On My Neck

SWORDS_

Polydor. Released 26 October 2009. UK Peak UK Chart Position: 55

Track-listing: Good Looking Man About Town/Don't Make Fun of Daddy's Voice/If You Don't Like Me, Don't Look at Me/Ganglord/My Dearest Love/The Never-Played Symphonies/Sweetie-Pie/Christian Dior/Shame Is the Name/Munich Air Disaster 1958/I Knew I Was Next/It's Hard to Walk Tall When You're Small/Teenage Dad on His

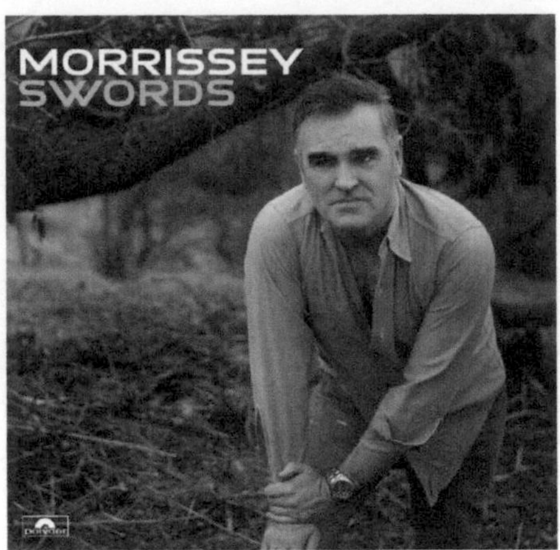

Estate/Children in Pieces/Friday Mourning/My Life is a Succession of People Saying Goodbye/Drive-In Saturday (live at the Orpheum Theater, Nebraska 11/507)/Because of My Poor Education

Limited edition bonus disc - Live in Warsaw (Stodola 7/7/09)
Track-listing: Black Cloud/I'm Throwing My Arms Around Paris/I Just Want to See the Boy Happy/Why Don't You Find Out for Yourself/One Day Goodbye Will Be Farewell/ You Just Haven't Earned it Yet, Baby/Life is a Pigsty/I'm OK by Myself

THE VERY BEST OF MORRISSEY

Major Minor. Released 25 April 2011. UK Peak UK Chart Position: 80

Track-listing: The Last of the Famous International

Playboys/You're Gonna Need Someone on Your Side/The More You Ignore Me, the Closer I Get/Glamorous Glue/Girl Least Likely To/Suedehead/Tomorrow/Boxers/My Love Life/Break Up the Family/I've Changed My Plea to Guilty/ Such a Little Thing Makes Such a Big Difference/Ouija Board, Ouija Board/Interesting Drug/November Spawned a Monster/Everyday Is Like Sunday/Interlude (solo version)/ Moonriver

THIS IS MORRISSEY

Parlophone (UK); Sire Records (US).
Released 6 July 2018.
Peak UK Chart Position: N/A

Track-listing: The Last of the Famous International Playboys/Ouija Board, Ouija Board/Speedway/Have-A-Go Merchant/Satellite of Love (Live)/Suedehead/Lucky Lisp/ Whatever Happens I Love You/You're The One For Me Fatty (Live)/Jack The Ripper/The Harsh Truth of the Camera Eye/Everyday Is Like Sunday

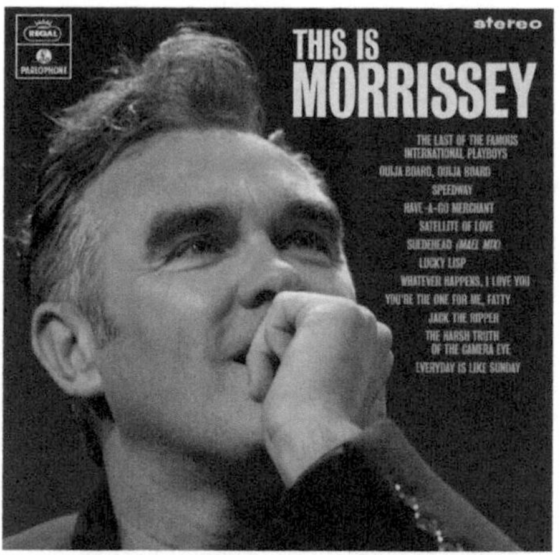

MINI ALBUMS

RARE TRACKS

Released 2008. Japan only

Track-listing: Lost/Heir Apparent/The Edges Are No Longer Parallel/This Is Not Your Country/Now I Am a Was/I Can Have Both

OTHER

VOLUME 5 – TOMORROW

(Steve Peck Mix) (1992)

MUSIC FROM GLASTONBURY THE FILM

First of the Gang to Die (2006)

THE SINGLES

Suedehead/I Know Very Well How I Got My Name. 12" single: Suedehead/I Know Very Well How I Got My Name/Hairdresser on Fire. CD and cassette: Suedehead/I Know Very Well How I Got My Name/Hairdresser on Fire/Oh Well, I'll Never Learn
HMV. Released 27 February 1988. UK
Chart Position: 5

Everyday is Like Sunday/Disappointed 12" single: Everyday Is Like Sunday/Sister I'm a Poet/Disappointed/Will Never Marry CD and cassette: Everyday Is Like Sunday/Sister I'm a Poet/Disappointed/Will Never Marry
HMV. Released 31 May 1988. UK
Chart Position: 9

The Last of the Famous International Playboys/Lucky Lisp. 12" single, CD and cassette: The Last of the Famous International Playboys/Lucky Lisp/Michaels Bones
HMV. Released 30 January 1989. UK
Chart Position: 6

Interesting Drug/Such a Little Thing Makes Such a Big Difference. 12" one-sided single: Interesting Drug/Such a Little Thing Makes Such a Big Difference 12" single, CD and cassette: Interesting Drug/Such a Little Thing Makes Such a Big Difference/Sweet and Tender Hooligan (live in Wolverhampton, 22/12/88)
HMV. Released 17 April 1989. UK
Chart Position: 9

Ouija Board, Ouija Board/Yes, I Am Blind 12" single: Ouija Board, Ouija Board/Yes, I Am Blind/East, West
HMV. Released 13 November 1989. UK
Chart Position: 18

November Spawned a Monster/He Knows I'd Love to See Him. 12" single, CD and cassette: November Spawned a Monster/He Knows I'd Love to See Him/Girl Least Likely To
HMV. Released 23 April 1990. UK
Chart Position: 12

Piccadilly Palare/Get Off the Stage. 12" single and CD: Piccadilly Palare/At Amber/Get Off the Stage
HMV. Released 8 October 1990. UK
Chart Position: 18

Our Frank/Journalists Who Lie. 12" single and CD: Our Frank/Journalists Who Lie/Tony the Pony
HMV. Released 11 February 1991. UK
Chart Position: 26

Sing Your Life/That's Entertainment. 12" single: Sing Your Life/That's Entertainment/The Loop
HMV. Released 1 April 1991. UK
Chart Position: 33

Pregnant for the Last Time/Skin Storm 12" single and CD: Pregnant for the Last Time/Skin Storm/Cosmic Dancer (live in Utrecht, 1/5/91)/Disappointed (live in Utrecht, 1/5/91)
HMV. Released 15 July 1991. UK
Chart Position: 25

My Love Life (UK version)/I've Changed My Plea to Guilty (UK version). 12" single

and CD: My Love Life (UK version)/I've Changed My Plea to Guilty (UK version)/ There's a Place in Hell for Me and My Friends (KROQ radio session). 12" single and CD: My Love Life (US version)/I've Changed My Plea to Guilty (US version)/ Skin Storm
HMV. Released 17 September 1991. UK Chart Position: 29

We Hate It When Our Friends Become Successful/Suedehead (live London, 4/10/91). 12" single (UK version): We Hate It When Our Friends Become Successful/Suedehead (live London, 4/10/91)/I've Changed My Plea to Guilty (live London, 4/10/91)/Pregnant for the Last Time (live London, 4/10/91). CD (UK version: We Hate It When Our Friends Become Successful/Suedehead (live London, 4/10/91)/I've Changed My Plea to Guilty (live London, 4/10/91)/Alsatian Cousin (live London, 4/10/91). 12" single and CD (US version): We Hate It When Our Friends Become Successful/Suedehead (live London, 4/10/91)/I've Changed My Plea to Guilty (live London, 4/10/91)/ Pregnant for the Last Time (live London, 4/10/91)/Alsatian Cousin (live London, 4/10/91)
HMV. Released 27 April 1992. UK Chart Position: 17

You're the One for Me, Fatty/Pashernate Love. 12" single: You're the One for Me, Fatty/Pashernate Love/There Speaks a True Friend
HMV. Released 6 July 1992. UK Chart Position: 19

Tomorrow/Let the Right One Slip In/ Pashernate Love. 12" single: Tomorrow/ Let the Right One Slip In/There Speaks a True Friend
Sire Records. Released Sept 1992. US. No. 1 Billboard Hot Modern Rock Tracks chart

Certain People I Know/Jack the Ripper 12" single and CD: Certain People I Know/ You've Had Her/Jack the Ripper
HMV. Released 7 December 1992. UK Chart Position: 35. UK

The More You Ignore Me, the Closer I Get/ Used to Be a Sweet Boy. 12 single and CD (UK version): The More You Ignore Me, the Closer I Get/Used to Be a Sweet Boy/I'd Love To (UK version). CD (US version): The More You Ignore Me, the Closer I Get/ Used to Be a Sweet Boy/I'd Love To (US version)
Parlophone. Released 28 February 1994. UK Chart Position: 8

Hold On to Your Friends/Moon River 12" single and CD: Hold On to Your Friends/Moon River (extended version)
Parlophone. Released 30 May 1994. UK Chart Position: 48. UK

Interlude/Interlude (Extended) (With Siouxsie Sioux). 12" single and CD: Interlude/Interlude (Extended)/Interlude (Instrumental)
Parlophone: Released 8 August 1994. UK Chart Position: 25

Now My Heart Is Full/Moon River CD version: Now My Heart Is Full/Moon River (extended)/Jack the Ripper (live in Paris 12/12/92)
Sire Records. Released 23 August 1994. US

Boxers/Have-a-Go Merchant. 12" single and CD: Boxers/Have-a-Go Merchant/ Whatever Happens, I Love You
Parlophone. Released 16 January 1995. UK Chart Position: 23

Dagenham Dave/Nobody Loves Us CD version: Dagenham Dave/Nobody Loves Us/You Must Please Remember

RCA. Released 21 August 1995. UK Chart Position: 26

The Boy Racer/London (live London, 26/2/95). CD 1 version: The Boy Racer/London (live London, 26/2/95)Billy Budd (live London, 26/2/95). CD 2 version: The Boy Racer/Spring-Heeled Jim (live London, 26/2/95)/Why Don't You Find Out for Yourself (live London, 26/2/95)
RCA. Released 27 November 1995. UK Chart Position: 36

Sunny/Black-Eyed Susan. Cassette version: Sunny/Black-Eyed Susan. CD version: Sunny/Black-Eyed Susan/A Swallow on My Neck
Parlophone. Released 11 December 1995. UK. Chart Position: 42

Alma Matters/Heir Apparent. 12" single and CD: Alma Matters/Heir Apparent/I Can Have Both
Island Records. Released 21 July 1997. UK Chart Position: 16

Roy's Keen/Lost. 12" single and CD: Roy's Keen/Lost/The Edges Are No Longer Parallel
Island Records. 6 October 1997. UK Chart Position: 42

Satan Rejected My Soul/Now I Am a Was 12" single and CD: Satan Rejected My Soul/Now I Am a Was/This Is Not Your Country
Island Records. Released 29 December 1997. UK. Chart Position: 39

Irish Blood, English Heart/It's Hard to Walk Tall When You're Small 12" single: Irish Blood, English Heart/It's Hard to Walk Tall When You're Small/Munich Air Disaster 1958/The Never Played Symphonies CD (UK version): Irish Blood, English Heart/Munich Air Disaster 1958/The Never Played Symphonies. CD (US version): Irish Blood, English Heart/It's Hard to Walk Tall When You're Small/Munich Air Disaster 1958/The Never Played Symphonies
Attack/Sanctuary. Released 10 May 2004 (UK) 4 May 2004 (US). Chart Position: 3 (UK); 36 (Billboard Alternative Songs)

First of the Gang to Die/My Life Is a Succession of People Saying Goodbye 12" single: First of the Gang to Die/My Life Is a Succession of People Saying Goodbye/Teenage Dad on His Estate/Mexico. CD (US): First of the Gang to Die/My Life Is a Succession of People Saying Goodbye/Teenage Dad on His Estate/Mexico. DVD: First of the Gang to Die (live Manchester, 22/5/04) (video)/First of the Gang to Die (audio)/Teenage Dad on His Estate (audio)/Mexico (audio)
Attack/Sanctuary. Released 12 July 2004 (UK); 13 July 2004 (US)Chart Position: 6

Let Me Kiss You/Don't Make Fun of Daddy's Voice (7" single and CD 1) CD 2 version: Let Me Kiss You/Friday Mourning/I Am Two People
Attack/Sanctuary. Released 11 October 2004. UK. Chart Position: 8

I Have Forgiven Jesus/No One Can Hold A Candle To You . CD version: I Have Forgiven Jesus/Slum Mums/The Public Image/I Have Forgiven Jesus
Attack/Sanctuary. Released 13 December 2004. UK. Chart Position: 10

Redondo Beach (live)/There Is A Light That Never Goes Out (live). CD version: Redondo Beach (live)/There Is A Light That Never Goes Out (live)/Noise Is The Best Revenge (Janice Long session 2004)
Attack/Sanctuary. Released March/April

2005. UK. Chart Position: 25

You Have Killed Me/Good Looking Man About Town (7" and CD). CD2 version: You Have Killed Me/Human Being/I Knew I Was Next/You Have Killed Me (video) US CD version: You Have Killed Me/Human Being/Good Looking Man About Town/I Knew I Was Next
Sanctuary. Released 27 March 2006 (UK); 28 March 2006 (US). Chart Position: 3 (UK); 1 (Billboard Hot 100 Singles)

The Youngest Was the Most Loved/If You Don't Like Me, Don't Look at Me (7" single and CD). Maxi single: The Youngest Was the Most Loved/Ganglord/A Song from Under the Floorboards/The Youngest Was the Most Loved (video). US single: The Youngest Was the Most Loved/If You Don't Like Me, Don't Look at Me/A Song From Under the Floorboards/ Ganglord/The Youngest Was the Most Loved (video)
Sanctuary. Released 6 June 2006 (UK); 27 June 2006 (US). Chart Position: 14 (UK); 11 (Billboard Hot 100 Singles)

In the Future When All's Well/Christian Dior (7" and CD). CD 2 version: In the Future When All's Well/I'll Never Be Anybody's Hero Now (live London, 28/5/06)/To Me You Are a Work of Art (live London, 28/5/06)/In the Future When All's Well (video)
Sanctuary. Released 21 August 2006. (UK) Chart Position: 17

I Just Want to See the Boy Happy/ Speedway (live London,17/9/02). 7" picture disc: I Just Want to See the Boy Happy/Late Night Maudlin Street (live London, 17/9/02). 12" single: I Just Want to See the Boy Happy/Sweetie-Pie/I Want the One I Can't Have (live London, 17/9/02)/Speedway (live London, 17/9/02)/ Late Night Maudlin Street (live London, 17/9/02). CD version: I Just Want to See the Boy Happy/Sweetie-Pie/I Want the One I Can't Have (live London, 17/9/02)/I Just Want to See the Boy Happy (video)
Sanctuary. Released 4 December 2006. UK

CD version: That's How People Grow Up/ The Last of the Famous International Playboys (live in NYC, 27/10/07). 7" single #1: That's How People Grow Up/The Boy with the Thorn in His Side (live in Omaha, 11/5/07). 7" single #2: That's How People Grow Up/Why Don't You Find Out for Yourself (live in Salt Lake City, 15/10/07)
Decca. Released 4 February 2008. UK Chart Position: 14

CD version: All You Need Is Me/Children in Pieces. 7" single #1: All You Need Is Me/ My Dearest Love. 7" single #2: All You Need Is Me/Drive-In Saturday (live Omaha 11/5/07)
Decca. Released 2 June 2008. UK. Chart Position: 24

CD version #1: I'm Throwing My Arms Around Paris/Because of My Poor Education. CD version #2: I'm Throwing My Arms Around Paris/Shame Is the Name. 7" single: I'm Throwing My Arms Around Paris/Death of a Disco Dancer (live Waukegan, 17/10/07)
Decca. Released 9 February 2009. UK. Chart Position: 21

CD version #1: Something Is Squeezing My Skull/This Charming Man (Live, BBC Radio Theatre Feb 2009). CD version #2: Something Is Squeezing My Skull/Best Friend on the Payroll (Live, BBC Radio Theatre Feb 2009). 7" single: Something Is Squeezing My Skull/I Keep Mine Hidden (Live, BBC Radio Theatre Feb 2009)
Decca. Released 27 April 2009. UK. Chart Position: 46

Everyday Is Like Sunday/November the Second/Everyday Is Like Sunday/Everyday Is Like Sunday (Top of the Pops - 9 June 1988) (2010 re-issue). 7" single #1: Everyday Is Like Sunday/Trash (live Cosa Mesa, 1/6/91). 7" single #2: Everyday Is Like Sunday/Everyday Is Like Sunday (live at the Hollywood Bowl, 8/6/07)
Major Minor. Released 27 September 2010. UK. Chart Position: 42

CD version: Glamorous Glue/Treat Me Like a Human Being/Glamorous Glue (video) 7" version: Glamorous Glue/Safe, Warm Lancashire Home. 7" picture disc: Glamorous Glue/Treat Me Like A Human Being
Major Minor. Released 18 April 2011. UK Chart Position: 69

Suedehead (Mael mix)/We'll Let You Know (live London, 1995)/Now My Heart Is Full (live London, 1995) (2012 Reissue)
EMI. Released April 2012 Record Store Day

The Last Of The Famous International Playboys/People Are The Same Everywhere (BBC live version 2011) (2013 Reissue). CD version: The Last Of The Famous International Playboys/Action Is My Middle Name (BBC live version 2011)
EMI. Released 8 April 2013. UK

7" picture disc: Satellite Of Love (live)/ You're Gonna Need Someone On Your Side/You Say You Don't Love Me (live) 12" single: Satellite Of Love (live)/You're Gonna Need Someone On Your Side/Vicar in a Tutu (live)/All You Need Is Me (live)
Parlophone. Released 28 January 2014. UK

World Peace Is None Of Your Business/ Istanbul/Earth Is The Loneliest Planet The Bullfighter Dies
Harvest/Capitol. Released 13 May 2014. US Chart Position: 83

Spent the Day in Bed/Judy Is a Punk (live)
BMG. Released 19 September 2017. UK Chart Position: 69

Jacky's Only Happy When She's Up on the Stage/You'll Be Gone (live)
BMG. Released 8 December 2017. UK

My Love, I'd Do Anything for You
BMG. Released 23 March 2018. UK

All the Young People Must Fall in Love
BMG. Released 6 July 2018. UK

E P ' S

At KROQ
Sire Records (US); Reprise (UK) Released 18 September 1991.

Track-listing: There's a Place in Hell for Me and My Friends/ My Love Life/Sing Your Life

Hulmerist
EMI. Released 1990. UK

Track-listing: The Last of the Famous International Playboys/ Sister I'm a Poet/Everyday Is Like Sunday/Interesting Drug/ Suedehead/Ouija Board, Ouija Board/November Spawned a Monster

Sing Your Life
EMI Japan. Released August 1991.

Track-listing: Sing Your Life/Our Frank/Sister I'm A Poet (live Wolverhampton, 22/12/88)

Live in Dallas
WEA. Released May 1992.

Track-listing: (intro: Wayward Sisters)/The Last Of The Famous International Playboys Interesting Drug/Piccadilly Palare/Trash/Sing Your Life/King Leer/Asian Rut/Mute Witness

November Spawned A Monster/Will Never Marry/Angel, Angel Down We Go Together/There's A Place In Hell For Me And My Friends/That's Entertainment/Our Frank Suedehead/Everyday Is Like Sunday/(exitus: Ave Maria)

The Malady Lingers On

EMI. Released November 1992.

Track-listing: Glamorous Glue/Certain People I Know/ Tomorrow (video edit)
We Hate It When Our Friends Become Successful/My Love Life (UK version of the song)
You're The One For Me, Fatty/Sing Your Life/Pregnant For The Last Time

Introducing Morrissey

WEA. Released August 1996.

Track-listing: (titles: excerpt from Glamorous Glue)/(intro: Hubert Parry -Jerusalem)/Billy Budd/Have-A-Go Merchant/ Spring-Heeled Jim/You're The One For Me, Fatty/The More You Ignore Me, The Closer I Get/Whatever Happens I Love You/We'll Let You Know/Jack The Ripper/Why Don't You Find Out For Yourself/The National Front Disco/Moonriver/Hold On To Your Friend/Boxers/Now My Heart Is Full/Speedway/ (exitus: Morrissey-Will Never Marry/excerpt from Seasick, Yet Still Docked)/(credits: excerpt Morrissey & Siouxsie-Interlude)

¡Oye Esteban!

WEA. Released 17 October 2000.

Track-listing: Everyday Is Like Sunday/Suedehead/Will Never Marry/November Spawned A Monster/Interesting Drug/ Last Of The Famous International Playboys/My Love Life/ Sing Your Life/Seasick, Yet Still Docked/We Hate It When Our Friends Become Successful/Glamorous Glue/Tomorrow/You're The One For Me, Fatty/The More You Ignore Me, The Closer I Get/Pregnant For The Last Time/Boxers/Dagenham Dave/ Boy Racer/Sunny

VIDEOS

Who Put The M In Manchester

Sanctuary. Released March 2005.

Track-listing: First Of The Gang To Die/Hairdresser On Fire/ Irish Blood, English Heart/The Headmaster Ritual/Subway Train/Everyday Is Like Sunday/I Have Forgiven Jesus/I Know It's Gonna Happen Someday/How Can Anybody Possibly Know How I Feel?/Rubber Ring/Such A Little Thing Makes Such A Big Difference/Don't Make Fun Of Daddy's Voice/The World Is Full Of Crashing Bores/Let Me Kiss You/No One Can Hold A Candle To You/Jack The Ripper/A Rush And A Push And The Land Is Ours/I'm Not Sorry/Shoplifters Of The World Unite/There Is A Light That Never Goes Out

Bonus Features: Irish Blood, English Heart (video)/First Of The Gang To Die (UK video)/First Of The Gang To Die (USA video)/I Have Forgiven Jesus (video)/Irish Blood, English Heart (live Move Festival 2004)/Everyday Is Like Sunday (live Move Festival 2004)/First Of The Gang To Die (live Move Festival 2004)/I Have Forgiven Jesus (live Move Festival 2004)/There Is A Light That Never Goes Out (live Move Festival 2004)

25Live

Eagle Rock. Released October 2013.

Track-listing: Alma Matters/Ouija Board, Ouija Board/Irish Blood, English Heart/You Have Killed Me/November Spawned A Monster/Maladjusted/You're The One For Me, Fatty/Still Ill People Are The Same Everywhere/Speedway/That Joke Isn't Funny Anymore/To Give (The Reason I Live)/Meat Is Murder/ Please, Please, Please, Let Me Get What I Want/Action Is My Middle Name/Everyday Is Like Sunday/I'm Throwing My Arms Around Paris/Let Me Kiss You/The Boy With The Thorn In His Side
Bonus material: The Kid's A Looker (Studio In Session)/ Scandinavia (Studio In Session)/Action Is My Middle Name (Studio In Session)/People Are The Same Everywhere (Studio In Session)/behind the scenes at Hollywood High/Grissle Bandage Present Lord Mudslide

JOHNNY MARR

ALBUMS

BOOMSLANG

Artistdirect/iMusic. Released 4 February 2003. UK. Peak UK Chart Position: N/A

Track-listing: The Last Ride/Caught Up/Down On the Corner/Need It/You Are the Magic/InBetweens/Another Day/Headland/Long Gone/Something to Shout About/Bangin' On

THE MESSENGER

Warner Bros. 25 February 2013. UK
Peak UK Chart Position: 10

Track-listing: The Right Thing Right/I Want the Heartbeat/European Me/Upstarts/Lockdown/The Messenger/Generate! Generate!/Say Demesne/Sun and Moon/The Crack Up/New Town Velocity/Word Starts Attack

PLAYLAND

New Voodoo. Warner Bros. Released 6 October 2014. UK
Peak UK Chart Position: 9. No. 153 (US)

Track-listing: Back in the Box/Easy Money/Dynamo/Candidate/25 Hours/The Trap/Playland/Speak Out Reach Out/Boys Get Straight/This Tension/Little King

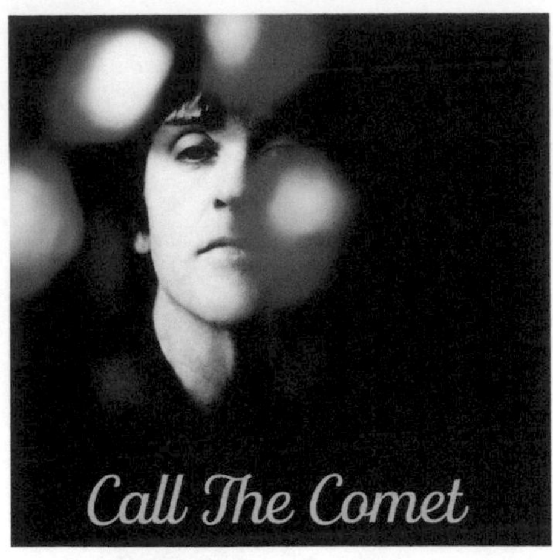

CALL THE COMET

New Voodoo. Warner Bros. Released 15 June 2018. UK
Peak UK Chart Position: 7

Track-listing: Rise/The Tracers/Hey Angel/Hi Hello/New Dominions/Day In Day Out/Walk Into the Sea/Bug/Actor Attractor/Spiral Cities/My Eternal/A Different Gun

LIVE SOLO ALBUMS

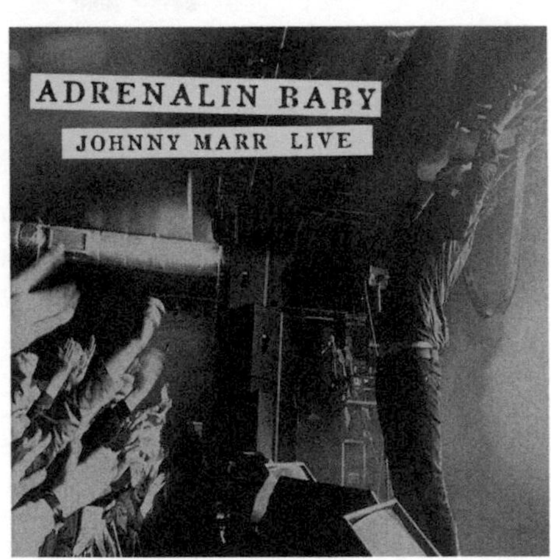

ADRENALIN BABY

New Voodoo. Warner Bros. Released 9 October 2015. UK

Track-listing: Playland/The Right Thing Right/Easy Money/25 Hours/New Town Velocity/The Headmaster Ritual/The Messenger/Back In The Box/Generate! Generate!/Bigmouth Strikes Again/Boys Get Straight/ Candidate/Getting Away With it/There Is A Light That Never Goes Out/Dynamo/I Fought The Law/How Soon Is Now?

SOLO SINGLES

Johnny Marr + the Healers

The Last Ride/Need It/Long Gone
Artistdirect/iMusic.
Released 2001. UK

Bangin' On/Here it Comes/Get Me Wrong
Artistdirect/iMusic.
Released 2003. UK
Peak UK Chart Position: 78

Down On the Corner (Radio edit)/Down On the Corner (Album version)
Artistdirect/iMusic. Released 2003. UK
Peak UK Chart Position: N/A

Johnny Marr

Upstarts/Physic Beginner
New Voodoo. Warner Bros. Released 2013. UK
Peak UK Chart Position: N/A

New Town Velocity/The It-Switch
New Voodoo. Warner Bros. Released 2013. UK
Peak UK Chart Position: N/A

Easy Money/Use Me Up
CD-R: Easy Money(Radio edit)/Use Me Up
New Voodoo. Warner Bros. Released 10 June 2014. UK
Peak Chart Position: N/A

Dynamo/Struck
New Voodoo. Warner Bros. Released 2014.UK
Peak UK Chart Position: N/A

Candidate/Exit Connection
New Voodoo. Warner Bros. Released 2014.UK
Peak UK Chart Position: N/A

I Feel You/Please Please Please Let Me Get What I Want (Live) (Alt. Version) I Feel You/I Feel You

New Voodoo. Warner Bros. Released 2015. UK Peak UK Chart Position: N/A

The Tracers
New Voodoo. Warner Bros. Released 2018. UK
Peak UK Chart Position: N/A

Hi Hello/Jeopardy
New Voodoo. Warner Bros. Released 2018. UK
Peak UK Chart Position: N/A

Spiral Cities/Spectral Eyes
Warner Bros. Released 9 November 2018. UK
Peak UK Chart Position: N/A

With Matt Johnson

Summer in the City
Warner Bros. Released 14 December 2014. UK
Peak UK Chart Position: N/A

With Electronic

Get The Message/Free Will
Factory. Released April 1991. UK
Peak UK Chart Position: 8. No. 1 (Billboard Modern Rock Tracks)

Tighten Up/Tighten Up (album version)
Warner Bros. Released July 1991. US
Peak US Chart Position: 6 (Billboard Modern Rock Tracks)

Feel Every Beat/Lean to the Inside/ Second to None
Factory. Released 9 September 1991. UK

Peak UK Chart Position: 39. No. 27 (Billboard Modern Rock Tracks)

Forbidden City/Imitation of Life
CD 1: Forbidden City/Imitation of Life/A New Religion
CD 2: Forbidden City/Imitation of Life/Getting Away with It
Parlophone. Released 24 June 1996. UK
Peak UK Chart Position: 14

CD 1: For You/All That I Need/I Feel Alright
CD 2: For You/Free Will (12" mix)/Disappointed/Get the Message (DNA Mix)
Parlophone. Released 16 September 1996. UK
Peak UK Chart Position: 16

CD 1: Second Nature/Turning Point/Feel Every Beat (12" remix)
CD 2: Second Nature/Second Nature (Plastik Mix)/Second Nature (Trance Atlantic Dub)/Second Nature (Sweet Remix)
Parlophone. Released 3 February 1997. UK
Peak UK Chart Position: 35

12" single: Vivid (radio edit)/Prodigal Son (Two Lone Swordsmen mix)/Prodigal Son (Harvey's a Star In Your Own Mind mix)
CD 1: Vivid (radio edit)/Haze (alt mix)/Prodigal Son (Harvey's a Star In Your Own Mind mix)
(UK CD 2) Vivid (album version)/Radiation/Prodigal Son (Inch remix)
Parlophone: 12 April 1999. UK
Peak UK Chart Position: 17

12" single: Late at Night (album version)/Make It Happen (original mix)/Make It Happen (Darren Price mix)
CD 1: Late at Night (radio edit)/Warning Sign/Make It Happen (Darren Price mix)
CD 2: Late at Night (album version)/King for a Day/Prodigal Son (Cevin Fisher mix)
Parlophone. Released 5 July 1999. UK
Peak UK Chart Position: N/A (Withdrawn)

With Modest Mouse

Dashboard/King Rat
Epic. Released 16 January 2007. UK
Peak UK Chart Position: 111. No. 61 (US)

Missed the Boat (radio edit)/Missed the Boat (album version)
Epic. Released 1 May 2007. UK
Peak UK Chart Position: N/A. No. 24 (US) (Billboard Hot Modern Rock Tracks)

Little Motel
Epic. Released 11 October 2007.UK
Peak UK Chart Position: N/A

People as Places as People
Epic. Released 2007. UK
Peak UK Chart Position: N/A

Satellite Skin/Guilty Cocker Spaniels
Epic. Released 26 May 2009. UK
Peak UK Chart Position: N/A

Autumn Beds/The Whale Song
Epic. Released 4 August 2009. UK
Peak UK Chart Position: N/A

Perpetual Motion Machine/History Sticks to Your Feet
Epic. Released 21 July 2009. UK
Peak UK Chart Position: N/A

With The Cribs

7" single 1: Cheat on Me/So Hot Now
7" single 2: Cheat on Me (live in Manchester)/We Were Aborted (live in Manchester)
CD version: Cheat on Me/Curse This English Rain
Wichita Recordings. Released 31 August 2009. UK; Warner Bros. (US)
Peak UK Chart Position: 80

We Share the Same Skies/City of Bugs" (Live in London)
Wichita Recordings. Released 6 November 2009. UK; Warner Bros. (US)
Peak UK Chart Position: N/A

With Bryan Ferry

The Right Stuff/The Right Stuff (Brooklyn mix)
12" single: The Right Stuff/The Right Stuff (dub mix)/The Right Stuff (original mix)
Virgin. Released 10 October 1987. UK
Peak UK Chart Position: 37

Kiss and Tell/Zamba
Virgin. Released 13 February 1988. UK; Reprise (US)
Peak UK Chart Position: 41. No. 31 (US)

Limbo (Latin mix)/Limbo (Brooklyn mix)
Virgin. Released 2 July 1988. UK; Reprise (US)
Peak UK Chart Position: 8

Mind Bomb
Epic. Released 11 July 1989. UK
Peak UK Chart Position: 4

Track-listing: Good Morning, Beautiful/Armageddon Days Are Here (Again)/The Violence of Truth/Kingdom of Rain/ The Beat(en) Generation/August & September/Gravitate to Me/Beyond Love

Dusk
Sony Records. Released 25 January 1993. UK
Peak UK Chart Position: 2

Track-listing: True Happiness This Way Lies/Love Is Stronger than Death/Dogs of Lust/This Is the Night/Slow Emotion Replay/Helpline Operator/Sodium Light Baby/ Lung Shadows/Bluer Than Midnight/Lonely Planet

Electronic_
Factory. Released 27 May 1991. UK
Peak UK Chart Position: 2. No. 109 (US)

Track-listing: Idiot Country/Reality/Tighten Up/The Patience of a Saint/Getting Away with It/Gangster**/ Soviet/Get the Message/Try All You Want/Some Distant Memory/Feel Every Beat*

** Getting Away with It did not appear on the first UK edition.*

*** Gangster was replaced by Getting Away with It in some territories*

iTunes bonus tracks: Lucky Bag/Free Will/Feel Every Beat/ Lean to the Inside/Second to None/Disappointed (original mix)/Disappointed (7" mix)/Feel Every Beat (DNA remix)/ Disappointed (12" remix)/Lucky Bag (Miami edit)/Idiot Country Two (AKA ultimatum mix)/Gangster (FBI mix)

2013 special edition
Track-listing (CD 1): Idiot Country/Reality/Tighten Up/The Patience of a Saint/Getting Away with It/Gangster/Soviet/ Get the Message/Try All You Want/Some Distant Memory/ Feel Every Beat
(CD2): Disappointed (Stephen Hague 7" version)/Second To None (2013 edit)/Lean To The Inside (2013 edit)/ Twisted Tenderness (guitar / vocal mix)/Idiot Country Two (12" Version-Edit)/Free Will (edit)/Until The End Of Time (edit)/Feel Every Beat (2013 edit)/Getting Away With It (instrumental)/Turning Point (edit)/Visit Me (edit)/Twisted Tenderness (instrumental)

Raise the Pressure
Parlophone. Released 8 July 1996. UK
Peak UK Chart Position: 8. No. 143 (US)

Track-listing: Forbidden City/For You/Dark Angel/One Day/ Until the End of Time/Second Nature/If You've Got Love/ Out of My League/Interlude/Freefall/Visit Me/How Long/ Time Can Tell
iTunes bonus tracks: Imitation of Life/A New Religion/All That I Need/I Feel Alright/Turning Point

Twisted Tenderness

Parlophone. 26 April 1999. UK; Koch Records (US) 2000
Peak UK Chart Position: 9

Track-listing: Make It Happen/Haze/Vivid/Breakdown/ Can't Find My Way Home/Twisted Tenderness/Like No Other/Late at Night/Prodigal Son/When She's Gone/Flicker

The 2000 US edition included three bonus tracks: King for a Day/Warning Sign/Make It Happen (album remix)

2001 Deluxe edition
Track-listing: Make It Happen/Haze/Vivid/Can't Find My Way Home/Twisted Tenderness/Like No Other/Late At Night/Prodigal Son/When She's Gone/Flicker
(Bonus disc): King for a Day/Warning Sign/Make It Happen (remix)/Haze (alt mix)/Prodigal Son (Star in Your Own Mind mix)/Radiation/Prodigal Son (Touched by the Hand of Inch)/Prodigal Son (Two Lone Swordsmen remix)/Prodigal Son (Harvey's Greatly Deluded mix)/Come Down (Cevin Fisher mix)

Get the Message: The Best of Electronic

EMI. Released 18 September 2006. UK; Rhino Records (US)
Peak UK Chart Position: 194

Track-listing: Forbidden City/Getting Away With It/Get The Message (single remix)/Feel Every Beat/Disappointed (single mix)/Vivid (radio edit)/Second Nature/All That I Need/Prodigal Son/For You/Imitation Of Life (2006 edit)/ Out Of My League/Like No Other/Twisted Tenderness/Late At Night (radio edit)
(DVD): Getting Away With It/Get The Message/Feel Every Beat/Disappointed/Forbidden City/For You/Vivid

With Modest Mouse

We Were Dead Before the Ship Even Sank

Epic. Released 20 March 2007. UK
Peak UK Chart Position: 47. No. 1 (US)

Track-listing: March into the Sea/Dashboard/Fire It Up/ Florida/Parting of the Sensory/Missed the Boat/We've Got Everything/Fly Trapped in a Jar/Education/Little Motel/ Steam Engenius/Spitting Venom/People as Places as People/Invisible

No One's First and You're Next

Epic. Released 4 August 2009. UK
Peak UK Chart Position: N/A

Track-listing: Satellite Skin/Guilty Cocker Spaniels/Autumn Beds/The Whale Song/Perpetual Motion Machine/History Sticks to Your Feet/King Rat/I've Got It All (Most)

With The Cribs

Ignore the Ignorant

Wichita Recordings. Released 7 September 2009. UK; Warner Bros. (US)
Peak UK Chart Position: 8

Track-listing: We Were Aborted/Cheat on Me/We Share the Same Skies/City of Bugs/Hari Kari/Last Year's Snow/ Emasculate Me/Ignore the Ignorant/Save Your Secrets/ Nothing/Victim of Mass Production/Stick to Yr Guns
iTunes bonus track: Is Anybody There?

With 7 Worlds Collide

7 Worlds Collide: Live at the St. James

Parlophone. Released 26 November 2001. UK
Peak UK Chart Position: N/A

Track-listing: Anytime/Take a Walk/The Climber/Loose Tongue/Down on the Corner/There Is a Light That Never Goes Out/Paper Doll/Turn and Run/Angels Heap/Edible Flowers/Stuff and Nonsense/I See Red/She Will Have Her Way/Parting Ways/Weather with You/Paradise (Wherever You Are)/Don't Dream It's Over

All tracks culled from a series of live shows recorded at the St. James Theatre in Auckland, New Zealand from April 2 to April 6, 2001.

DVD version:
Track-listing: Fall at Your Feet/Anytime/Hole in the Ice/ Paper Doll/The Climber/Take a Walk/Last to Know/Down on the Corner/There Is a Light That Never Goes Out/ Private Universe/Parting Ways/Driving Me Mad/Turn and Run/Loose Tongue/She Will Have Her Way/Angels Heap/ Edible Flowers/|Stuff and Nonsense/Four Seasons in One Day/Suffer Never/Cry Wolf/History Never Repeats/I See Red/Paradise (Wherever You Are)/Weather with You/Don't Dream It's Over

GUEST APPEARANCES

Billy Bragg

Talking with the Taxman About Poetry

Go Discs: Released 4 October 1986. UK
Peak UK Chart Position: 8

Track-listing: Greetings to the New Brunette/Train Train/The Marriage/Ideology/Levi Stubbs' Tears/Honey, I'm a Big Boy Now/There Is Power in a Union/Help Save the Youth of America/Wishing the Days Away/The Passion/The Warmest Room/The Home Front

2006 Bonus Disc Reissue

Track-listing: Sin City/Deportees/There is Power in a Union (instrumental)/The Tracks of My Tears/Wishing the Days Away" (alt version)/The Clashing of Ideologies (alt version)/Greetings to the New Brunette (demo version)/A Nurse's Life is Full of Woe/Only Bad Signs/Hold the Fort

Don't Try This at Home

Go Discs: Released 28 September 1991. UK
Peak UK Chart Position: 8

Track-listing: Accident Waiting to Happen/Moving the Goalposts/Everywhere/Cindy of a Thousand Lives/You Woke Up My Neighbourhood/Trust/God's Footballer/The Few/Sexuality/Mother of the Bride/Tank Park Salute/Dolphins/North Sea Bubble/Rumours of War/Wish You Were Her/Body of Water

Bloke on Bloke

Cooking Vinyl. Released 28 June 1997. UK
Peak UK Chart Position: 72

Track-listing: The Boy Done Good/Qualifications/Sugar Daddy (Smokey Gets in Your Ears mix)/Never Had No One Ever/Sugardubby (remix by Grant Showbiz of the William Bloke track)/Rule Nor Reason/Thatcherites

Reaching to the Converted

Cooking Vinyl. Released 11 September 1999. UK
Peak UK Chart Position: 41

Tracks: Shirley/The Boy Done Good/Walk Away Renée

Bryan Ferry

Bête Noire

Virgin. Released 2 November 1987 UK. Reprise (US)
Peak UK Chart Position: 9. No. 63 (US)

Track-listing: Limbo/Kiss and Tell/New Town/Day for Night/Zamba/The Right Stuff/Seven Deadly Sins/The Name of the Game/Bête Noire

Avonmore

BMG. Released 17 November 2014. UK
Peak UK Chart Position: 19. No. 72 (US)

Tracks: Loop de Li/Midnight Train/Soldier of Fortune/Driving Me Wild/Avonmore/One Night Stand/Send in the Clowns

Talking Heads

Naked

Sire Records. 15 March 1988. US
Peak US Position: 19. No. 3 (UK)

Tracks: Ruby Dear/(Nothing But) Flowers/Mommy Daddy You and I/Cool Water

Kirsty MacColl

Kite

Virgin. Released 20 May 1989. UK
Peak UK Chart Position: 34

Track-listing: Innocence/Free World/Mother's Ruin/Days/No Victims/Fifteen Minutes/Don't Come the Cowboy With Me Sonny Jim!/Tread Lightly/What Do Pretty Girls Do?/Dancing in Limbo/The End of a Perfect Day/You and Me Baby

2001 reissue bonus tracks: You Just Haven't Earned It Yet, Baby/La Forêt de Mímosas/Complainte Pour Ste Catherine

Electric Landlady
Virgin. Released 6 July 1991. UK
Peak UK Chart Position: 17

Track-listing: Walking Down Madison/All I Ever Wanted/ Children of the Revolution/Halloween/My Affair/Lying Down/He Never Mentioned Love/We'll Never Pass This Way Again/The Hardest Word/Maybe It's Imaginary/My Way Home/The One and Only

2005 reissue bonus tracks: Don't Go Near the Water/One Good Thing/Darling, Let's Have Another Baby/My Affair (Bass Sexy remix)/Walking Down Madison (6 am Ambient remix)

Titanic Days
Virgin. Released 12 April 1994. UK

Co-write on Can't Stop Killing You

The Pretenders

Packed!
Sire Records. 14 May 1990

Co-write on When Will I See You

Pet Shop Boys

Behaviour
Parlophone. Released 22 October 1990. UK

Tracks: This Must Be the Place I Waited Years to Leave/My October Symphony

Bilingual
Parlophone. Released 2 September 1996. UK

Tracks: Up Against It

Release
Parlophone. Released 1April 2002. UK

Tracks: Home and Dry/I Get Along/Birthday Boy/E-Mail/ Love Is a Catastrophe/The Night I Fell in Love/You Choose

Yes
Parlophone. Released 18 March 200. UK

Tracks: Beautiful People/Did You See me Coming/Building a Wall/Pandemonium

Banderas

Ripe
London Records. Released 1991. UK
Peak UK Chart Position: 40

Track-listing: This Is Your Life/Comfort of Faith/May This Be Your Last Sorrow/First Hand/Why Aren't You in Love With Me?/She Sells/Too Good/Don't Let That Man/It's Written All Over My Face/Never Too Late

Stex

Spiritual Dance (1992)

Moodswings

Horizontal (2006)

Tracks: Storm in a Teacup/Into The Blue/Clair De Lune

K-Klass

Universal (1993)

Tracks: La Cassa

Electrafixation

Burned (1995)

Tracks: Lowdown/Too Far Gone

M People

Fresco (October 1997)

Tracks: Rhythm and Blues/Believe It

Beck

Midnite Vultures

DGC. Released 23November 1999. UK
Peak UK Chart Position: 19. No. 34 (US)

Track-listing: Sexx Laws/Nicotine & Gravy/Mixed Bizness/Get Real Paid/Hollywood Freaks/Peaches & Cream/Broken Train/Milk & Honey/Beautiful Way/Pressure Zone/Debra (Ed Green, Hansen, John King, Michael Sim

Bert Jansch

Crimson Moon

Castle Communications: Released 15 August 2000. UK

Track-listing: Caledonia/Going Home/Crimson Moon/Downunder/October Song/Looking for Love/Fool's Mate/The River Bank/Omie Wise/My Donald/Neptune's Daughter/Singing the Blues

Oasis

Heathen Chemistry (July 2002)

Tracks: (Probably) All in the Mind/Born on a Different Cloud/Better Man

Beth Orton

Daybreaker (July 2002)

Co-write on Concrete Sky

The Charlatans

Live It Like You Love It (2002)

Tracks: Weirdo

Pearl Jam

2/23/03 – Perth, Australia (2003)

Tracks: Fortunate Son

Quando Quango

Pigs + Battleships (2003 CD reissue)

Tracks: Atom Rock (remix)/Triangle

Karl Bartos

Off the Record (2013)

Tracks: Musica Ex Machina

Lisa Germano

Lullaby for Liquid Pig (2003)

Tracks: Paper Doll/Into the Night

In the Maybe World (2006)

Tracks: Into Oblivion/Wire

Tweaker

2 A.M. Wakeup Call (2004)

Tracks: The House I Grew Up In

Jane Birkin

Fictions (2006)

Tracks: Home/Living in Limbo/Waterloo Station/My Secret/ Mother Stands for Comfort

Transit Kings

Living in a Giant Candle Winking at God (2006)

Tracks: America is Unbelievable

Crowded House

Time on Earth (June 2007)

Tracks: Don't Stop Now/Even a Child

John Frusciante

The Empyrean (2009)

Tracks: Enough of Me/Central

Robyn Hitchcock

Propellor Time (2010)

Tracks: Ordinary Millionaire

Edwyn Collins

Losing Sleep (2010)

Tracks: Come Tomorrow, Come Today

Hans Zimmer

Inception OST (Soundtrack) (2010)

Track-listing: Half Remembered Dream/We Built Our Own World/Dream Is Collapsing/Radical Notion/Old Souls/528491/Mombasa/One Simple Idea/Dream Within a Dream/Waiting for a Train/Paradox/Time

The Amazing Spider-Man 2 (Soundtrack) (2013)

Track-listing: I'm Electro/There He Is/I'm Spider-Man/My Enemy/Ground Rules/Look At Me/You Need Me/So Much Anger/I Need To Know/Sum Total/I Chose You/We're Best Friends/Still Crazy/You're That Spider Guy/It's On Again/ Phosphorescent
Song For Zula/That's My Man/Here/Honest/Electro (remix)

Freeheld (Soundtrack) (2015)

Track-listing: On The Case/Can I Have Your Number?/ House Hunting/Can't Leave Her/The Decision/Justice/ Remembering

Pajama Club

Pajama Club (2011)

Tracks: Can't Put It Down Till It Ends/Go Kart

Malka Spigel

Every Day Is Like the First Day (2012)

Track-listing: Ammonite/Every Day Is Like the First Day/ Lost In Sound/See It Sideways/European Weather/Dream Time/Finding You/No More Running/Chasing Shadows/

Back In The Old City/Two Dimensions In A Single Frame/ After The Rain

Noel Gallagher's High Flying Birds

Chasing Yesterday (2015)

Tracks: Ballad of the Mighty I

Who Built the Moon (2017)

Tracks: If Love Is the Law

Chris Spedding

Joyland (2015)

Tracks: Heisenberg

Blondie

Pollinator (2017)

Tracks: My Monster (+ writing credit)

ANDY ROURKE

ALBUMS

Bona Drag (October 1990

Tracks: Piccadilly Palare/Interesting Drug/November Spawned a Monster/Such a Little Thing Makes Such a Big Difference/The Last of the Famous International Playboys/ He Knows I'd Love to See Him/Lucky Lisp

SINGLES

The Last of the Famous International Playboys/Lucky Lisp (January 1989)

12" single bonus track: Michaels Bones

Interesting Drug/Such a Little Thing Makes Such a Big Difference (April 1989)
November Spawned a Monster/He Knows I'd Love to See Him (April 1990)

12" single bonus track: Girl Least Likely To

Piccadilly Palare/Get Off the Stage (October 1990)

With Sinéad O'Connor

I Do Not Want What I Haven't Got

Ensign. Released 20 March 1990. UK; Chrysalis (US)
Peak UK Chart Position: 1. No. 1 (US)

Track-listing: Feel So Different/I Am Stretched on Your Grave/Three Babies/The Emperor's New Clothes/Black Boys on Mopeds/Nothing Compares 2 U/Jump in the River/You Cause as Much Sorrow/The Last Day of Our Acquaintance/I Do Not Want What I Haven't Got

With The Pretenders

Last of the Independents

Sire Records. Released 9 May 1994. UK

Tracks: Night in My Veins/Money Talk/Revolution/ Tequila/Every Mother's Son/Rebel Rock Me/Love Colours

With Ian Brown

THE SMITHS

The World is Yours

Fiction. Polydor. Released 15 October 2007. UK

Track-listing: The World Is Yours/On Track/Sister Rose/Save Us/Eternal Flame/The Feeding of the 5000/Street Children/Some Folks Are Hollow/Goodbye To the Broken/Me And You Forever/Illegal Attacks/The World Is Yours (reprise)

With Freebass

It's a Beautiful Life (2010)

Track-listing: Not Too Late/The Only Ones Alone/Lady Violence/World Won't Wait/Kill Switch, Pt. 141/Stalingrad/Secrets And Lies/She Said/The God Machine/Plan B

Two Worlds Collide (2010)

Track-listing: Intro/You Don't Know (This About Me)/The Milky Way Is Our Playground/Dark Starr/Live Tomorrow You Go Down/Thats Life

You Don't Know This About Me (The Artur Baker Remixes) (2010)

Track-listing: You Don't Know This About Me (Arthur Baker Vocal remix)/You Don't Know This About Me (Arthur Baker Instrumental remix)/You Don't Know This About Me (Two Worlds Collide mix)/You Don't Know This About Me (Two Worlds Collide Instrumental mix)/You Don't Know This About Me (Arthur Baker A Capella remix)

Two Worlds Collide (The Instrumental Mixes) (2010)

Track-listing: You Don't Know This About Me (Instrumental mix)/The Milky Way Is Our Playground (Instrumental mix)/Dark Starr (Instrumental mix)/Live Tomorrow You Go Down (Instrumental mix)

D.A.R.K.

Science Agrees (2016)

Track-listing: Curvy/Chynamite/Gunfight/Steal You Away/High Fashion/Watch Out/Miles Away/The Moon/Underwater/Loosen The Noose

MIKE JOYCE

ALBUMS

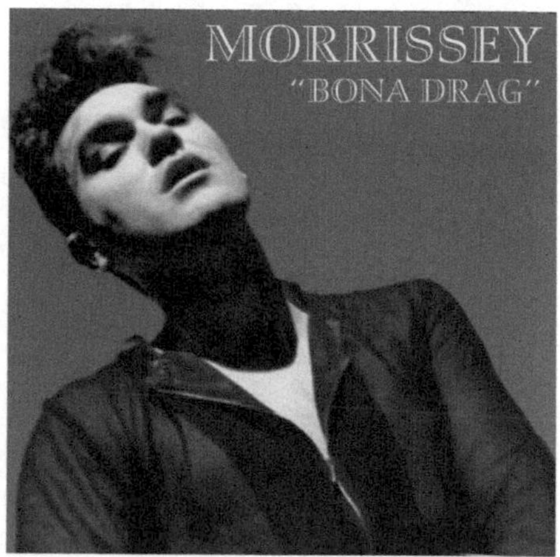

Bona Drag (October 1990)

Tracks: Interesting Drug/The Last of the Famous International Playboys/Ouija Board, Ouija Board/Lucky Lisp

SINGLES

The Last of the Famous International Playboys/Lucky Lisp (January 1989) (12" single bonus track: Michaels Bones)

Interesting Drug/Such a Little Thing Makes Such a Big Difference (April 1989)

CRAIG GANNON

SINGLES

Panic (July 1986)

Ask (October 1986)

ALBUMS

THE WORLD WON'T LISTEN

Tracks: Panic/Ask/London/Half a Person/You Just Haven't Earned It Yet, Baby (Golden Lights on post-1992 reissues)

LOUDER THAN BOMBS

Tracks: Half a Person/London/Panic/Ask/You Just Haven't Earned It Yet, Baby/Golden Lights

RANK

All tracks

THE SMITHS

BEST . . . I

Tracks: Half a Person/Panic

SINGLES

Tracks: Panic/As

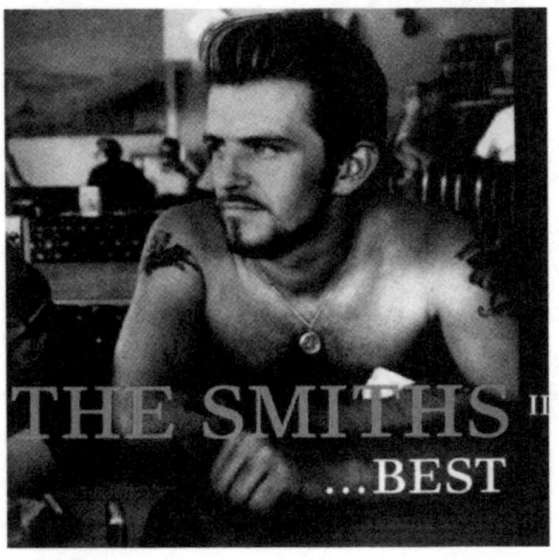

BEST II

Tracks: Ask

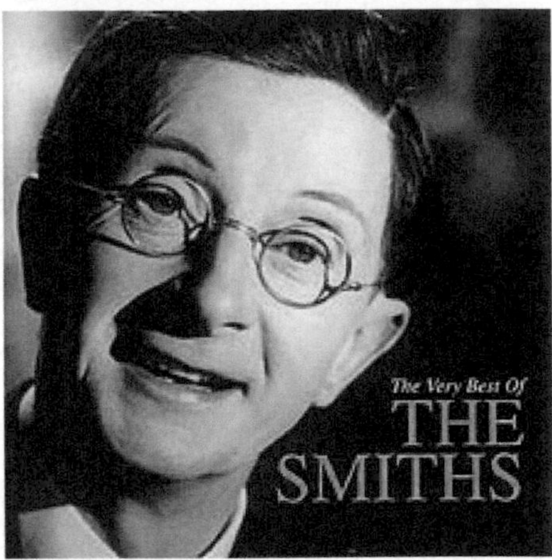

THE VERY BEST OF THE SMITHS

Tracks: Panic/Ask

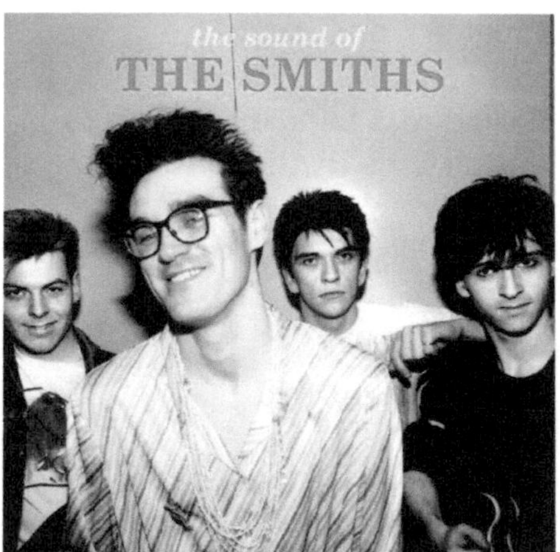

THE SOUND OF THE SMITHS

Tracks: Panic/Ask/You Just Haven't Earned It Yet Baby/Half a Person/London (live version)

With Morrissey

Singles

The Last of the Famous International Playboys/Lucky Lisp (January 1989) (12" single bonus track: Michaels Bones)

Interesting Drug/Such a Little Thing Makes Such a Big Difference (April 1989)

Albums

Bona Drag (October 1990)

Tracks: Such a Little Thing Makes Such a Big Difference/Interesting Drug/The Last of the Famous International Playboys/Lucky Lisp

World of Morrissey (February 1995)

Tracks: The Last of the Famous International Playboys

Suedehead: The Best Of Morrissey (September 1997)

Tracks: The Last of the Famous International Playboys/Interesting Drug

My Early Burglary Years (September 1998)

Tracks: Michaels Bones

The Best of Morrissey (November 2001)

Tracks: The Last of the Famous International Playboys/Interesting Drug

Greatest Hits (February 2008)
Tracks: The Last of the Famous International Playboys

With Terry Hall

Home

Anxious Records. Released 12 September 1994. UK
Peak UK Chart Position: 95

Track-listing: Forever J/You/Sense/I Drew a Lemon/Moon on Your Dress/No No No/What's Wrong with Me/Grief Disguised as Joy/First Attack of Love/I Don't Got You

Singles from Home:

Forever J/Forever J (Pulp mix)/Suburban Cemetery/Guess It's

THE SMITHS

Not a Great Day to Be Me

Anxious Records. Released August 1994. UK

Peak UK Chart Position: 67

Sense/God Only Knows/This Guy's in Love With You

Anxious Records. Released 12 November 1994. UK
Peak UK Chart Position: 54

EPs

Rainbows EP

Anxious Records. Released 28 October 1995. UK
Peak UK Chart Position: 62

Track-listing: Chasing a Rainbow/Mistakes/See No Evil (live)/Ghost Town (live)

Laugh

Southsea Bubble Company. Released 6 October 1997. UK
Peak UK Chart Position: 50

Track-listing: Love to See You/Sonny and His Sister/Ballad of a Landlord/Take It Forever/Misty Water/A Room Full of Nothing/Happy Go Lucky/For the Girl/Summer Follows Spring/I Saw the Light

2009 reissue bonus tracks: Ballad of a Landlord (acoustic version)/Working Class Hero (live)/Close to You/Music to Watch Girls By/Bang Went Forever/Love to See You (acoustic version)/Misty Water (acoustic version)/ Interview

Singles from Laugh

Ballad of a Landlord/Music to Watch Girls By/Close to You

Southsea Bubble Company. Released 14 June 1997. UK
Peak UK Chart Placing: 50

With Robert Lloyd

Me & My Mouth
Virgin. Released 1990. UK

Peak UK Chart Position: N/A
Tracks: Not Forever/Sweet Georgia Black/Of Course You Can't/Man Oh Man/Hey Roberta

Singles from Me & My Mouth

Funeral Stomp/Strayed/The Last Laugh/All the Time in the World

Virgin. Released 1990. UK

Peak UK Chart Position: N/A

Nothing Matters/Mama Nature's Skin
Virgin. Released 1990. UK

Peak UK Chart Position: N/A

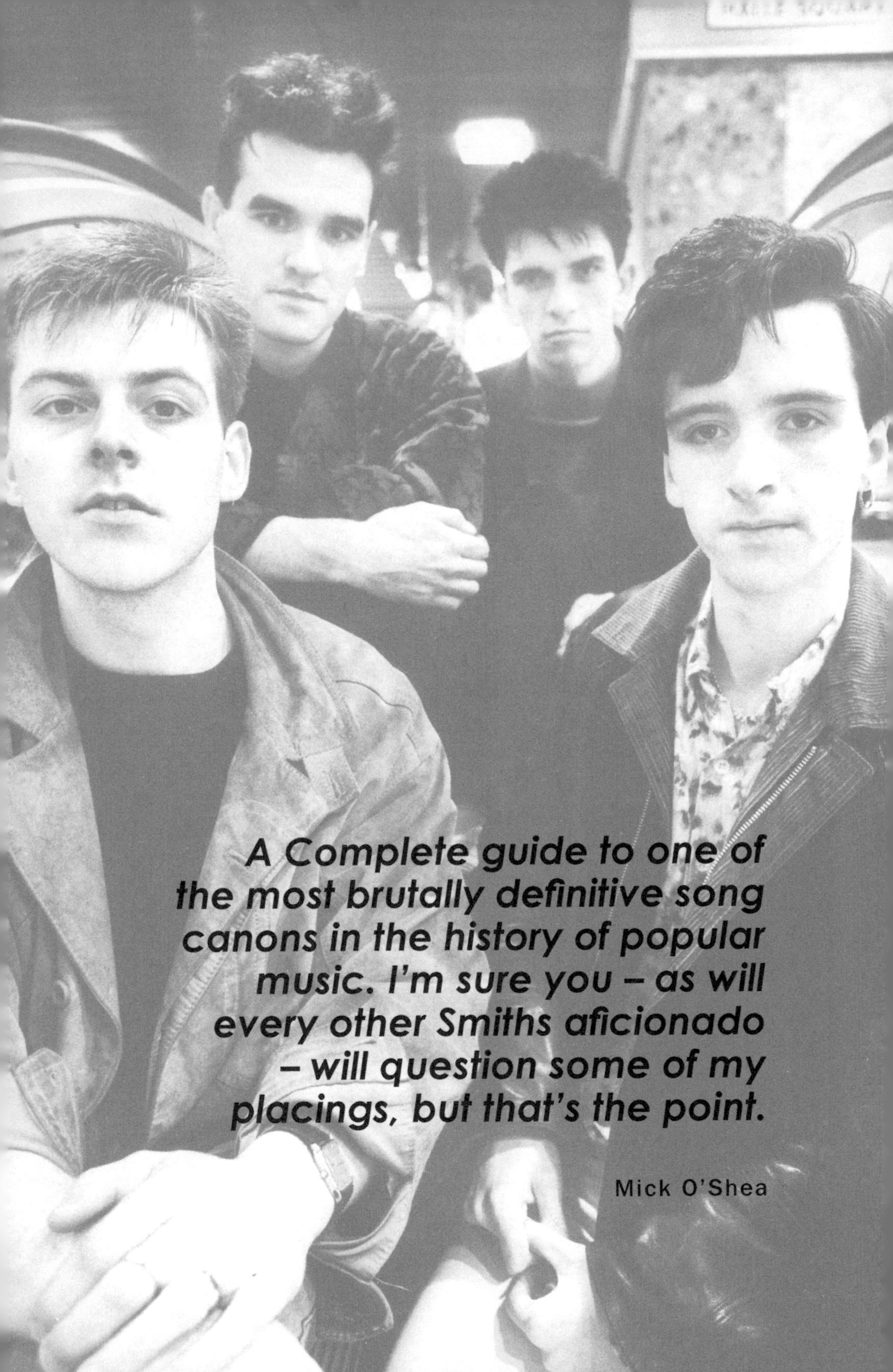
A Complete guide to one of the most brutally definitive song canons in the history of popular music. I'm sure you – as will every other Smiths aficionado – will question some of my placings, but that's the point.
Mick O'Shea

PART THREE

THE SMITHS TOP TRACKS

In descending order I give you a complete guide to one of the most brutally definitive song canons in the history of popular music. I'm sure you – as will every other Smiths aficionado –will question some of my placings. But surely that's the point. And there are worse ways to while away a rain-soaked October day that ruminate over the hits and misses that made The Smiths the most singular band of the Eighties...

#73. 'Golden Lights' (B-side to 12 inch version of 'Ask')

'Golden Lights' was a 1965 UK Top 30 hit for a long-forgotten Dusty Springfield wannabe called Lynn Annette Ripley, who went by the stage name 'Twinkle' Morrissey would proclaim the cover "an act of playful perversity," but such impish obstinacy could and should have been put to better use. Even in the inclusion of Kirsty MacColl's dulcet tones couldn't lift it above a turd-polishing exercise.

#72. 'Accept Yourself' (12 inch version of 'This Charming Man')

Additional tracks on 12 inch singles are by and large poor fare, but 'Accept Yourself' plumbs the direst of depths. I thought it crap the first time of hearing – at the time of release - and my opinion hasn't changed in the interim. Indeed, It's a toss-up as to whether it deserves bottom billing, but moving on . . .

#71. 'The Draize Train' (B-side to 12 inch version of 'Panic')

Not the first instrumental offering Mozzer and Co. thrust upon us, but most definitely the least appealing. Rumour has it that Mozzer refused to put words to the tune simply because he thought it to be the weakest thing Marr had ever come up with. Not quite . . . but pretty close.

#70. 'Meat Is Murder' (Meat Is Murder)

Meat Is Murder is a great album, so how ironic that the title track should prove the weakest song on there. Morrissey's long-standing advocacy of animal rights is honourable enough, and while 'Meat Is Murder' still features regularly in his solo sets, it's a meandering dry dirge in need of lashings of gravy.

THE SMITHS

#69. 'Work Is a Four-Letter Word' (B-side to 'Girlfriend in a Coma')

Morrissey and Marr's relationship was already strained to breaking point by the time The Smiths headed into the studio for what was to prove the band's final studio session in May 1987, so hearing Mozzer announce he wanted to cover this Cilla Black trifle from the 1968 film pushed him beyond the point of no return. It wasn't that he had any personal antipathy to Cilla per se, he couldn't bring himself to play along to her songs. Such was his displeasure that he fled to LA and wouldn't clap eyes on his nemesis again for 21 years. So far as we know, Cilla remained blissfully unaware of her proving the inadvertent cause behind the break-up, which Mozzer has since deemed "pretty much to her credit."

#68. 'Death at One's Elbow' (Strangeways, Here We Come)

One doesn't normally equate whimsical seaside organ with The Smiths and with good reason. Indeed their attempt to introduce faux zydeco shuffles to their fourth and final album was worthy of a night spent in Strangways to consider their folly.

#67. 'Money Changes Everything' (B-side to 'Big Mouth Strikes Again')

The second instrumental to feature is a decent enough ditty but given its teasing title one expects to hear Mozzer come bursting in at any moment with either a rant about the state of the nation's then current fiscal situation or bemoan his not finding enough cash down the back of the sofa to take the bus into town. Marr would ultimately cash in on the tune by handing it to Bryan Ferry, who, having added words, scored a hit with 'The Right Stuff.'

#66. 'I Keep Mine Hidden' (B-side to 12 inch version of 'Girlfriend in a Coma')

This rather mediocre effort about the virtues of guarding one's emotions was spawned from the same Smiths-snuffing session as 'Work Is a Four-Letter Word' – reportedly the last song the band wrote together. Also, what's with the totally un-Smiths whistling solo at the beginning? I've made the mistake of refreshing my memory by listening to it on *YouTube* and it's stuck in my head now.

#65. 'Back to the Old House' (B-side to 'What Difference Does It Make?')

My local's the Old House at Dorking, and after listening to this run-of-the-mill lament for childhood innocence, I suddenly feel like drowning my sorrows in Guinness.

#64. 'Well I Wonder' (Meat Is Murder)

Did you know of all the songs from the first three Smiths albums 'Well I Wonder' is the only one they never attempted to play live? Well, I wonder . . . Well, I don't to be honest' cos they had far better songs in their repertoire.

#63. 'Paint a Vulgar Picture' (Strangeways, Here We Come)

Everybody remembers George Michael's 'Freedom '90', but The Smiths were railing about corporate entities within the music and media industries happy to put cash

before creativity while Yoggy was still trying to shake off his Wham image. But having said that, George does it better #62. 'Jeane' (B-side to 'This Charming Man')
Joe Strummer and Mick Jones were happy to go the extra mile when it came to a penning a B-side – The Smiths not so much as 'Jeanne' readily exemplifies. True, it was an early stab at songcraft on Morrissey and Marr's part but save for a not-to-be-forgotten airing on some naff kids TV show – with Mozzer trading lines with Sandie Shaw – this one was swiftly consigned to the 'must try harder' file.

#61. 'What's the World' (B-side to 'Sweet and Tender Hooligan')

Technically The Smiths didn't record this James cover – from the latter Mancunian act's debut EP, Jimone – as it's a live recording from a show at Glasgow's Barrowlands in September 1985. It's unusual for a headline act to cover a song by one of their support acts, but it was all about sharing the love.

#60. 'Oscillate Wildly' (B-side to UK 12 inch version of 'How Soon Is Now?')

For a guy fond of hearing his own voice it's surprising how many instrumentals The Smiths recorded. 'Oscillate Wildly' was the first and best of the bunch . . . by far.

#59. 'Wonderful Woman' (B-side to 12 inch version of 'This Charming Man')

Morrissey's tongue-in-cheek ode to his fellow Mancunian, best chum, and muse, photographer and radical feminist Linder Sterling. Speaking with Simon Goddard for the latter's highly-insightful Mozipedia, Mozzer explained how the 'Wonderful Woman' was an "incredibly vicious person [yet] had a magnetic ray to me." At the end of the day it's another early B-side that was soon discarded and maybe rightly so.

#58. 'Girl Afraid' (B-side to 12 inch version of 'Heaven Knows I'm Miserable Now')

It's been argued elsewhere that 'Girl Afraid' might have fared better had Morrisey's lyric been left to haunt the studio mixing desk. Marr's slinky guitar riff certainly deserved than this at any rate. Mozzer reportedly took his inspiration for the lyric from the 1943 comedy-drama, Old Acquaintance, starring yet another of his beloved Hollywood divas, Bette Davis.

#57. 'This Night Has Opened My Eyes' (Hatful of Hollow)

Did you know Shelagh Delaney is one of Morrissey's favourite writers? No, really? Well, Shelagh does really need to take a bow here as her lines feature in many a Smiths/ Morrissey song. However, she was a Salford lass after all. 'This Night Has Opened My Eyes' takes its unveiled inspiration from Delaney's – a morose 'kitchen sinker' questioning class, race, gender and sexual orientation in mid-twentieth-century Britain. Just your average theme for any Smiths ditty then.

#56. 'Asleep' (B-side to 'The Boy with the Thorn in His Side')

It would be discourteous to say we've left the chaff behind, but that's oft the dilemma

when collating a rundown of a stupendous canon such as The Smiths. 'Asleep' is one of the band's finer ballads – it's also the first Morrissey and Marr collaboration where the latter opts to express to encapsulate the song's theme via piano rather than his customary guitar. Go Johnny, Go!

#55. 'Vicar in a Tutu' (The Queen Is Dead)

'Vicar in a Tutu' could be described as being a delightful interlude of comic relief midway through side two of *The Queen Is Dead* – sandwiched as is it is betwixt 'Bigmouth Strikes Again' and 'The Boy with the Thorn in His Side', and 'There Is a Light That Never Goes Out' and 'Some Girls Are Bigger Than Others'. It's an all right song, but for me 'Vicar in a Tutu' takes something away from what is undoubtedly The Smiths' finest hour. What, you don't agree? Best get penning your own Smiths book then . . .

#54. 'Miserable Lie' (The Smiths)

My least fave track on *The Smiths* – if only because of Morrissey's ridiculous falsetto throughout. If I'd have been a fly on the wall at Strawberry Studios I'd have buzzed some advice into the bequiffed one's earhole – "drop this one, Moz; it's miserable . . . and not in a good way."

#53. 'Rusholme Ruffians' (Meat Is Murder)

I suppose Rusholme had its fair share of ruffians, but for anyone that hails from Manchester, or grew up within a 30-mile radius of the city, Rusholme – or Wilmslow Road to be precise – conjures up images of curry. Mmmmmm, where was I...? Oh yeah, this is one where Rourke's groovy bass strut overshadows the Morrissey/ Marr show. Also, who doesn't love the live version on *Rank* which adeptly morphs out of Elvis' 'Marie's the Name (Of His Latest Flame)'. Now, chicken tikka pathia, anyone . . .?

#52. 'I Won't Share You' (Strangeways, Here We Come)

Often referred to as being The Smiths' 'Let It Be' song, 'I Won't Share You' is a haunting ballad built around an all-too-familiar chord progression that Marr uses on other songs within the Smiths canon yet transcends above the norm thanks to its being played on the autoharp – an instrument not usually associated with The Smiths. A rather excellent way to bring an album to a close once all's said and done. One can almost imagine the boys playing it atop the old Affleck's Palace.

#51. 'Sweet and Tender Hooligan' (B-side to 12 inch version of 'Sheila Take a Bow')

One of the better B-sides from the band's oeuvre and would have been better still had Mozzer took his nail scissors to the lyrics to fit with Marr's jingly/jangly fretwork. Sometimes less is more.

#50. 'Suffer Little Children' (The Smiths)

Morrissey's fascination with the Moors Murders is perhaps understandable given that Ian Brady and Myra Hindley carried out their harrowing crimes more or less on his doorstep, but his referencing three of the victims in the lyric to 'Suffer Little Children' obviously didn't sit well with their relatives. (At the time he and Marr were penning the song Pauline Read and Keith Bennet had yet been attributed to Brady and Hindley); the eerily haunting children's laughter echoing behind Marr's droning guitar merely adding to everyone's discomfiture and would make for an unsettling inclusion on any band's back-catalogue.

Boots and Woolworths refused to stock both the album and single ('Suffer Little Children also features as the B-side to 'Heaven Knows I'm Miserable Now'), but Ann West (mother of Lesley Ann Downey) subsequently accepted the band's intentions were honourable.

#49. 'Barbarism Begins at Home' (Meat Is Murder)

This one comes in for criticism from certain quarters for Andy Rourke's funky slap bass, but I really The longest Smiths song at seven minutes, which is either a sign of how deeply they cared about child abuse or an indication of how desperate they were to fill out Side Two of *Meat Is Murder*. Unlikely slap-bass enthusiast Andy Rourke plays the funk, never exactly this band's speciality.

#48. 'I Don't Owe You Anything' (The Smiths)

One of the criticisms aimed at The Smiths debut long player is John Porter's production, which can be described as mediocre at best – particularly on 'I Don't Owe You Anything'. And the fact that he was only allowed near a single track on both *Meat Is Murder* and *The Queen Is Dead* kind of says what the band thought of his efforts. Mozzer's fave Sixties

rave, Sandie Shaw, chose the song as the B-side to her version of 'Hand in Glove', which, seeing as it provided her with her first UK Top 30 placing in 15 years, meant she pretty much owed *The Smiths* everything.

#47. 'These Things Take Time' (B-side to 12 inch version of 'What Difference Does It Make?')

One of The Smiths' better seemingly throwaway 12 inch bonus tracks, but perhaps Marr's choppy riff deserved a more cutting lyric. Just saying . . .

#46. 'The Headmaster Ritual' (Meat Is Murder)

To my mind, this is another example of Marr's magic being senselessly negated by Morrissey's senseless yodelling – WTF?!? In essence, this, the second album opener, was Morrissey's jaundiced view of his schooldays at St Mary's Tech, which understandably struck a chord with many of the band's following – despite many of those same Smithites having remained within the educational system by going on to uni.

#45. 'Nowhere Fast' (Meat Is Murder)

The song where Morrisey declares he'd like to drop his trousers to the Queen, a salacious act that every sensible child would supposedly understand. Not quite as seditious as the Sex Pistols' attack on our reigning sovereign of seven years earlier perhaps, but an eyebrow-raiser all the same – especially if Mozzer chose not to don his undercrackers while carrying out his fantasy flash.

#44. 'Rubber Ring' (B-side to 12 inch version of 'The Boy with the Thorn in His Side')

Morrissey has often said how he lost himself in music at a very early age and fell hopelessly in love with the voices emanating from either the radio or the record player – regardless of their gender – and that pop music had allowed him to transcend his otherwise mundane existence. In 'Rubber Ring' he rather vaingloriously attempts to exalt the power of his songs to not only lift his fans above their own drudgery but save their lives. Can a song save lives? Answers on a postcard, please.

#43. 'Unhappy Birthday' (Strangeways, Here We Come)

If it wasn't for the effects-laden electric thrash and harmonium, 'Unhappy Birthday' wouldn't have looked out of place on either *The Smiths* or *Meat Is Murder*. Marr says the song is introspective yet wistful – two adjectives that perfectly sum up Morrissey both as a man and a songsmith.

#42. 'Never Had No One Ever' (The Queen Is Dead)

An offbeat 6/8 groove that doesn't initially smack you in the face yet somehow manages to burrow itself inside your mind. Hardly surprising it would become a firm live favourite amongst Smithites.

#41. 'That Joke Isn't Funny Anymore' (Meat Is Murder)

While speaking with *Melody Maker* shortly after *Meat Is Murder*'s release, Morrissey said how 'That Joke Isn't Funny Anymore'

was in response to the ongoing journalistic mockery of his songwriting that dwelt "on the unhappy side of life" and to persistent attempts to expose him as a 'fake'. Marr says it's one of his favourite Smiths songs, but the fans didn't agree as it barely scraped into the UK Top 50.

#40. 'A Rush and a Push and the Land Is Ours' (Strangeways, Here We Come)

This eerie piano ramble sets the tone for what was to prove Moz and Co's final studio album. Morrissey's obsession with the writings of Oscar Wilde is well-known, but the title is undoubtedly an oblique tip of the cap to the poet's mother, Jane, a staunch Irish nationalist, who, under the pseudonym 'Speranza' (the Italian word for hope), wrote poetry for the revolutionary Young Irelanders.

#39. 'I Started Something I Couldn't Finish' (Strangeways, Here We Come)

Somewhat ironically, by the time 'I Started Something I Couldn't Finish' was released as a single The Smiths had announced they were splitting up. It's also rather fitting that Morrissey couldn't even decide if he was happy with the finished track as in the original demo he can be heard asking producer Stephen Street if they should have another run-through.

#38. 'Is It Really So Strange?' (B-side to 'Sheila Take a Bow')

An above average mid-tempo number that Morrissey and Marr reportedly wrote while on a promo visit to LA and subsequently recorded for an end-of-year John Peel session; its quasi-rockabilly overtones proving particularly popular with American audiences.

#37. 'What She Said' (B-side to 'Shakespeare's Sister')

'What She Said' was lifted from *Meat Is Murder* as a B-side for 'Shakespeare's Sister' which didn't. It's a fast-paced rocker driven along by Joyce's drums and fuelled by another of Marr's blistering riffs.

#36. 'Unloveable' (B-side to 12 inch version of 'Big Mouth Strikes Again')

Marr apparently penned the tune to this woefully underrated number the same night he came up with 'Some Girls Are Bigger Than Others' before – as was his habit – dutifully recording both tunes onto a cassette and posting them off to Mozzer to add a lyric.

35. 'London' (B-side to 12 inch version of 'Shoplifters of the World Unite')

Craig Gannon might have only been in The Smiths for six months, but the guitarist nonetheless left his mark – most notably for providing a twin-guitar sonic attack on 'London' which the band's B-side trilogy (along with 'Half a Person' and 'Is It Really So Strange?') warning of the pitfalls of falling for the capital's alluring lights. That the band would make a move to London before hightailing it back to Manchester within the year suggests an autobiographical slant.

HOW SOON IS NOW?

THE SMITHS

#34. 'You Just Haven't Earned It Yet, Baby' (The World Won't Listen)

Undoubtedly one of The Smiths more commercial efforts, 'You Just Haven't Earned It Yet', Baby' was inspired by – or so Morrissey would have us believe – a direct quote from Rough Trade's head honcho Geoff Travis (though it has since transpired that Travis' quote ended on 'yet' rather than 'baby'. Despite its undeniable brilliance, the song would become something of a bugbear for fans owing to its shameless inclusion on the compilation album, *The World Won't Listen*. This, of course, could have all been part of Travis' retribution . . .

#33. 'Stretch Out and Wait' (B-side to 12 inch version of 'Shakespeare's Sister')

'Stretch Out and Wait' isn't just another of Morrissey's ramblings about the sexual act, it's by far his finest lyrics relating to the subject suitably accompanied by some of Marr's finest acoustic noodlings.

#32. 'Pretty Girls Make Graves' (The Smiths)

Morrissey lifted the title for 'Pretty Girls Make Graves' from Jack Kerouac's 1958 novel *The Dharma Bums*, and in turn provided a Seattle-based post-punk outfit their name. The song's pretty much a thinly-disguised critique of hetero society, with Mozzer's Polish pal Anna Jablonska (who supposedly dressed only in authentic Victorian clothes) playing the cruel woman.

#31. 'I Want the One I Can't Have' (Meat Is Murder)

Stephen Street knew how to get the best from Morrissey but was having one of those days while The Smiths were recording 'I Want the One I Can't Have' as it was his accepting Mozzer's gloriously off-key vocal that prevented the song's release as a single. It's nonetheless a cracking punk romp about, yes, you've guessed it, unrequited love.

#30. 'The Hand That Rocks the Cradle' (The Smiths)

'The Hand That Rocks the Cradle' is the first song Morrissey and Marr ever wrote together. The lyric was lifted from Mozzer's poem of the same name, while the riff is a blatant rip-off of Patti Smith's 'Kimberly'. However, we'll forgive Marr's plagiarism seeing as it was at a Patti Smith gig at the Manchester Apollo at the fag-end of August 1978 that he first encountered his future songwriting collaborator.

#29. 'Shoplifters of the World Unite'

Mozzer would have us believe that 'Shoplifters of the World Unite' isn't about picking up a Snickers and sticking it in your coat pocket but rather about "spiritual shoplifting, cultural shoplifting, taking things and using them to your own advantage." Moreover, according to Smiths scholar Simon Goddard, the lyric contains lines appropriated from songs by Joni Mitchell and Rickie Lee Jones amongst others. Stop thief!!

#28. 'Some Girls Are Bigger Than Others' (The Queen Is Dead)

Johnny Marr describes 'Some Girls Are

Bigger Than Others' as a "beautiful piece of music" and he'll get no argument from me. The song has taken on significance as it was only played live once – at what was to prove The Smiths final live show (Brixton Academy, December 12, 1986)

#27. 'Last Night I Dreamt That Somebody Loved Me' (Strangeways, Here We Come)

'Last Night I Dreamt That Somebody Loved Me' was the third and final single from *Strangeways, Here We Come*, and also serves as the album's show-stopping climax. Unsurprisingly, the backdrop of crowd noises – from the miners' strike of 1984 – 85 (lifted from a BBC sound effects album) – was cut from the 7 inch single to make it more radio-friendly. Speaking with *Select* magazine in December 1993, Marr said how the last time he'd met up with Morrissey, the latter had said how 'Last Night . . .' was his favourite Smiths song.

#26. 'Death of a Disco Dancer' (Strangeways, Here We Come)

'Death of a Disco Dancer' is a grim elegy to the sufferings of the mid-Eighties gay community with Morrissey purportedly substituting 'disco dancer' for 'homosexual', while ruminating on the rise of gay AIDS casualties and homophobic violence. Mozzer actually plays piano on the song – the only Smiths recording to feature him playing a musical instrument. Marr once commented to *Q* Magazine that the keyboard drone on the song was like "Goldfinger on bad acid, which is kind of The Smiths in a nutshell". Indeed, it is . . .

#25. 'Frankly Mr. Shankly' (The Queen Is Dead)

'Frankly, Mr Shankly' isn't an ode to the legendary Liverpool manager, Bill, but rather a rant aimed at Rough Trade's head honcho Geoff Travis set to a burlesque music-hall air driven along by Andy Rourke's jaunty bass. Speaking about the song to *Mojo*, Travis said how he saw the lyric being "part of Morrissey's desire to be somewhere else". In his eponymously-titled autobiography, however, Morrissey caustically opines that Travis "had zero appreciation for the songs that had saved him from life's lavatory."

#24. 'Still Ill' (The Smiths)

The Smiths enjoyed playing this death-or-glory rallying call as 'Still Ill' is second only to 'Hand in Glove' in terms of live performances. The lyric also provided Mark Gill with the title of the 2017 Morrissey biopic *England Is Mine*, which covers his pre-Smiths years. Definitely worth a watch

#23. 'Bigmouth Strikes Again' (The Queen Is Dead)

'Bigmouth Strikes Again' is The Smiths answer to the Stones' 'Jumping Jack Flash' – at least that's how Johnny Marr tells it. It's also another of Mozzer's rants at a demanding and merciless media in which the protagonist – Morrissey? - compares himself to Joan of Arc. The shrill Chipmunks-esque backing vocals are punningly credited to 'Ann Coates' (Ancoats is an affluent area of Manchester) is actually Morrissey tuned to a higher pitch.

#22. 'Cemetry Gates' (The Queen Is Dead)

Speaking about 'Cemetry Gates' during a 1997 interview with *Guitar* magazine,

Marr said how he'd wrote the song in the hope that it would meet expectations to his and Morrissey's being lauded as 'The Great New Songwriters' at the time of the band's signing to Rough Trade. Mozzer's fascination with death is well-known, of course. "I have a dramatic, unswayable, unavoidable obsession with death," he told *Spin* magazine in 1988. "If there was a magical, beautiful pill that would retire you from this world, I think I would take it." The misspelling of 'Cemetery' was an unintentional error on Mozzer's part as he's always had trouble with the spelling.

#21. 'Hand in Glove' (The Smiths)

'Hand in Glove' is undoubtedly one of the classic debut singles ever. The Smiths were certainly proud of the song, with Morrissey going to far as to cite the couplet "Though we may be hidden by rags, we have something they'll never have" as being his favourite Smiths lyric. At the time of the single's May 1983 release, he brazenly declared that he expected the single to be a massive hit. This was not to be, alas, as the record stalled at a miserly #124 on the UK chart.

#20. 'Girlfriend in a Coma' (Strangeways, Here We Come)

'Girlfriend in a Coma', the lead single from *Strangeways, Here We Come,* was inspired by Jamaican singing duo Bob and Marcia's 1970 UK hit 'Young, Gifted and Black', which Morrissey and Marr both adored. The promo video (which proved a surprise MTV hit) features Morrissey performing alone alongside footage from the 1964 subculture classic, *The Leather Boys*, starring Colin Campbell and Rita Tushingham. The reason for Marr, Rourke, and Joyce's absence in the video is owing to The Smiths' split.

#19. 'Sheila Take a Bow'

'Sheila Take a Bow' saw The Smiths go Glam. According to Smiths folklore, Mozzer intended on bringing in Sandie Shaw as a second vocalist. However, when Shaw arrived at Solid Bond Studios in Marble Arch (owned by Paul Weller) to record the song Morrissey was absent owing to his suffering from the lurgy. Mike Joyce recalls Shaw being 'frantic' at the news, and of her calling Morrissey on the phone to get the song's melody. Shaw's version was ultimately scrapped. It was to prove a wise move on someone's part as 'Sheila' gave The Smiths their highest chart placing during the band's lifetime.

#18. 'You've Got Everything Now' (The Smiths)

The version of 'You've Got Everything Now' that appears on The Smiths suffers from poor production, but the one they recorded for Kid Jenson for the latter's highly-rated radio show is proof positive of the song's true potential.

#17. 'William, It Was Really Nothing'

'William, It Was Really Nothing' is Mozzer's anti-marriage song from a male viewpoint. 'I thought it was about time there was a male voice speaking directly to another male saying that marriage was a waste of time," he said around the time of the song's release, ". . . 'that, in fact, it was 'absolutely nothing.'" Speculation still abounds that the song was directed at The Associates' doomed frontman Billy MacKenzie,

HANDSOME
DEVIL

the theory being largely based on The Associates' belated 1993 riposte 'Stephen, You're Really Something'. Something that Morrissey has never confirmed. It's such a shame that Mozzer chose to rip open his shirt to reveal the words 'MARRY ME' etched on his chest during a performance on *Top Of The Pops*.

#16. 'Handsome Devil' (The Smiths)

When The Smiths recorded their first Peel Session in May 1983, the venerable DJ prefaced the band's appearance saying how Mozzer and Co were being touted as the "latest prophets of Northern doom". Powered by Marr's gleefully sinister rockabilly riff, 'Handsome Devil' shows The Smiths at their very best, yet the song would see the band enmired in a scandal owing to outspoken Conservative MP Geoffrey Dickens claiming the song was about paedophilia. Morrissey didn't take this slur kindly. Speaking to *NME* in early September 1983, he scoffed at Dickens' spurious claim saying, "This piece makes me out to be a proud child-molester and I don't even like children."

#15. 'Shakespeare's Sister'

Mozzer would subsequently lay the blame for the poor showing of 'Shakespeare's Sister' on the UK chart (the song peaked at a modest #26 following its release in March 1985) at Geoff Travis' door. "'Shakespeare's Sister' – regardless of what many people feel – was the song of my life," he told *Record Mirror*. "I put everything into that song and I wanted it more than anything else to be a huge success and – as it happens – it wasn't. We can talk about independents and majors till the end of the day, but ultimately, when you make a good record, you want it to be heard. The song's title was lifted from Virginia Woolf's feminist classic *A Room of One's Own*, and in turn provided Siobhan Fahey and Marcella Detroit with a name to hang their songs on.

#14. 'What Difference Does It Make?' (The Smiths)

For some inexplicable reason Mozzer hates the lyric to 'What Difference Does It Make?' saying he finds them "facile, mildly embarrassing, and very Simon Le Bon", and that had the Duran Duran frontman penned the lyric he would have probably covered the song. Go figure.

#13. 'Please, Please, Please Let Me Get What I Want' (B-side to 'William, It Was Really Nothing')

Mozzer apparently regretted not releasing 'Please, Please, Please Let Me Get What I Want' as a single in its own right. "Hiding it away on a B-side was sinful," he told *Melody Maker* in 1987. "I feel sad about it now although we did include it on *Hatful Of Hollow* by way of semi-repentance." He then went on to add that when the band first played it to Geoff Travis, the latter had questioned the song's brevity. "They kept asking, 'Where's the rest of the song?', but to me, it's like a very brief punch in the face. Lengthening the song would, to my mind, have simply been explaining the blindingly obvious."
Though Mozzer did not object when Slow Moving Millie's 2011 cover of the song was featured in a John Lewis Christmas commercial, he took umbrage over its being used for advertising celebrated TV chef Gordon Ramsay's Channel 4 show *Christmas Cookalong Live*. Having settled for $14,800 damages, he donated the cash to fund an organisation that campaigns against foie

gras and its distributors.

#12. 'The Boy With the Thorn in His Side' (The Queen Is Dead)

The 'boy' the song is Mozzer himself while the 'thorn' digging into his ribs is the music industry. Speaking with the actress Margi Clarke, he said how the song was a veiled attack against all those that had tried to do him and The Smiths wrong. From a musical standpoint, 'The Boy With The Thorn In His Side' breaks new ground – primarily owing to Marr's lavish layering of flamenco-style guitar. It was also the first Smiths single to be accompanied by a promo video – even if the end result was pretty naff.

#11. 'Ask'

'Ask' is undoubtedly a great song, but Smithites still feel aggrieved that Steve Lillywhite supposedly ruined Marr and Gannon's intricate fretwork on the original mix. John Porter was all for the band bringing in Kirsty MacColl to provide backing vocals, but Morrissey's decision to have Kirsty's hubby (Lillywhite) produce the song left him feeling somewhat aggrieved. While it's not beyond the realms of possibility that Porter's more complex vision of 'Ask' will be unearthed, Lillywhite's version can hardly be viewed as a failure. Any ideas as to the identity of the "buck-toothed girl from Luxembourg?"

#10. 'How Soon Is Now?' (Meat Is Murder)

And so we arrive at the Top 10. Marr apparently penned 'How Soon Is Now?' about Morrissey's crippling shyness. The song – the longest within the Smiths' canon – has, of course, since become an anthem for the alienated and socially isolated. The song struck a nerve with audiences everywhere and is rightly viewed as a classic. Marr purposely strove to pen an intro that would be instantly recognisable and there's little argument that he didn't achieve his aim. Richard Butler's post-Psychedelic Furs outfit Love Spit Love's cover version (which featured as a bonus track on the band's 1997 second album, *Trysome Eatone*) was used as the theme song of the US TV series *Charmed*. In a perfect world the Halliwell sisters would have surely called upon the Book of Shadows to bring about a Smiths reunion.

#9. 'The Queen Is Dead' (The Queen Is Dead)

You just have to wonder at Johnny Marr's self-effacement. Instead of taking the kudos for letting his creativity run wild while toying around with his wah-wah pedal during a marathon jam session he admits to stumbling upon the tune by accident whilst trying to do the "Detroit thing" in paying homage to the Motor City's punk trailblazing MC5. Mozzer's lyric talks of the protagonist breaking into a palace – presumably Buck House – armed with a sponge and a spanner. '"The Queen Is Dead' is six-and-a-half minutes of genius, but while admiring Mozzer's anti-monarchic musings, there's no arguing the Sex Pistols did it better. Yet it was nonetheless nice to see the flowers ended up poking out of Mozzer's behind rather than end up ditched in a dustbin.

#8. 'Panic'

'Panic' sees The Smiths go T-Rex and there's nothing wrong with that in my eyes – even if Marr's rip-off of 'Metal Guru' was maybe a tad too obvious for the purists. And who knew the 'hang the DJ' refrain referred to Steve Wright? The song came about owing to

Wright (who at the time was with Radio One) tactlessly playing Wham's 'I'm Your Man' after a news report on the Chernobyl disaster in April 1986. To be fair to Wright, he was only adhering to the playlist on that given day. Yet while there's no arguing he was and still is an irritating twat, he inadvertently sowed the seed for a creative masterpiece.

#7. 'Half a Person' (B-side to 'Shoplifters of the World Unite')

The conundrum with Mozzer's lyrics is that that whenever they're delivered in the first person you're never sure whether he's drawing on his own experiences. There are dozens of songs about kids doing a 'Dick Wittington' and heading for London in the hope of a better future, but none are quite so poignant. Marr rates 'Half a Person' as being "The best songwriting moment me and Morrissey ever had." Few would argue with that, but I'm one of the few as you will have guessed from its placing.

#6. 'Heaven Knows I'm Miserable Now'

Morrissey singing about being miserable, or about misery in general is what he based his 36-year-and-counting career on. But misery does love company, which probably explains why 'Heaven Knows I'm Miserable Now' was to prove The Smiths' greatest hit during the band's existence. Mozzer and Marr came up with the song in a cockroach-infested New York hotel room – well, if you can be miserable there, you can be miserable anywhere. Marr conjured up the riff while trying out the brand-spanking cherry-red Gibson ES-355 that Sire Records' head honcho Seymour Stein gifted to him in the hope of adding The Smiths to his label's roster – a ploy which worked. Way to go, Seymour!

#5. 'I Know It's Over' (The Queen Is Dead)

'I Know It's Over' is celebrated by Smithites as being the bleakest or saddest song in The Smiths' perennial glass-half-empty repertoire – and that takes some doing! Mozzer and Marr apparently tossed this one out the same autumnal evening they came up with 'Frankly, Mr Shankly' and 'There Is a Light That Never Goes Out'. Most bands spend their entire feckin' careers without coming up with anything to match one of these. And one likes to think the beers were on Joyce and Rourke that night.

#4. 'Stop Me If You Think That You've Heard This One Before' (Strangeways, Here We Come)

This one featuring so prominently might confuse a fair number of Smithites, but certain songs stir differing emotions or memories. Me and a bunch of my mates were enjoying a long weekend in London in May 1988 (to see Burnley contest the long-forgotten Sherpa Van Trophy against Wolves at Wembley. We ended up gate-crashing a party somewhere – Islington, I think – and what just as the tension was mounting amongst the locals at our intrusion someone popped this onto the CD player. Cue dancing!! 'Stop Me . . .' was to prove The Smiths' most high-profile American hit – largely due to MTV placing the promo video on heavy rotation. Said video features Mozzer – accompanied by a cluster of adoring suedeheads sporting Smiths shirts cycling around Manchester. One of the buildings they idle past is the now-legendary Salford Lads Club (in

Ordsall), which has become something of a shrine for all Smithites.

#3. 'This Charming Man'

It's hard to imagine The Smiths ever coming under record company pressure. Yet with 'Hand in Glove' having failed to set the chart alight as Geoff Travis had clearly been hoping, the band had to deliver – and deliver they did. Marr came up with 'This Charming Man' especially for an impending John Peel session – the same night he came up with 'pretty Girls Make Graves' and 'Still Ill' Little wonder Rough Trade co-opted it as the follow-up single. Mozzer lifted the line, "A jumped-up pantry boy, who never knew his place" from the 1972 film adaptation of the homoerotic play, *Sleuth*, starring Laurence Olivier and Michael Caine.
Acquiescing to their label's wishes was a brave move on the band's part as at the time of the single's release in October 1983 there was no place in the pop world for homoerotic paeans – especially those crooned by a celibate gay guy proclaiming himself a "prophet for the fourth gender". And yet Mozzer's evocative vocal coupled with Marr's jumped-up jangly guitar punctured our hearts like . . . well, like a bicycle on a hillside desolate.

#2. 'There Is a Light That Never Goes Out' (The Queen Is Dead)

Andy Rourke once referred to 'There Is a Light That Never Goes Out' as being the UK indie scene's 'Candle in the Wind', and had Elton John and Bernie Taupin penned it would surely have enjoyed a far better UK chart placing than the rather desultory #25. This is often regarded as being the jewel within The Smiths' crown, and rightly so. Indeed, I would have installed it at #1 if it wasn't for another Mozzer/Marr composition having already tugged my heartstrings to snapping point. According to Marr's recollections the song took just 40 minutes to write from start to finish – although lifting the intro from the Stones' cover of Marvin Gaye's 'Hitch Hike' probably saved a bit of time. Johnny also says that while he never expected 'There Is a Light That Never Goes Out' to become an anthem, he knew instantly that it was the best song he'd ever heard.

#1. 'Reel Around the Fountain' (The Smiths)

Speaking to *Rolling Stone* in October 1986, Mozzer said how 'Reel Around the Fountain' was "about a loss of innocence" (and not child-molesting as the UK tabloid muckrakers would have had us believe). For me, the song conjures up images of yesteryear; going out to a pub, club, or gig with my mates with The Smiths serving as part of the soundtrack to my unfolding life story. I thought those halcyon days would stretch out forever. They didn't, of course, but I still get a tingling sensation remembering being in my bedroom, slipping album, *The Smiths*, from its sleeve and gently placing the needle onto the start of side one and hearing the lush production of 'Reel Around The Fountain' for the first time; Mozzer's haunting lyric floating over Marr's slow-burn guitar. All in all, 358 seconds of pop music in its purest unadulterated form.

PREPARED BY

DATE

THE QUEEN

7 PANIC

I WANT THE ONE ...

VICAR

7 THERE IS A LIGHT

ASK

RUSHOLME ...

8 FRANKLY ...

THE BOY ...

5 WHAT SHE SAID

IS IT REALLY SO STRANG

9 NEVER ...

CEMETRY GATES

LONDON

5 MEAT IS MURDER

I KNOW IT'S OVER

DRAIZE TRAI

HOW SOON

STILL IL

7 BIG MOUTH

LOUCESTER LEISURE CE

Bruton Way, Glouceste

MAIN HALL

Phil McIntyre presents

THE SMITHS

plus support

Saturday 18th October 1

Doors Open 7.00

TICKET £6.50

(£4.50 on production of UB.40 o

STANDING

Nº 1 20

TO BE RETAINED

PART FOUR

THE SMITHS GIG GUIDE

* Indicates bootleg recordings.

1982

Oct 4: The Ritz. Manchester, UK

Songs played: The Hand That Rocks the Cradle/Suffer Little Children/Handsome Devil/I Want a Boy for My Birthday

1983

Jan 25: Manhattan (a.k.a. Manhattan Sound). Manchester, UK

Possible songs played: The Hand That Rocks the Cradle/ Handsome Devil/I Want a Boy for My/ Birthday/What Do You See in Him?/These Things Take Time/What Difference Does it Make? *

Feb 4: The Haçienda. Manchester, UK

Set-list: These Things Take Time/What Difference Does it Make?/The Hand That Rocks the Cradle/Handsome Devil/Jeane/What Do You See in Him?/ Hand in Glove/Miserable Lie *

Feb 21: Rafters. Manchester, UK

Set-list not known.

Mar 23: The Rock Garden. London, UK

Set-list not known.

May 6: University of London Union. London, UK

Set-list not known.

May 21: Electric Ballroom. London, UK

You've Got Everything Now/Accept Yourself/What Difference Does it Make?/Reel Around the Fountain/These Things Take Time/I Don't Owe You Anything/Hand in Glove/The Hand That Rocks the Cradle/Handsome Devil/Miserable Lie *

June 2: Miner's Gala. Cannock Chase, UK

Set-list not known.

June 3: Fighting Cocks. Birmingham, UK

You've Got Everything Now/Handsome Devil/Accept Yourself/What Difference Does it Make?/Reel Around the Fountain/Wonderful Woman/ These Things Take Time/I Don't Owe You Anything/Hand in Glove/Miserable Lie *

THE SMITHS

June 4: Brixton Ace. London, UK

*You've Got Everything Now/Handsome Devil/Accept Yourself/Reel Around the Fountain/These Things Take Time/Miserable Lie **

June 29: Brixton Ace. London, UK

*You've Got Everything Now/Handsome Devil/Reel Around the Fountain/What Difference Does it Make?/Wonderful Woman/These Things Take Time/Hand in Glove/I Don't Owe You Anything/Miserable Lie **

June 30: University of Warwick. Coventry, UK

Set-list not known.

July 1: Midnight Express Club. Bournemouth, UK

*You've Got Everything Now/Handsome Devil/Reel Around the Fountain/What Difference Does it Make?/Wonderful Woman/These Things Take Time/Hand in Glove/I Don't Owe You Anything/Miserable Lie/Accept Yourself **

July 6: The Haçienda. Manchester, UK

*You've Got Everything Now/Handsome Devil/Reel Around the Fountain/What Difference Does it Make?/Wonderful Woman/These Things Take Time/I Don't Owe You Anything/Hand in Glove/Miserable Lie **

July 7: The Rock Garden. London, UK

*You've Got Everything Now/Handsome Devil/Reel Around the Fountain/What Difference Does it Make?/Wonderful Woman/These Things Take Time/I Don't Owe You Anything/Hand in Glove/Miserable Lie/Accept Yourself **

Aug 7: Lyceum Ballroom. London, UK

*You've Got Everything Now/Handsome Devil/What Difference Does it Make?/Reel Around the Fountain/These Things Take Time/Hand in Glove/I Don't Owe You Anything/Hand in Glove/Miserable Lie **

Aug 9: Dingwalls. London, UK

*You've Got Everything Now/What Difference Does it Make?/Handsome Devil/Wonderful Woman/Reel Around the Fountain/These Things Take Time/I Don't Owe You Anything/Hand in Glove/Miserable Lie/Accept Yourself/Hand in Glove/Handsome Devil **

Aug 11: Warehouse. Leeds, UK

*You've Got Everything Now/What Difference Does it Make?/Handsome Devil/Wonderful Woman/Reel Around the Fountain/These Things Take Time/I Don't Owe You Anything/Hand in Glove/Miserable Lie/Accept Yourself/Hand in Glove **

Aug 19: Gala Ballroom. Norwich, UK

*You've Got Everything Now/What Difference Does it Make?/Handsome Devil/Wonderful Woman/Reel Around the Fountain/These Things Take Time/I Don't Owe You Anything/Hand in Glove/Miserable Lie/Accept Yourself/Hand in Glove/Handsome Devil **

Aug 30: Dingwalls. London, UK

*You've Got Everything Now/What Difference Does it Make?/Pretty Girls Make Graves/Handsome Devil/Wonderful Woman/Reel Around the Fountain/Miserable Lie/These Things Take Time/I Don't Owe You Anything/Hand in Glove/Miserable Lie/Accept Yourself/Hand in Glove/Handsome Devil **

Sept 3: Woods Leisure Centre. Colchester, UK

Set-list not known.

Sept 15: The Venue. London, UK

*Handsome Devil/You've Got Everything Now/These Things Take Time/This Charming Man/Reel Around the Fountain/Miserable Lie/Still Ill/I Don't Owe You Anything/Hand in Glove/What Difference Does it make?/Accept Yourself/Hand in Glove/Handsome Devil **

Sept 16: Moles Club. Bath, UK

Set-list not known.

Sept 25: Lyceum Ballroom. London, UK

*Pretty Girls Make Graves/Wonderful Woman/Miserable Lie/Reel Around the Fountain/I Don't Owe You Anything/Hand in Glove/What Difference Does it Make?/These Things Take Time/Hand in Glove **

Sept 29: Gum Club (at Fernando's). Blackburn, UK

Set-list not known.

Sept 30: University of Birmingham. Birmingham, UK

*You've Got Everything Now/This Charming Man/Handsome Devil/Still Ill/Reel Around the Fountain/Pretty Girls Make Graves/Miserable Lie/I Don't Owe You Anything/Hand in Glove/What Difference Does it Make?/These Things Take Time/Hand in Glove/Accept Yourself **

Oct 1: City of London Polytechnic. London, UK

Set-list not known.

Oct 5: Institute of Contemporary Arts. London, UK

*You've Got Everything Now/This Charming Man/Handsome Devil/Still Ill/Reel Around the Fountain/Pretty Girls Make Graves/Miserable Lie/I Don't Owe You Anything/Hand in Glove/What Difference Does it Make?/These Things Take Time/Hand in Glove **

Oct 14: Bangor University. Bangor, UK

Set-list not known.

Oct 17: University of Sheffield. Sheffield, UK

You've Got Everything Now/Still Ill/This Charming Man/These Things Take Time/Pretty Girls Make Graves/Reel Around the Fountain/Miserable Lie/This Night Has Opened my Eyes/What Difference Does it Make?/Handsome Devil/Hand In Glove

Oct 21: North East London Polytechnic. London, UK

*These Things Take Time/This Charming Man/What Difference Does it |Make?/This Night Has Opened my Eyes/Pretty Girls Make Graves/Miserable Lie/Reel Around the Fountain/Hand in Glove/Handsome Devil/You've Got Everything Now/Hand in Glove **

Oct 22: Liverpool Polytechnic. Liverpool, UK

*Handsome Devil/Still Ill/This Charming Man/What Difference Does it Make?/Pretty Girls Make Graves/This Night Has Opened my Eyes/Hand in Glove/Reel Around the Fountain/Miserable Lie/You've Got Everything Now/Hand in Glove **

Oct 27: Kingston Polytechnic. London, UK

Set-list not known.

Oct 28: King's College London. London, UK

*Handsome Devil/Still Ill/This Charming Man/Pretty Girls Make Graves/Miserable Lie/This Night Has Opened my Eyes/ What Difference Does it Make?/Reel Around the Fountain/Hand in Glove **

Nov 10: Portsmouth Polytechnic. Portsmouth, UK

Set-list not known.

Nov 16: Leicester Polytechnic. Leicester, UK

*Handsome Devil/Still Ill/This Charming Man/What Difference Does it Make?/ This Night Has Opened my Eyes/Pretty Girls Make Graves/Hand in Glove/Reel Around the Fountain/These Things Take Time/Miserable Lie/Accept Yourself/This Charming Man/You've Got Everything Now/Hand in Glove **

Nov 17: Westfield College. London, UK

*Handsome Devil/Still Ill/This Charming Man/Pretty Girls Make Graves/This Night Has Opened my Eyes/What Difference Does it Make?/Hand in Glove/Reel Around the Fountain/Miserable Lie/Accept Yourself/This Charming Man/You've Got Everything Now **

Nov 18: Edge Hill College. Ormskirk, UK

*Handsome Devil/Still Ill/This Charming Man/Pretty Girls Make Graves/This Night Has Opened my Eyes/What Difference Does it Make?/ Wonderful Woman/Hand in Glove/Reel Around the Fountain/Miserable Lie/You've Got Everything Now/This Charming Man **

Nov 24: The Haçienda. Manchester, UK

*Handsome Devil/Still Ill/This Charming Man/Pretty Girls Make Graves/Reel Around the Fountain/Miserable Lie/This Night Has Opened my Eyes/ What Difference Does it Make?/Hand in Glove/You've Got Everything Now/These Things Take Time/This Charming Man/Accept Yourself/Hand in Glove **

Dec 6: Assembly Rooms. Derby, UK

*Handsome Devil/Still Ill/This Charming Man/Pretty Girls Make Graves/Reel Around the Fountain/What Difference Does it Make?/Miserable Lie/ This Night Has Opened my Eyes/Hand in Glove/You've Got Everything Now/These Things Take Time **

Dec 9: SFX. Dublin, Ireland

Set-list not known.

Dec 19: Electric Ballroom. London, UK

*Hand in Glove/Still Ill/Barbarism Begins at Home/This Night Has Opened my Eyes/Pretty Girls make Graves/You've Got Everything Now/What Difference Does it Make?/Miserable Lie/This Charming Man/Back to the Old House/Reel Around the Fountain/Handsome Devil/Accept Yourself/This Charming Man **

Dec 31: Danceteria. New York City, NY. USA

Set-list not known.

1984

Jan 12: Trianon Palace. Versailles, France

William, It Was Really Nothing/What She Said/Nowhere Fast/Reel Around the Fountain/Heaven Knows I'm Miserable Now/How Soon Is Now?/Still Ill/Rusholme Ruffians/This Charming Man/Barbarism Begins at Home/I Want the One I Can't Have/Hand in Glove/What Difference Does It Make?/Handsome Devil/Miserable Lie

Jan 31: University of Sheffield. Sheffield, UK

*Hand in Glove/Heaven Knows I'm Miserable Now/Girl Afraid/This Charming Man/Pretty Girls Make Graves/Still Ill/I Don't Owe You Anything/ Miserable Lie/This Night Has Opened my Eyes/Barbarism Begins at Home/Back to the Old House/What Difference Does it Make?/Reel Around the Fountain/You've Got Everything Now **

Feb 1: North Staffordshire Polytechnic. Stoke-on-Trent, UK

Set-list not known.

Feb 2: University of Warwick. Coventry,

UK

Set-list not known.

Feb 12: Lyceum Ballroom. London, UK

*Hand in Glove/Heaven Knows I'm Miserable Now/Girl Afraid/This Charming Man/Pretty Girls Make Graves/Still Ill/This Night Has Opened my Eyes/Barbarism Begins at Home/Back to the Old House/What Difference Does it Make?/You've Got Everything Now **

Feb 14: University of East Anglia. Norwich, UK

*Hand in Glove/Heaven Knows I'm Miserable Now/Girl Afraid/This Charming Man/Pretty Girls Make Graves/Still Ill/This Night Has Opened my Eyes/Barbarism Begins at Home/Back to the Old House/What Difference Does it Make?/You've Got Everything Now **

Feb 15: Rock City. Nottingham, UK

*Hand in Glove/Heaven Knows I'm Miserable Now/Girl Afraid/This Charming Man/Pretty Girls Make Graves/Still Ill/This Night Has Opened my Eyes/Barbarism Begins at Home/Back to the Old House/What Difference Does it Make?/You've Got Everything Now/Reel Around the Fountain/Hand in Glove **

Feb 16: University of Leicester. Leicester, UK

*Hand in Glove/Heaven Knows I'm Miserable Now/Girl Afraid/This Charming Man/Pretty Girls Make Graves/Still Ill/This Night Has Opened my Eyes/Barbarism Begins at Home/Back to the Old House/What Difference Does it Make?/You've Got Everything Now **

Feb 18: University of Essex. Colchester, UK

*Hand in Glove/Heaven Knows I'm Miserable Now/Girl Afraid/This Charming Man/Pretty Girls Make Graves/Still Ill/This Night Has Opened my Eyes/Barbarism Begins at Home/Back to the Old House/What Difference Does it Make?/You've Got Everything Now/Reel Around the Fountain/Hand in Glove **

Feb 21: Town Hall. Bournemouth, UK

*Hand in Glove/Heaven Knows I'm Miserable Now/Girl Afraid/This Charming Man/Pretty Girls Make Graves/Still Ill/This Night Has Opened my Eyes/Barbarism Begins at Home/Back to the Old House/What Difference Does it Make?/Reel Around the Fountain/You've Got Everything Now/Handsome Devil **

Feb 22: University of Reading. Reading, UK

*Hand in Glove/Heaven Knows I'm Miserable Now/Girl Afraid/This Charming Man/Pretty Girls Make Graves/Still Ill/This Night Has Opened my Eyes/Barbarism Begins at Home/Back to the Old House/What Difference Does it Make?/You've Got Everything Now **

Feb 23: Swansea University. Swansea, UK

*Hand in Glove/Heaven Knows I'm Miserable Now/Girl Afraid/This Charming Man/Pretty Girls Make Graves/Still Ill/This Night Has Opened my Eyes/Barbarism Begins at Home/Back to the Old House/What Difference Does it Make?/Reel Around the Fountain/You've Got Everything Now/Handsome Devil **

Feb 24: University of Bristol. Bristol, UK

*Hand in Glove/Heaven Knows I'm Miserable Now/Girl Afraid/This Charming Man/Pretty Girls Make Graves/Still Ill/This Night Has Opened my Eyes/Barbarism Begins at Home/Back to the Old House/What Difference Does it Make?/Reel Around the Fountain/You've Got Everything Now **

Feb 25: Brighton Polytechnic. Brighton, UK

Hand in Glove/Heaven Knows I'm Miserable Now/Girl Afraid/This Charming Man/Pretty Girls Make Graves/Still Ill/This Night Has Opened my

*Eyes/Barbarism Begins at Home/Back to the Old House/What Difference Does it Make?/Reel Around the Fountain/You've Got Everything Now/Handsome Devil **

Feb 27: University of Kent. Canterbury, UK

*Hand in Glove/Heaven Knows I'm Miserable Now/Girl Afraid/This Charming Man/Pretty Girls Make Graves/Still Ill/This Night Has Opened my Eyes/Barbarism Begins at Home/Back to the Old House/What Difference Does it Make?/Reel Around the Fountain/You've Got Everything Now/Handsome Devil **

Feb 28: Victoria Hall. Stoke-on-Trent, UK

*Hand in Glove/Heaven Knows I'm Miserable Now/Girl Afraid/This Charming Man/Pretty Girls Make Graves/Still Ill/This Night Has Opened my Eyes/Barbarism Begins at Home/Back to the Old House/What Difference Does it Make?/Reel Around the Fountain/You've Got Everything Now/Handsome Devil **

Feb 29: University of Leeds. Leeds, UK

*Hand in Glove/Heaven Knows I'm Miserable Now/Girl Afraid/This Charming Man/Pretty Girls Make Graves/Still Ill/This Night Has Opened my Eyes/Barbarism Begins at Home/Back to the Old House/What Difference Does it Make?/Reel Around the Fountain/You've Got Everything Now/Handsome Devil **

Mar 2: University of Glasgow. Glasgow, UK

Hand in Glove/Heaven Knows I'm Miserable Now/Girl Afraid/This Charming Man/Pretty Girls Make Graves/Still Ill/This Night Has Opened my Eyes/Barbarism Begins at Home/Back to the Old House/What Difference Does it Make?/Reel Around the Fountain/You've Got Everything Now/Handsome Devil *

Mar 3: University of Dundee. Dundee, UK

*Hand in Glove/Heaven Knows I'm Miserable Now/Girl Afraid/This Charming Man (instrumental)/Pretty Girls Make Graves/Still Ill/This Night Has Opened my Eyes/Barbarism Begins at Home/Back to the Old House/What Difference Does it Make?/Reel Around the Fountain/You've Got Everything Now/Handsome Devil **

Mar 4: Fusion Club. Aberdeen, UK

Hand in Glove/Heaven Knows I'm Miserable Now/Girl Afraid/This Charming Man/Pretty Girls Make Graves/Still Ill/This Night Has Opened my Eyes/Barbarism Begins at Home/Back to the Old House/What Difference Does it Make?/Reel Around the Fountain/You've Got Everything Now/Handsome Devil

Mar 5: Coaster's. Edinburgh, UK

*Hand in Glove/Heaven Knows I'm Miserable Now/Girl Afraid/This Charming Man/Pretty Girls Make Graves/Still Ill/This Night Has Opened my Eyes/Barbarism Begins at Home/Back to the Old House/What Difference Does it Make?/Reel Around the Fountain/You've Got Everything Now **

Mar 7: Mayfair Ballroom. Newcastle-upon-Tyne, UK

*Hand in Glove/Heaven Knows I'm Miserable Now/Girl Afraid/This Charming Man/Pretty Girls Make Graves/Still Ill/This Night Has Opened my Eyes/Barbarism Begins at Home/Back to the Old House/What Difference Does it Make?/Reel Around the Fountain/You've Got Everything Now/Handsome Devil **

Mar 8: Middlesbrough Town Hall. Middlesbrough, UK

*Hand in Glove/Heaven Knows I'm Miserable Now/Girl Afraid/This Charming Man/Pretty Girls Make Graves/Still Ill/This Night Has Opened my Eyes/Barbarism Begins at Home/Back to the Old House/What Difference Does it Make?/Reel Around the Fountain/You've Got Everything Now/Handsome Devil **

Mar 9: Lancaster University. Lancaster, UK

*Hand in Glove/Heaven Knows I'm Miserable Now/Girl Afraid/This Charming Man/Pretty Girls Make Graves/Still Ill/This Night Has Opened my Eyes/Barbarism Begins at Home/Back to the Old House/What Difference Does it Make?/Reel Around the Fountain/You've Got Everything Now/Handsome Devil **

Mar 10: Lanchester Polytechnic. Coventry, UK

Hand in Glove/Heaven Knows I'm Miserable Now/Girl Afraid/This Charming Man/Pretty Girls Make Graves/Still Ill/This Night Has Opened my Eyes/Barbarism Begins at Home/Back to the Old House/What Difference Does it Make?/Reel Around the Fountain/You've Got Everything Now/Handsome Devil

Mar 12: Hammersmith Palais. London, UK

*Miserable Lie/Heaven Knows I'm Miserable Now/This Charming Man/Girl Afraid/Pretty Girls Make Graves/Still Ill/This Night Has Opened my Eyes/Barbarism Begins at Home/Back to the Old House/What Difference Does it Make?/I Don't Owe You Anything (feat Sandi Shaw)/Reel Around the Fountain/Hand in Glove/You've Got Everything Now/Handsome Devil/These Things Take Time **

Mar 13: Free Trade Hall. Manchester, UK

*Hand in Glove/Heaven Knows I'm Miserable Now/Girl Afraid/This Charming Man/Pretty Girls Make Graves/Still Ill/This Night Has Opened my Eyes/Barbarism Begins at Home/Back to the Old House/What Difference Does it Make?/I Don't Owe You Anything (feat Sandi Shaw)/Reel Around the Fountain/Hand in Glove/You've Got Everything Now/Handsome Devil/These Things Take Time **

Mar 14: University of Liverpool. Liverpool, UK

*Hand in Glove/Still Ill/Heaven Knows I'm Miserable Now/This Charming Man/Girl Afraid/Pretty Girls Make Graves/This Night Has Opened my Eyes/Barbarism Begins at Home/Back to the Old House/What Difference Does it Make?/Reel Around the Fountain/You've Got Everything Now/Handsome Devil **

Mar 15: University of Hull. Hull, UK

*Hand in Glove/Still Ill/Heaven Knows I'm Miserable Now/This Charming Man/Girl Afraid/Pretty Girls Make Graves/This Night Has Opened my Eyes/Barbarism Begins at Home/Back to the Old House/What Difference Does it Make?/Reel Around the Fountain/You've Got Everything Now/Handsome Devil **

Mar 17: Loughborough University. Loughborough, UK

Set-list not known.

Mar 18: De Montfort Hall. Leicester, UK

*Hand in Glove/Still Ill/Heaven Knows I'm Miserable Now/This Charming Man/Girl Afraid/Pretty Girls Make Graves/This Night Has Opened my Eyes/Barbarism Begins at Home/Back to the Old House/What Difference Does it Make?/Reel Around the Fountain/You've Got Everything Now/Handsome Devil/These Things Take Time **

Mar 19: Sheffield City Hall. Sheffield, UK

Hand in Glove/Still Ill/Heaven Knows I'm Miserable Now/Pretty Girls Make Graves/Back to the Old House/Barbarism Begins at Home/This Charming Man/Reel Around the Fountain/Handsome Devil/What Difference Does It Make?

Mar 20: Tower Ballroom. Birmingham, UK

*Hand in Glove/Still Ill/Heaven Knows I'm Miserable Now/This Charming Man/Girl Afraid/Pretty Girls Make Graves/This Night Has Opened my Eyes/Barbarism Begins at Home/Back to the Old House/What Difference Does it Make?/I Don't Owe You Anything/You've Got Everything Now/Handsome Devil/These Things Take Time **

Apr 21: Theater de Meervaart. Amsterdam, Netherlands

THE SMITHS

*Hand in Glove/Heaven Knows I'm Miserable Now/Girl Afraid/This Charming Man/Barbarism Begins at Home/ This Night Has Opened my Eyes/Miserable Lie/Still Ill/I Don't Owe You Anything/What Difference Does it Make?/ Handsome Devil/You've Got Everything Now/These Things Take Time **

Apr 22: Breekend Festival. Bree, Belgium

*Hand in Glove/Heaven Knows I'm Miserable Now/Girl Afraid/This Charming Man/Barbarism Begins at Home/ This Night Has Opened my Eyes/Still Ill/Handsome Devil/ What Difference Does it Make?/You've Got Everything Now/These Things Take Time **

Apr 24: Rote Fabrik. Zürich, Switzerland

*Hand in Glove/Heaven Knows I'm Miserable Now/Girl Afraid/This Charming Man/Barbarism Begins at Home/ This Night Has Opened my Eyes/Still Ill/Handsome Devil/ What Difference Does it Make?/You've Got Everything Now/These Things Take Time/Miserable Lie/Pretty Girls Make Graves/Hand in Glove **

May 4: Markthalle. Hamburg, Germany

*Hand in Glove/Heaven Knows I'm Miserable Now/Girl Afraid/This Charming Man/Pretty Girls Make Graves/Still Ill/Barbarism Begins at Home/This Night Has Opened my Eyes/Miserable Lie/You've Got Everything Now/ Handsome Devil/What Difference Does it Make?/These Things Take Time/This Charming Man/Hand in Glove/ Barbarism Begins at Home **

May 9: L'Eldorado. Paris, France

*Hand in Glove/Heaven Knows I'm Miserable Now/Girl Afraid/This Charming Man/Barbarism Begins at Home/ Pretty Girls Make Graves/This Night Has Opened my Eyes/Still Ill/You've Got Everything Now/Handsome Devil/Miserable Lie/These Things Take Time/What Difference Does it Make?/Barbarism Begins at Home/ Hand in Glove **

May 17: Ulster Hall. Belfast, UK

*Hand in Glove/Heaven Knows I'm Miserable Now/Girl Afraid/This Charming Man/Barbarism Begins at Home/ Pretty Girls Make Graves/Still Ill/This Night Has Opened my Eyes/You've Got Everything Now/I Don't Owe You Anything/Miserable Lie/These Things Take Time/What Difference Does it Make?/Handsome Devil **

May 18: SFX. Dublin, Ireland

*Hand in Glove/Still Ill/This Charming Man/This Night Has Opened my Eyes/Heaven Knows I'm Miserable Now/ Miserable Lie/I Don't Owe You Anything/Barbarism Begins at Home/Reel Around the Fountain/What Difference Does it Make?/These Things Take Time/Hand in Glove/You've Got Everything Now/Handsome Devil **

May 19: SFX. Dublin, Ireland

*Still Ill/Hand in Glove/Pretty Girls Make Graves/This Charming Man/This Night Has Opened my Eyes/Heaven Knows I'm Miserable Now/Miserable Lie/I Don't Owe You Anything/Barbarism Begins at Home/Reel Around the Fountain/What Difference Does it Make?/Jeane/These Things Take Time/Hand in Glove/You've Got Everything Now/Handsome Devil **

May 20: Savoy Theatre. Cork, Ireland

*Still Ill/Hand in Glove/Pretty Girls Make Graves/This Charming Man/This Night Has Opened my Eyes/Heaven Knows I'm Miserable Now/Miserable Lie/I Don't Owe You Anything/Barbarism Begins at Home/Reel Around the Fountain/What Difference Does it Make?/Jeane/These Things Take Time/Hand in Glove/You've Got Everything Now/Handsome Devil/What Difference Does it Make? **

June 3: Provinssirock Festival. Seinäjoki, Finland

*Hand in Glove/Nowhere Fast/William, It Was Really Nothing/Heaven Knows I'm Miserable Now/This Charming Man/This Night Has Opened my Eyes/Still Ill/I Don't Owe You Anything/Barbarism Begins at Home/ Miserable Lie/You've Got Everything Now/Handsome Devil/Jeane/What Difference Does it Make?/These Things Take Time **

June 10: Jubilee Gardens (GLC "Jobs for a Change Festival). London, UK

*Nowhere Fast/Girl Afraid/This Charming Man/William, It Was Really Nothing/Heaven Knows I'm Miserable Now/I Don't Owe You Anything/Still Ill/Jeane/Barbarism Begins at Home/Hand in Glove/What Difference Does it Make?/ You've Got Everything Now/Pretty Girls Make Graves/ Miserable Lie **

June 12: Market Hall. Carlisle, UK

*Nowhere Fast/Girl Afraid/Handsome Devil/This Charming Man/William, It Was Really Nothing/Heaven Knows I'm Miserable Now/Still Ill/I Don't Owe You Anything/Jeane/Barbarism Begins at Home/Hand in Glove/What Difference Does it Make?/You've Got Everything Now/Pretty Girls Make Graves/Miserable Lie/These Things Take Time **

June 13: Barrowlands. Glasgow, UK

*Nowhere Fast/Girl Afraid/Handsome Devil/William, It Was Really Nothing/This Charming Man/Heaven Knows I'm Miserable Now/Still Ill/I Don't Owe You Anything/Jeane/Barbarism Begins at Home/Hand in Glove/Pretty Girls Make Graves/Miserable Lie/What Difference Does it Make?/You've Got Everything Now **

June 14: Caley Palais. Edinburgh, UK

*Nowhere Fast/Girl Afraid/Handsome Devil/This Charming Man/William, It Was Really Nothing/Heaven Knows I'm Miserable Now/Still Ill/I Don't Owe You Anything/Jeane/Barbarism Begins at Home/Hand in Glove/Pretty Girls Make Graves/Miserable Lie/What Difference Does it Make?/You've Got Everything Now **

June 15: Caird Hall. Dundee, UK

Nowhere Fast/Girl Afraid/Handsome Devil/William, It Was Really Nothing/This Charming Man/Heaven Knows I'm Miserable Now/Still Ill/I Don't Owe You Anything/Jeane/Barbarism Begins at Home/Hand in Glove/Pretty Girls Make Graves/Miserable Lie/What Difference Does it Make?/You've Got Everything Now

June 16: Capital Theatre. Aberdeen, UK

Nowhere Fast/Girl Afraid/Handsome Devil/William, It Was Really Nothing/This Charming Man/Heaven Knows I'm Miserable Now/Still Ill/I Don't Owe You Anything/Jeane/Barbarism Begins at Home/Hand in Glove/Pretty Girls Make Graves/Miserable Lie/What Difference Does it Make?/You've Got Everything Now

June 17: Eden Court Theatre. Inverness, UK

Nowhere Fast/Girl Afraid/Handsome Devil/William, It Was Really Nothing/Heaven Knows I'm Miserable Now/Still Ill/I Don't Owe You Anything/Jeane/Barbarism Begins at Home/Hand in Glove/Pretty Girls Make Graves/Miserable Lie/What Difference Does it Make?/You've Got Everything Now

June 20: Opera House Theatre. Blackpool, UK

*Nowhere Fast/Girl Afraid/Handsome Devil/This Charming Man/William, It Was Really Nothing/Heaven Knows I'm Miserable Now/Still Ill/I Don't Owe You Anything/Jeane/Barbarism Begins at Home/Hand in Glove/Pretty Girls Make Graves/Miserable Lie/What Difference Does it Make?/You've Got Everything Now **

June 22: Cornwall Coliseum. St Austell, UK

*Nowhere Fast/Girl Afraid/Handsome Devil/This Charming Man/William, It Was Really Nothing/Heaven Knows I'm Miserable Now/Still Ill/I Don't Owe You Anything/Jeane/Barbarism Begins at Home/Hand in Glove **

June 23: Glastonbury, CND Festival. Pilton, UK

*Nowhere Fast/Girl Afraid/Handsome Devil/William, It Was Really Nothing/Heaven Knows I'm Miserable Now/Still Ill/I Don't Owe You Anything/Jeane/Barbarism Begins at Home/Hand in Glove/Pretty Girls Make Graves/Miserable Lie/What Difference Does it Make?/You've Got Everything Now **

Sept 24: Gloucester Leisure Centre. Gloucester, UK

*William, It Was Really Nothing/Handsome Devil/Nowhere Fast/How Soon is Now?/Barbarism Begins at Home/Rusholme Ruffians/This Charming Man/Reel Around the Fountain/Jeane/You've Got Everything Now/Girl Afraid/Heaven Knows I'm Miserable Now/Still Ill/These Things Take Time/Please Please Please, Let me Get What I Want/Hand in Glove/Miserable Lie **

Sept 25: Cardiff University. Cardiff, UK

*William, It Was Really Nothing/Handsome Devil/Nowhere Fast/How Soon is Now?/Barbarism Begins at Home/Rusholme Ruffians/This Charming Man/Reel Around the Fountain/Jeane/You've Got Everything Now/Girl Afraid/Heaven Knows I'm Miserable Now/Still Ill/These Things Take Time/Please Please Please, Let me Get What I Want/Hand in Glove/Miserable Lie **

Sept 26: Mayfair. Swansea, UK

William, It Was Really Nothing/Handsome Devil/Nowhere Fast/How Soon is Now?/Barbarism Begins at Home/

*Rusholme Ruffians/This Charming Man/Reel Around the Fountain/Jeane/You've Got Everything Now/Girl Afraid/ Heaven Knows I'm Miserable Now/Still Ill/These Things Take Time/Please Please Please, Let me Get What I Want/ Hand in Glove/Miserable Lie **

Nov 11: Savoy. Waterford, Ireland

*Please Please Please, Let Me Get What I Want/William, It Was Really Nothing/What She Said/Nowhere Fast/Pretty Girls Make Graves/Reel Around the Fountain/Heaven Knows I'm Miserable Now/This Night Has Opened my Eyes/How Soon is Now?/Still Ill/I Want the One I Can't Have/Miserable Lie/This Charming Man/Hand in Glove/ Jeane/These Things Take Time/What Difference Does it Make? **

Nov 12: SFX. Dublin, Ireland

*William, It Was Really Nothing/Handsome Devil/ Nowhere Fast/How Soon is Now?/I Want the One I Can't Have/Barbarism Begins at Home/Girl Afraid/Rusholme Ruffians/This Charming Man/Still Ill/Heaven Knows I'm Miserable Now/Jeane/You've Got Everything Now/These Things Take Time/Please Please Please, Let me Get What I Want/Hand in Glove **

Nov 13: SFX. Dublin, Ireland

*Please Please Please, Let Me Get What I Want/William, It Was Really Nothing/What She Said/Nowhere Fast/Reel Around the Fountain/Heaven Knows I'm Miserable Now/ Rusholme Ruffians/This Charming Man/How Soon is Now?/Still Ill/Barbarism begins at Home/I Want the One I Can't Have/Miserable Lie/Hand in Glove/What Difference Does it Make?/Jeane/These Things Take Time **

Nov 16: Savoy. Limerick, Ireland

William, It Was Really Nothing/What She Said/Nowhere Fast/Reel Around the Fountain/Rusholme Ruffians/This Charming Man/How Soon is Now?/Still Ill/Barbarism Begins at Home/I Want the One I Can't Have/Miserable Lie/Hand in Glove/What Difference Does it Make?/Jeane/ These Things Take Time/Handsome Devil

Nov 17: Leisureland. Galway, Ireland

Please Please Please, Let Me Get What I Want/William, It Was Really Nothing/What She Said/Nowhere Fast/Pretty Girls Make Graves/Reel Around the Fountain/Heaven Knows I'm Miserable Now/This Night Has Opened my Eyes/How Soon is Now?/Still Ill/I Want the One I Can't Have/Miserable Lie/This Charming Man/Hand in Glove/ These Things Take Time/What Difference Does it Make?

Nov 18: Savoy. Cork, Ireland

*Please Please Please, Let Me Get What I Want/William, It Was Really Nothing/What She Said/Nowhere Fast/Reel Around the Fountain/Heaven Knows I'm Miserable Now/ Rusholme Ruffians/How Soon is Now?/Still Ill/I Want the One I Can't Have/Miserable Lie/Hand in Glove/What Difference Does it Make? **

Nov 20: Leisure Centre. Letterkenny, Ireland

*How Soon is Now?/Still Ill/This Charming Man/I Want the One I Can't Have/Handsome Devil/Hand in Glove/ What Difference Does it Make?/Jeane/You've Got Everything Now * (recording incomplete)*

Nov 21: University of Ulster. Coleraine, UK

Set-list not known.

Nov 22: Ulster Hall. Belfast, UK

Set-list not known.

Dec 1: Parc des Expositions de Villepinte. Paris, France

*William, It Was Really Nothing/What She Said/Nowhere Fast/Reel Around the Fountain/Heaven Knows I'm Miserable Now/How Soon is Now?/Still Ill/Rusholme Ruffians/This Charming Man/Barbarism Begins at Home/I Want the One I Can't Have/Miserable Lie/Hand in Glove/What Difference Does it Make?/Handsome Devil/ Miserable Lie **

1985

Feb 27: Golddiggers. Chippenham, UK

William, It Was Really Nothing/ I Want the One I Can't Have/What She Said/Handsome Devil/How Soon is Now?/Shakespeare's Sister/Heaven Knows I'm Miserable

*Now/That Joke isn't Funny Anymore/Rusholme Ruffians/Hand in Glove/The Headmaster Ritual/Nowhere Fast/Still Ill/Stretch Out and Wait/You've Got Everything Now/Meat Is Murder/Reel Around the Fountain/Barbarism Begins at Home/Miserable Lie **

Feb 28: Guildford Civic Hall. Guildford, UK

*William, It Was Really Nothing/ I Want the One I Can't Have/What She Said/Handsome Devil/How Soon is Now?/Shakespeare's Sister/Heaven Knows I'm Miserable Now/That Joke isn't Funny Anymore/Rusholme Ruffians/Hand in Glove/The Headmaster Ritual/Nowhere Fast/Stretch Out and Wait/Still Ill/Meat Is Murder/Miserable Lie/Barbarism Begins at Home **

Mar 1: Brixton Academy. London, UK

*William, It Was Really Nothing/ I Want the One I Can't Have/What She Said/Handsome Devil/How Soon is Now?/Shakespeare's Sister/Heaven Knows I'm Miserable Now/That Joke isn't Funny Anymore/Stretch Out and Wait/Rusholme Ruffians/Hand in Glove/The Headmaster Ritual/Nowhere Fast/Still Ill/Meat Is Murder/Miserable Lie/Barbarism Begins at Home/You've Got Everything Now/These Things Take Time **

Mar 3: Portsmouth Guildhall. Portsmouth, UK

*William, It Was Really Nothing/ I Want the One I Can't Have/What She Said/Handsome Devil/How Soon is Now?/Shakespeare's Sister/Heaven Knows I'm Miserable Now/That Joke isn't Funny Anymore/Reel Around the Fountain/Rusholme Ruffians/Hand in Glove/The Headmaster Ritual/Nowhere Fast/Still Ill/Meat Is Murder/Miserable Lie/Barbarism Begins at Home/You've Got Everything Now **

Mar 4: The Hexagon. Reading, UK

*William, It Was Really Nothing/ I Want the One I Can't Have/What She Said/Handsome Devil/How Soon is Now?/Shakespeare's Sister/Heaven Knows I'm Miserable Now/That Joke isn't Funny Anymore/Reel Around the Fountain/Rusholme Ruffians/Hand in Glove/The Headmaster Ritual/Nowhere Fast/Still Ill/Meat Is Murder/Barbarism Begins at Home/Miserable Lie **

Mar 6: Arts Centre. Poole, UK

*William, It Was Really Nothing/ I Want the One I Can't Have/What She Said/Handsome Devil/How Soon is Now?/Shakespeare's Sister/Heaven Knows I'm Miserable Now/That Joke isn't Funny Anymore/Reel Around the Fountain/Rusholme Ruffians/Hand in Glove/The Headmaster Ritual/Nowhere Fast/Still Ill/Meat Is Murder/Miserable Lie **

Mar 7: Brighton Dome. Brighton, UK

*William, It Was Really Nothing/ I Want the One I Can't Have/What She Said/Handsome Devil/How Soon is Now?/Shakespeare's Sister/Heaven Knows I'm Miserable Now/That Joke isn't Funny Anymore/Reel Around the Fountain/Rusholme Ruffians/Hand in Glove/The Headmaster Ritual/Nowhere Fast/Meat Is Murder/Still Ill/Miserable Lie **

Mar 8: Winter Gardens. Margate, UK

*Nowhere Fast/Barbarism Begins at Home/Still Ill/How Soon is Now?/Shakespeare's Sister/Handsome Devil/The Headmaster's Ritual/Reel Around the Fountain/That Joke isn't Funny Anymore/Hand in Glove/Rusholme Ruffians/I Want the One I Can't Have/What She Said/William, It Was Really Nothing/Meat Is Murder/Miserable Lie **

Mar 11: Gaumont. Ipswich, UK

*William, It Was Really Nothing/Nowhere Fast/I Want the One I Can't Have/What She Said/How Soon is Now?/Stretch Out and Wait/Heaven Knows I'm Miserable Now/That Joke isn't Funny Anymore/Handsome Devil/The Headmaster Ritual/Shakespeare's Sister/Rusholme Ruffians/Hand in Glove/Still Ill/Meat Is Murder/Barbarism Begins at Home/Miserable Lie **

Mar 12: Nottingham Royal Concert Hall. Nottingham, UK

*William, It Was Really Nothing/Nowhere Fast/I Want the One I Can't Have/What She Said/Handsome Devil/How Soon is Now?/Heaven Knows I'm Miserable Now/Stretch Out and Wait/That Joke isn't Funny Anymore/Shakespeare's Sister/Rusholme Ruffians/The Headmaster Ritual/Still Ill/Hand in Glove/Meat Is Murder/Barbarism Begins at Home/Miserable Lie **

Mar 16: Victoria Hall. Stoke-on-Trent, UK

*William, It Was Really Nothing/Nowhere Fast/I Want the One I Can't Have/Handsome Devil/What She Said/How Soon is Now?/Heaven Knows I'm Miserable Now/Stretch Out and Wait/That Joke isn't Funny Anymore/Shakespeare's Sister/Rusholme Ruffians/The Headmaster Ritual/Still Ill/Hand in Glove/Meat Is Murder/Miserable Lie/Barbarism Begins at Home **

THE SMITHS

Mar 17: Birmingham Hippodrome. Birmingham, UK

William, It Was Really Nothing/Nowhere Fast/I Want the One I Can't Have/What She Said/Hand in Glove/How Soon is Now?/Stretch Out and Wait/That Joke isn't Funny Anymore/Shakespeare's Sister/Rusholme Ruffians/The Headmaster Ritual/Still Ill/Meat Is Murder/Miserable Lie/Barbarism Begins at Home *

Mar 18: Apollo Theatre. Oxford, UK

William, It Was Really Nothing/Nowhere Fast/I Want the One I Can't Have/What She Said/Hand in Glove/How Soon is Now?/Stretch Out and Wait/That Joke isn't Funny Anymore/Shakespeare's Sister/Rusholme Ruffians/The Headmaster Ritual/Still Ill/Meat Is Murder/Miserable Lie/Barbarism Begins at Home/You've Got Everything Now/Handsome Devil *

Mar 22: Sheffield City Hall. Sheffield, UK

William, It Was Really Nothing/Nowhere Fast/I Want the One I Can't Have/What She Said/Hand in Glove/How Soon is Now?/Stretch Out and Wait/That Joke isn't Funny Anymore/Shakespeare's Sister/Rusholme Ruffians/The Headmaster Ritual/Still Ill/Meat Is Murder/Miserable Lie/Barbarism Begins at Home/You've Got Everything Now/Handsome Devil *

Mar 23: Middlesbrough Town Hall. Middlesbrough, UK

William, It Was Really Nothing/Nowhere Fast/I Want the One I Can't Have/What She Said/Hand in Glove/How Soon is Now?/Stretch Out and Wait/That Joke isn't Funny Anymore/Shakespeare's Sister/Rusholme Ruffians/The Headmaster Ritual/Still Ill/Meat Is Murder/Miserable Lie/Barbarism Begins at Home/You've Got Everything Now *

Mar 24: Newcastle City Hall. Newcastle upon Tyne, UK

William, It Was Really Nothing/Nowhere Fast/I Want the One I Can't Have/What She Said/Hand in Glove/How Soon is Now?/Stretch Out and Wait/That Joke isn't Funny Anymore/Shakespeare's Sister/Rusholme Ruffians/The Headmaster Ritual/Still Ill/Handsome Devil/Meat Is Murder/Miserable Lie/Heaven Knows I'm Miserable Now/Barbarism Begins at Home *

Mar 27: Royal Court Theatre. Liverpool, UK

William, It Was Really Nothing/Nowhere Fast/I Want the One I Can't Have/What She Said/Hand in Glove/How Soon is Now?/Stretch Out and Wait/That Joke isn't Funny Anymore/Shakespeare's Sister/Rusholme Ruffians/The Headmaster Ritual/Still Ill/Meat Is Murder/Heaven Knows I'm Miserable Now/Barbarism Begins at Home/Miserable Lie *

Mar 28: St George's Hall. Bradford, UK

William, It Was Really Nothing/Nowhere Fast/I Want the One I Can't Have/What She Said/Hand in Glove/How Soon is Now?/Stretch Out and Wait/That Joke isn't Funny Anymore/Shakespeare's Sister/Rusholme Ruffians/The Headmaster Ritual/Still Ill/Heaven Knows I'm Miserable Now/Meat Is Murder/Handsome Devil/Barbarism Begins at Home/Miserable Lie *

Mar 29: Derngate Theatre. Northampton, UK

William, It Was Really Nothing/Nowhere Fast/I Want the One I Can't Have/What She Said/Hand in Glove/How Soon is Now?/Stretch Out and Wait/That Joke isn't Funny Anymore/Shakespeare's Sister/Rusholme Ruffians/The Headmaster Ritual/Still Ill/Meat Is Murder/Heaven Knows I'm Miserable Now/This Charming Man/Handsome Devil *

Mar 31: Palace Theatre. Manchester, UK

William, It Was Really Nothing/Nowhere Fast/I Want the One I Can't Have/What She Said/Hand in Glove/How Soon is Now?/Stretch Out and Wait/That Joke isn't Funny Anymore/Shakespeare's Sister/Rusholme Ruffians/The Headmaster Ritual/Still Ill/Meat Is Murder/Heaven Knows I'm Miserable Now/Handsome Devil/Barbarism Begins at Home/Miserable Lie/You've Got Everything Now *

Apr 1: De Montfort Hall. Leicester, UK

William, It Was Really Nothing/Nowhere Fast/I Want the One I Can't Have/What She Said/Hand in Glove/How Soon is Now?/Stretch Out and Wait/That Joke isn't Funny Anymore/Shakespeare's Sister/Rusholme Ruffians/The Headmaster Ritual/Still Ill/Meat Is Murder/Heaven Knows I'm Miserable Now/Handsome Devil/Miserable Lie/Barbarism Begins at Home *

Apr 4: Bristol Hippodrome. Bristol, UK

*William, It Was Really Nothing/Nowhere Fast/I Want the One I Can't Have/What She Said/Hand in Glove/ How Soon is Now?/Stretch Out and Wait/That Joke isn't Funny Anymore/Shakespeare's Sister/Rusholme Ruffians/ The Headmaster Ritual/Still Ill/Meat Is Murder/Heaven Knows I'm Miserable Now/Handsome Devil/Miserable Lie **

Apr 6: Royal Albert Hall. London, UK

*How Soon is Now?/Nowhere Fast/I Want the One I Can't Have/What She Said/Hand in Glove/How Soon is Now?/ Stretch Out and Wait/That Joke isn't Funny Anymore/ Shakespeare's Sister/Rusholme Ruffians/The Headmaster Ritual/You've Got Everything Now/Handsome Devil/ Still Ill/Meat Is Murder/ William, It Was Really Nothing / Heaven Knows I'm Miserable Now/Barbarism Begins at Home (feat Pete Burns)/Miserable Lie **

May 14: Teatro Tendastrisce. Rome, Italy

*William, It Was Really Nothing/Nowhere Fast/I Want the One I Can't Have/What She Said/How Soon is Now?/ Stretch Out and Wait/That Joke isn't Funny Anymore/ Shakespeare's Sister/Rusholme Ruffians/The Headmaster Ritual/Hand in Glove/Still Ill/Meat Is Murder/Heaven Knows I'm Miserable Now/Handsome Devil/This Charming Man/Miserable Lie/You've Got Everything Now **

May 16: Studio 54. Barcelona, Spain

*William, It Was Really Nothing/Nowhere Fast/I Want the One I Can't Have/What She Said/How Soon is Now?/ This Charming Man/That Joke isn't Funny Anymore/ Shakespeare's Sister/Rusholme Ruffians/The Headmaster Ritual/Hand in Glove/Still Ill/Meat Is Murder/Heaven Knows I'm Miserable Now/Handsome Devil/Miserable Lie/Barbarism Begins at Home/You've Got Everything Now **

May 18: Paseo de Camiones. Madrid, Spain

*William, It Was Really Nothing/Nowhere Fast/I Want the One I Can't Have/What She Said/How Soon is Now?/Handsome Devil/That Joke isn't Funny Anymore/ Shakespeare's Sister/Rusholme Ruffians/The Headmaster Ritual/Hand in Glove/Still Ill/Meat Is Murder/Heaven Knows I'm Miserable Now/Miserable Lie/Barbarism Begins at Home/This Charming Man/You've Got Everything Now **

June 7: Aragon Ballroom. Chicago, IL. USA

*William, It Was Really Nothing/Nowhere Fast/I Want the One I Can't Have/What She Said/How Soon is Now?/Handsome Devil/That Joke isn't Funny Anymore/Stretch Out and Wait/ Shakespeare's Sister/Rusholme Ruffians/The Headmaster Ritual/Hand in Glove/Still Ill/Meat Is Murder/Please Please Please, Let Me get What I Want/Heaven Knows I'm Miserable Now/This Charming Man/Miserable Lie **

June 8: Royal Oak Music Theatre. Detroit, MI. USA

*William, It Was Really Nothing/Nowhere Fast/I Want the One I Can't Have/What She Said/Handsome Devil/How Soon is Now?/That Joke isn't Funny Anymore/Stretch Out and Wait/Shakespeare's Sister/Rusholme Ruffians/ The Headmaster Ritual/Hand in Glove/Still Ill/Meat Is Murder/Please Please Please, Let Me get What I Want/ Heaven Knows I'm Miserable Now/This Charming Man/ Miserable Lie **

June 9: Kingswood Music Theatre. Vaughan, Canada

*William, It Was Really Nothing/Nowhere Fast/I Want the One I Can't Have/What She Said/Handsome Devil/ How Soon is Now?/That Joke isn't Funny Anymore/ Stretch Out and Wait/Shakespeare's Sister/Rusholme Ruffians/The Headmaster Ritual/Hand in Glove/Still Ill/ Meat Is Murder/Heaven Knows I'm Miserable Now/This Charming Man/ Please Please Please, Let Me get What I Want/Miserable Lie **

June 11: Warner Theatre Washington, D.C. USA

*William, It Was Really Nothing/Nowhere Fast/I Want the One I Can't Have/What She Said/Handsome Devil/ How Soon is Now?/That Joke isn't Funny Anymore/ Stretch Out and Wait/Shakespeare's Sister/Rusholme Ruffians/The Headmaster Ritual/Hand in Glove/Still Ill/ Meat Is Murder/Heaven Knows I'm Miserable Now/This Charming Man/ Please Please Please, Let Me get What I Want/Miserable Lie/You've Got Everything Now **

June 12: Tower Theatre. Upper Darby, PA. USA

THE SMITHS

William, It Was Really Nothing/Nowhere Fast/I Want the One I Can't Have/What She Said/Handsome Devil/ How Soon Is Now?/That Joke Isn't Funny Anymore/ Stretch Out and Wait/Shakespeare's Sister/Rusholme Ruffians/The Headmaster Ritual/Hand in Glove/Still Ill/ Meat Is Murder/Heaven Knows I'm Miserable Now/This Charming Man/Please, Please, Please Let Me Get What I Want/Miserable Lie/Barbarism Begins at Home

June 14: Opera House. Boston, MA. USA

*William, It Was Really Nothing/Nowhere Fast/I Want the One I Can't Have/Jeane/What She Said/How Soon Is Now?/That Joke Isn't Funny Anymore/Stretch Out and Wait/Shakespeare's Sister/Rusholme Ruffians/ The Headmaster Ritual/Hand in Glove/Still Ill/Meat Is Murder/Heaven Knows I'm Miserable Now/This Charming Man/Please, Please, Please Let Me Get What I Want/Miserable Lie/Barbarism Begins at Home **

June 17: Beacon Theatre. New York City, NY. USA

*William, It Was Really Nothing/Nowhere Fast/I Want the One I Can't Have/What She Said/How Soon Is Now?/ That Joke Isn't Funny Anymore/Stretch Out and Wait/ Shakespeare's Sister/Rusholme Ruffians/The Headmaster Ritual/Hand in Glove/Still Ill/Meat Is Murder/Heaven Knows I'm Miserable Now/This Charming Man/Please, Please, Please Let Me Get What I Want/Miserable Lie/ Jeane/Barbarism Begins at Home **

June 18: Beacon Theatre. New York City, NY. USA

*Meat Is Murder/The Headmaster Ritual/Reel Around the Fountain/Shakespeare's Sister/Nowhere Fast/I Want the One I Can't Have/This Charming Man/That Joke Isn't Funny Anymore/Stretch Out and Wait/ Heaven Knows I'm Miserable Now/What She Said/Still Ill/How Soon is Now?/William, It Was Really Nothing/Please, Please, Please Let Me Get What I Want/Rusholme Ruffians/ Miserable Lie/Jeane/Barbarism Begins at Home **

June 21: H. J. Kaiser Auditorium. Oakland, CA. USA

*William, It Was Really Nothing/Nowhere Fast/I Want the One I Can't Have/What She Said/How Soon Is Now?/ That Joke Isn't Funny Anymore/Stretch Out and Wait/ Shakespeare's Sister/Rusholme Ruffians/Jeane/ Please, Please, Please Let Me Get What I Want/ Miserable Lie/ Barbarism Begins at Home/Meat Is Murder **

June 25: San Diego State University Open Air Theater. San Diego, CA. USA

*Meat Is Murder/The Headmaster Ritual/Shakespeare's Sister/Hand in Glove/Nowhere Fast/I Want the One I Can't Have/This Charming Man/That Joke Isn't Funny Anymore/Stretch Out and Wait/ Heaven Knows I'm Miserable Now/What She Said/Still Ill/How Soon is Now?/William, It Was Really Nothing/Jeane/Please, Please, Please Let Me Get What I Want/Rusholme Ruffians/Miserable Lie/Barbarism Begins at Home **

June 27: Hollywood Palladium. Los Angeles, CA. USA

*Meat Is Murder/Hand in Glove/Shakespeare's Sister/ The Headmaster Ritual/Hand in Glove/Nowhere Fast/I Want the One I Can't Have/This Charming Man/That Joke Isn't Funny Anymore/Stretch Out and Wait/ Heaven Knows I'm Miserable Now/What She Said/Still Ill/How Soon is Now?/William, It Was Really Nothing/Jeane/ Please, Please, Please Let Me Get What I Want/Rusholme Ruffians/Miserable Lie/Barbarism Begins at Home **

June 28: Hollywood Palladium. Los Angeles, CA. USA

*Meat Is Murder/Hand in Glove/I Want the One I Can't Have/Nowhere Fast/ Shakespeare's Sister/That Joke Isn't Funny Anymore/Stretch Out and Wait/ Heaven Knows I'm Miserable Now/What She Said/Still Ill/How Soon is Now?/Jeane/The Headmaster Ritual/Reel Around the Fountain/William, It Was Really Nothing/This Charming Man/Miserable Lie **

June 29: Irvine Meadows Amphitheatre. Irvine, CA. USA

*Meat Is Murder/Hand in Glove/I Want the One I Can't Have/Nowhere Fast/ Shakespeare's Sister/That Joke Isn't Funny Anymore/Stretch Out and Wait/ Heaven Knows I'm Miserable Now/What She Said/Still Ill/How Soon is Now?/Jeane/The Headmaster Ritual/Reel Around the Fountain/William, It Was Really Nothing/This Charming Man/Miserable Lie/Barbarism Begins at Home **

Sept 22: Magnum Leisure Centre. Irvine, UK

Shakespeare's Sister/I Want the One I Can't Have/What She Said/What's the World/Nowhere Fast/The Boy With the Thorn in His Side/Frankly Mr Shankly/Bigmouth Strikes Again/That Joke Isn't Funny Anymore/Stretch Out and Wait/Still Ill/Rusholme Ruffians (Marie's the

*Name) Has Latest Flame (medley)/How Soon is Now?/ The Headmaster Ritual/Meat Is Murder/Heaven Knows I'm Miserable Now/Hand in Glove/William, It Was Really Nothing/Miserable Lie **

Sept 24: Edinburgh Playhouse. Edinburgh, UK

*Shakespeare's Sister/I Want the One I Can't Have/What She Said/What's the World/Nowhere Fast/The Boy With the Thorn in His Side/Frankly Mr Shankly/Bigmouth Strikes Again/That Joke Isn't Funny Anymore/Stretch Out and Wait/Still Ill/Rusholme Ruffians (Marie's the Name) Has Latest Flame (medley)/How Soon is Now?/ The Headmaster Ritual/Meat Is Murder/Heaven Knows I'm Miserable Now/Hand in Glove/William, It Was Really Nothing/Miserable Lie **

Sept 25: Barrowlands. Glasgow, UK

*Shakespeare's Sister/I Want the One I Can't Have/What She Said/What's the World/Nowhere Fast/The Boy With the Thorn in His Side/Frankly Mr Shankly/Bigmouth Strikes Again/That Joke Isn't Funny Anymore/Stretch Out and Wait/Still Ill/Rusholme Ruffians (Marie's the Name) Has Latest Flame (medley)/Heaven Knows I'm Miserable Now/Meat Is Murder/This Charming Man/Hand in Glove/ William, It Was Really Nothing/Miserable Lie **

Sept 26: Caird Hall. Dundee, UK

*Shakespeare's Sister/I Want the One I Can't Have/What She Said/What's the World/The Boy With the Thorn in His Side/Nowhere Fast/That Joke Isn't Funny Anymore/ Stretch Out and Wait/Frankly Mr Shankly/Bigmouth Strikes Again/Still Ill/Rusholme Ruffians (Marie's the Name) Has Latest Flame (medley)/Heaven Knows I'm Miserable Now/Meat Is Murder/This Charming Man/ Hand in Glove/William, It Was Really Nothing/Miserable Lie **

Sept 28: Clickimin Centre. Lerwick, UK

*Shakespeare's Sister/I Want the One I Can't Have/What She Said/Nowhere Fast/What's the World/The Boy With the Thorn in His Side/That Joke Isn't Funny Anymore/ Stretch Out and Wait/Frankly Mr Shankly/Bigmouth Strikes Again/Still Ill/Rusholme Ruffians (Marie's the Name) Has Latest Flame (medley)/Heaven Knows I'm Miserable Now/Meat Is Murder/This Charming Man/ Hand in Glove/Miserable Lie **

Sept 30: Capital Theatre. Aberdeen, UK

*Shakespeare's Sister/I Want the One I Can't Have/What She Said/What's the World/Nowhere Fast/The Boy With the Thorn in His Side/That Joke Isn't Funny Anymore/ Stretch Out and Wait/Frankly Mr Shankly/Bigmouth Strikes Again/How Soon is Now?/Still Ill/Rusholme Ruffians (Marie's the Name) Has Latest Flame (medley)/ Heaven Knows I'm Miserable Now/Jeane/Meat Is Murder/ This Charming Man/Hand in Glove/William, It Was Really Nothing/Miserable Lie **

Oct 1: Eden Court Theatre. Inverness, UK

*Meat Is Murder/Shakespeare's Sister/I Want the One I Can't Have/What She Said/What's the World/Nowhere Fast/The Boy With the Thorn in His Side/That Joke Isn't Funny Anymore/Stretch Out and Wait/Heaven Knows I'm Miserable Now/Frankly Mr Shankly/Bigmouth Strikes Again/Rusholme Ruffians (Marie's the Name) Has Latest Flame (medley)/How Soon is Now?/Asleep/Hand in Glove/This Charming Man/William, It Was Really Nothing/Miserable Lie **

1986

Jan 31: Newcastle City Hall (Red Wedge Tour). Newcastle upon Tyne, UK

Shakespeare's Sister/I Want the One I Can't Have/The Boy With the Thorn in His Side/Bigmouth Strikes Again

Feb 8: Royal Court Theatre. Liverpool, UK

*Shakespeare's Sister/I Want the One I Can't Have/Vicar in a Tutu/Frankly Mr Shankly/Rusholme Ruffians (Marie's the Name) Has Latest Flame (medley)/The Boy With the Thorn in His Side/Cemetry Gates/Nowhere Fast/What She Said/There is a Light That Never Goes Out/Bigmouth Strikes Again/William, It Was Really Nothing/Meat Is Murder/Stretch Out and Wait **

Feb 10: National Stadium. Dublin, Ireland

*Shakespeare's Sister/I Want the One I Can't Have/Vicar in a Tutu/Rusholme Ruffians (Marie's the Name) Has Latest Flame (medley)/Cemetry Gates/Still Ill/Stretch Out and Wait/That Joke Isn't Funny Anymore/Nowhere Fast/What She Said/The Boy With the Thorn in His Side/There is a Light That Never Goes Out/Bigmouth Strikes Again/Meat Is Murder/William, It Was Really Nothing/Heaven Knows I'm Miserable Now/Miserable Lie **

THE SMITHS

Feb 11: Fairways Hotel. Dundalk, UK

*Shakespeare's Sister/I Want the One I Can't Have/Vicar in a Tutu/Rusholme Ruffians (Marie's the Name) Has Latest Flame (medley)/Cemetry Gates/Still Ill/Stretch Out and Wait/That Joke Isn't Funny Anymore/Nowhere Fast/What She Said/The Boy With the Thorn in His Side/Bigmouth Strikes Again/Hand in Glove **

Feb 12: Whitla Hall, Queen's University Belfast. Belfast, UK

*Shakespeare's Sister/I Want the One I Can't Have/Vicar in a Tutu/Rusholme Ruffians (Marie's the Name) Has Latest Flame (medley)/Cemetry Gates/Still Ill/Stretch Out and Wait/That Joke Isn't Funny Anymore/Nowhere Fast/What She Said/The Boy With the Thorn in His Side/There is a Light That Never Goes Out/Bigmouth Strikes Again/Meat Is Murder/William, It Was Really Nothing/Heaven Knows I'm Miserable Now/Hand in Glove **

July 16: Barrowlands. Glasgow, UK

*Bigmouth Strikes Again/Panic/Vicar in a Tutu/Frankly Mr Shankly/There is a Light That Never Goes Out/Ask/I Want the One I Can't Have/Never Had No One Ever/Cemetry Gates/The Boy With the Thorn in His Side/Is It Really So Strange?/Shakespeare's Sister/What She Said/That Joke Isn't Funny Anymore/The Queen Is Dead/I Know It's Over/Rusholme Ruffians (Marie's the Name) Latest Flame (medley)/William, It Was Really Nothing **

July 17: Mayfair Ballroom. Newcastle upon Tyne, UK

*Bigmouth Strikes Again/Panic/Vicar in a Tutu/Frankly Mr Shankly/There is a Light That Never Goes Out/Ask/I Want the One I Can't Have/Never Had No One Ever/Cemetry Gates/The Boy With the Thorn in His Side/Is It Really So Strange?/Shakespeare's Sister/Stretch Out and Wait/That Joke Isn't Funny Anymore/The Queen Is Dead/I Know It's Over/Rusholme Ruffians (Marie's the Name) Latest Flame (medley)/Hand in Glove **

July 19: G-Mex Centre. Manchester, UK

*Bigmouth Strikes Again/Panic/Vicar in a Tutu/Frankly Mr Shankly/There is a Light That Never Goes Out/Ask/I Want the One I Can't Have/Never Had No One Ever/Cemetry Gates/The Boy With the Thorn in His Side/Is It Really So Strange?/Shakespeare's Sister/Stretch Out and Wait/That Joke Isn't Funny Anymore/The Queen Is Dead/I Know It's Over/Rusholme Ruffians (Marie's The Name) Latest Flame (medley)/Hand in Glove **

July 20: University of Salford. Salford, UK

*Panic/Shakespeare's Sister/Frankly Mr Shankly/Vicar in a Tutu/Ask/I Want the One I Can't Have/Cemetry Gates/Never Had No One Ever/Is It Really So Strange?/The Boy With the Thorn in His Side/There is a Light That Never Goes Out/That Joke Isn't Funny Anymore/What She Said; Rubber Ring (medley)/The Queen Is Dead/Money Changes Everything/I Know It's Over/Bigmouth Strikes Again/Rusholme Ruffians (Marie's The Name) Latest Flame (medley)/Hand in Glove **

July 30: Centennial Hall. London, Canada

*Panic/Still Ill/I Want the One I Can't Have/Vicar in a Tutu/Frankly Mr Shankly/Is It Really So Strange?/Cemetry Gates/What She Said; Rubber Ring (medley)/There is a Light That Never Goes Out/The Boy With the Thorn in His Side/That Joke Isn't Funny Anymore/Ask/Shakespeare's Sister/William, It Was Really Nothing/How Soon is Now?/Heaven Knows I'm Miserable Now/The Queen Is Dead/Money Changes Everything/Please, Please, Please Let Me Get What I Want/Bigmouth Strikes Again/Hand in Glove **

July 31: Kingswood Music Theatre. Vaughan, Canada

*Panic/Still Ill/I Want the One I Can't Have/Vicar in a Tutu/Frankly Mr Shankly/Is It Really So Strange?/Cemetry Gates/What She Said; Rubber Ring (medley)/There is a Light That Never Goes Out/The Boy With the Thorn in His Side/That Joke Isn't Funny Anymore/Ask/Shakespeare's Sister/William, It Was Really Nothing/How Soon is Now?/Heaven Knows I'm Miserable Now/The Queen Is Dead/Money Changes Everything/Please, Please, Please Let Me Get What I Want/Bigmouth Strikes Again/Hand in Glove **

Aug 2: Congress Centre. Ottawa, Canada

Bigmouth Strikes Again/Still Ill/I Want the One I Can't Have/Frankly, Mr. Shankly/Vicar in a Tutu/Panic/Never Had No One Ever/Shakespeare's Sister/Stretch Out and Wait/The Boy With the Thorn in His Side/Cemetry Gates/William, It Was Really Nothing/What She Said; Rubber Ring (medley)/Is It Really So Strange?/There Is a Light That Never Goes Out/That Joke Isn't Funny Anymore/The Queen Is Dead
(in all likelihood this running order has been edited)

Aug 3: Université de Montréal. Montreal, Canada

Bigmouth Strikes Again/Still Ill/I Want the One I Can't Have/Frankly, Mr. Shankly/Vicar in a Tutu/Panic/Never Had No One Ever/Shakespeare's Sister/Stretch Out and Wait/The Boy With the Thorn in His Side/Cemetry Gates/What She Said; Rubber Ring (medley)/Is It Really So Strange?/There Is a Light That Never Goes Out/That Joke Isn't Funny Anymore/The Queen Is Dead/Money Changes Everything/How Soon Is Now?/Heaven Knows I'm Miserable Now/Hand in Glove

Aug 5: Great Woods Performing Arts Center. Mansfield, MA. USA

*How Soon is Now?/Hand in Glove/I Want the One I Can't Have/Still Ill/Frankly Mr Shankly/Panic/Never Had No One Ever/Stretch Out and Wait/The Boy With the Thorn in His Side/Cemetry Gates/What She Said; Rubber Ring (medley)/Is It Really So Strange/There Is a Light That Never Goes Out/That Joke Isn't Funny Anymore/The Queen Is Dead/Money Changes Everything/I Know It's Over/Heaven Knows I'm Miserable Now/Bigmouth Strikes Again **

Aug 6: Hudson River Park, Pier 84. New York City, NY. USA

*How Soon is Now?/I Want the One I Can't Have/Still Ill/Frankly Mr Shankly/Panic/Never Had No One Ever/Stretch Out and Wait/The Boy With the Thorn in His Side/Cemetry Gates/What She Said; Rubber Ring (medley)/Hand in Glove/Is It Really So Strange/There Is a Light That Never Goes Out/That Joke Isn't Funny Anymore/The Queen Is Dead/Money Changes Everything/I Know It's Over/Heaven Knows I'm Miserable Now/Bigmouth Strikes Again **

Aug 8: Charles E. Smith Center. Washington, D.C. USA

*There Is a Light That Never Goes Out/Still Ill/I Want the One I Can't Have/Vicar in a Tutu/Frankly Mr Shankly/Panic/Stretch Out and Wait/The Boy With the Thorn in His Side/Shakespeare's Sister/Cemetry Gates/Never had No One Ever/What She Said; Rubber Ring (medley)/That Joke Isn't Funny Anymore/Meat Is Murder/The Queen Is Dead/How Soon is Now?/Heaven Knows I'm Miserable Now/Bigmouth Strikes Again **

Aug 11: Music Hall, Public Auditorium. Cleveland, OH. USA

There Is a Light That Never Goes Out/Still Ill/I Want the One I Can't Have/How Soon is Now?/Frankly Mr Shankly/Panic/Stretch Out and Wait/The Boy With the Thorn in His Side/Shakespeare's Sister/Cemetry Gates/Never had No One Ever/What She Said; Rubber Ring (medley)/That Joke Isn't Funny Anymore/Meat Is Murder/The Queen Is Dead/Money Changes Everything/I Know It's Over/Hand in Glove/Bigmouth Strikes Again

Aug 12: Fulton Theater. Pittsburgh, PA. USA

*Still Ill/I Want the One I Can't Have/There Is a Light That Never Goes Out/How Soon is Now?/Frankly Mr Shankly/Panic/Stretch Out and Wait/The Boy With the Thorn in His Side/Is It Really So Strange?/Cemetry Gates/Never had No One Ever/What She Said; Rubber Ring (medley)/That Joke Isn't Funny Anymore/Meat Is Murder/The Queen Is Dead/Money Changes Everything/I Know It's Over/Hand in Glove/Bigmouth Strikes Again **

Aug 14: Fox Theatre. Detroit, MI. USA

*Still Ill/I Want the One I Can't Have/There Is a Light That Never Goes Out/How Soon is Now?/Stretch Out and Wait/The Boy With the Thorn in His Side/Is It Really So Strange?/Cemetry Gates/Never had No One Ever/What She Said; Rubber Ring (medley)/That Joke Isn't Funny Anymore/Meat Is Murder/The Queen Is Dead/Money Changes Everything/I Know It's Over/Hand in Glove/Bigmouth Strikes Again **

Aug 15: Aragon Ballroom. Chicago, IL. USA

*Still Ill/I Want the One I Can't Have/There Is a Light That Never Goes Out/How Soon is Now?/Frankly Mr Shankly/Panic/Stretch Out and Wait/The Boy With the Thorn in His Side/Is It Really So Strange?/Cemetry Gates/Never had No One Ever/What She Said; Rubber Ring (medley)/That Joke Isn't Funny Anymore/Meat Is Murder/The Queen Is Dead/Money Changes Everything/I Know It's Over/Hand in Glove/Bigmouth Strikes Again **

Aug 16: Performing Arts Center. Milwaukee, WI. USA

Still Ill/I Want the One I Can't Have/There Is a Light That Never Goes Out/How Soon is Now?/Frankly Mr Shankly/Panic/Stretch Out and Wait/The Boy With the Thorn in His Side/Is It Really So Strange?/Cemetry Gates/Never had No One Ever/What She Said; Rubber Ring (medley)/That Joke Isn't Funny Anymore/Meat Is Murder/The Queen Is Dead/Money Changes Everything/I Know It's

*Over/Hand in Glove/Bigmouth Strikes Again **

Aug 22: Arlington Theater. Santa Barbara, CA. USA

*Still Ill/I Want the One I Can't Have/There Is a Light That Never Goes Out/How Soon is Now?/Frankly Mr Shankly/Panic/Stretch Out and Wait/The Boy With the Thorn in His Side/Is It Really So Strange?/Cemetry Gates/Never had No One Ever/What She Said; Rubber Ring (medley)/That Joke Isn't Funny Anymore/Meat Is Murder/The Queen Is Dead/Money Changes Everything/I Know It's Over/Hand in Glove **

Aug 23: Hearst Greek Theatre. Berkeley, CA. USA

*Still Ill/I Want the One I Can't Have/There Is a Light That Never Goes Out/How Soon is Now?/Frankly Mr Shankly/Panic/Stretch Out and Wait/The Boy With the Thorn in His Side/Is It Really So Strange?/Cemetry Gates/Never had No One Ever/What She Said; Rubber Ring (medley)/That Joke Isn't Funny Anymore/Meat Is Murder/Shakespeare's Sister/The Queen Is Dead/Money Changes Everything/I Know It's Over/Hand in Glove/Bigmouth Strikes Again **

Aug 25: Universal Amphitheatre. Los Angeles, CA. USA

*Still Ill/I Want the One I Can't Have/There Is a Light That Never Goes Out/How Soon is Now?/Frankly Mr Shankly/Panic/Stretch Out and Wait/The Boy With the Thorn in His Side/Is It Really So Strange?/Cemetry Gates/Never had No One Ever/What She Said; Rubber Ring (medley)/That Joke Isn't Funny Anymore/Meat Is Murder/Rusholme Ruffians; (Marie's the Name) His Latest Flame (medley)/Heaven Knows I'm Miserable Now/The Queen Is Dead/Money Changes Everything/I Know It's Over/Hand in Glove/Bigmouth Strikes Again **

Aug 26: Universal Amphitheatre. Los Angeles, CA. USA

*Please Please Please, Let Me Get What I Want/Still Ill/I Want the One I Can't Have/There Is a Light That Never Goes Out/How Soon is Now?/Frankly Mr Shankly/Panic/Stretch Out and Wait/The Boy With the Thorn in His Side/Is It Really So Strange?/Cemetry Gates/Never had No One Ever/What She Said; Rubber Ring (medley)/That Joke Isn't Funny Anymore/Meat Is Murder/Heaven Knows I'm Miserable Now/Reel Around the Fountain/The Queen Is Dead/Money Changes Everything/I Know It's Over/Hand in Glove/Bigmouth Strikes Again **

Aug 28: Irvine Meadows Amphitheatre. Irvine, CA. USA

*Please Please Please, Let Me Get What I Want/Still Ill/I Want the One I Can't Have/There Is a Light That Never Goes Out/How Soon is Now?/Frankly Mr Shankly/Panic/Stretch Out and Wait/The Boy With the Thorn in His Side/Is It Really So Strange?/Cemetry Gates/Never had No One Ever/What She Said; Rubber Ring (medley)/That Joke Isn't Funny Anymore/Meat Is Murder/Heaven Knows I'm Miserable Now/The Queen Is Dead/Money Changes Everything/I Know It's Over/Hand in Glove/Bigmouth Strikes Again **

Aug 29: San Diego State University Open Air Theater. San Diego, CA. USA

*Panic/I Want the One I Can't Have/There Is a Light That Never Goes Out/How Soon is Now?/Frankly Mr Shankly/Still Ill/Stretch Out and Wait/The Boy With the Thorn in His Side/Is It Really So Strange?/Cemetry Gates/Never had No One Ever/What She Said; Rubber Ring (medley)/That Joke Isn't Funny Anymore/Meat Is Murder/Heaven Knows I'm Miserable Now/The Queen Is Dead **

Aug 31: Mesa Amphitheatre. Phoenix, AZ. USA

Set-list not known.

Sept 3: University of Colorado Boulder Events Center. Boulder, CO. USA

*Still Ill/I Want the One I Can't Have/There Is a Light That Never Goes Out/How Soon is Now?/Frankly Mr Shankly/Panic/Stretch Out and Wait/The Boy With the Thorn in His Side/Is It Really So Strange?/Cemetry Gates/Never had No One Ever/What She Said; Rubber Ring (medley)/That Joke Isn't Funny Anymore/Meat Is Murder/Rusholme Ruffians; (Marie's the Name) His Latest Flame (medley)/The Queen Is Dead **
(Recording cuts off at close of "The Queen Is Dead")

Sept 5: Cullen Performance Hall. Houston, TX. USA

The Queen Is Dead/Panic/I Want the One I Can't Have/Rusholme Ruffians; (Marie's the Name) His Latest Flame (medley)/There Is a Light That Never Goes Out/Still Ill/William, It Was Really Nothing/Cemetry Gates/Stretch Out and Wait/Never had No One Ever/Is It Really So Strange?/That Joke Isn't Funny Anymore/Meat Is Murder/What She Said; Rubber Ring (medley)/I Know It's Over/

Money Changes Everything/How Soon is Now?/Hand in Glove/Bigmouth Strikes Again

Sept 6: Bronco Bowl. Dallas, TX. USA

The Queen Is Dead/Panic/I Want the One I Can't Have/Rusholme Ruffians; (Marie's the Name) His Latest Flame (medley)/There Is a Light That Never Goes Out/Still Ill/Frankly Mr Shankly/Cemetry Gates/Stretch Out and Wait/Never had No One Ever/Is It Really So Strange?/That Joke Isn't Funny Anymore/Meat Is Murder/What She Said; Rubber Ring (medley)/I Know It's Over/Money Changes Everything/How Soon is Now?/Hand in Glove/Bigmouth Strikes Again

Sept 8: McAlister Auditorium, Tulane University. New Orleans, LO. USA

*The Queen Is Dead/Panic/I Want the One I Can't Have/Rusholme Ruffians; (Marie's the Name) His Latest Flame (medley)/There Is a Light That Never Goes Out/Still Ill/The Boy with The Thorn in His Side/Cemetry Gates/Stretch Out and Wait/Never had No One Ever/Is It Really So Strange?/That Joke Isn't Funny Anymore/Meat Is Murder/What She Said; Rubber Ring (medley)/I Know It's Over/Money Changes Everything/How Soon is Now?/Hand in Glove/Bigmouth Strikes Again **

Sept 10: Bayfront Arena. St. Petersburg, FL. USA

Set-list not known.

Oct 13: Sands Centre. Carlisle, UK

*The Queen Is Dead/Panic/I Want the One I Can't Have/Vicar in a Tutu/There Is a Light That Never Goes Out/Rusholme Ruffians; (Marie's the Name) His Latest Flame (medley)/Frankly Mr Shankly/The Boy with The Thorn in His Side/What She Said; Rubber Ring (medley)/Ask/Is It Really So Strange?/That Joke Isn't Funny Anymore/Never Had No One Ever/Cemetry Gates/London/Meat Is Murder/I Know It's Over/The Draize Train/How Soon is Now?/Still Ill/Bigmouth Strikes Again **

Oct 14: Middlesbrough Town Hall. Middlesbrough, UK

*The Queen Is Dead/Panic/I Want the One I Can't Have/Vicar in a Tutu/There Is a Light That Never Goes Out/Ask/Rusholme Ruffians; (Marie's the Name) His Latest Flame (medley)/Frankly Mr Shankly/The Boy with The Thorn in His Side/What She Said; Rubber Ring (medley)/Ask/Is It Really So Strange?/Never Had No One Ever/Cemetry Gates/London/Meat Is Murder/I Know It's Over/The Draize Train/How Soon is Now?/Still Ill/Bigmouth Strikes Again **

Oct 15: Wolverhampton Civic Hall. Wolverhampton, UK

*The Queen Is Dead/Panic/I Want the One I Can't Have/Vicar in a Tutu/There Is a Light That Never Goes Out/Ask/Rusholme Ruffians; (Marie's the Name) His Latest Flame (medley)/Frankly Mr Shankly/The Boy with The Thorn in His Side/What She Said; Rubber Ring (medley)/Is It Really So Strange?/Never Had No One Ever/Cemetry Gates/London/Meat Is Murder/I Know It's Over/The Draize Train/How Soon is Now?/Still Ill/Bigmouth Strikes Again **

Oct 17: Cornwall Coliseum. St Austell, UK

*The Queen Is Dead/Panic/I Want the One I Can't Have/Vicar in a Tutu/There Is a Light That Never Goes Out/Ask/Rusholme Ruffians; (Marie's the Name) His Latest Flame (medley)/Frankly Mr Shankly/The Boy with The Thorn in His Side/What She Said; Rubber Ring (medley)/Is It Really So Strange?/Never Had No One Ever/Cemetry Gates/London/Meat Is Murder/I Know It's Over/The Draize Train/How Soon is Now?/Still Ill/Bigmouth Strikes Again **

Oct 18: Leisure Centre. Gloucester, UK

*The Queen Is Dead/Panic/I Want the One I Can't Have/Vicar in a Tutu/There Is a Light That Never Goes Out/Ask/Rusholme Ruffians; (Marie's the Name) His Latest Flame (medley)/Frankly Mr Shankly/The Boy with The Thorn in His Side/What She Said; Rubber Ring (medley)/Is It Really So Strange?/Never Had No One Ever/Cemetry Gates/London/Meat Is Murder/I Know It's Over/The Draize Train/How Soon is Now?/Still Ill/Bigmouth Strikes Again **

Oct 19: Newport Centre. Newport, UK

*The Queen Is Dead/Panic/I Want the One I Can't Have/Vicar in a Tutu/There Is a Light That Never Goes Out/Rusholme Ruffians; (Marie's the Name) His Latest Flame (medley)/Frankly Mr Shankly/The Boy with The Thorn in His Side/The Draize Train **

Oct 21: Nottingham Royal Concert Hall.

SALFORD LADS
CLUB

Nottingham, UK

*The Queen Is Dead/Panic/I Want the One I Can't Have/ Vicar in a Tutu/There Is a Light That Never Goes Out/ Ask/Rusholme Ruffians; (Marie's the Name) His Latest Flame (medley)/Frankly Mr Shankly/The Boy with The Thorn in His Side/What She Said; Rubber Ring (medley)/ Is It Really So Strange?/Never Had No One Ever/Cemetry Gates/London/Meat Is Murder/I Know It's Over/The Draize Train/How Soon is Now?/Still Ill/Bigmouth Strikes Again **

Oct 23: Kilburn National Ballroom. London, UK

*The Queen Is Dead/Panic/I Want the One I Can't Have/ Vicar in a Tutu/There Is a Light That Never Goes Out/ Ask/Rusholme Ruffians; (Marie's the Name) His Latest Flame (medley)/Frankly Mr Shankly/The Boy with The Thorn in His Side/What She Said; Rubber Ring (medley)/ Is It Really So Strange?/Never Had No One Ever/Cemetry Gates/London/Meat Is Murder/I Know It's Over/The Draize Train/How Soon is Now?/Still Ill/Bigmouth Strikes Again **

Oct 24: Brixton Academy. London, UK

*The Queen Is Dead/Panic/I Want the One I Can't Have/ Vicar in a Tutu/There Is a Light That Never Goes Out/ Ask/Rusholme Ruffians; (Marie's the Name) His Latest Flame (medley)/Shakespeare's Sister/Frankly Mr Shankly/ The Boy with The Thorn in His Side/What She Said; Rubber Ring (medley)/Is It Really So Strange?/Cemetry Gates/London/Meat Is Murder/I Know It's Over/The Draize Train/How Soon is Now?/Still Ill/Bigmouth Strikes Again **

Oct 26: London Palladium. London, UK

*The Queen Is Dead/Panic/I Want the One I Can't Have/ Vicar in a Tutu/There Is a Light That Never Goes Out/ Ask/Rusholme Ruffians/Shakespeare's Sister/Frankly Mr Shankly/The Boy with The Thorn in His Side/What She Said; Rubber Ring (medley)/Is It Really So Strange?/ Cemetry Gates/London/Meat Is Murder/I Know It's Over/ The Draize Train/How Soon is Now?/Still Ill/Bigmouth Strikes Again **

Oct 27: Preston Guild Hall. Preston, UK

The Queen Is Dead (Set terminated after Morrissey was struck with a coin)

Oct 30: Free Trade Hall. Manchester, UK

*Ask/The Queen Is Dead/Panic/How Soon Is Now?/Vicar in a Tutu/Rusholme Ruffians; (Marie's the Name) His Latest Flame (medley)/Frankly Mr Shankly/The Boy with The Thorn in His Side/There Is a Light That Never Goes Out/Cemetry Gates/Is It Really So Strange?/What She Said; Rubber Ring (medley)/That Joke Isn't Funny Anymore/London/Meat Is Murder/Still Ill/The Draize Train/I Know It's Over/Bigmouth Strikes Again **

Dec 12: Brixton Academy (Artists Against Apartheid benefit). London, UK

*Ask/Bigmouth Strikes Again/London; Miserable Lie (medley)Some Girls Are Bigger than Others/The Boy with The Thorn in His Side/Shoplifters of the World Unite/ There Is a Light That Never Goes Out/Is It Really So Strange?/Cemetry Gates/This Night Has Opened My Eyes/ Still Ill/Panic/The Queen Is Dead/William, It Was Really Nothing/Hand in Glove **

1987

Feb 7. San Remo Festival. San Remo, Italy

Shoplifters of the World Unite/There Is a Light That Never Goes Out/The Boy With the Thorn in His Side/Panic/Ask (Mimed performance)

THE SMITHS

THE PHOTOGRAPHER

I hope you enjoy these old photographs of The Smiths shot a long time ago as I learned how to use my first Nikon. Over the years they've been in various newspapers, magazines and books but, to me, they are images that bring back great memories of just some of the many musicians I shot at the start of my career as a photographer. I was initially based in Manchester – spending lots of time at the fabled Hacienda club and the Manchester Apollo. I eventually moved back south and started working on shows in London, but while the artists were arguably bigger, it was never quite the same. Over the years I was lucky to work on a long list of iconic artists – Madonna, Prince, Miles Davis, Nina Simone, James Brown and many more!

Of course, it's The Smiths images that have become most well-known and its odd that one posed photo on a damp winter day in Salford should haunt me for the next 30 years. The session was on a Friday 13th that fell in December 1985 – a dark winters day in Salford.

Everyone seems to know these photos of The Smiths. What you might call a 'Marmite' band: you either love them or hate them! I for one was, and more than 30 years later still am, a massive fan.

When I was first starting as a photographer in the early Eighties everything was happening in Manchester; a city of rain, sex and rock and roll.The Hacienda had just opened and Manchester dominated the English music scene. I met some very clever, talented people and was lucky to shoot some great musicians – from the older established stars to the new pretenders. Factory Records' bands led the way in terms of mystique but whilst New Order were kings of the patch it was The Smiths that took the crown of the Manchester music scene.

Trying to describe The Smiths 'live' is a tough one, as it was always such a great show. An adoring crowd with Morrissey in total command of the whole audience! I was really lucky to see The Smiths live several times and get the opportunity to work with them. The jangle of Johnny's guitar makes me smile a decade later...

I photographed them in concert several times and sent the shots down to Rough Trade – their record company. The first show was at the Free Trade Hall and was truly magnificent. A riotous moving audience meant taking photos was hard and I only had two lenses and one roll of film! I couldn't get anywhere near the front to shoot so I managed to climb up the side of the stage and hide in the lighting rigging. Hardly ideal and I only had 36 shots to work with. Later, the NME voted the image of Morrissey's rear with flowers hanging from his jeans as one of the most famous photos in 50 years. However, my favourite of these from that first show is the one of him flaying the flowers above his head – shot from the side of the stage.

I got the chance to capture several concerts and a couple of BBC appearances.

THE SMITHS

For 20 years the negatives sat in the same brown envelope in a drawer but the photos have become better known over the last 15 years – coinciding with a renewed interest in The Smiths.

A year or so after The Free Trade Hall show I had a call from Rough Trade asking me to do a session with the band for a possible album sleeve. At the time, I was still, at best, a novice photographer and this is a session that really should have gone to Anton Corbin or Pennie Smith. I was given a great opportunity at the time and I've always been glad of this.

The Queen is Dead shoot itself was in December in Salford – it was a damp dark day and it should really have been cancelled as the light was so poor for photography. We spent a bit of time at a couple of locations but the Salford Lads club was the key one. You can even see Johnny shivering in some of the images. Somehow, the casual poses and the grim weather give the photos a certain natural and gritty character. I love the way Morrissey stands there, arms folded, smirking slightly like the Mona Lisa.

For years fans have gone back to the Salford Lads Club and it has become a shrine to The Smiths fans who pose for their own version of the photo. Just as Beatles fans pose on the Abbey Road zebra crossing.

The Salford Lads Club committee at the time were unhappy with the album title and it is only over the last 16 years that the Lads Club has made Smiths fans far more welcome. When we did the original shoot the club was shut as it was daytime. I've been lucky to be allowed into the Lads Club in this new phase and the warmth of welcome from the old members has been very touching. They welcome and humour me – I'm allowed to make my own tea there... In fact, I am now the only Honorary Member of the Salford Lads Club and enjoy visiting when I can. If I didn't live 200 miles away it would be far more often!

I find it all a bit funny that the film was processed in a darkroom set up in my bedroom with my chemicals stored in old pop bottles yet now there's a print in the National Portrait Gallery collection, The Manchester Art Gallery and the Salford Art Gallery.

For me a pleasure is the fact that these photos are enjoyed years later. I love the fact that there are now signed prints as far afield as Australia, Japan and Los Angeles and that they are given pride of place.

I've been pleased to donate prints several times to the Abbey Road Cancer Research auction and various other charities. I was given a great chance and have always felt it 'right' to give back to others with these photos. I enjoyed going back to the Salford Lads Club on three occasions to shoot Smiths fans posing for the Sue Ryder Hospice – who were so kind to my father and also to the Alzheimers Society. In 2015 I gave the Salford Lads Club one of my Smiths images for a fundraising T shirt – this raised £60,000 in a year for a trip for teenagers from the Salford Lads Club to visit Native Indians in South Dakota.

Stephen Wright
www.smithsphotos.com

Photographs signed by Stephen Wright are available and shipped worldwide.

With thanks to Severine, Paul, Mark, Colin, Elliot, Leslie Mick, Damian, David, Tim, Julian, Will, Neal at the MEN, the gentleman at the SLC and my patient parents...

SALFORD LADS
CLUB

SALFORD LADS
CLUB

SALFORD LADS
CLUB

PART FIVE

THE SMITHS IN PICTURES

BY STEPHEN WRIGHT

BOXING DAY 1985

MORRISSEY of The SMITHS
(Photo by Andy Catlin)

STEVEN,

A sweeter set of pictures were never taken. I smiled for a full minute (phone Roy Castle, that's a record); I quite fancy Southport's wet sands next, or the tropical shores of Belle Vue. It must be done. Fatal Regret: I should have worn my mud-coloured cardigan. Oh well. We shall meet when Venus is under Capricorn, so keep your lenses dry, and Thank You.

MORRISSEY

The SMITHS c/o Rough Trade Records,
61-71 Collier Street, London N1 9BE

THE SMITHS

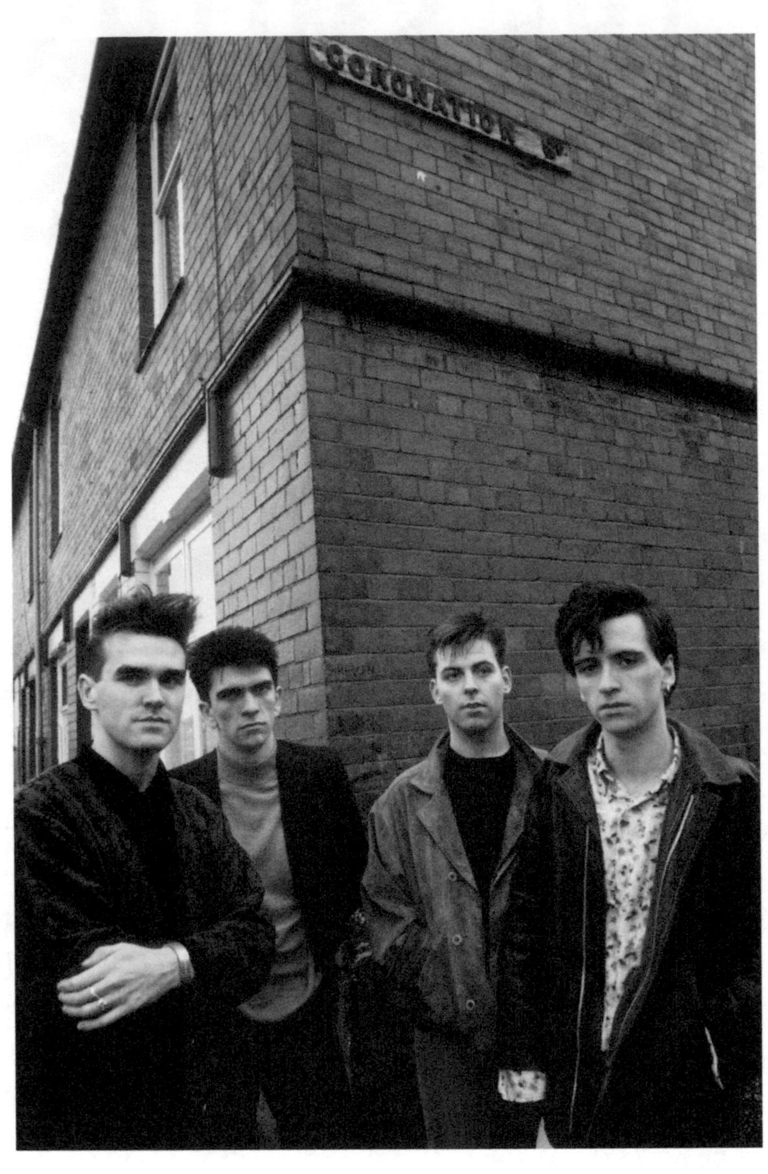

CORONATION ST

THE SMITHS

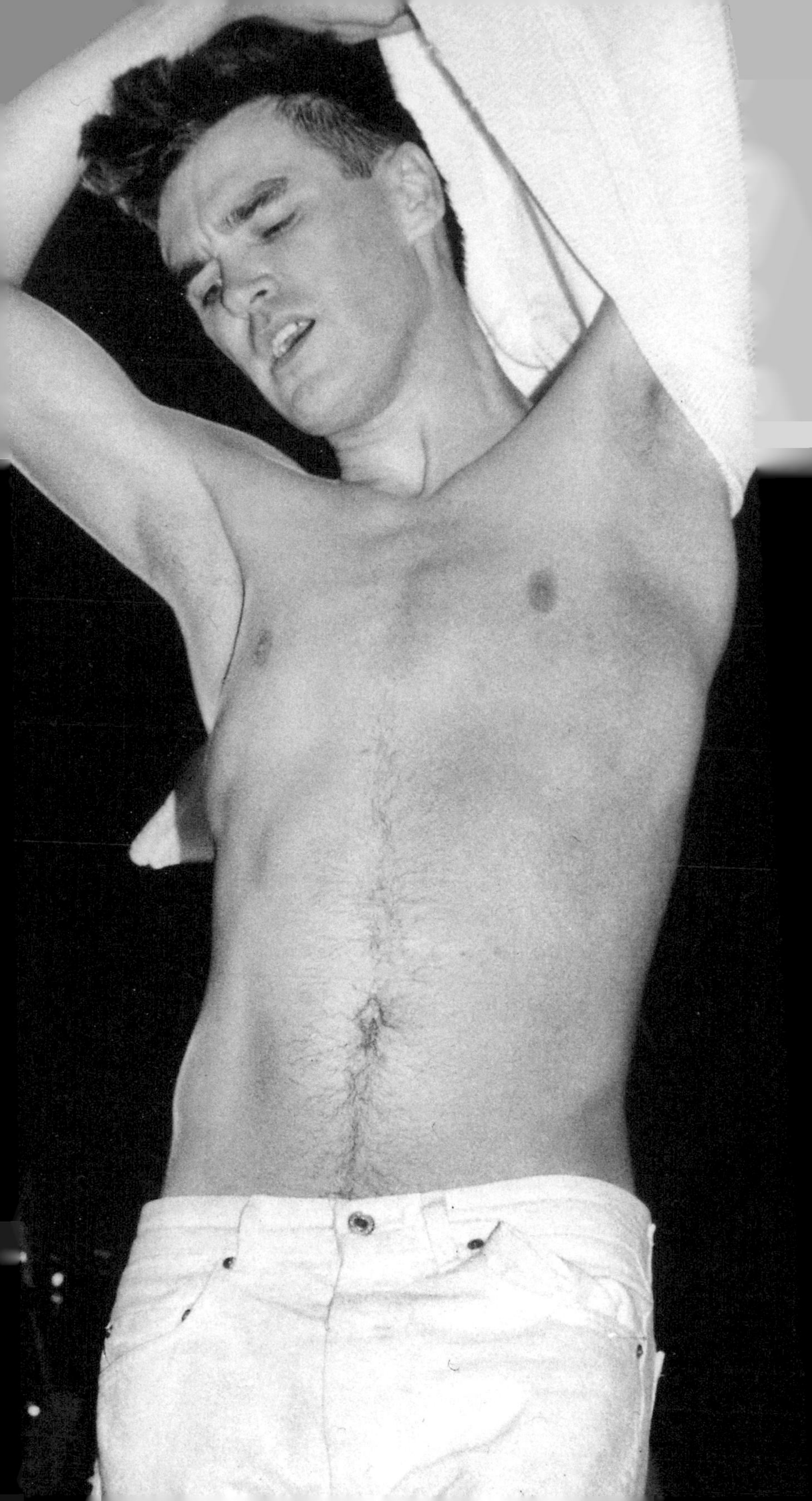

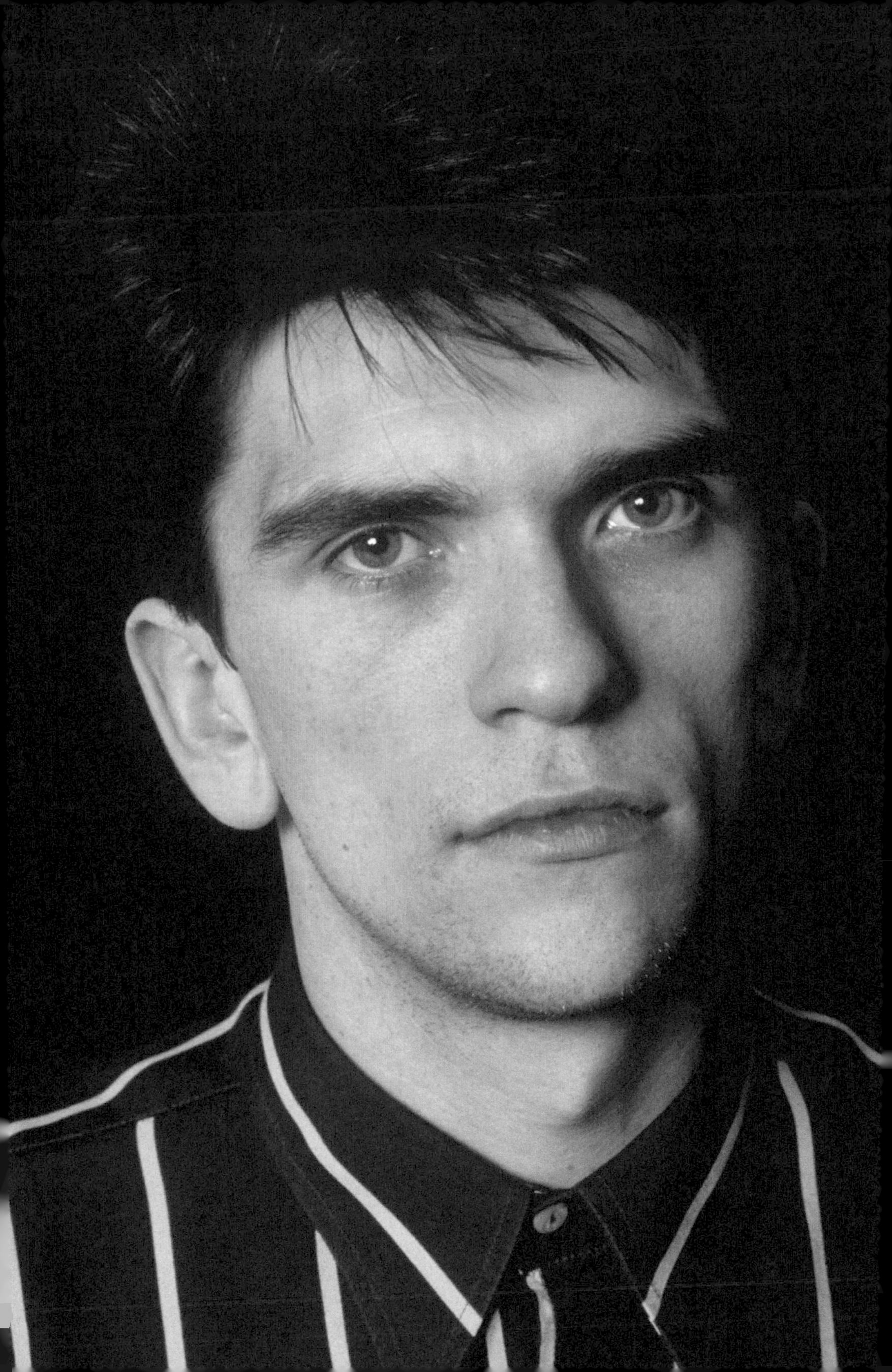

CORONATION ST
SALFORD LADS
CLUB

Premier

SALFORD LA
CLUB

SECRET AFFAIR

THE CHORDS

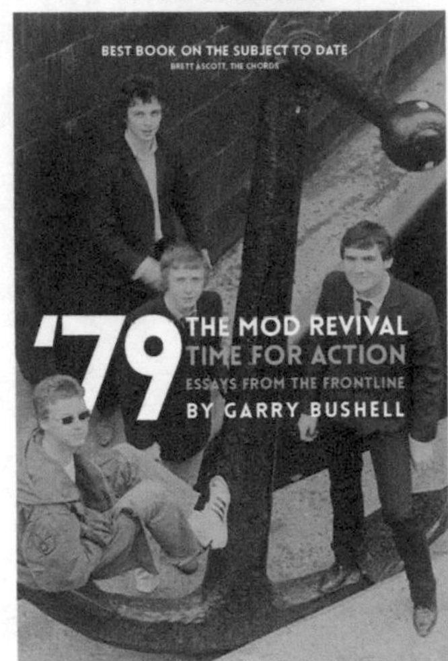

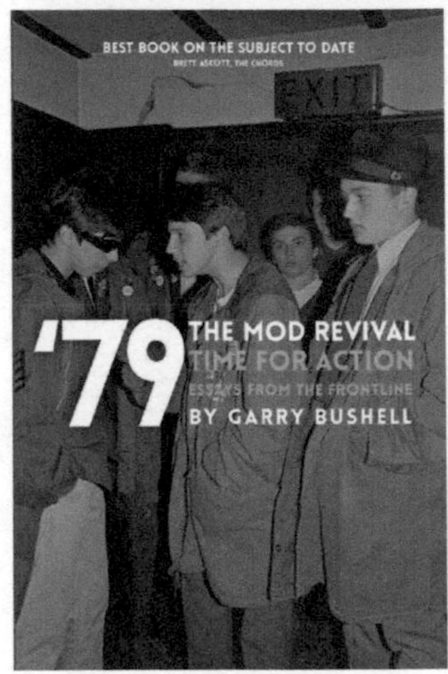

MODS AT BRIDGE HOUSE

PURPLE HEARTS

Louis The PA
Fish and chips saloon. Hot & cola
POCKET GUIDE TO
SKA
MICK O' SHEA
POCKET GUIDE TO
MOD
PAUL ANDERSON
DEAD STRAIGHT MUSIC GUIDES